PERSPECTIVES
Sociolinguistics and TESOL

PERSPECTIVES
Sociolinguistics and TESOL

Nessa Wolfson
University of Pennsylvania

NEWBURY HOUSE PUBLISHERS
A Division of Harper & Row, Publishers, Inc.

*Cambridge, New York, Philadelphia, San Francisco, Washington, D.C.
London, Mexico City, São Paulo, Singapore, Sidney*

Director: Laurie E. Likoff
Production Coordinator: Cynthia Funkhouser
Cover Design: Wanda Lubelska Design
Compositor: The Composing Room of Michigan, Inc.
Printer and Binder: Malloy Lithographing, Inc.

NEWBURY HOUSE PUBLISHERS
A division of Harper & Row, Publishers, Inc.

Language Science
Language Teaching
Language Learning

Perspectives: Sociolinguistics and TESOL

Library of Congress Cataloging in Publication Data

Wolfson, Nessa.
  Perspectives : sociolinguistics and TESOL.

  Bibliography: p. 289
  Includes index.
  1. Sociolinguistics. 2. English language—Social
aspects. 3. English language—Study and teaching—
Foreign speakers. I. Title.
P40.W59 1989   401'.9   88-12545
ISBN 0-06-632572-2

63-25724   91 92 9 8 7 6 5 4 3

Dedication

This book is dedicated to televised ballgames because they kept my husband busy while I was writing it. It is also dedicated to His Majesty, my husband, without whom I could not possibly survive, let alone write books. His love and support during the writing of this book were manifested in more ways than I can say without writing a whole other book on the subject. He even cooked our dinners, forcing himself to put aside expectations concerning sex roles, rights, and obligations inculcated in him from early childhood. In short, he looked after me in countless ways. He never failed to shout when I tried to get some writing done at night by sneaking out of bed once I thought he was asleep. He always caught me and saved me from myself, and he deserves all the dedication I have to give.

Preface

The first draft of this book was begun in 1982. Having spent a number of years before that creating and developing a Ph.D. program in educational linguistics, including a master's degree program in TESOL, I became aware that the field was in critical need of a textbook in sociolinguistics that would give an overview of the field in response to the needs of future ESL instructors.

With Dell Hymes as dean, it was not difficult to gain support in giving a strong sociolinguistics orientation to the educational linguistics program at the University of Pennsylvania. Thus, courses were specifically designed to teach those aspects of sociolinguistics most relevant to TESOL students, as well as to doctoral students who would themselves become university instructors in applied linguistics programs throughout the world. Indeed, the only serious problem we faced was the total lack of textbooks that could give our students background information that was both concrete and pertinent to their needs.

After years of attempting to make do with what little existed in the way of relevant articles, and with sociolinguistics texts that had no relevance to TESOL at all, I at last decided to write the needed book myself. By 1983, a first draft had been produced. However, while the manuscript was still rough and incomplete, I became Chair of the Language in Education Division at the University of Pennsylvania's Graduate School of Education. Administrative responsibilities at this level are heavy and time-consuming, and I had no choice but to put the unfinished manuscript aside. It was only five years later, when, in the spring of 1987, I was granted a sabbatical leave, that I was able to go back to work on this book.

At first, I assumed that two or three months of solid work would suffice to revise and update the original draft. Two things had happened in the interim, however, that made my original estimate completely unrealistic. On the one hand, a great deal of important research had been conducted during those five years, and on the other, my own knowledge and perspectives had undergone considerable development. In the end, I found that it was necessary not to revise and update, but to completely rewrite the book, a project that took very nearly a year. I can only hope that the book which has finally emerged will make a valuable contribution to the growing field of sociolinguistics and TESOL.

Over the past decade, research in sociolinguistics has come to have an ever-increasing impact on the field of TESOL. To a great extent, this development has been due to the growing recognition that second language acquisition is, in fact, the acquisition of what Dell Hymes has called communicative competence. That is, becoming an effective speaker of a new language not only involves learning new vocabulary in addition to rules of pronunciation and grammar but must also include the ability to use these linguistic resources in ways that are socially appropriate among speakers of the target language. Members of the TESOL profession are therefore in need of empirically valid analyses upon which to base instruction in this area—analyses that can be provided only by sociolinguistic research. Such research also gives teachers of English necessary insights into the variation in speech behavior among the many communities in which English is spoken as a native language, thus making it possible for them to present the relevant facts to their students.

In addition to the pressing need for information regarding the appropriate use of the language in specific social contexts, it is critical that members of the TESOL profession be fully informed of the many sociopolitical implications involved in the teaching of the most widely used international language of our era. The increasing linguistic and cultural diversity within English-speaking countries has serious consequences, and the role of TESOL in bilingual education, for example, is of utmost importance. The fact that English is taught as a foreign language throughout the world, and that it has been adopted as the second, and often the official language of many developing nations, means that nonnative speakers now outnumber native speakers. An important aspect of sociolinguistics is the investigation of the complex and varied problems caused by the unprecedented spread of the English language. A clear understanding of these problems is essential to the background of TESOL professionals so that they may be prepared to meet the need for effective and appropriate instruction in the many different settings in which the English language is taught.

The purpose of this book is to provide a critical overview of those aspects of sociolinguistics most relevant to members of the TESOL profession. The first part of the book deals with face-to-face interaction. Early chapters deal with cross-cultural differences in speech behavior, problems in the analysis of sociolinguistic rules, descriptions of speech behavior in native English-speaking communities, and the implications of this kind of analysis for gaining insight into cultural patterns. Differences in language use are examined in chapters on miscommunication, language and sex, social variation, and dialects and standards. Chapters on bilingual education, multilingualism, and the spread of English complete the second half of the book, covering the workings of language contact, choice, use, maintenance, and change at the societal level.

Perspectives: Sociolinguistics and TESOL is primarily intended as a textbook to be used in sociolinguistics courses within programs leading to master's degrees in TESOL or in applied linguistics. In addition, the book should also be of value in general graduate or advanced undergraduate courses in sociolinguistics, sociology, linguistics, intercultural communication, speech communication, and education. It is hoped that the book will prove useful to researchers and instructors in the fields mentioned above, since it contains a considerable amount of new material, and reviews research on major, current sociolinguistic issues, including an historical overview and a critical discussion of research methods. It should be pointed out here that this textbook is intended for readers who have had an introductory course in linguistics. If students have not had such a background, an introductory linguistics text may be used in conjunction with this book.

As the first comprehensive textbook in the area, *Perspectives: Sociolinguistics and TESOL* will, I hope, fill a critical gap in the field of English language teaching.

It is customary to make acknowledgments and express gratitude to all those who have given help and support during the writing of a book. My own list is so long that the acknowledgments could easily take up a separate preface. To begin with, there is no one among the faculty, students, and office staff in Penn's Language in Education Program who does not deserve thanks for patience and emotional support. Although my responsibilities as Chair make it difficult, I've sometimes managed to slip out of the office early or to take an extra day at home so that I could finish up last-minute revisions before the book went to press. In doing this, I had a lot of cooperation.

Sandra Gill, my teaching assistant during the semester I did most of the writing, was always cheerful, helpful, and incredibly resourceful in tracking down references for me. She proofread every chapter I wrote and made helpful comments throughout. Sandi's assistance went far beyond the call of duty; even after her graduation from Penn's TESOL Program, she voluntarily continued to work with me on the final chapters. She deserves more thanks than I can find words to express.

Three other teaching assistants were very helpful. Susan Failer read and commented on the first draft, and Lisa Basille and Julie Spiegel aided by pulling together some of the most recent research findings I wanted to include.

Among the staff, thanks go to our former secretary, Angel Mattos, who typed sections of the earlier draft, and to our administrative assistant, Lorraine Hightower, who helped with printing and copying. Catherine Stemmler, our newest staff assistant, deserves special mention. She typed in pages of additional references for me, and when, at the very last moment, I decided to make a revision that required renumbering and reprinting most of the manuscript, Cathy rose to the occasion and accomplished it all with efficiency and cheerfulness, seeing to it that the revision reached the publisher on the very day it had been promised.

John Irwin, our school's computer expert, saved Chapter 3 for me when I thought it had been wiped out through a disk error. His patience and effectiveness on this and many other occasions are much appreciated.

When one is lucky enough to have faculty colleagues who are also dear friends, it is difficult to describe how much their backing means. To begin with, they all did their best not to disturb me at home while I was writing, and when they did call, they always felt guilty and apologized. In addition, there was no one who did not find ways to encourage and support me.

Specifically, I want to thank Ann Williams, who has been an outstanding administrative coordinator, and who did her best to take on as many of my burdens as possible, thus helping me to find some extra time in which to write. Ann also gave aid by reading the first chapters of the new book and telling me it made her sorry she hadn't gone into TESOL instead of getting an MBA. I don't believe her, but it was gratifying nonetheless.

My faculty colleagues in the educational linguistics program, Teresa Pica and Nancy Hornberger, read, listened, discussed, and commented on chapters I was rewriting, as did my friend Virginia Hymes. Their insights and encouragement have helped enormously. My intellectual debt to Dell Hymes—teacher, friend, and colleague—will be apparent throughout this book.

Teresa Pica, director of the educational linguistics program, did much more than her share of administration and advising, going far out of her way to help me find the time I needed to write. My colleague Morton Botel willingly substituted for me by acting as Chair while I was on leave last spring. Many other colleagues have offered support, both emotional and substantive. Susan Lytle never failed to offer words of encouragment. In a moment of crisis, Ed Boe gave me his disk drive when mine broke, a minor example of his sustained support.

Long breakfast conversations with my friend Jenny Glusker provided me with the opportunity I needed to discuss what I was writing and the decisions I had to make concerning organization and presentation of material. A crystallographer rather than a linguist by profession, Jenny has nevertheless written enough books to know just what I was facing, and her advice was always sound.

One of the benefits of having had to put aside the rewriting and completing of this book for five years was that I was able to test it with my own classes and those of several colleagues. Although the original draft was rough, incomplete, and outdated, it was nevertheless useful in being the only relevant overview in existence. Rough as it was, therefore, I used it with successive classes in my course in sociolinguistics. When Nancy Hornberger joined our faculty and took over the course, she found it on my syllabus and began to use it herself, and when Cheri Micheau taught the course for us, she had her students read it as well. In addition, Leslie Beebe, Chair of Applied Linguistics at Teachers College, Columbia, used parts of the original draft with her classes there. Thus, the first rough draft of the book was class-tested numerous times with many different groups of students, both at the University of Pennsylvania and at Columbia University. The comments of the instructors and the feedback from students regarding clarity and accessibility of the material were most encouraging. I wish to thank both faculty and students for their warm responses.

Leslie Berriman, my sponsoring editor at Newbury House, deserves special appreciation for her never-failing patience and her expert advice and encouragement. It is rare to find an editor who has the ability to offer such a combination of personal warmth with professional expertise.

Last, but never least, I want to express loving gratitude to my family. In dedicating this book to him, I have already spoken of my husband's steadfast support. In addition, all of my children gave substantive help as well as emotional comfort. Danielle Wolfson read many of the rewritten chapters, making trenchant comments regarding both style and content. Dan Wolfson provided invaluable computer assistance, patiently helping me out of all sorts of trouble. Dan also proofread what I thought was the final revision of a tricky chapter, and forced me to revise it even more. Mark Wolfson read and commented on the first draft, engaging me in discussions that always proved fruitful. And, finally, I owe deep appreciation to Miriam Wolfson, who typed a large section of the original draft and who did a great deal of printing. Like her brothers and her sister-in-law, she helped me learn to use the computer, showed me how to solve problems, and gave technical assistance with the machinery.

I won't pretend that I could have managed to write this book without the support that was so generously given by all concerned.

Contents

Introduction   **1**

Chapter 1:   Sociolinguistic Relativity   **14**
Introduction   14
Sociolinguistic Diversity   15
The Consequences of Sociolinguistic Diversity Across Cultures   23
Sociolinguistic Diversity Within English-Speaking Communities   27
Conclusion   30

Chapter 2:   Communicative Competence and Rules of Speaking   **34**
Introduction   34
The Unconscious Nature of Sociolinguistic Rules   37
The Inadequacy of Intuition   40
Communicative Competence   44
Language and Community   48
Conclusion   53

Chapter 3:   Investigating Spoken Interaction   **55**
Introduction   55
The Philosophic Tradition   56
Ethnomethodology   60
The Notion of Face   67
Elicitation as a Method of Sociolinguistic Research in TESOL   68
The Use of Spontaneous Speech Data in Research in TESOL   72
Conclusion   78

Chapter 4:   The Sociolinguistic Behavior of English Speakers   **79**
Introduction   79
Forms of Address   79
Apologies   86
Requests   92

The Telephone   95
Disapproval   98
Refusals   100
The Expression of Gratitude   102
Greetings   104
Partings   105
Conclusion   107

Chapter 5:   An In-Depth Analysis of Speech Behavior   109
Introduction   109
Speech Behavior—Surface Forms and the Reflection of Cultural
    Values: The Investigation of Compliments   110
The Unrecognized Need for Negotiation: A Look at Invitations   118
Conclusion   124

Chapter 6:   Speech Behavior and Social Dynamics   125
Introduction   125
Speech Behavior and Negotiation of Roles   128
THE BULGE: A Theory of Social Interaction   129
Conclusion   139

Chapter 7:   Miscommunication   140
Introduction   140
Sociolinguistic/Pragmatic Transfer   141
Pragmatic Transfer Among Immigrants in Australia   141
The Study of Transfer in Apologies   143
The Study of Transfer in Refusals   146
The Study of Transfer in Requests   150
Pragmatic Transfer in the Expression of Gratitude   154
Interactional Sociolinguistics   156
TESOL and the Study of Miscommunication Across Cultures   159

Chapter 8:   Language and Sex   162
Introduction   162
Sexism in Language   164
Gender-Related Language Differences   176
Implications for Second Language Teaching   182
Conclusion   186

Chapter 9:   Social Class Variation in English–Speaking Communities   **188**
Variation by Social Class, Region, and Style   188
The Department Store Study   189
The New York City Study   190
Attention to Speech   191
Frequency   192
Hypercorrection   192
Subjective Reaction Tests   193
Linguistic Insecurity   194
Theoretical Foundations   195
A New Theory of Language Change   195
A Critique of the Theory   197
Urban Language Studies   197
The Norwich Study   198
Progress in Belfast   199
Reading and Speaking   200
Methodology   201
Methodological Problems and Alternatives   206
Conclusion   209

Chapter 10:   Dialects and Standards   **211**
Introduction   211
Standard English   212
Nonstandard English   214
The Deficit/Difference Controversy   217
Black Community Attitudes   220
The Ann Arbor Case   223
Bidialectalism   224
Ethnic Identity and Dialect Diversity   225
Nonnative English Speaker Attitudes Toward Dialects and Standards   228
Conclusion   230

Chapter 11:   Bilingual Education   **231**
Introduction   231
Early Approaches to the Education of Language-Minority Children   235
History of Bilingual Education in the Twentieth Century   236
Philosophical Differences   240
The Submersion Approach   240
English as a Second Language   241
The Immersion Model   242
Transitional Bilingual Education   244
Maintenance Bilingual Education   246

Controversies Over Bilingual Education   247
Conclusion   255

Chapter 12:   Multilingualism   **257**
Introduction   257
The Origins of Linguistic Diversity   258
Bilingualism   260
Ethnic Diversity and Linguistic Imposition   264
Problems of Linguistic Inequality   265
Pidgins and Creoles   268
The Post-Creole Continuum   273
Conclusion   274

Chapter 13:   English as a World Language   **275**
Why English?   275
Immigrant Groups   276
Yiddish: Case History of an Immigrant Language   277
Postcolonial Societies   281
English in India   282
English as a Foreign Language   286
English as a Shared Resource   287

Bibliography   **289**

Author Index   **313**

Subject Index   **317**

Introduction

Sociolinguistics, the study of the interplay of linguistic, social, and cultural factors in human communication, is of fundamental importance to the profession of TESOL (Teachers of English to Speakers of Other Languages). Whether we focus on the role of English in the world, on the contexts in which English may be acquired, or on the norms and patterns which condition its use and interpretation, the fact remains that the concerns of TESOL are linked to those of sociolinguistics at every level. Thus, both the field of sociolinguistics and its relevance to TESOL are grounded in the fact that language is intrinsic to human interaction. It is the purpose of this book to provide an overview of sociolinguistic principles and findings which are most closely related to the concerns of those whose profession involves the teaching of English as a second or foreign language.

The teaching of a second language necessarily involves a degree of intercultural communication, and this in turn leads to questions concerning social rules and cultural values which might otherwise not arise. Language teachers cannot help but become aware of differences in communicative conventions between one group and another. Language, both as medium and subject of study, is more than a system of sounds, meaning units, and syntax, more than simply a tool for getting meaning across. More than anything else, language is social behavior, and it is upon this fact that sociolinguistics is predicated.

Because language teaching is, by its very nature, concerned with understanding and interpreting cultural meaning, the connection between the two fields would seem to be both natural and inevitable. Yet the inclusion of sociolinguistics courses in programs designed to train ESL (English as a Second Language) teachers is a relatively new phenomenon. Only a few short years ago, the theoretical outlook and research orientation of scholars in the field was focused on the relationship between psychology and linguistics, or, as the approach came to be called, psycholinguistics. In seeking to understand the developmental aspects of second language acquisition, few researchers concerned themselves seriously at that time with the sociocultural aspects of language learning. But TESOL, itself a vigorous and growing area of applied linguistics, could not long remain immune to the rapidly expanding interest in the social aspects of language use which gathered momentum in the late 1960s and early 1970s. The above-mentioned connection between sociolinguistics and TESOL could not fail to be noticed. Scholars and practitioners of TESOL had much to offer and much to learn. Indeed, a fascination with the sociocultural

1

aspects of language behavior, and the opportunity to interact with people from cultures other than one's own, often serve as an initial attraction to the field. The knowledge and the sensitivity to different cultures which spring from such experience may well engender deeper interest and inspire scholarly research into what is, after all, a relatively new field of study. Thus, we come full circle with the ESL specialist as both learner and contributor in the endeavor to understand language as sociocultural behavior, which is, when all is said, sociolinguistics.

From the point of view of the wide variety of research encompassed by this field, it may be helpful to regard sociolinguistics as a sort of telescope through which language behavior may be studied in its sociocultural context. In looking through the small end of the telescope, we view speech at the level of face-to-face interaction, and this type of study is, indeed, called microsociolinguistics. By looking through the large end of the sociolinguistic telescope, we are able to see the workings of language contact, choice, use, maintenance, and change at the societal level, a field of study known as the sociology of language or macrosociolinguistics. To complete the metaphor it is necessary to point out that the focus of the sociolinguistic telescope can be adjusted to the strength appropriate to the object of study. Thus, it is possible to collect and analyze data on the frequency and distribution of a single sound (e.g., the occurrence of (r) in the speech of New Yorkers), on the use of a verb tense in narrative (e.g., the historical present), on the syntactic or semantic structure of a speech act (e.g., complimenting among speakers of American English), or on the structure of conversation generally (e.g., turn-taking). A wider focus permits examination of the structure of an entire speech situation, such as a cocktail party or a funeral, while the view through the larger end of the telescope can take in the speech behavior of an entire community or even a nation. Although detail must sometimes be sacrificed for breadth, it is always possible to readjust the focus.

For the sake of clarity, this book begins not with the smallest unit of analysis but rather with a discussion of sociolinguistic relativity, the issue most immediately relevant to those involved in communicating across cultures. What sociolinguistic relativity means is that each community has its own unique set of conventions, rules, and patterns for the conduct of communication and that these must be understood in the context of a general system which reflects the values and the structure of the society. No two societies are quite alike in this respect, although some have more in common than others. The central point behind the notion of sociolinguistic relativity is that no group has a monopoly on correct sociolinguistic behavior, for such judgments can be based only upon the rules one begins with. Lack of knowledge about the sociolinguistic rules which guide the behavior of an interlocutor from a different cultural background can lead to serious breakdowns in communication. For this reason, it is of prime importance for language learners to be made aware, insofar as possible, of the rules which obtain among native speakers of the target language. Where, as is most often the case, sociolinguistic rules have not yet been adequately analyzed and described, language learners and others who are involved in intercultural communication can at least be made sensitive to the fact that these patterns exist, and can be guided in ways to minimize misunderstandings. The first half of this book thus takes up issues which may be subsumed under the rubric "microsociolinguistics." Here we deal with the analysis of rules of speaking, the kinds of miscommunication which may arise through differences in rule systems, and in general with questions concerning the nature and acquisition of *communicative competence*. This important term, introduced into the literature by Dell Hymes in 1972, refers to the ability of native speakers to use the resources of their language(s) in ways that are not only linguistically accurate but also socially appropriate. Thus, each group knows its own communicative conventions, but since no two groups are quite the same in this respect, we cannot appeal to a universal system.

In describing speech behavior, there are a number of terms which will be useful to the reader. *Dialect*, for example, is a term which appears very often in linguistic literature and which, owing to its negative connotation in everyday usage, is quite frequently misunderstood. Indeed, in order to avoid confusion, many linguists prefer to make use of the term *variety*. Since the term *dialect* does appear in the literature, however, both terms will be used here. From the point of view of sociolinguistic description, a dialect is best regarded as a regional variant. That is, the dialect or variety of a language used by particular speakers is determined in large part by where they come from. Thus, New Englanders have a different set of pronunciation patterns than do people who come from the southeast of the United States, and the speech of New Yorkers differs from both. Pronunciation is one of the most obvious differences separating regional dialects, but syntactic and semantic patterns also differ, as do some sociolinguistic rules. Used in this sense, *dialect* is a neutral term and no value judgments are made by linguists in describing the speech of one region or another. Unless they were born abroad or have moved around a good deal, all native speakers of English must necessarily come from one dialect area or another. However, while linguists are deliberately nonjudgmental in this regard, there is no point in denying that some regional dialects are seen as having more *prestige* (or higher social status) than others. Clearly they do, and speakers, keenly aware of this, may make an effort, conscious or not, to change their native speech patterns in order to disguise what they consider to be low status or, to use the most common sociolinguistic term, *stigmatized* features. Not only is it the case that some regional dialects enjoy greater prestige than others, but it is also true that within each region greater prestige is attached to the speech habits of the upper socioeconomic groups than to those of the lower. Social stratification is reflected in pronunciation as well as in syntax and vocabulary choice, and this too is so well known that speakers will, in certain circumstances, attempt to model their speech on that of the prestige group. This phenomenon and its consequences, as well as its relationship to second language learning, will be described in detail in the chapter dealing with social class variation. In addition to the foregoing types of variation, we may also recognize varieties of a language which can be distinguished according to the function to which speech is put. The term most commonly used to refer to such a functional variety is *register*. If one thinks of all the different contexts in which language is used, it becomes obvious that, depending upon the situation, different styles of speech are appropriate. Indeed, the ability to vary one's speech with the situation is an important aspect of native speaker communicative competence, the knowledge of what to say to whom and in which situations. Thus, the same speaker will normally choose a different means of self-expression when addressing a large audience of strangers than when engaged in a spirited conversation with close personal friends. When we wish to refer to situational variation in speech, the term speech *style* is used. From what we have learned through observation and through anthropological studies of cultures around the world, it would appear that stylistic variation in speech is universal. This being the case, it stands to reason that learners of English will, so far as they are able, vary their speech behavior in an attempt to speak appropriately in the differing speech situations in which they find themselves. Thus, there is much merit in Tarone's (1979) suggestion that second language acquisition researchers pay special attention to stylistic variation in the speech of language learners (their interlanguage) in order to get a true picture of their sociolinguistic competence. The term *register* is most often used to describe the speech varieties which pertain to specific occupations or domains. Thus, we think of the register of a lawyer, a kindergarten teacher, or a sportscaster, each in a particular professional setting, and we would have very little difficulty in recognizing which features of speech were typical of each. Since register and style both involve the selection of speech forms appropriate to a given situation, and since participating members of a given speech community move from one situation to another during the course of their daily lives, it is obvious that speakers must control a considerable range of forms of speech. The ability to use the appropriate register or speech style is of particular importance to language learners, as Halliday et al. (1964) and Ervin-Tripp (1972) have pointed out. The choice of items from the wrong style or register and the mixing of items from different styles and registers are among the most frequent mistakes made by learners of a language.

All this is not to suggest that comprehensive, empirically based sociolinguistic analyses of the varieties of speech used by English speakers, or, indeed, by those of any language, are already in existence. Much work remains to be done before it is possible to give a truly adequate account of the linguistic features appropriate to the many contexts in which speakers interact. Because the methods used in the investigation of sociolinguistic behavior have a critical effect on the validity of the results obtained, a knowledge of the advantages and disadvantages of different means of collecting and analyzing data is vital to our ability to assess the findings reported in the literature. Wherever relevant, questions pertaining to methodology will be taken up and the different approaches used by researchers will be described. In this connection, it will be argued that speech is best studied within the framework of the context in which it occurs. Other methods for the collection of data on speech behavior may provide a useful complement to the study of spontaneous speech, making it possible to compare and to generalize findings from more limited samples. The position taken here, however, is that nothing can replace the investigation of speech as it actually takes place. This viewpoint is based on the unarguable fact that speech does not take place in a social or situational vacuum. It occurs in specific places, on specific occasions, about specific topics, and to specific others. And the forms an individual speaker may use will vary greatly, depending on all these factors. Without taking such situational variables into account, we cannot hope to obtain a realistic understanding of the range, distribution, and function of the forms we wish to study and teach. It is up to the sociolinguist to discover how women and men of differing ages, regional, social, educational, and ethnic backgrounds use speech in differing situations and with a variety of interlocutors. In order to get a realistic picture of the factors that condition how people interact, it is best to base analyses on data gathered through the observation of naturally occurring or spontaneous speech. The underlying sociolinguistic principle is that individuals have, as a part of their competence as native speakers, a repertoire of speech styles, registers, and behaviors which they vary according to the rules of appropriateness which exist in the speech communities of which they are members. No one speaks the same way all the time.

Perhaps the most significant contribution to the development of the study of speech in use has been the theoretical framework called the *ethnography of speaking* proposed by Dell Hymes in 1962. While many frameworks used in the analysis of speech behavior have provided analytic dimensions, concepts, terms, and methods that have contributed added richness to research in the field of sociolinguistics and TESOL, none has proved so comprehensive, relevant, or fruitful as that set forth by Hymes in the ethnography of speaking.

For this reason, although we will describe other frameworks of analysis relevant to work in TESOL in a later chapter, an explanation, albeit brief, of what is meant by the ethnography of speaking is fundamental to an understanding of the issues and questions that have provided the major inspiration for a great part of the scholarly research into sociolinguistics and TESOL. As Hymes has put it, the ethnography of speaking

> . . . fills the gap between what is usually described in grammars, and what is usually described in ethnographies. Both use speech as evidence of other patterns; neither brings it into focus in terms of its own patterns. In another sense, this is a question of what a child internalizes about speaking, beyond rules of grammar and a dictionary, while becoming a full-fledged member of its speech community. *Or, it is a question of what a foreigner must learn about a group's verbal behavior in order to participate appropriately and effectively in its activities.* The ethnography of speaking is concerned with the situations and uses, the patterns and functions, of speaking as an activity in its own right. (Hymes 1962:101, emphasis mine)

As Hymes goes on to explain, the rationale for engaging in such research includes the uncovering of cross-cultural patterns and differences in the use of speech. Although Hymes himself does not explicitly state the connection, the cross-cultural study of language use is an area critical to language learning and provides the foundation for virtually all of the sociolinguistic research undertaken by scholars within the field of TESOL. Hymes himself states the purpose of engaging in the ethnography of speaking in the following words:

> Why undertake such field work? The reasons are several: because the phenomena are there, ready to be brought into order; *so that systematic descriptions can give rise to a comparative study of the cross-cultural variations in a major mode of human behavior (a "comparative speaking" beside comparative religion, comparative law, and the like)*, and give it its place in theory; for the contribution to other kinds of concern, such as studies of the formation of personality in early years. (Hymes 1962:102, emphasis mine)

A linguist with considerable training and interest in anthropology, Hymes was disturbed by the fact that anthropologists rarely provided descriptions of the speech behavior of the groups they studied. This meant that it was possible to read an anthropological account, or an ethnography, without learning anything about the use of speech in the society under investigation. At the same time, Hymes noted, linguists, concerned with the details of language structure, paid little or no attention to the context in which speech is embedded or to the sociocultural factors which condition its use. In order to gain a full picture of culture on the one hand and language on the other, Hymes urged scholars in both anthropology and linguistics to join forces in examining speech behavior as both the primary realization of language and a major factor of cultural organization. More recently, the field of language teaching, and most specifically that of TESOL, has been heavily influenced by the seminal notions such as that of communicative competence originally introduced by Hymes. Thus, although scholars within the field of sociolinguistics and TESOL have adopted and, indeed, originated a variety of research paradigms, most of the underlying questions and dimensions of analysis are those proposed by Hymes.

Useful sets of categories and components for analyzing and describing the patterns of speaking in a given speech community are set forth by Hymes (1962, 1972a, 1974a) and have provided a basic framework for the study of sociolinguistic rules. To begin with, Hymes gives a taxonomy of technical terms for use in the investigation of the ways and rules of speaking in a given speech community. The most general descriptive term, *speech situation*, includes contexts such as "ceremonies, fights, hunts, meals, lovemaking and the like" (Hymes 1974a:51). But, although speech situations provide the context in which speech occurs, such situations are not in themselves governed by specific sets of rules for the conduct of speech. The term *speech event*, on the other hand, is intended to be technical and refers to specific activities involving speech, such as a private conversation, a classroom lecture, or a political debate: "The term speech event will be restricted to activities, or aspects of activities, that are directly governed by rules or norms for the use of speech. An event may consist of a single speech act, but will often comprise several" (Hymes 1974a:52). The term *speech act* "is the minimal term of the set just discussed. . . . It represents a level distinct from the sentence, and not identifiable with any single portion of other levels of grammar, nor with segments of any particular size defined in terms of their levels of grammar . . . a sentence interrogative in form may be now a request, now a command, now a statement; a request may be manifested by a sentence that is now interrogative, now declarative, now imperative in form; and one and the same sentence may be taken as a promise or a threat, depending on the norm of interpretation applied to it" (Hymes 1974a:52–53). A speech act may therefore be culturally defined as a complaint, a compliment, an apology, or a refusal, and competent native speakers will have little difficulty in identifying them as such. A given speech act or event is, as Hymes points out, conditioned by rules of conduct and interpretation, and the ability to use these rules appropriately is a critical part of the communicative competence of the native speaker. Hymes further points out that a good ethnographic means for identifying speech events is to begin with words that name them. Thus, starting from culturally named speech situations, events, and acts in English, it is possible to analyze speech behavior on a number of levels. Work has been done, for example, on narratives in American English (e.g., Labov and Waletzky 1967, Labov et al. 1968, Labov 1972, Wolfson 1976, 1978a, 1979a), as well as on jokes (Sacks 1974), on ritual insults among groups of black teenagers in Harlem (Labov 1972, Labov et al. 1968), on forms of address (e.g., Brown and Ford 1961, Ervin-Tripp 1969), as well as on a number of other forms of speech behavior which will be discussed in detail in the first six chapters of this book.

To recapitulate, then, Hymes proposes a taxonomy that can serve as a starting point for the investigation of the way speech is used in a given society or community. The minimal unit of analysis, the speech act, and larger sequences, called speech events, are both governed by rules for appropriate use. Speech acts and events are embedded in the more general speech situation which provides the context for rule-governed speech behavior but which is not itself so governed.

The paradigm Hymes proposes for approaching research in ethnography of speaking "requires discovering a relevant frame or context, identifying the items which contrast within it, and determining the dimensions of contrast for the items within the set so defined" (Hymes 1962:103). In order to provide a comprehensive framework for such analysis, Hymes (1972a) has proposed a set of components of speech which can be subsumed under the acronym SPEAKING. It is important to understand that while the rules of speaking may take the form of statements of relationship among components, any of the following components may be used as a starting point so that the others are viewed in relation to it. Clearly, a comprehensive list of this sort must include some overlap. This is intended since different components of speech may be more relevant to some analyses than to others. Hymes lists 16 components which, for the sake of ease of memory, he groups into eight categories which, taken together, spell out the word *speaking*. A brief description of these components will serve to demonstrate the factors which need to be taken into account in a descriptive analysis of speech:

1. Setting: This refers to the time, place,and physical circumstances in which speech takes place.

2. Scene: Here Hymes refers to the psychological setting of speech or to what may be seen as the cultural definition of an occasion.

Together, Setting and Scene are combined into the component called "Act Situation" and recalled by the first letter of the acronym, *S*.

P which stands for "Participants," includes the following four components, which may have relevance to the analysis:

3. Speaker or sender of a message.

4. Addressor: Since in some societies, the speaker is not the same person who actually gives the message, this component is included for use where necessary.

5. Hearer or receiver or audience.

6. Addressee: It should be noted that in some instances the addressee is not a person. People in English-speaking societies speak to animals, for example, and may even address such inanimate objects as walls.

Together, these four components may be referred to as "Participants," represented by the letter *P*. Put simply, Hymes's view of participants has to do with who is talking and who is listening. Obviously, the relevant attributes of participants may change or be very different for different speech acts and events. Therefore, while participants should be seen as intrinsic to an analysis of speech behavior, the researcher will need to investigate the dimensions of contrasts included under this category in light of the specific subject of study.

7. Purposes or outcomes.

8. Goals.

The above two components may be subsumed under the term *Ends*, or *E* in the acronym, and have to do with what the speaker intends to accomplish and to what degree he or she does, in fact, accomplish the intended purpose.

9. Message Form: This component is fundamental to all rules of speaking since it involves the description of how something is said. Since the way things are said is part of what is said, it is not possible to analyze speech without first looking at the form itself.

10. Message Content: This refers to the topic or what is being talked about. Clearly, content is interdependent with form, and both are central to the analysis of the speech act or event being investigated.

Together, Message Form and Message Content have to do with what is said and in what order. According to Hymes, they can be combined and subsumed under the heading "Act Sequence," or *A* in the mnemonic SPEAKING.

11. Keys: This has to do with the manner or spirit in which something is said (e.g., serious, joking, sarcastic, playful). As Hymes points out, when the key in which something is said is in conflict with its overt form or content, the key will override these.

12. Channels: This refers to whether the medium of communication is spoken or written (since both oral and written forms are included in Hymes's framework). To elaborate further, talk may take place in face-to-face interaction or by means of the telephone, for example. Writing may be by hand or typewritten, and may further take the form of a memo, a formal letter, or similar vehicles.

13. Forms of Speech has to do with the languages or codes, varieties, and registers which may be used.

Both Channels and Forms of Speech are joined as means or agencies of communication and are therefore labeled "Instrumentalities," or *I*.

14. Norms of Interaction refers to the specific behaviors that are considered appropriate for different kinds of speaking in different societies. Because they have to do with rules and constraints on what participants may say or write to one another, they necessarily involve the analysis of social structure and of social relationships.

15. Norms of Interpretation involve the way different kinds of speech are regarded and understood by members of a given group and therefore involve what Hymes calls the belief system of the community. Where norms of interpretation are different, they often lead to miscommunication across cultures.

Norms of Interaction and Norms of Interpretation are grouped together as "Norms," or *N*.

16. Genres: These refer to categories of communication, such as poems, curses, prayers, jokes, proverbs, myths, commercials, or form letters, and will often coincide with speech events. "Genres" form the letter *G* in the acronym SPEAKING.

In analyzing the use of appropriate speech use for a society, it is often helpful to state rules of speaking in terms of the relationships among the various components listed above. Any one of the components described may serve as a point of departure and thus be held constant, while each of the others is viewed in relationship to it. Clearly, the list of components given by Hymes is intended to be a comprehensive one and will necessarily include factors which are relevant to some societies and not to others. Therefore, it should never be assumed that these components of speech are intended to be used as a checklist in the sense that each needs to be accounted for each time a rule of speaking is under analysis. Rather, they are meant to provide an overall picture of the possible variables that may operate to form the basis of analysis. It would therefore not be productive for any investigator to attempt to describe the rules which operate to condition the ways in which specific speech acts or events are realized. The acronym SPEAKING has been offered as a tool to help investigators remember the many components of speech which might be operative in a given situation and is in no sense presented as a mechanical device against which analyses of speech behavior should be gauged. As Hymes (1974a) explicitly says:

> Ethnographic material so far investigated indicates that some sixteen or seventeen components have sometimes to be distinguished. No rule has been found that requires specification of all simultaneously. There are always redundancies, and sometimes a rule requires explicit mention of a relation between only two, message form and some other. (It is a general principle that all rules involve message form, if not by affecting its shape, then by governing its interpretation.) Since each of the components may sometimes be a factor, however, each has to be recognized in the general grid. (Hymes 1974a:59)

Having described, however briefly, the theoretical background which has been most influential in informing a great part of the sociolinguistic work to be discussed in detail in the first six chapters of this book, we then move on to somewhat broader societal issues.

While a discussion of issues regarding language and sex spans both micro- and macrosociolinguistics, the enormity of the sociopolitical issues which are implicated in this area of work have led to the decision to include it in the second section. One of the most important, and until recently, least studied, variables conditioning speech behavior is that of gender. Although early travelers' accounts and anthropologists' descriptions made mention of differences in men's and women's language in non-Western cultures, little attention was paid to such distinctions in the Western languages spoken by the scholars themselves. (For a notable exception, see Jespersen 1922.) Conventional wisdom held that women did indeed speak differently from men and that these differences reflected women's lesser ability to think logically as well as their "delicacy" of feeling. It was not until the women's movement of the 1960s that these and other stereotypes began to be put to the test of empirical investigation. Once begun, the systematic study of the ways in which language is used by, about, and to women has burgeoned into a dynamic field of study in its own right. Along with the investigation of sex as a sociolinguistic variable came a strong impetus to analyze and publicize the many ways in which language reflects the deeply ingrained sexism of our society. In the chapter devoted to language and sex, we will look at the research findings from this growing literature. The subject is included here not only for its intrinsic interest but because research findings in this area have serious implications for education in general and for TESOL in particular. On the one hand, English language teaching materials (e.g., the very textbooks used to teach nonnative speakers) have been found to reflect a serious sexist bias. On the other hand, if it is true that there are differences in the language used by male and female speakers of English, then this is important information for materials developers and ESL teachers. It would not do, after all, for students to be taught to express themselves inappropriately in this respect. Here, too, it may be that second language acquisition researchers familiar with sociolinguistic methods and findings will have an important contribution to make. For, just as variation in style seems to be a universal aspect of language behavior, there is reason to believe that the fact that differences along the lines of sex have been documented for speakers of English and a number of other languages, both Western and non-Western, may well indicate that sex is a universal sociolinguistic variable. If this is true, it would be an important finding. One interesting way of looking at such potential differences would be to analyze the interlanguage of male and female learners by replicating some of the studies reported in the language and gender literature. Here, as in so many other areas, sociolinguists and ESL specialists have much to gain from one another.

Social variation in language has been one of the major foci of the field of sociolinguistics since its inception in the early 1960s, and no textbook in sociolinguistics would be complete without a description of the research that has been done in this area. Since Labov's groundbreaking study, *The Social Stratification of English in New York City*, was published in 1966, a great deal of interest and attention has been devoted to investigating the patterns which both condition and reflect social status in speech behavior. In Chapter 8 we will review the most well known and influential of these studies and discuss their implications for language teaching and learning in the context of TESOL.

By no means do all native speakers of English speak what is known as Standard English, and it is important for ESL instructors, of both children and adults, to know as much as possible about the educational implications of linguistic diversity and related controversies over school achievement, as well as about nonstandard dialects themselves. Teachers of English as a foreign or second language, working in countries where English is not the native language, can benefit from this information also, since neither the sociolinguistic principles nor the issues underlying the controversies are limited to the setting under discussion. Indeed, not only does knowledge of this area shed light on many of the most confusing and disturbing aspects of American society, it also provides insights into troublesome questions about linguistic purity in general. The chapter on dialects and standards will take up these problems and their implications for TESOL.

Concern over the educational problems of children from minority group backgrounds has been, like the renewed concern over women's issues, linked to the civil rights movement which gained momentum in the second half of the twentieth century. From the point of view of language teaching, one of the most important pieces of social legislation to come out of this movement was the Bilingual Education Act of 1968. What this has meant for the education of children from non-English-speaking backgrounds has depended largely upon the form of bilingual education to which they were exposed. Chapter 10, which presents an overview of the history of bilingual education in this country, together with a description of the various approaches and models and the philosophical positions leading to their development, will give perspectives on the implications of these endeavors to the profession of TESOL.

If concerns over the language problems of women and of minority group members may be seen as sociolinguistics at the societal or macrolevel, then issues having to do with multilingualism and with the spread of English epitomize this perspective. The ways in which languages come into contact through migration and conquest, the types of multilingualism which result, and the effects of power and of social inequality on language attitudes, choice, and use are all topics of great relevance to English language teachers. In the chapter on multilingualism, we examine the ways in which various language situations come about and the problems and opportunities they pose. Although linguistic diversity is everywhere apparent, it is in third world countries, still struggling toward political, economic, and social stability, that it presents the most critical challenge. Here we are reminded that the political boundary lines of many newly independent nations of the developing world were created to suit the convenience of colonial administrations, and that these political boundaries often reflect little or no relationship to ethnic or linguistic

borders. Language planning and language policies in developing nations are generally aimed at technological and economic advancement and at political unification
in the face of often extreme ethnolinguistic diversity and frequently of longstanding
interethnic hostility. Decisions regarding language choice in instruction, as well as
in the sphere of government and commerce, are crucial to hopes and expectations
of equality of educational opportunity and of socioeconomic mobility engendered
by political independence from colonial rule. For this reason, finally, we turn to
the overwhelming implications for TESOL of the spread of English throughout the
world. Here we must take into consideration the historical forces which set the
stage, as well as the political, economic, and technological developments which
have led to the worldwide acceptance of English as the major language of wider
communication.

Patterns of language shift are illustrated through a description of the immigrant
experience in the United States, taking the decline of the Yiddish language as an
example of how American nativism combined with social, educational, and economic incentives has led to the linguistic, although not necessarily the ethnic,
assimilation of minority groups. Since the 1980s have already witnessed the largest
wave of immigration to the United States since the 40-year period ending with
World War I, we have much to gain from a careful appraisal of that era.

As the exemplar par excellence of the language problems and controversies
resulting from the colonial and postcolonial experience, India's linguistic situation
is described in some detail. Here we come to a discussion of the political issues
surrounding the teaching of English as a second language and of the implications for
TESOL of the growing acceptance of nonnative institutionalized varieties of English (see Bailey and Gorlach 1982, Pride 1982, Kachru 1982b). Thus, the final
chapters of the book will provide a background on the issues, problems, and
solutions concerned with multilingualism and with the spread of English, topics that
are of considerable concern to TESOL.

In this regard, it is important to point out that the term *nonnative speaker of
English,* one which we will, in fact, use frequently in the chapters to follow, covers
a number of very different groups. Traditionally, it has been the custom to make a
rough division between those nonnative speakers who use English as a second
language (ESL speakers) and those for whom it is learned and used as a foreign
language (EFL speakers). As the use of the English language has spread, however
(see Fishman et al.1977), this distinction becomes more and more difficult to make.
When we begin to think of all the various nonnative speaking groups which have
incorporated the use of the English language into their daily lives, the picture
becomes complex indeed. Maintaining the distinction has its uses, however, and in
the chapters to follow we will set forth some examples of English users of different
categories in order to give a sense of the breadth of the field with which we are
dealing. The traditional distinction, that between ESL and EFL, can be broken
down in a number of ways. To put it simply, there are people all over the world who
study English as a foreign language, just as students in the United States study
French or Spanish in order to learn to communicate in another language and to read

the literature that has been produced in it. Thus, students in European countries and in, for example, Japan or Korea have their normal school instruction in their national language, and increasingly choose or are required to study English as a subject. For some of these students, the knowledge of English becomes increasingly important as they choose professions in which the English language has become the international means of communication. Frequently, students from these countries decide to study abroad, and because of the growing importance of the English language, a considerable number of these students choose to do their undergraduate or graduate work in one of the English-speaking countries such as the United States, the United Kingdom, or Australia. It is with the foreign students in the United States, here to learn English and to pursue their studies, that much of the early part of this book is concerned. When we come to the category known as ESL, we are, in actuality, speaking of two very different groups. On the one hand, there is a large and ever-growing number of immigrants in the United States and in other English-speaking countries for whom English is not the native language, but who must and do learn to speak it as a second language in order to earn their livelihoods and to interact generally in the mainstream culture. Further, there are a great number of emerging nations, frequently former British colonies, which, as mentioned above, have chosen to retain the English language for purposes of communication within their national borders.

With English as the official or coofficial language of approximately 25 percent of the world's nations, with the number of nonnative speakers now approximately equal to the number of native speakers, and with English now the internationally recognized language of diplomacy, communication, science and technology, media, postal systems, and transportation, the teaching of English has assumed major importance. It is the aim of this book to provide an introduction to sociolinguistics which will, in some small way, help to prepare professionals in TESOL for the heavy responsibility they have undertaken.

1

Sociolinguistic Relativity

INTRODUCTION

The principle underlying the investigation of patterns and conventions of language behavior, known as sociolinguistic rules or rules of speaking, is that these are far from universal across cultural groups. This principle will be referred to as sociolinguistic diversity. There is considerable evidence for this principle. Indeed, sociolinguistic studies, particularly those conducted within the framework of the ethnography of speaking, provide striking evidence that speech communities vary greatly with respect to rules of speaking or sociolinguistic rules, however one wishes to designate these patterns (Hymes 1962, Gumperz and Hymes 1964, 1972, Bauman and Sherzer 1974). Thus, the norms and values which inform speakers' knowledge as to what is appropriate to say to whom, and under which conditions, show considerable variation from community to community around the world, not only from one language group to another but within language groups as well. This phenomenon, sociolinguistic relativity, has important implications for language learning and for intercultural communication generally. Everyone recognizes that languages are different from one another in such areas as phonology, syntax, and lexicon. When people learn a new language, they expect to have to learn new rules of pronunciation and grammar and to memorize a new vocabulary. What is often not taken into account, however, is that the individual who wishes to acquire the ability to interact effectively with native speakers of the target language must also learn the rules of speaking of the speech community which uses it.

The cause of intercultural misunderstanding, then, is twofold. To begin with, people coming from different sociocultural backgrounds tend to have very different value systems, and these are manifested in speech as well as in other sorts of social behavior. These differences often lead to misunderstanding. What is even more critical is that the diversity in value systems and in the ways in which these are expressed is usually not well understood. When people coming from different backgrounds interact, they tend to judge each other's behavior according to their own value systems. The more we know about other cultures, the more we are able to recognize that being different is not a question of being better or worse—it is merely a question of being different. This principle, which is usually referred to as cultural relativity, when extended to the evaluation of sociolinguistic rules, may be referred to as sociolinguistic relativity. The adoption of such a point of view would aid greatly in reducing the negative results of the sorts of misunderstanding which are bound to arise when people interact across cultures. But in order to adopt this perspective, we must first understand how sociolinguistic diversity manifests itself. Some illustrations of the kinds of differences that exist, and of reactions to these differences, will help to clarify the situation.

SOCIOLINGUISTIC DIVERSITY

Inculcated in early childhood as part of the socialization process, appropriate speech usage within the context of a given society is so linked to such attributes as good manners, honesty, sincerity, and good character generally that it is often difficult for language learners, and for native speakers with whom they interact, to accept the notion of diversity along these lines. Indeed, if there is anything universal about rules of speaking, it is the tendency of members of one speech community to judge the speech behavior of others by their own standards. It is exactly this lack of knowledge about sociolinguistic diversity which lies at the root of most intercultural misunderstanding. Since how people speak is part of what they say, language learners may well find themselves in the position of being unable to interpret the meaning of what native speakers say to them even though all the vocabulary is quite familiar. With no other frame of reference at their disposal, nonnative speakers have little choice but to interpret what they hear according to the rules of speaking of their own native speech communities. And since the rules are very likely to be quite different, misunderstandings are almost inevitable. The result may be amusement or contempt, but it is just as likely to be disappointment, shock, or even serious insult.

Thomas (1983) discusses the problem of sociolinguistic miscommunication. For Thomas, "pragmatic failure" is "the inability to understand what is meant by what is said." As is often the case in the literature on cross-cultural differences, the term *pragmatics* is used instead of the term *sociolinguistics* for descriptions of patterns having to do with interpersonal interaction, or what we have called *microsociolinguistics*. Although there is virtually no difference in meaning between these two terms as we are using them here, it is true that the term *pragmatics* derives from a different tradition of scholarship within philosophy and formal linguistics, and although it must be considered a part of sociolinguistics, the study of pragmatics has a narrower scope. It does not, for example, cover issues having to do with language problems at the societal level, issues which we will deal with under the rubric of "macrosociolinguistics." For our purposes, the terms *sociolinguistic* and *pragmatic* rules may be used interchangeably. Thomas, for example, defines pragmatics as "language in use". The term *sociolinguistics* may be defined in exactly the same words. Coming from a somewhat different tradition, heavily influenced by anthropology and sociology, many sociolinguists would tend to look for the ways in which sociolinguistic diversity is organized, while the scholar involved in what is called pragmatics may tend instead to look for universals of human behavior. From the point of view of TESOL, and of applied linguists concerned with miscommunication across cultures and with how best to help language learners, the distinctions between the two terms are of very minor import.

What is particularly interesting about Thomas's description of what she calls pragmatic failure is that she identifies two very different sources of cross-cultural miscommunication and makes a distinction between the two with respect to difficulty of analysis and possible remedies, in terms of both the responsibility of teachers and the responses of language learners. For this reason, Thomas's dichotomy provides us with a useful starting point for our discussion of types and sources of sociolinguistic differences leading to miscommunication between language learners and native speakers of the target language.

The first of the categories Thomas identifies is what she calls "pragmalinguistic failure," as opposed to what she terms "sociopragmatic failure." Thomas uses the term *failure* rather than *error* because, although grammar can, she says, be judged according to prescriptive rules, the nature of pragmatic or sociolinguistic patterns is such that it is not possible to say that "the pragmatic force of an utterance is 'wrong.' All we can say is that it failed to achieve the speaker's goal." In the case of what Thomas calls "pragmalinguistic failure," language learners translate an utterance from their first language into the target language but fail to get their meaning across because the communicative conventions behind the utterances used are different. For example, it is typical in English to make indirect requests by using a question form, such as "Can you pass the salt?" or "Why don't you close the window?" As every native speaker of English knows, these are not requests for information, they are requests for action. If, however, a native speaker of English, learning another language such as Russian, were to translate such an indirect request literally, the Russian addressee would not be able to interpret the utterance as a request and would instead hear it as a question. Thus, the force of the utterance would be lost and the English-speaking learner of Russian would have failed to make his or her meaning understood. This, as Thomas points out, is more a linguistic problem than a pragmatic one since it has little to do with speakers' perceptions of what constitutes appropriate behavior and a great deal to do with knowing how to phrase a request so that it will be interpreted as a request rather than as an information question.

Numerous examples of what Thomas categorizes as pragmalinguistic failure exist in the literature. One of these is cited by Richards (1980:418), who has this to say:

> A crucial goal for conversationists is to interpret the intended speech act appropriately. The following example of a telephone conversation between a professor (A) and a foreign student (B) illustrates the student's failure to interpret the intended speech act:
>
> A: Hello, is Mr Simatapung there please?
> B: Yes.
> A: Oh . . . may I speak to him please?

B: Yes.
A: Oh . . . are you Mr. Simatapung?
B: Yes, this is Mr. Simatapung.

Here B answers A's question as if it were an existential question rather than a summons.

One very useful point made by Thomas in her categorization of "pragmalinguistic" failure has to do directly with the teaching of the rules she describes. "In general, I would suggest that the foreign learner is not noticeably more sensitive about having pragmalinguistic failure pointed out to him/her, than about having grammatical errors corrected. Insofar as s/he is prepared to learn the language at all, s/he is usually willing, if not able, to try to conform to the pragmalinguistic norms of the target language."

The second type of "pragmatic failure" that Thomas identifies is the type we are most concerned with here. What Thomas calls "sociopragmatic failure" has to do with knowing what to say and whom to say it to. This goes directly to the issue of what we refer to when we speak of sociolinguistic diversity. Many of the misunderstandings we have been dealing with stem from what Thomas identifies as differences in evaluations regarding what she terms "size of imposition," "tabus," "cross-culturally different assessments of relative power or social distance," and "value judgements." By separating out what she sees as major areas in which there exist differences in cultural rules regarding speech behavior, Thomas provides a useful way of looking at the types of diversity which exist across cultures and which, when encountered in cross-cultural interactions, often lead to problems. Although these categories are not exhaustive, we will find them represented among the examples of cross-cultural diversity given below.

Japanese students and immigrants living in the United States, for example, report that they find it strange and rather offensive when Americans extend an invitation to a social gathering by indicating when and where it will take place and then adding some sort of phrase like "Come if you want to." Since Japanese rules of speaking require that a potential guest be urged to accept an invitation, while American rules impose a constraint on pinning people down to accepting possibly unwanted invitations, and since neither group is likely to be aware of the other's rules, it is difficult to avoid misunderstandings. In a case like this, the Japanese feels hurt and uncertain whether the invitation is really sincerely meant.

This particular problem seems to arise with a number of nonnative speakers from other areas and language backgrounds as well. Arabic speakers, for example, report a similar difficulty with American invitations which leave the decision about whether to attend up to the person being invited. A further problem having to do with social visits encountered by Arabic speakers, as well as members of a number of other cultures, is that the conventions for the behavior of host and guest follow very different patterns. As guests, nonnative speakers from these areas of the world expect that, when they do go to visit someone, refreshments will be urged on them repeatedly, while they, following the rules taught to them since childhood, are expected to refuse again and again. An American host, used to a very different pattern of behavior, is unlikely to make an offer of refreshments more than once or twice. If guests refuse to accept anything to eat or drink, they may or may not be seen as rude (since the hosts will almost certainly have prepared food and drink to offer), but they *are* likely to be taken at their word. The outcome is apt to be guests who are hungry and confused, and hosts who are rather annoyed that the refreshments they have prepared have gone untasted and unappreciated.

Nonnative speakers' responses to what are seen as violations of the obligations of host and guest occur in examples of questions Malaysian students reported they felt should not have been asked of a guest by a host, such as "Do you want something to drink?" or "Have you eaten?" The Malaysian students, in their report on "inappropriate questions" (part of a class research project), go on to explain, saying: "In Malay culture, it is not appropriate to ask these questions when someone visits your house. It is understood that we must serve our guest something to drink or eat, regardless if they want it or not" (Jamaluddin et al. 1986). An example of the sort of misunderstanding that so frequently occurs when nonnative speakers visit American homes is given by Rubin (1983:14): "An anecdote was recounted about an Arab speaker's first encounter with some Americans. On his first visit to an American home, he was served some delicious sandwiches. When the hostess came to offer seconds, he refused. Much to his chagrin, the hostess didn't repeat the offer. Thus the Arab sat there, confronted by some lovely sandwiches which he couldn't eat."

In light of other descriptions of cross-cultural diversity in the offering of refreshments to guests, it would appear that the pattern described for Americans holds for the British as well. Thomas (1983), for example, makes a somewhat similar point with respect to the behavior of Ukranian hosts in contrast to norms in the United Kingdom. Thomas's example has to do not with the initial offer of food but with repeated offers of more and more. Taking the viewpoint of the British guest in the Ukraine, she describes a situation in which the guest is put in almost the opposite position of the foreign guest in the United States: "Thus, in the Ukraine it may happen that a guest is pressed as many as seven or eight times to take more food, whereas in the UK it would be unusual to do so more than twice. . . . Indeed, British recipients of such hospitality sometimes feel that their host is behaving *impolitely* by forcing them into a bind, since they run out of polite refusal strategies long before the Ukrainian host has exhausted his/her repertoire of polite insistence strategies."

One of the most common problems in communicating across cultures is that speech communities vary considerably with respect to what is considered appropriate to talk about. Comparing her own rules as a British speaker of English with sociolinguistic behavior in the Ukraine, Thomas remarks that there it is perfectly acceptable to ask directly about a stranger's "income, politics, religion, marital status, etc.," whereas among the British, such questions are regarded as intrusive.

Richards (1980:424) also makes reference to the need for language learners to know "which topics have language specific conversational restrictions. They need to know, for instance what one can request in English without causing offense, the degree to which other people's statements and beliefs can be disagreed with, as well as the topics one can talk about on first encounter with a stranger of equal status, of higher status, and of the same sex. Thus common questions from Asians on first encounters such as 'Are you married?' and 'How old are you?' may deviate from topic norms for English speakers, as does the common question from Arabs, 'How much did that cost?' "

What is considered appropriate in terms of topics for such speech events as conversational narratives, jokes, questions, and even sermons or lectures may be very different across cultures, as may topics for any sort of discussion. However, it is always necessary, in considering specific sociolinguistic rules, to recognize that these taboos are rarely categorical. Rather, it is reasonable to assume that constraints on topic, like most sociolinguistic rules, are usually conditioned heavily by the situation in which the talk takes place and the social identity of the participants vis-á-vis one another.

Societies may also differ in the attributes by which relative power and status are accorded to their members. In Japan, for example, a man's status depends to a large degree on the prestige of the organization with which he is affiliated. Independent businessmen, no matter how successful, may well be regarded with less esteem than a middle-level administrator working for a large and well-known company. An example of this difference in the assessment of social status comes from Christopher (1982), who says:

> The fact that mere membership in the bureaucracy automatically confers prestige upon someone reflects perhaps the most important single aspect of social status in Japan; far more than in the United States, it is acquired not by individual achievement but by group affiliation. A number of years ago, at a breakfast meeting with a representative group of "young" Tokyo businessmen, I was particularly impressed by a handsome, compact man in his late thirties who had parlayed some innovative ideas into a profitable business of his own. Apparently I concentrated my attention upon him somewhat too heavily. In any case, when the breakfast was over, one of the people who had helped to arrange it politely pointed out that there had been other, more important people present—namely, middle level executives from some of Japan's biggest corporations. None of these cautious corporate types had struck me as being nearly as imaginative as the entrepreneur, and certainly none of them had accomplished as much personally as he had. But in the Japanese scheme of things they carried more weight because the great institutions to which they belonged shed a kind of glory upon them that the medium-sized company the young entrepreneur had created could not match. (Christopher 1982:147)

Status is so important in Japan, and the rules for interaction are so heavily conditioned by relative status, that it is critical for members of the society to know exactly where they stand in regard to one another. Indeed, one of the first things Japanese men do upon being introduced for the first time is to exchange business cards, thus providing one another with information about occupation and institutional affiliation which will enable them to judge each other's status and speak with the appropriate degree of deference. Again, a comment from Christopher (1982) will illustrate the point:

> As a people, the Japanese have a far more highly developed sense of hierarchy than Americans and manifest it far more openly. When three or four well-fed, wisecracking top executives of an American corporation board an airplane, it may take a bystander a bit of time to figure out which one of them is the boss. But when a group of executives from a Japanese firm board a plane, it's invariably immediately obvious who is top dog; he's the one who gets the window seat, whose briefcase is carried by someone else and whose bows to his colleagues follow their bows to him. (Christopher 1982:141)

Relative values such as "politeness, perspicuousness" may be ranked in a different order by different cultures." With respect to "ground rules," Thomas means that what is said cannot always be taken at face value. Thus, when a Latin American speaker of Spanish promises to have something done "*mañana*," it is not to be interpreted literally. As Thomas points out, this is not because the Spanish speaker is untruthful or unreliable, but because the community ground rules call for this response, which, as every communicatively competent member of the society knows, can be intrepreted approximately as "soon." Another example of different ground rules, to use Thomas's term, is the English greeting "How are you?" which is to be interpreted not as a question requiring a long account of the addressee's state of health and/or emotions but rather as a polite way of saying hello. In many societies, however, greeting routines do involve just this sort of response and, indeed, may require a long series of questions and answers on the part of both participants regarding the health and well-being of each member of the other's family. Not to engage in such a lengthy greeting exchange would be considered a serious breach of etiquette and might well undermine the relationship. It is interesting to note that in some societies where greetings consist of long verbal exchanges of the type just mentioned, it is not appropriate to interpret the questions literally, and one is expected to say that all is well, whether it is or not, just as is the case in most native English-speaking communities. As Irvine (1974) explains in her description of greeting structure among the Wolof of Senegal: "The questions used in a greeting are stereotypes and are followed by stereotyped responses. If asked about a kinsman's health, the respondent will say he is well even if the kinsman is on his deathbed; the true information about him will only emerge later in the conversation, after the greeting is over" (Irvine 1974:171).

In speaking of cross-cultural differences in values as a source of pragmatic failure, Thomas points out that "in some cultures certain relative values may systematically prevail over others. Thus, in culture X 'generosity' may be systematically valued above 'succinctness'; in culture Y 'approbation' may outweigh 'truthfulness.'" This is a very good point and one which could be elaborated on with an almost infinite number of examples, particularly from the literature concerned with sociolinguistic studies of non-Western societies. In her description of sociolinguistic norms in Malagasy, the language spoken in Madagascar, Keenan (1974) gives an excellent example of the ways in which values are reflected in norms of speech behavior. "For example" Keenan says, "one is expected [in many social situations] to avoid open and direct confrontation with another. One is expected not to affront another, not to put an individual in an uncomfortable or unpleasant situation." Thus, truthfulness is less important than the avoidance of confrontation. Obviously, however, there are situations in which direct speech is necessary, and, interestingly enough, it is the women in this community who operate outside the community norms. As Keenan tells it: "In particular they [women] are associated with the direct and open expression of anger towards others. Their social behavior contrasts sharply with men in this respect. Men tend not to express their sentiments openly. . . . In short they avoid creating unpleasant face-to-face encounters. Women, on the other hand, tend to speak in a more straightforward manner. They express feelings or anger or criticism directly to the relevant party." Keenan then goes on to describe how this difference in the speech behavior of men and women is made use of by men, who, though they follow the norms themselves, use women: "In other words, men often use women to confront others with some unpleasant information. Women communicate sentiments which men share but dislike expressing" (Keenan 1974:137–138). Thus, although indirectness and non-confrontation are the ideal, women as "norm-breakers" serve the community in important ways. This example of the difference in speech behavior between men and women in Malagasy society should also serve to remind us that cultural norms for speech behavior vary not only across cultures but also within them. As we have seen in the Japanese example, societies vary in the extent to which the rules for appropriate speech behavior reflect social status. Such attributes as age and gender and occupation often have powerful effects, and this must be kept in mind by language instructors. There are many societies in which it is inappropriate for a younger person to speak when an elder is present. The same is true for the behavior expected of women in mixed sex gatherings. This could have serious consequences for classroom language instruction. With respect to norms of speech behavior between men and women, it is often the case that women are constrained by rules which do not permit them to disagree with men or even to compete with them. Putting a husband and wife into the same class, or a wife into a higher proficiency level, may, although reasonable from the pedagogical point of view, create a situation which is counterproductive in terms of the actual learning process.

To return to examples of diversity owing to differing values, the issue of when and when not to express gratitude is particularly revealing. From a study of the expression of gratitude in South Asian languages (Apte 1974) we learn that speakers of Marathi and Hindi follow very different patterns from those of Europeans in this respect. The concept of gratitude is closely connected with that of indebtedness, and thanks are never given unless the speaker feels that the addressee has, in some way, performed a service that he or she was not under obligation to give. Thus, Apte tells us, gratitude is never expressed in commercial transactions between salespeople and customers: "in situations involving exchanges of goods, no verbalization of gratitude takes place. Neither the customer nor the shopkeeper will therefore exchange phrases equivalent to 'thank you'" (Apte 1974:69). As a number of scholars have pointed out, the fact that South Asians do not engage in thanking routines in service encounters in Western countries, where such expressions of gratitude are formulaic, often causes them to be stigmatized as ungrateful or boorish. However, as Apte goes on to explain, the value system in South Asia is such that it is considered a duty to help family members and close friends, and for this reason "any verbalization of gratitude is considered taboo, and it is insulting or looked down upon when family members or close friends interact with each other" (Apte 1974:79). One point of similarity with middle-class Americans should be mentioned in this context. That is, while it is true that Americans, like other Westerners, do engage in exchanges of gratitude in service encounters, it is not always the case that a direct expression of gratitude is the appropriate response for a service performed for one by a close family member. As we will discuss more fully in Chapter 4, it would be unusual among most Americans for a husband or a child to thank the mother of the family for cooking dinner or for performing other regular household services, although they are clearly the beneficiaries of her work. What is done instead in cases such as this is to offer a compliment about the tastiness of the food or the cleanliness of the house. One wonders whether some such patterns do not also exist in the South Asian culture described by Apte. Nevertheless, it is fair to say that Western assessments of obligations for which no gratitude need be expressed do vary considerably from those of South Asia, and this is certainly a difference in value systems that could easily lead to misunderstanding.

A somewhat similar difference in value assessments and their corresponding potential for miscommunication occurs in the way Japanese combine expressions of gratitude with those of apologies. As Coulmas (1981a) points out, thanks and apologies in Japanese are often expressed together through use of the same lexical item, *sumimasen*:

> In Japanese textbooks *arigato* ("thanks") is usually described as the most general and commonly used gratitude expression. The Japanese, however, seem to use *sumimasen* more often than *arigato* where Europeans would say "thank you." Upon receiving a gift, we would not normally say *excuse me* or *I'm sorry*. In such a situation *sumimasen* is, by contrast, quite appropriate. We can translate it, according to context, either as "thank you" or as "I'm sorry." That the Japanese language has such a polyfunctional word is, however, clearly not the end of the analysis. . . . when the Japanese express appreciation, what they are saying is that the respective matter is not over until the benefactor has been somehow repaid. The speaker of *sumimasen* acknowledges his indebtedness toward his interlocutor. The Japanese conception of gifts and favors

focusses on the trouble they have caused the benefactor rather than the aspects which are pleasing to the recipient. When leaving after a dinner invitation we might say, *thank you so much for the wonderful evening*. Under similar circumstances, one of the things the Japanese guest could and frequently does say is *o-jama itashimashita* ("I have intruded on you"). (Coulmas 1981a:82–83)

THE CONSEQUENCES OF SOCIOLINGUISTIC DIVERSITY ACROSS CULTURES

While many of the illustrations of cross-cultural variation in speech behavior given above could seem to be merely trivial differences in etiquette, it must be recognized that such differences may have far-reaching consequences for the success of a relationship. More important, such intercultural misunderstandings go much deeper and cover a far broader range of situations than social interaction alone. If the episode is part of a commercial or diplomatic negotiation, the repercussions may be quite serious for the success of the enterprise involved.

An example of the way in which seemingly trivial differences in sociolinguistic patterns may have serious consequences involves the expression of approval. As we will describe in detail in Chapter 4, Americans customarily give compliments with far greater frequency and in a far wider range of speech situations than is common in most other cultures. In cross-cultural interactions, nonnative speakers are often surprised by the American custom of praising the belongings, accomplishments, and appearance of others, and in consequence they may react by regarding Americans with mistrust. In situations where they receive the sort of compliments which are a frequent aspect of interactions among Americans, nonnative speakers may interpret these as effusive, insincere, and possibly motivated by ulterior considerations. In some cases, the effect of this deeply ingrained American habit of offering compliments may turn out to be far more serious than one would imagine. One instance of the sort of misunderstandings which might occur, and of their potential gravity, came about a few years ago when Jimmy Carter visited France during his term of office as president of the United States. On being asked to say a few words to newsmen after talks with some local government officials, Carter commented on what a fine job one of the officials was doing. The French public took instant umbrage. Unaware of the American custom of making favorable remarks in public about the accomplishments of fellow politicians, newspaper reporters wrote editorials in which they stated that Carter's remarks were an attempt to interfere in the internal politics of France and expressed themselves as being seriously provoked by what they took to be yet another example of American imperialism (Wolfson 1981a:117–124).

Another, even more striking example of the way in which sociolinguistic misunderstandings may lead to serious and even critical consequences has to do with the failure of American officials, during the war in Vietnam, to convince the

North Vietnamese that they were sincere in their desire to negotiate a peace settle-
ment. As Rubin (1983) says:

> In the United States, negotiations with North Vietnam were often misin-
> terpreted. The President often said, "I'll talk peace *anywhere, anytime.*" I think
> that one meaning which can be attributed to this sentence is "no I won't". The
> reason for this interpretation is that in most United States areas, when a person
> says "drop in anytime," this is not an invitation. Rather, if one really wanted to
> extend an invitation, one would need to specify when and where to meet. By
> saying "anywhere, anytime" without being more specific, the President made
> his willingness to negotiate seem dubious. (Rubin 1983:11)

This analysis of the misinterpretation placed on the president's invitation to
talk with the North Vietnamese is insightful and almost certainly accurate. The fact
that a great proportion of "invitations" in American society are reached through
negotiation by both participants is a frequent cause of misunderstanding since
nonnative speakers, told to "drop in anytime" frequently interpret this as a true
invitation and are hurt and distressed when they are brought to realize that no social
commitment was ever intended or made. A more detailed discussion of the ways in
which Americans accomplish the act of inviting is given in Chapter 4.

Christopher (1982), observing that the Japanese have a strong dislike of enter-
ing into direct confrontations and a horror of placing others in an embarrassing
position, points out that Japanese businesspersons find it almost impossible to
respond to any suggestion with a definite "no." What the Japanese will do instead
is resort to a vague sort of reply to the effect that the matter needs further study.
They do this to save face for their interlocutor, but this may not be understood, and,
indeed, an American negotiating partner may completely misinterpret the vagueness
for compliance and assume that the proposition has been accepted. Along these
lines, Christopher gives still another example, reported also in Takahashi and Beebe
(1987), of the way in which cross-cultural miscommunication can lead to serious
consequences at high governmental levels:

> Sometimes such vagueness reflects nothing more than a polite way of saying
> that the proposition in question is a nonstarter; sometimes it presages a genuine
> search for a compromise solution. The obvious danger, however, is that such
> calculated and artificial imprecision can mislead an unwary foreigner into con-
> cluding that he has received some form of commitment—an error in judgment
> classically exemplified in a 1970 summit meeting between President Richard
> Nixon and the late Prime Minister Eisaku Sato. At that meeting, Nixon, for
> domestic political reasons, put heavy pressure upon Sato to curtail Japan's
> proliferating textile exports to the United States. In response, Sato used a
> Japanese phrase which, loosely translated, means "I'll do my damnedest." All
> that Sato meant to convey was that he would look into the problem and see if
> there was some way he could alleviate it without too many ugly repercussions.
> To Nixon, however, it sounded as though Sato had promised to remedy the
> situation. And so, when Sato failed to take really effective action, Nixon bitterly
> concluded that he had been double-crossed.

The reason for this misunderstanding, which had serious adverse consequences for Japanese–U.S. relations, was apparently never made clear to Nixon.

Misunderstandings due to different sets of values and their expression may have embarrassing outcomes in commercial negotiations as well as in political ones. If one Asian value, that of not putting people into an awkward position by refusing them directly, is misunderstood, so too is the value placed upon modesty, humility, and reserve. To illustrate the sort of embarrassment which may occur in business interactions between members of Chinese and British speech communities, respectively, Craig (1979) gives us the following example of a true event recounted to her:

> A rich merchant went to London and was entertaining some very important European guests. He had the affair catered at a famous hotel. In the Chinese manner, he said that he was sorry that the food and drink were not very fine. (This was intended to pay respect to the guests and it actually means that nothing is considered good enough for the honourable people who are being entertained. This is proper Chinese etiquette.) Some hotel employees overheard these remarks and the management, feeling quite insulted, proceeded to sue the merchant for defaming the character of the hotel. (Craig 1979:2–3).

Thus, one of the most serious difficulties for speakers interacting across cultures is that they are not only prone to misinterpret the intentions of those from other backgrounds with whom they interact, but, as in the example given above, their own behavior is also open to serious misinterpretation. The result is that they not only take offense but frequently give it quite inadvertently. It would be possible to find endless examples of misunderstandings resulting from differences in rules of speaking, and many will appear in the following pages. Indeed, when one considers the enormous potential for such intercultural misunderstandings, it seems amazing that international diplomacy and business negotiations succeed as well as they appear to. Of course, since neither government officials nor individuals affiliated with other international organizations usually publicize their failures, and since it is unlikely that the causes of the great majority of such failures in communication are even recognized, we will never know about most of the problems which have arisen in this way.

Because sociolinguistic rules of speaking are very largely unconscious, we are rarely aware of their existence unless they are brought to our attention through the shock of having them broken. When it happens that nonnative speakers do break sociolinguistic rules, natives, as we have seen, often react very negatively. Tolerance of sociolinguistic violations is uncommon precisely because the rules are so much a part of unconscious expectations concerning proper behavior. People do not normally take offense or make negative character judgments when a nonnative speaker mispronounces a word or when grammatical errors are made; indeed, such differences as those which result in a foreign accent are often found very charming. Errors in rules of speaking are a very different matter. An inappropriate question or the failure to utter the customary apology, compliment, or congratulation will not be judged as an error natural to the process of language learning or, indeed, of intercultural differences, but as a personal affront. The student from Eastern Europe who asks her professor how much money he earns for a living is likely to provoke a feeling of outrage. The Japanese student who bows frequently, maintaining a formal relationship with classmates, is likely to be regarded as obsequious or insincere. The Latin American who repeatedly begs for special consideration with respect to grades, giving as her excuse the illness of family members, or the Arabic speaker who openly asks help from fellow Arabic-speaking students in their native language, may well create negative value judgments on the part of instructors. Thus, because sociolinguistic relativity is so little understood, the nonnative speaker is seen not as an imperfect language learner but as intrusive or unfriendly or dishonest, or as having a host of other negative characteristics.

As Thomas (1983) puts it:

> Grammatical errors may be irritating and impede communication, but at least, as a rule, they are apparent in the surface structure, so that H (the hearer or addressee) is aware that an error has occurred. Once alerted to the fact that S (the speaker) is not fully grammatically competent, native speakers seem to have little difficulty making allowances for it. Pragmatic failure, on the other hand, is rarely recognized as such by non-linguists. If a non-native speaker appears to speak fluently (i.e., is grammatically competent), a native speaker is likely to attribute his/her apparent impoliteness or unfriendliness, not to any linguistic deficiency, but to boorishness or ill-will. While grammatical error may reveal a speaker to be a less than proficient language-user, pragmatic failure reflects badly on him/her as a person. Misunderstandings of this nature are almost certainly at the root of unhelpful and offensive national stereotyping: "the abrasive Russian/German," "the obsequious Indian/Japanese," "the insincere American," and "the standoffish Briton."

As we have attempted to point out, negative judgments based on the lack of understanding of cross-cultural variation in speech behavior tends to be reciprocal in nature. That is, if native speakers form negative impressions of people from cultures different from their own, nonnative speakers' judgments of native speakers are likely to be equally strong for the same reasons, and it is not uncommon for a foreigner to express anger or hurt toward an entire society on the basis of exactly this sort of misunderstanding. During a recent project at the University of Pennsylvania, a sociolinguistics class conducted an investigation into the question of what constitutes inappropriate questions in various societies. Several members of the class who came from Malaysia reported that they and their Malaysian informants were often shocked and hurt by questions asked by Americans. Any questions regarding sex, for example, are absolutely taboo among Malaysians, and, according to the students and their informants, there are no exceptions to this rule. Therefore, a question asked by an American and considered highly inappropriate to Malaysians was "Have you ever kissed your boyfriend?" Rules of behavior are strongly influenced by the Islamic religion in Malaysia, and two other examples of questions asked by Americans and considered inappropriate were the following: "Why don't you drink?" and "Why can't you shake hands with me?" As the authors of the research report explain: "These questions are considered inappropriate because it is a question of lawful or unlawful in the eyes of the Islamic religion. We cannot drink or touch hands of people of opposite sex except when they are wearing gloves. Malay people know about these rules already; as a result, they do not ask these types of questions. Americans who are not familiar with Islam will ask these types of questions" (Jamaluddin et al. 1986).

Reactions to violations of sociolinguistic rules are negative and even quite harsh, because most individuals take their own behavior patterns for granted and are unaware that rules of speaking are far from universal. Yet in every society there are some things that are simply not said or asked and others that are absolutely required in certain situations, and it is assumed that every well-brought-up person knows these rules of behavior. Each speech community has, as part of its collective wisdom, the unquestioned assumption that its own ways of speaking are the correct, proper, honest, and good ways. For this reason, even people whose occupations lead them to interact frequently with people of different cultural backgrounds are prone to regard sociolinguistic rule breaking as a manifestation of a flawed character, and if they have had what they see as negative experiences with numerous members of a particular group, they are apt to stigmatize everyone who belongs to it.

SOCIOLINGUISTIC DIVERSITY WITHIN ENGLISH-SPEAKING COMMUNITIES

Writing in the late 1980s, when the use of English has spread to the point where approximately half its speakers are nonnative, one would not want to suggest that the kind of miscommunication just described is limited to interactions between native speakers and language learners, or, indeed, that there is just one set of rules for all English-speaking communities. As was mentioned in the introduction to this book, there are large numbers of people who, while not native speakers, nevertheless have an excellent command of English and use it regularly in the course of their daily lives. In addition to the millions of immigrants to English-speaking countries, there are considerable proportions of English-speaking people in all the nations that have adopted English as an official or an additional language. It would be inaccurate and even insulting to categorize members of these groups as English learners, for many are at least as fluent in the language as any native speaker, and, indeed, there is important literary and scholarly work being written in English by Africans and Asians who are not native speakers. All of these groups have their own rules of speaking, most of them based on the rules of speaking of their native communities. When a language becomes "nativized" or "indigenized" (Kachru 1982a) as an institutionalized second language and is used for purposes of national communication, it is to be expected that the sociolinguistic patterns of the speech community using it will be reflected in this tongue as they are in the native tongue(s). As Akere (1982) puts it in describing Nigerian English:

> What has happened here in Nigeria . . . and in other places where some cultural assimilation of the English language has taken place (say for example, in India) is that the resources of a second language are superimposed on an intricate system of social and kinship relationships, and on a completely different pattern of cultural outlook and social expectations. The differences in cultural outlook and social expectations between British society, on the one hand and indigenous Nigerian cultures, on the other hand, become quite obvious in the resulting pattern of address forms and greetings that characterize Nigerian English. . . The intracultural variations in the uses of these linguistic forms in Nigerian English may be assumed to be systematically related to the constituents of subculture patterns. These include aspects of the social structure, cultural definitions of the situation of action, respect and deference in social relationships, the cultural philosophy and the value system, and their patterned interrelations.

There has been considerable controversy regarding what this means in terms of language teaching. Many experts believe that it is important for people learning English as a second language (for use within their own societies) to be taught a native variety of English such as the prestige variety of British or of American English. The idea here is that people should learn the vocabulary, syntax, and phonology that will be most widely understood around the world, and that to teach English learners a nonnative variety would be to limit their potential for interacting at an international level. This argument has been most forcefully expressed by Prator (1968), who takes this position against the teaching of indigenous models of English:

> In one developing country after another the government is making strenuous efforts to establish an indigenous language (Filipino, Bahasa Indonesia, Malay, Hindi, Sinhalese, Arabic, Swahili, etc.) as the preferred medium of communication within the national boundaries. As more and more of these attempts are successful, the importance of English and French will increasingly reside in their usefulness as channels to the outside world. The shift in the role of the latter two languages is accelerated by the internationalization of economic development programs, the vastly augmented dependence of men everywhere on science and technology, and the oft-cited shrinkage of the world. The present moment in history appears to be a singularly inappropriate time to set about the deliberate cultivation of varieties of French and English that would have less international viability than the currently taught varieties. (Prator 1968:469)

The counterargument, and the one which has gained increasing favor with most applied linguists (e.g., Halliday et al. 1964), is that the so-called new Englishes, or the nonnative institutionalized varieties of English (NIVES, as Williams 1987 calls them), are perfectly legitimate linguistic systems in and of themselves.

That they have developed in a somewhat different manner phonologically, syntactically, and semantically has to do with the very natural influences of the first languages of their speakers. These new varieties of English are, however, perfectly well suited for the purposes which they serve within the individual societies that use them. Furthermore, the prestige forms of these new varieties of English are quite intelligible to other speakers of English around the world, both native and nonnative.

What all this means in terms of sociolinguistics is that communicative competence in the target language could mean many things, depending on the identity of the students and their purpose in learning English. For one thing, different native speaking communities have different rules of speaking, just as they have different phonological rules, and therefore the model, when it comes to sociolinguistic behavior, cannot be thought of in terms of the English language as a whole, but rather in terms of the various speech communities that use it. Given that we have selected a specific speech community, we must still be cautious in our consideration of the need for English learners to acquire the sociolinguistic rules of the native target language speech community. That is, while learners who expect to interact with native speakers need to be aware of their sociolinguistic patterns, we would not want to waste students' time in attempting to teach native-speaker sociolinguistic behavior to those whose use of English will probably be primarily confined to situations in which English is spoken mainly for the purposes of communication across ethnolinguistic boundaries within the country in question. Thus, although the goal of communicative competence for language learners makes sense in certain ways, the type of competence will vary depending on the purpose of the learner. Knowing about the sociolinguistic patterns of middle-class Americans may be of extreme importance to the businessperson, diplomat, or student who expects to interact extensively with native speakers of American English.

For Indians, Nigerians, and citizens of other nations which have chosen to adopt English as an official or additional language, the situation is rather different. The great majority of people within such countries use English primarily for the purpose of commercial, political, judicial, or scientific interactions with their own countrymen who may come from different linguistic backgrounds. While we would not want to minimize the differences between the various ethnolinguistic groups within a country such as India, we must nevertheless recognize that members of different groups within the same general area will tend to share a great deal in terms of sociolinguistic behavior. It makes sense that the target speech community for these learners of English as a second language be the prestige group of nonnative English speakers within their own societies. Knowledge of rules of speaking for native speakers of, for example, American English may be of interest to these learners from the point of view of understanding the occasional tourist with whom they may come into contact and also of being able to understand the cultural implications of the American literature they read, and indeed, of the television shows and movies with which they will come into contact. This motivation for understanding sociocultural rules could just as easily be given for Americans who wish to gain insight into the English literature and films imported here from Nigeria or India. The point here is that knowledge of the sociolinguistic rules of native speakers is not of major consideration to all learners of English everywhere in the world. Before designing a curriculum for a particular population of language learners, it is important to be quite clear about the purpose to which the language will be put in order to avoid attempting to teach irrelevant information. Above all, we must remember that among the 600 million or so speakers of English in the world today, there is enormous cultural diversity and that different sociolinguistic rules will be relevant for different groups.

Indeed, even among native speakers of English there are striking sociolinguistic differences, owing to such factors as differences in regional, socioeconomic, ethnic, and educational background. It is well known that such differences as these often give rise to negative stereotypes. To Americans, the British seem cold; to Britons, Americans appear brash, and so on and on. If such misunderstandings occur among native speakers who may be seen as sharing at least some aspects of a common cultural tradition, it is easy to imagine how much greater potential for miscommunication exists when interactions take place between native and nonnative speakers or among nonnative speakers coming from different parts of the world. Differences in pronunciation and syntax may, of course, impede communication, and, as with "foreign accents," these distinctions tend to serve the purpose of warning interlocutors of one another's differing origins. Still, because they share a language, people often assume a similarity in outlook and especially in sociolinguistic rules, and may, as we have seen, form very negative judgments of the other group when this is found not to be the case.

CONCLUSION

From the point of view of language teaching in general and of TESOL in particular, the implications of what has been said are critical. Ability to interact successfully in a foreign language speech community depends on communicative competence, of which sociolinguistic rules are an important aspect.

The issue of whether or to what extent sociolinguistic rules can or should be taught in ESL classrooms is a controversial one. Since, until very recently, there has been little in the way of empirical information concerning these rules for any native English-speaking community, only a limited attempt at such teaching was actually possible. Materials writers and teachers, caught up in the wave of enthusiasm for including sociocultural information in classroom language instruction, have, it is true, tried to use their own knowledge as native speakers to provide students with such information. But, as we will discuss more fully in the next chapter, intuitions about sociolinguistic behavior is often very unreliable. To a large extent, the kinds of information that have been included in such curricula have been based on community norms rather than on actual use. In the last few years, researchers in the field of applied sociolinguistics have worked hard to provide badly needed analyses, and a good deal has been accomplished. However, we are still very far from being able to write anything resembling a complete description of sociolinguistic behavior for any English-speaking community.

Controversies over what to teach are, however, minor in comparison with those over whether this kind of material can be taught, on the one hand, and whether it should be taught, on the other. From the point of view of language learners, it seems clear that much of the sociocultural information they need in order to become communicatively competent in the target language must be learned by exposure and by actual interactions with native speakers. For foreign students residing in the host community, a certain amount of exposure through the media, and through contact with native speakers, including teachers, is inevitable. As far as language teaching is concerned, however, it is unclear whether rules of this nature can actually be taught in conventional ways. My own view is that the acquisition of sociolinguistic rules can be greatly facilitated by teachers who have the necessary information at their command and who have the sensitivity to use their knowledge in order to guide students and help them to interpret values and patterns which they would otherwise have difficulty in interpreting. While we would not want to be in the position of trying to change the value systems of people from other cultures, or to attempt to persuade them to model their personal behavior on our own, we know that language learners would benefit greatly from information on how to interpret and respond to native speaker sociolinguistic behavior. Thomas (1983) expresses a position very close to my own when she says:

> It is not the responsibility of the language teacher qua linguist to enforce Anglo-Saxon standards of behavior, linguistic or otherwise. Rather, it is the teacher's job to equip the student to express her/himself in exactly the way s/he chooses to do so—rudely, tactfully, or in an elaborately polite manner. What we want to prevent is her/his being *unintentionally* rude or subservient. It may, of course, behoove the teacher to point out the likely consequences of certain types of linguistic behavior. (Thomas 1983:96)

Other specialists in TESOL have gone much further, indicating that we do students a serious disservice in not teaching sociolinguistic rules. Yorio (1980), for example, says:

> Along with items chosen for their high usefulness and productivity value, teachers should endeavor to make their students aware of, and sensitive to, the sociolinguistic variables that play a role in different types of situational frames. These are strategies which the learner will be able to use in actual situations long after he has left the language classroom. We might, in fact, do students a disservice by presenting idioms and formulas as more or less inflexible lists of items. . . . Learners must be made aware of the differences and similarities

between English and their native language. Teachers must be careful so that
students do not see these discussions as brain-washing designed to eliminate
their native identity. It is not a question of intrinsic quality of one set of
conventions over another, it is a question of intrinsic difference. The teacher's
task is to add a new set of conventions to the already existing set, not to replace
one for the other. (Yorio 1980:441)

Holmes and Brown (1977) go even further, saying that it is clearly the teacher's responsibility to provide feedback to students concerning the appropriate or
inappropriate use of English, since the students themselves are likely to be unaware
of many of their errors in this area" (Holmes and Brown 1977:72).

Thus we see that applied linguists are well aware of the sensitivity involved in
correcting the social behavior of others, particularly adults who have their own sets
of values and rules, and who know themselves to be perfectly competent in their
own native speech communities. It would seem reasonable that the analysis of these
patterns of speech behavior and the use of these research findings could be of
considerable use to both teachers and students. The important point that we must
always keep in mind is the meaning of sociolinguistic relativity—that there is no
right and wrong when it comes to sociolinguistic diversity. There are conventions
which, when understood, will enable language learners to interpret rather than
misunderstand, and to make their own meanings clear rather than miscommunicate.
If students can be guided to understand the values, patterns, and conventions of the
target language community, they will be in a position to communicate effectively
with its members.

Although much of the information presented in the following chapters bears on
the needs of learners who will be interacting with native speakers of American
English, it is to be hoped that all those who teach English will come away with
perspectives and information that will be useful to them. This does not mean that the
patterns to be described in the next chapters are in any sense universal, but rather
that they are to be seen as examples of what sociolinguistic rules are, how one can
go about analyzing them, and what one may learn about a speech community by
studying the rules of speaking that obtain within it. As with any other aspect of
language teaching, the use to which such material is put must fit the needs of the
learners.

To come back to our original point, we must recognize that the phenomenon
that we are calling sociolinguistic relativity is a very difficult concept to accept, and
that differences in communicative or sociocultural conventions are all too often
interpreted as intentional rudeness. Indeed, some adult language learners are never
able to reconcile themselves to such differences or to accept the possibility that the
issue is not between kinds of behavior that are right or wrong, but between different
norms of behavior. Fortunately, most learners do come to appreciate this fact and,
especially when guided by well-trained instructors, may make the attempt to adapt,
learn to interpret, and, under some circumstances, even decide to emulate to some

degree the behavior of the host community when interacting with its members. Obviously, language learning does not require that people change their personalities or their most deeply ingrained principles concerning correct behavior; what is needed is for the learners to come to understand what is meant by the words and expressions they hear, and to be able to respond to them appropriately so that unnecessary miscommunication can be avoided.

CHAPTER 2

Communicative
Competence and Rules of
Speaking

INTRODUCTION

Given the description of the problem so far, it might seem that the best way to avoid intercultural misunderstandings would be to disseminate as much information as possible regarding the diversity of sociolinguistic behavior. The more people know about the many kinds of patterns that exist around the world, and the more the public is made aware of the way negative judgments and stereotypes come into being through lack of awareness about other value systems, the more hope there is of building tolerance. Members of the first language community need to be warned of potential pitfalls just as second language learners do. Intercultural communication must operate in both directions. A recognition that there are patterns of behavior which are neither better nor worse than one's own, but simply different, would go a long way toward creating an atmosphere of tolerance in which people could work toward understanding one another. In some respects, this sort of educational effort is possible even now. School children could learn about differences in sociolinguistic rules in social studies classes, just as they now learn about differences in other aspects of culture. That is to say, an attitude of tolerance toward sociolinguistic differences could be fostered. Until we have more than what Sherzer (1977) has called "a growing collection of ethnographic tidbits from around the world" regarding how language behavior is organized in different societies, however, we can do little more. This is unfortunate since it would be both interesting and instructive for native English speakers to learn how their own language use is patterned. For nonnative speakers of English (NNES) who need to interact with members of NE communities, such insights into sociolinguistic rules could prove vital. From the point of view of both groups, concrete information in this area would greatly enhance people's ability to evaluate what is meant by what is said, thus avoiding unnecessary misunderstanding. Ultimately, the analysis of rules of speaking both across and within different societies will provide us with the sort of knowledge upon which to build this aspect of intercultural understanding. At present, however, we are not yet at the stage where this course of action is possible in any systematic way. To begin with, since most sociolinguistic rules are largely below the level of conscious or intuitive analysis, and since not enough research has been done to describe them, there is not yet enough information available even within TESOL to enable curriculum writers or teachers to help language learners to identify potential problems. A considerable amount of research is currently under way that is specifically designed to meet the needs of English language learners for as much information as possible concerning the sociolinguistic rules of the speech communities whose language they are attempting to acquire so that they may learn to interpret the intent of what is said to them and to adapt to a new set of communicative conventions. Until very recently, most of the research into the sociocultural aspects of speech behavior has been carried out in societies very different from those in which English is the dominant native language. In developing the English-oriented research projects so critical to TESOL, we cannot help but expose theoretical and methodological problems which are far less apparent when the society under study is very different from that of the investigator. As Sherzer (1977) has put it in a critical assessment of the ethnography of speaking:

> USA-oriented research is crucial in several respects. It provides a testing ground for all of the theoretical and methodological issues. . . . One aspect of this testing ground, of course, is that analyses are open to constant critical scrutiny by all members of the society. Modern societies like that of the United States are particularly challenging to ethnography, which has developed most of its technique and approach in relatively small, relatively homogeneous societies. In complex societies such as that of the United States, members of the community, as well as analysts, often have to work out and understand communicative patterns that are much more variable, overlapping, and changing than those typically found in the more homogeneous and tradition-oriented societies in which anthropologists have tended to carry out field research. But the United States provides more than a testing ground for method and theory. It is also a testing ground for practice and application. One of the motivations for the ethnography of speaking in particular, and sociolinguistics more generally, has been relevance in the solution of social problems, especially those concerned with communication. It has been argued that by carrying out ethnography of speaking research in various communities as well as in such institutions as law, medicine, and education, we will have a better understanding of the reasons for conflict and failure. Important research initiatives in this direction can be cited. But much more research is needed. There is still a woefully small amount of published, available information dealing with the ethnography of speaking in our own society. (Sherzer 1977:53)

In this chapter I will attempt to describe some of the problems involved in analyzing sociolinguistic rules. In doing so, I will take the perspective of the sociolinguist concerned with applying research findings to language learning and teaching. In order for rules and patterns of use to be made available for application, valid descriptions of them must exist. And in order for analyses to be valid and therefore useful to the field, it must be recognized that most of these aspects of speech behavior are below the level of conscious awareness of speakers, no matter how well trained in linguistics or in language teaching. When we turn to our native speaker intuitions for ways of describing how we speak, we very quickly learn that these, although useful in many ways, are inadequate as tools of description. As we will see in the pages that follow, there is a great deal of empirical evidence to show that great differences exist between the intuitive reports of native speakers and their own use of speech when actually recorded and analyzed.

In spite of the difficulties involved in describing sociolinguistic behavior, most language teaching specialists agree that the aim of second language instruction should be to facilitate learners' acquisition of communicative competence, the ability to speak both accurately and appropriately. We will discuss how this aim has been interpreted by scholars in the field of applied linguistics, and what problems remain to be solved.

One issue to which we will devote some attention is the frequent blurring of the distinction between language and community. This is a crucial problem for TESOL since, as we will see, the lack of correspondence between the two can lead to some serious problems not only in terms of the analysis of sociolinguistic rules but in terms of the generalizability and usefulness of such analyses for language teaching and learning.

If sociolinguistics is to be of value to the field of language acquisition, the problems involved in carrying out research in this area, as well as those concerned with making use of findings, must be open to question and discussion. We need to be clear about what we know and what we do not know so that the validity and the practical implications of the analyses reported can be openly and thoroughly evaluated by those who wish to make use of them.

Before beginning our discussion, it will be useful to have a solid definition of *culture* and of what it means to be a competent member of a given culture. The explanation given by Ward Goodenough, one of the most eminent linguistic anthropologists of our day, will provide us with a background to the description of sociolinguistic principles which follows:

> As I see it, a society's culture consists of whatever it is one has to know or believe in order to operate in a manner acceptable to its members, and do so in any role that they accept for any one of themselves.
>
> Given such a definition, it is obviously impossible to describe a culture properly simply by describing behavior or social, economic and ceremonial events and arrangements as observed material phenomena . . . What is required is to construct a theory of the conceptual model which they represent and of which they are artifacts. We test the adequacy of such a theory by our ability to interpret and predict what goes on in a community as measured by how its members, our informants, do so. A further test is our ability ourselves to behave in ways which lead to the kind of responses from the community's members which our theory would lead us to expect. Thus tested, the theory is a valid

statement of what you have to know in order to operate as a member of the society and is, as such, a valid description of its culture. . .

Indeed, we may define a language in precisely the same terms in which we have already defined a culture. It consists of whatever it is one has to know in order to communicate with its speakers as adequately as they do with each other and in a manner which they will accept as correspondng to their own. . . .

In this sense, a society's language is an aspect of its culture. This is contradicted in no way by the fact that two communities speaking what passes for the same language may otherwise have somewhat different cultures. (Goodenough 1964:36–37)

We begin this chapter, then, on a note of considerable optimism and reasonable caution. There is much to be gained by the inclusion of sociolinguistics in language acquisition, but we must recognize that there is also much to be lost unless we are aware of the limitations involved in the study of speech as social behavior.

THE UNCONSCIOUS NATURE OF SOCIOLINGUISTIC RULES

Rules of speaking and, more generally, norms of interaction are, as we have pointed out, both culture-specific and largely unconscious. What this means is that native speakers, although perfectly competent in the uses and interpretation of the patterns of speech behavior which prevail in their own communities, are, with the exception of a few explicitly taught formulas, not even aware of the patterned nature of their own speech behavior. That is, native speakers are very well able to judge the correctness and appropriateness of the speech behavior of those with whom they interact, so that when a rule is broken, when someone not fully socialized into the culture in question (such as a nonnative speaker or a child) says something which is incorrect or inappropriate, the native speaker recognizes the deviation and responds to it in whatever way seems most reasonable under the circumstances. Children are frequently corrected, even by strangers. Nonnative speakers, depending on their level of proficiency and on the relationship of the interlocutors, will sometimes be corrected, sometimes negatively judged, as we have described above. However, what native speakers are not able to do with any degree of accuracy is to describe their own rules of speaking. It has been demonstrated many times that when native speakers are asked to explain or to identify forms which they or others in their community use in a given speech situation, their responses do not necessarily coincide with speech behavior which is actually observed and recorded.

Although it has been proved again and again that native speaker opinions concerning language use are frequently quite inaccurate, this fact is not easy to accept. Even researchers and people who have had wide experience in language teaching are often resentful of the idea that they themselves are not really conscious of how they speak. Many reject the notion entirely and insist that they are perfectly capable, as native speakers, of instructing their students in sociolinguistic rules. Others rely for their research on the responses of other native speakers for information about the forms people use in certain specific situations without recognizing that the intuitions of other native speakers are neither better nor worse than their own. What underlies the belief that most people have in the accuracy of their intuitions about language use is both good and bad for language pedagogy. That is, most people are extremely interested in language. The good part of this is that language is generally seen as fascinating. People love to play with it and create new and different ways of using it. What is difficult for the sociolinguistic researcher is that people also have strong (but often mistaken) opinions concerning their own speech behavior and are frequently disbelieving and even angry when these opinions are shown to be inaccurate. Knowing themselves to be competent users of their language(s), most people, including language teachers, make the assumption that they know exactly what they do and do not say in a given situation. In actual fact, speakers do have strong and well-formed ideas about what they *should* say, but this is not at all the same as knowing what they *do* say. Speech norms, or community ideals concerning appropriate speech behavior, cannot be equated with speech use which is the behavior itself. Perhaps some examples from the sociolinguistic literature will help to throw light on this point.

At the level of language use, one of the most obvious facts about speech behavior has to do with which language a speaker is using. It would seem, on the surface, that speakers could be in no doubt on this point. Yet research shows that the reverse is the case. People who are bilingual or bidialectal often switch from one of their codes or languages to the other without being in the least aware of it. Indeed, so common is this phenomenon that there is an entire area of research within sociolinguistics which specializes in investigating what is called "code-switching." In a study done in Hemnesberget, a small town in Norway, Blom and Gumperz (1972) investigated the way inhabitants switched between their local dialect, Rana-mal, and Bokmal, the standard Norwegian dialect taught in school and used in church, in interactions with officials, and in the mass media. Through anthropological investigation, including extensive observation and interviews with members of the community, Blom and Gumperz found that most townspeople had a strong and positive sense of local pride, and that this loyalty to their local identity was openly manifested in opinions strongly favoring the use of the local language. Indeed, use of their native dialect was regarded as an important sign that community members had a common culture and heritage. Use of Ranamal, they said, signals friendliness, equality, and, above all, local identity. When the researchers tape-recorded a friendly gathering, however, they found that there was a considerable amount of switching from Ranamal to Bokmal for stylistic purposes:

> The social character of the style switch was clearly revealed when the tape-recorded conversations were played back to other Hemnes residents. One person who had been working with us as a linguistic informant at first refused to

believe that the conversations were recorded locally. When he recognized the voices of the participants, he showed clear signs of disapproval. Apparently, he viewed the violation of co-occurrence rules as a sign of what is derogatorily called *knot* "artificial speech" in colloquial Norwegian. Some of the participants showed a similar reaction when they heard themselves on tape. They promised to refrain from switching during future sessions. Our analysis of these later sessions, however, revealed that when an argument required that the speaker validate his status as an intellectual, he would again tend to use standard forms in the manner shown by Berit and Ola. Code selection rules thus seem to be akin to grammatical rules. Both operate below the level of consciousness and may be independent of the speaker's overt intentions. (Blom and Gumperz 1972:430)

If speakers are unconscious of their own and others' switching from language to language, how much less likely is it that they will notice variation in the details of their pronunciation? In his classic study, *The Social Stratification of English in New York City,* William Labov (1966) demonstrated that New Yorkers show the same lack of conscious awareness about their own speech as do residents of Hemnesberget. Labov isolated five phonological variables [(r), (eh), (oh), (th), and (dh)] and, through the use of large-scale interviewing, obtained tape-recorded samples of the speech of people from differing socioeconomic backgrounds as they responded to a set of interview tasks designed to elicit different speech styles. He found that all speakers varied their pronunciation of these variables depending on the formality of the task. Subjects were more conscious of their pronunciation when asked to read than when asked to answer the interviewer's questions, for example, and varied their pronunciation accordingly. No matter what their socioeconomic background, all subjects varied their pronunciation toward the direction of the more formal speech of the highest socioeconomic group when asked to read. Labov found that the second highest status group did the most extreme style shifting, using in their most careful speech an even higher frequency of prestige pronunciation than did the top socioeconomic group whose speech they were attempting to emulate. This famous example of overcorrection, or what Labov has called "hypercorrection," will be discussed in further detail in the chapter dealing with social variation in speech. What is interesting for the purpose of the present discussion is that Labov found speakers to be extremely sensitive to social class difference in the speech of others, while at the same time completely unconscious of their own speech patterns:

. . . New Yorkers showed surprisingly consistent response to the subjective reaction test. In their reactions to the speech of other New Yorkers, they detected certain stigmatized features with great regularity, and showed close agreement in the recognition of prestige markers. . . .

In the conscious report of their own usage, however, New York respondents are very inaccurate. . . . When the average New Yorker reports his own usage, he is simply giving us his norm of correctness. No conscious deceit plays a part in this process. It appears that most New Yorkers have acquired a set of governing norms which they use in the audio-monitoring of their own speech. . . The audio-monitoring norm is the form which is perceived by the speaker himself as he speaks. He does not hear the actual sound which he produces, but the norm which he imposes. . .

New Yorkers also showed a systematic tendency to report their own speech inaccurately. Most of the respondents seemed to perceive their own speech in terms of the norms at which they were aiming rather than the sound they actually produced. (Labov 1966).

Thus we see that whether the speech behavior in question has to do with something as large and seemingly obvious as which language people are speaking, or whether it has to do with fine details of pronunciation, speakers are largely unconscious of the sociolinguistic rules they follow.

THE INADEQUACY OF INTUITION

Language choice and pronunciation are not the only aspects of language about which speakers have internalized norms. As mentioned earlier, speakers have strong opinions about speech behavior at all levels, and, as exemplified by the studies described above, these opinions about what is right and wrong, good and bad, are reflections of community norms or attitudes and have little to do with the actual use of the individual who expresses them.

This discrepancy between norms and behavior is readily seen in the study of speech acts. In responding to questions about how they go about giving invitations, for example, the native speakers of American English sampled by Wolfson et al. (1983) described themselves as using forms which were rarely or never heard in observations of actual interactions, and expressed strong disapproval of forms which they were heard to use all the time. If the researchers had chosen to inform these speakers of their actual behavior, they would no doubt have expressed the same sort of shock and dismay that residents of Hemnesberget did when it was proved to them that their own patterns of language use were contrary to cherished ideals.

Perhaps worse, if the researchers had chosen to investigate the forms used in giving invitations by asking speakers of middle-class American English what they would say in a given situation, the data collected in this way would not have corresponded well with that which was gathered through the observation and recording of the spontaneous speech of the same group. It is important to recognize that academic training in cultural and/or linguistic analysis does not, in itself, put individuals in a position to be objective about their own speech behavior, or about the patterns which obtain even in their own speech communities.

The inadequacy of native speaker intuitions may be seen at all levels of language analysis. An interesting example of the way linguists themselves must test their intuitions empirically is given in the description of a study of sex differences in language done in Amsterdam (Brouwer et al. 1979). In a seminar on language and sex, a group of linguists at the Institute of General Linguistics of the University of Amsterdam began to look into the ways in which men's and women's speech differ in Dutch. Using their intuitions about speech use in their own language, as well as what they were able to find in the literature, they developed a list of features which they thought distinguished men's and women's speech behavior in Dutch. They then tested their hypothesis by tape recording several hundred interactions in which men and women ordered train tickets in the Central Station in Amsterdam. The interactions recorded were between travelers of both sexes and varying age groups and socioeconomic backgrounds and two different ticket sellers, one a young man and the other a young woman. What the investigators found was that it was not the sex of the speaker which made the difference as to which speech features were used, but rather the sex of the addressee. As the authors say in their report of the research: "All of the kinds of utterances that women are characteristically supposed to use more often than men—utterances indicating insecurity and politeness—were used more often by both women and men when speaking to the male ticket seller" (Brouwer et al. 1979:47).

We will look more closely at these findings in the chapter on language and gender. For the purposes of this argument, however, it is important to point out that even such supposedly transparent aspects of language use as the differences in men's and women's speech have been found, once empirical analysis is done, to be very different from what native speakers would have expected. As Brouwer et al. explicitly say in the conclusion to their study: "The results of our investigation of speech differences between the sexes are very different from what intuition had led us to expect. It appears that an intuitive approach has evident shortcomings" (Brouwer et al. 1979:47).

A systematic investigation of a particular feature of speech may well lead to a conclusion about its use which differs sharply from the attitudes and beliefs expressed by speakers. The investigation of a verb tense used in American English narrative (Wolfson 1976, 1978a, 1979a, 1982a) demonstrates this point particularly well. The historical present tense is the use of the present tense to narrate events which occurred prior to the moment of speaking. Explanations concerning the use of the historical present tense, which are to be found in the scholarly literature as well as in grammar books, tend to be based on written data rather than on speech. Where speech usage is mentioned, there are often serious contradictions and inaccuracies. According to popular wisdom gleaned from interviews with native speakers of varying socioeconomic backgrounds, the use of this feature is associated with the nonstandard usage of lower-class speakers. Given examples ("Yesterday I was walking down the street and a guy comes up to me and says . . ."), native speakers reported that they recognized this form but did not themselves use it. Frequent mention was made of sloppy or "low-class" speech associated with this form. Yet observation and analysis of tape-recorded narratives demonstrated that the use of this form depended not on speaker background but on speech situation. Many of those who had denied using the historical present tense were found to use it quite consistently. When presented with the evidence, in the form of tape recordings of their own stories, most subjects reacted with shocked displeasure. Middle-class Americans tended to regard their own use of the historical present tense as carelessness; the negative evaluation remained unchanged. Yet the fact is that the conversational historical present tense is a device used by all good storytellers in our society. Here again is a linguistic feature which native speakers, both laymen and scholars, thought they understood and which they clearly did not. It was only by collecting a great many narratives as they occurred in everyday conversation that it was possible to analyze the feature and discover its true discourse function. The organization of the narrative into episodes was found to be the purpose for switching between past and historical present tenses.

From the point of view of TESOL and, more specifically, the use of discourse analysis in the investigation of second language acquisition, the study of verb tense use has particular relevance. That is, if we are to analyze the errors of second language learners, it is necessary to base such analysis on a comparison not with what prescriptive grammar books say but with what native speakers of the target language actually do. Researchers can otherwise gain a very false picture of the linguistic competence of language learners.

A case in point is a study of verb tense errors by learners of English through the use of discourse analysis. In analyzing the way learners of English avoid the difficulty of using the past tense, Godfrey (1980) bases learners' error rates on what he takes to be discourse level constraint violations. In doing so he makes the assumption that there is, in spoken English, a discourse constraint such that the speaker must continue to use the same verb tense throughout a narration as long as the reference to time remains the same. In view of the finding that the alternation between past tense and historical present tense in conversational narrative serves to give structure to the story, it is interesting that Godfrey recognized a very similar pattern in the nonnative speaker data he analyzed. In case after case, Godfrey points out that advanced learners make "errors" by breaking tense continuity at episode boundaries. Given the analysis of the conversational historical present tense presented above, it would appear that rather than making errors, the nonnative speakers in Godfrey's sample may have attained a high level of control over the use of this tense.

The fact that tense switching in narrative has been shown not to be a violation or an error in English, but rather to be in exact conformity with native speaker usage, serves to emphasize the need to understand the rules of the target language before attempting to analyze the errors made by language learners. If native speaker usage is to be the model for second language learners, we must know much more about how native speakers use the features we wish to investigate. The fact that well-trained researchers, doing sophisticated analyses of discourse, are capable of mistaking targetlike usage for learning errors is good evidence of the inadequacy of native speaker intuitions regarding language use.

Another aspect of the problem posed by the inadequacy of native speaker intuitions for TESOL, and, indeed, for the field of language teaching generally, has to do with the textbooks and curriculum materials designed to teach the spoken language to nonnative speakers. Given that there exist very few empirically based descriptions of native speaker use, it is not surprising that these materials are themselves based on grammatical rules derived from analyses of the written language or, as is often the case, from the intuitions of the authors. Since a great many of the grammatical choices made by native speakers in spontaneous everyday conversation are dependent on sociolinguistic context, and since these distinctions are not intuitively obvious, materials designed for the purpose of teaching language learners are often both artificial and misleading.

An excellent example of the contrast between the rules given in ESL textbooks and the actual use of native speakers is demonstrated in the work of Pica (1983) on the use of the article in American English. Having gone through a representative sample of textbook explanations of rules for article usage, a notoriously difficult aspect of English grammar for nonnative speakers to master, Pica then did two ethnographic studies of native speaker use. In the first study, Pica collected examples of article use in speech events having to do with the requesting and giving of directions and, in the second study, with the ordering of food in restaurants. In both studies, Pica found that native speakers varied their use of the articles *a* and *the* depending on the setting of the interaction and on various other features of the context. The variation in the actual article use she found by observing and recording native speakers interacting spontaneously was not only not reflected but often contradicted in the rules given in the textbooks she examined. In the conclusion to her analysis, Pica says:

> Comparison of article use in the natural data and usage rules in the instructional materials has indicated that article use may have more to do with communication and communicative competence than with grammar and linguistic competence. In the sentence-level examples of grammars and textbooks, *a* and *the* could be interchanged without resulting in a loss of grammaticality; on the other hand, in the natural data of requesting and giving directions, even though participants spoke in grammatically correct utterances, communication broke down when articles were used in reference to items in one participant's experience but not in another's.
>
> Comparison with the natural data of speech events has also shown that the instructional materials used by ESL students (and their teachers) present a seemingly complete but actually partial description of the article system. Findings of the comparison study suggest that ESL students might use article rules correctly according to the dictates of a grammar or textbook, but inappropriately according to the demands of a communicative context. (Pica 1983:231)

It would be possible to go on and on giving examples of studies which purposely or inadvertently prove that native speaker intuitions are of limited extent and certainly do not include the ability to describe actual patterns of speech behavior. The point to be emphasized is that it is useful, and, indeed, necessary, for us to know the rules of speaking of a community in a way that will permit us to describe them objectively for the purposes of language teaching and the assessment of the language proficiency of learners. It is critical for specialists in language teaching and learning to recognize that because so many of these rules are not available to our intuitions as native speakers, we must determine what they are by empirical investigation.

If it is difficult for most of us to accept the fact that rules of speaking are different both across cultures and within them, and that speech behavior is appropriate or not relative to the context rather than because of any intrinsic value that may pertain to a particular form or expression, then it is doubly difficult to accept the idea that we are not in a position to describe the rules of speaking of our own speech community. In spite of such clear demonstrations as the ones given above, many people who are themselves involved in sociology or linguistics do not hesitate to give analyses based on intuitions, with, perhaps, a few examples drawn from memory or even from actual speech. These analyses, when systematically investigated, frequently turn out to be inaccurate. Intuitions into sociolinguistic rules, whether at the level of general behavior or at much more specific levels of analysis into the use of certain linguistic features in different contexts, are notoriously unreliable.

Before leaving the topic of native speaker intuition, it is important to make the point that while often inadequate with respect to our ability to report what we say and how we say it, our intuitions are unquestionably valuable and important in many ways. That is, while we do not have the ability to describe speech use objectively, we are very capable of recognizing inaccuracies and inappropriate speech behavior. Further, and even more important to the analysis of sociolinguistic rules, we often have good insights into the meanings behind various means of expression. We know a great deal about what is appropriate in various sorts of interactions and we can bring this knowledge to the analysis of patterns of use, once we have a good collection of examples of speech used in spontaneous daily interactions. What is important to remember is that while our intuitions as native speakers are far from adequate to the description of sociolinguistic rules, we would be completely unable to make sense of these rules if we had no intuitions at all. Inadequacy is not the same as absence of knowledge. We do not know enough about the way language is used, but this does not mean that we do not know a great deal.

COMMUNICATIVE COMPETENCE

As Hymes (1974a, 1975) points out, a child who had acquired the competence to produce any and all the sentences of his native language, and who was likely to say any sentence without reference to social context or rules, would be considered a social monster. The point is that the ability to produce correct sentences does not, in itself, constitute knowledge of a language. Whether the language learner is a small child acquiring his or her first language, or anyone learning a new language, the fact remains that language acquisition involves not linguistic competence alone but what Hymes (1967, 1972b) has called *communicative competence*. As we have pointed out in earlier chapters, this term, along with the concept to which it refers, has gained wide acceptance in the field of TESOL and of applied linguistics generally. Researchers, writers of language teaching materials, and most language instructors have become convinced that successful language acquisition involves learning what to say to whom and in which circumstances, as well as the ability to follow the rules of grammar and pronunciation.

Paulston (1974a,b) was one of the earliest specialists in language teaching to take up Hymes's notion of communicative competence and to advocate the need to incorporate rules of speaking into second language classroom teaching. As she says, "I have come to think that it is every bit as important that we teach the appropriate forms of social usage as the linguistic forms themselves." As she points out, it is typical of TESOL curricula to include instruction in the grammatical rules for information questions, but what is not taught is what questions are appropriate to ask. She goes on to suggest that one reason such information is not taught is that there are strong constraints on teaching rules of social behavior to adults. But, as she points out, and as we have seen in detail in the last chapter, "we do our students a disservice if we don't teach them the social rules along with the linguistic rules as long as we remember not to imply any moral superiority of one rule over the other" (Paulston 1974a:3). What Paulston does not say is that most of the rules for appropriate speech behavior have not yet been investigated empirically and that the only information teachers who wish to take this approach have available to them is to use their own intuitions about what is and is not appropriate in a given situation. As we discussed above, these intuitions, while extremely valuable in terms of getting at the norms of native speakers, are very unreliable when it comes to actual insights into spontaneous use. In recommending that communicative competence be taught, Paulston makes suggestions regarding teaching methods which she calls communicative. These include the use of grammar lessons that involve the meaningful use of language and of role-plays to give students practice in interacting in situations which are based on real-life activities, such as opening a bank account. Such activities may be useful and are certainly an improvement over language lessons in which no attempt is made to give students an opportunity to engage in meaningful communication. Paulston's suggestion is also an early and important example of the problems which arose in the attempt to apply the theoretical principles of communicative competence to language instruction. My intention is not to find fault with Paulston's pioneering work in this field. The fact that she was one of the first to recognize and attempt to implement these principles was an extremely significant beginning, and she is to be admired as one of the forerunners in recognizing the importance of these principles to the field of TESOL. Indeed, Paulston was one of the first scholars in the United States to become involved in the application of Hymes's theoretical notion of communicative competence to second language teaching through what has come to be called the communicative approach to language teaching.

During the mid-1970s and early 1980s, many articles appeared in the applied linguistics literature supporting the rationale for introducing communicative competence as a goal of language teaching. Materials development, syllabus design, and proficiency assessment all became imbued with the new communicative approach to language teaching. Almost immediately, problems began to surface, as it was discovered that acceptance of a theoretical principle is one thing and putting it into operation is quite another.

Not all the new communicative approaches to language teaching were based specifically or solely on Hymes's notion of communicative competence. Indeed, various aspects of the theories of numerous other scholars concerned with language behavior were brought into play in the new approaches to communicative language teaching, and the term *communicative competence* itself began to be redefined by scholars in the field of language teaching. Almost immediately, it became clear that some serious problems would have to be worked out before satisfactory solutions could be found to implement the theoretical concepts embraced by the notion of communicative competence. For many teachers and curriculum developers, there was uncertainty about what exactly was to be included under the rubric of "communicative competence." In many cases, the term, as originally defined by Hymes, was completely misinterpreted, so that grammatical competence was regarded as something separate from communicative competence instead of an intrinsic part of what speakers need to know in order to communicate effectively. Frequently, such misinterpretations resulted in the creation of teaching materials and syllabi that concentrated heavily on guiding learners in their efforts to get their meanings across, but paid little attention to helping them to become accurate language users with respect to grammar or phonology. As Brumfit (1980b) pointed out:

> The whole "communicative" movement in language teaching has been a reaction, in a variety of ways, to too narrow and "syntactic" an interpretaton of language teaching. . . . The so-called "humanistic" approaches to language teaching, popular particularly in the United States, . . . are attempts to increase the social and personal value of the language learning process. Such responses, coming from experienced teachers have been received sympathetically on a wide front, but there is no systematic approach to language in society by which they can readily be explained or to which they can really be referred.

Thus, scholars writing about language teaching methodology have sometimes interpreted communicative competence to mean a focus on spontaneity of expression (e.g., Rivers 1973), while others have recognized that the term as Hymes intended it to be interpreted had more to do with the elaboration of the social rules of language use. In spite of these difficulties, however, most scholars in the field of TESOL, motivated by the need to translate theory into practice, correctly took the goal of communicative competence to mean that it was necessary to design materials based on the functional use of language, to make materials more authentic and meaningful, and to give students the opportunity to learn to use language spontaneously and appropriately in social context. Many (e.g., Widdowson 1978) stressed the need to gear language teaching to the needs and interests of the learners and to move away from a mechanical, decontextualized presentation of grammar and pronunciation rules.

Canale and Swain (1980) reviewed the theoretical model on which the term *communicative competence* rests and, for the sake of clarity in translating the concept itself into areas that could be operationalized at the level of syllabus design and curriculum development, identified three components. Disturbed over the fact that many models of communicative language teaching have tended to represent grammatical competence separately from communicative competence, and to focus on meaning and function at the expense of attention to form, Canale and Swain are careful to include grammatical accuracy as one of the three major aspects of communicative competence. As they put it, "Just as Hymes . . . was able to say that there are rules of grammar that would be useless without rules of language use, so we feel that there are rules of language use that would be useless without rules of grammar" (Canale and Swain 1980:5).

In proposing a "theoretical framework for communicative competence," Canale and Swain (1980:28) include three components: grammatical competence, sociolinguistic competence, and strategic competence. Under sociolinguistic competence, Canale and Swain identify what they suggest are two sets of rules: sociocultural rules of use and rules of discourse. As they explain this distinction:

> Sociocultural rules of use will specify the ways in which utterances are produced and understood *appropriately* with respect to the component of communicative events outlined by Hymes. . . . The primary focus of these rules is on the extent to which certain propositions and communicative functions are appropriate within a given sociocultural context depending on contextual factors such as topic, role of participants, setting, and norms of interaction. A secondary concern of such rules is the extent to which appropriate attitude and register or style are conveyed by a particular grammatical form within a given sociocultural context. . . . the rules of discourse in our framework is the combination of utterances and communicative functions and not the grammatical well-formedness of a single utterance nor the sociocultural appropriateness of a set of propositions and communicative functions in a given context. (Canale and Swain 1980:30)

The third of the components of communicative competence outlined by Canale and Swain is what they call "strategic competence." Here they call attention to both verbal and nonverbal communication strategies that can help language learners to cope with or remedy breakdowns in communication which result from lack of proficiency in the language. Included in strategic competence are such items as paraphrase, when the speaker does not know or remember a word or phrase, ways to address someone when the speaker is uncertain of the addressee's status, and so on. The teaching of strategic competence, they argue, will encourage learners to communicate even when they are unsure of the exact way to express themselves.

The objective of the framework proposed by Canale and Swain (1980) and by Canale (1983) is to "prepare and encourage learners to exploit in an optimal way their limited communicative competence in the second language in order to participate in actual communication situations" (Canale 1983:17).

The recognition of the need and the usefulness of moving away from context-free grammar exercises and working to guide students to learn to communicate in meaningful ways was a critical step for applied linguistics. It was, however, not without its problems, and many of these are still far from resolved. Some of the problems have had to do with conceptualizing and operationalizing the notion of communicative competence so that it could become truly workable in a second language teaching situation. Other problems were less obvious but no less severe. Recognizing a need and working out ways to meet it from the instructional point of view are important; what is equally important is that the content one has decided to make use of be available.

Having accepted the necessity to include sociolinguistic information in language instruction, therefore, textbook writers and teachers turned to the literature in sociolinguistics for the information they needed to apply. Unfortunately, too little research into sociolinguistic rules had been done, leading to a situation in which the TESOL profession wanted and needed to apply information that did not yet exist. Some work had been done, of course, and in the following chapters I will both present early research findings and describe the results of more recent investigations into sociolinguistic rules and patterns. What is important to understand is that the field of sociolinguistics was, itself, in a very early stage of development. Many problems regarding research methodology had yet to be worked out. In the following sections, I will outline some of the more salient problems in the collection and analysis of the sort of sociolinguistic information needed by the field of second language teaching, and will attempt to describe the difficulties involved in providing what we might think of as a grammar of sociolinguistic rules.

LANGUAGE AND COMMUNITY

When one confronts the need for sociolinguistic information which can be applied to language teaching and learning, one is immediately faced with a number of unresolved issues. Although inherent in the field itself, these problems were made much more obvious once an attempt was made to put sociolinguistic findings to use. There is a vast difference between doing scholarly research with the intention of adding to the general knowledge in the field, and doing the same work with the purpose of making it available to people outside the field who have a need for specific information. Once research findings are put to the test of relevance for an applied field, problems which may have seemed unimportant assume a very different perspective. So it is with work in sociolinguistics. As long as the work was being done to add to our general knowledge as social scientists, problems having to do with the generalizability of findings, for example, could be regarded as academic questions to be pondered and debated. Now that these same findings are actually being put to use in the construction of curriculum materials and in actual classroom teaching, the issue becomes a much more concrete problem. The one thing we must avoid is to mislead people not directly connected with sociolinguistic research into believing that what has been done is faultless, or ready for dissemination without serious critical evaluation. To disseminate information of this kind without making clear that there are problems of validity to be solved could prove disastrous since it might easily undermine the entire endeavor. In the next section, I will try to point out what the specific problems are and why they are relevant to the application of sociolinguistic research findings to the classroom.

To begin with, there is the very critical issue of identifying the object of study. This may, on the face of it, seem absurd. How can trained researchers with a strong background in their discipline have difficulty in defining who and what they are trying to investigate? The answer is a complicated one, but necessary to the understanding of sociolinguistics and its application to the field of language teaching. As we know, sociolinguistic research involves the study of language in its social context. But, like grammatical and phonological rules, the sociolinguistic rules or, as they are often called, the rules of speaking that are such a critical part of what we have come to call communicative competence are different not only from language to language but also from society to society and from subgroup to subgroup. Since this is the case, it follows that the patterns of speech behavior that constitute a large part of a native speaker's communicative competence must be learned in the context of *specific* social units. The questions that must be addressed first, then, are: How are we to define these units? Within how inclusive a group shall we look for common rules of speaking—at the level of a village or at that of an entire nation? Clearly, some rules have wider application than others, but until we put our questions to the test of systematic, empirical investigations, we cannot know how far a particular rule can be applied. What we do know is that we must begin in specific places or communities in which we can be relatively certain that everyone shares the same norms and the same rules for what Hymes calls the "conduct and interpretation of speech" (Hymes 1974a). In the attempt to identify groups which do share at least one language and the rules for their use, sociolinguists have for many years depended upon the concept of *speech community*. The term itself is not a new one; indeed it has been used by linguists for generations. What is new is the redefinition of the concept by sociolinguists.

From the sociolinguistic point of view, a single speech community may have, as part of its repertoire, two or more languages. Conversely, speakers of a single language often participate in more than one speech community, each with its own norms and rules of speaking. Where speech community may be said to correspond to geographical area, this fact is not, on the surface, particularly difficult to deal with. The English-speaking world, to take a relatively simple example, is made up of a large number of speech communities. Where boundaries happen to coincide with territory or with political lines, the situation appears to be relatively straightforward. It is widely recognized, for example, that the British and the Australians differ sharply from the Americans in many aspects of language use, although all three nations are predominantly English-speaking. And anyone who has lived in one of the other English-speaking nations, or who has interacted extensively with its people, knows that pronunciation, grammar, and lexicon are not the only distinguishing features. Norms and values differ, and these differences are reflected in differing rules of speech behavior. However, it is also the case that within political and geographic boundaries, we have a great variety of smaller social groupings, and these are much less easy to define. Although most of us are well aware that language use both reflects and helps to create and maintain social differences, there is little agreement as to the criteria that define and distinguish specific social units. What is at issue here is the very serious and complex problem which must be faced in defining the basic notion of speech community.

As a starting point, we can say that scholars agree that members of a speech community must share at least one language. But as Hymes (1972b) points out: "The sharing of grammatical (variety) rules is not sufficient. There may be persons persons whose English I can grammatically identify but whose messages escape me. I may be ignorant of what counts as a coherent sequence, request, statement requiring an answer, requisite or forbidden topic, marking of emphasis or irony, normal duration of silence, normal level of voice, etc. . ." (Hymes 1972b:54).

Thus, Hymes points again to the fact that the social rules of interaction are no less important than linguistic rules if people are to understand each other. Given this fact, Hymes says: "Tentatively, a *speech community* is defined as a community sharing rules for the conduct and interpretation of speech, and rules for the interpretation of at least one linguistic variety. Both conditions are necessary." (Hymes 1972b:54).

Taken together, the two quotations from Hymes make clear that what is at issue in the definition of speech community is that not all speakers of a language do share the same rules of speaking, and, therefore, not all may be said to belong to the same speech community. It is important to make this argument again and again because it is one which is, unfortunately, often misunderstood or ignored. It is critical that researchers and teachers understand that it is unrealistic to speak of investigating or teaching the rules of speaking for English or, indeed, for any language. Depending on the group studied, the rules are likely to be different from group to group within the same language.

In this connection, it may be useful to mention a distinction made by the Czech linguist Neustupny (1971), who conceptualizes language groups along two dimensions. On the one hand, he says, we have what is called a *Sprachbund* (language area) and, on the other, what he has called a *Sprechbund* (speech area). Under language area, Neustupny classifies all speakers of the "same" language, regardless of specific regional or social variations. In this sense, all native speakers of English belong to one language area. On the other hand, Neustupny recognizes that the rules for the appropriate use of language are extremely variable and that there will always be subgroups within language areas. Furthermore, coming from Central Europe as he does, he is well aware that many sociolinguistic rules hold *across* language areas, such that people living in a particular geographic region may speak different languages but share the rules for what topics are appropriate, for speech conduct in various settings, and so on. Underlying this classification, of course, is the recognition that different sociolinguistic rules will have wider or narrower application. For example, it may well be that the rules for the use of address terms—whether you address interlocutors by their titles and last names or by their first names—often have very wide distribution, so that Hungarians, following their own rules would, in speaking Czech, use the very forms considered appropriate. The same might be said for the rules governing the sorts of questions considered appropriate to ask of a stranger. It may well happen that a large number of communities in a general geographic area will share these rules for language behavior, even though they speak mutually unintelligible languages. These communities would, in Neustupny's classification, belong to the same speech area but to different language areas. As we will see in our discussion of sociolinguistic transfer, the learners' generalization of rules from native to target language, the distribution of such patterns across language groups which inhabit or come from the same "speech area," may prove to be a critical factor. The similarities and differences in rules of speaking among the various subgroups that make up a language community lead to some extremely difficult questions. If a speech community is to be defined by shared rules, and if these rules are largely unconscious, where do we begin? Even where we notice patterns of use, how can we tell how far they extend? The simplest answer is to begin by looking for groups that have some sort of preexisting definition apart from speech usage. But, as Irvine (1986) asks: "What are the social characteristics of this unit? . . . I would suggest that the concept of the speech community was still an abstracted, idealized notion that runs into practical problems when you try to operationalize it in conducting fieldwork. . ." (Irvine 1986).

As Irvine points out, Hymes himself is very cautious in this regard, admitting that we cannot know in advance what social unit might correspond to the speech community and that in each case this is something which must be empirically tested. For Irvine, the problem had to do with fieldwork in anthropological linguistics or, more specifically, in the ethnography of speaking. For applied linguists studying the sociolinguistic patterns of a vast and complex population of native speakers in order to describe them to language learners, the problem is even more severe.

If our concern is to describe rules of speaking which obtain across subgroups and which have a wide enough frame of reference to be useful to the language learner, we are faced with an inescapable circularity in the definition of our object of study. That is, a speech community is defined as a group that shares rules for the conduct and interpretation of speech, but there is no feature external to speech which can be used as a criterion of membership. What we have, then, is simply an equation between shared language(s) and speech conduct, on the one hand, and speech community, on the other hand. Furthermore, when the language under consideration is, like English, that of a complex, industrialized society, the notion of speech community must be used at a level of abstraction that ignores many subtle distinctions. The decision to focus on the broader category rather than on small self-defined groupings has to do with the purpose of the investigation; this in turn will determine the methods to be used.

Given that the purpose of our investigations is to discover patterns of interaction that will be of use to nonnative speakers in their acquisition of communicative competence, we must work out the rules of speaking that cut across the specific patterns of extralinguistically identifiable local groups. Language learners need to know about the general norms and speech behavior common to mainstream middle class speakers if that is the group with whom they plan to interact. In this connection, however, it must be recognized that many language learners are immigrants and refugees who live and work with speakers of nonstandard varieties of English. While their own socioeconomic aspirations may well lead them to want to learn the forms of the prestige group, this is not always possible. The point is that many smaller groups exist both within the mainstream and outside it. Furthermore, much of the mainstream population belongs not to independent subgroups or networks (see Milroy 1980) but to series of neighborhood, occupational, religious, political, and social groups whose memberships may overlap only slightly or not at all. Whether such groups as these share certain sociolinguistic rules peculiar to themselves is an empirical question. If, however, our aim is to uncover norms and patterns of speech behavior common to the broader population of native speakers of American English, we must, for heuristic purposes, assume the existence of a broader speech community than the type usually studied by anthropologists. It is important to recognize from the beginning that our construct of the speech community under study is, of necessity, much less fine-grained than it would be if our purpose were to investigate intergroup differences. As Irvine points out in her discussion of the problems regarding the concept of speech community encountered by ethnographers of speaking: "If speech communities are organized in ever-widening nested series and always correspond to some social aggregate, it doesn't matter which aggregate you pick. The choice of social locus is somewhat arbitrary; at whatever level you bound your social universe, you can find sociolinguistic system" (Irvine 1986:11).

An instructive example of the distinction under discussion can be found in the work of Paulston (1974b, 1976). In urging that communicative competence be recognized as the goal of language teaching, Paulston (1974b) gives examples of her own accidental sociolinguistic transfer in cross-cultural interaction between Swedes and Americans:

> Occasionally, faulty rule sharing will lead to complete breakdown in communication. Here is an example from my recent stay in Sweden, where I was born and raised. We (my American husband and children) celebrated Thanksgiving by having my immediate family (Swedish) and friends for a traditional turkey dinner. I was busy in the kitchen and came belatedly into the living room just after my sister-in-law had arrived. In impeccable Swedish I asked her politely, "Do you know everyone?" Any native American would correctly interpret such a question to mean that I wanted to know if she had been introduced to those guests she had not previously met. She looked at me sourly and said, "I don't know everyone but if you are asking me if I have greeted everyone, I have." Fussed as I was, and in such an archetypal American situation, I had momentarily forgotten that proper Swedish manners demand that guests do not wait to be introduced by a third party, but go around the room,

shake hands with everyone and say their names aloud to those they have not previously met. Any child knows that, so my sister-in-law felt that I had reprimanded her for bad manners, for faulty sharing of a systematic set of social interactional rules. Clearly, the meaning of an interaction is easily misinterpreted if the speakers don't share the same set of rules. Hence the necessity for teaching those rules.

In comparing Swedish and American rules, Paulston makes the implicit assumption that all Swedes share the rules for greeting which she describes, and this may indeed be the case. In writing for an audience of sociolinguists, however, the same scholar chooses a much finer analytical grid to demonstrate differences in sociolinguistic rules for second-person pronoun selection in Swedish, each used by a different social class. Like most sociolinguistic rules, those for pronoun selection are unconscious. However, since members of different social classes are actually following different rules, interactions between groups frequently involve a good deal of miscommunication, "The fact that the two do exist, with a tendency to separate along class lines, is not recognized, and there are constant complaints from encounters where the speakers apply different sets of rules with no recognition of the difference" (Paulston 1976:369).

Thus, depending on the purpose of the research and the uses to which it will be put, the same sociolinguist can decide to use a larger or smaller unit of analysis on which to focus. In this sense, the term *speech community* may be seen as a construct which has boundaries in the sense that its members share sociolinguistic rules, but which might be broadened or narrowed, depending on what the investigator is attempting to find out.

Since the unit of analysis may vary depending upon the judgment of the researcher, we must be especially careful to define the boundaries we have chosen to focus upon. The validity of our results depends not only upon how we go about our work but, to a great extent, upon the identification of the boundaries we have chosen to work within.

CONCLUSION

From the point of view of language teaching in general and of TESOL in particular, the implications of what has been said are many-faceted. The ability of a second language learner to interact successfully in a foreign speech community depends on the extent of his or her communicative competence, of which rules of speaking are an important aspect. These sociolinguistic patterns are, however, not objectively known to native speakers, including the teachers and materials writers who are most in need of applying them.

It is important for language specialists, as for all speakers, to recognize that however well able we may be to function appropriately in our own native speech communities, we must not make the mistake of believing that the way we handle the linguistic and social resources at our command is completely open to our conscious knowledge. We have good insights into what we do and why we behave in certain ways, but much is hidden from us too. Part of the reason for the inadequacy of our intuitions regarding speech behavior has to do with the very ease and naturalness of the process. We do not notice which muscles we use when we walk or what rules we use when we talk. Socialized as we all are into culture-specific ways of speaking, few of our interactional patterns are even noticeable to us. Thus, although our native speaker intuitions are extremely useful in analyzing data collected from the stream of ongoing speech, we cannot trust them to predict how people will speak in given situations. The only way of getting at this sort of knowledge is through systematic analysis of everyday speech as it is used in as broad a range of speech situations as possible.

When we turn to sociolinguistic analyses for information about rules of speaking, we are immediately confronted with the fact that there are many unresolved problems to be worked out. We must be clear about whose rules of speaking are being studied, and how far we can generalize from what has been learned in our application of these findings to second language instruction. Further, we must be aware that sociolinguistics is a young field and that although a great deal has been done, we are very far from being able to write anything approaching a grammar of sociolinguistic rules for any group.

To have discussed these problems openly and in detail is not to suggest that they cannot be solved or that what already exists in the sociolinguistic literature is not valuable both in itself and for what it can offer us with respect to insights, information, and inspiration for further research. Much of what remains to be done will, I hope, come from students who, seeing the need and the value of the work, as well as the problems involved in doing it, will devote their time and energy to adding to the description and dissemination of information about rules of speaking. Such descriptions will be valuable not only to language learners but to everyone interested in understanding sociolinguistic regularities and the creativity with which speakers make use of their own unconscious patterns in order to accomplish the work of ongoing social interaction.

CHAPTER
3

Investigating Spoken Interaction

INTRODUCTION

The analysis of sociolinguistic rules of speaking is the analysis of the patterns and functions of language in use. In order to make sense of the research into the ways in which people use language in interacting with one another, we must first recognize that there are a number of ways of looking at language and that different research paradigms and traditions have fed into the work that is currently being undertaken by scholars whose primary interest is in investigating ongoing speech or conversation. While no single way of looking at language represents the sum total of what might be investigated, there are a number of frameworks which have been put forth, each presenting or emphasizing different sets of dimensions of language use and each making use of different (though occasionally overlapping) terminology. The fact that researchers concerned with understanding and describing spoken interaction have made use of different research paradigms stems largely from the fact that scholars from a variety of academic disciplines have each brought the research traditions of those disciplines to bear on what is essentially the same subject matter. Thus, present-day analyses of verbal interaction include the work of scholars from various disciplinary backgrounds, including philosophy, sociology, anthropology, folklore, and linguistics. In addition, much of the sociolinguistic work most relevant to TESOL has been interdisciplinary, making use of research methods drawn from different disciplines and adapting them to suit needs for specific types of information. A book of this scope cannot provide a detailed description of all the various frameworks that have been put forward for the analysis of speech, since each would require at least book-length treatment in itself. From the point of view of TESOL and of applied linguistics generally, however, it is useful to have background knowledge about some of the more widely used analytic frameworks for describing speech use, along with the scholars and terminology associated with them. A brief introduction to the most commonly mentioned traditions of analysis will be given here so that when these names, terms, and concepts are used in the description of various studies of speech in use, readers will recognize their source and be in a position to evaluate the findings within the context of the analytic framework(s) upon which such studies have drawn.

The approach to the analysis of language in use known as the ethnography of speaking as formulated by Dell Hymes (1962, 1967, 1971b, 1972a, 1974a, 1974b) is fundamental to the entire enterprise of investigating communicative competence and therefore has, in many ways, informed most of the research in sociolinguistics and TESOL. For this reason, this framework for the investigation of language use was described in some detail in the introduction to this book. Because the concepts and technical terms proposed by Hymes are so deeply embedded in the sociolinguistic literature in the field of TESOL, it would have been impossible to delineate the field without beginning with a description of Hymes's framework. For this reason, the ethnography of speaking, especially as it relates to sociolinguistic research relevant to TESOL, was discussed at some length in the introduction to this book. No other sequence would have sufficed to prepare readers to understand the issues and findings so far described. Since this is the case, and since Hymes's perspective has already been described and will be mentioned throughout, it must be recognized as basic to the underlying fabric of this book. The tradition of work which Hymes has initiated will therefore be assumed to be understood and will not be included among the various frameworks to be surveyed below.

While it is true that a considerable amount of work has been done by ethnographers of speaking on rules of speaking in a wide variety of societies (Gumperz and Hymes 1972, Bauman and Sherzer 1974), we will limit ourselves here to a discussion of those findings and frameworks of analysis which have had specific relevance for research in TESOL, except where an example from a different culture serves to throw light upon the cross-cultural validity of the analytic frameworks to be described. Such counterevidence of universality in speech behavior is of particular importance to ESL specialists for whom cross-cultural communication is of intrinsic concern.

THE PHILOSOPHIC TRADITION

This analytic framework is primarily associated with what is known as "speech act theory" and has its origins in the work of philosophers of language such as Austin (1962) and Searle (1975). Some of the concepts and terminology to be found in the recent literature in applied linguistics were developed within this tradition, and many have proved useful in the analysis of sociolinguistic problems in language acquisition.

It was Austin (1962) who pointed out that some utterances in a language are, in themselves, acts. On this basis, Austin posited the existence of a set of verbs in English which he termed "performatives" because a speaker may, by using one of them in the first person present, perform an act. Examples of such utterances are "I sentence you to ten years in prison," "I warn you to obey," "I promise to be at the meeting," or "I beg you to help me." In each of the foregoing examples, the speaker explicitly performs an act solely through speaking. The verbs such as *sentence*, *warn*, *promise*, and *beg* belong to the category which Austin termed "performative" verbs. It was also noted that forms of speech which do not contain explicit performative verbs may nevertheless serve to perform acts implicitly. That is, the utterance may perform an act without explicitly naming it. An example of such an implicitly performed speech act would be a promise which does not actually contain the verb *promise* but implies that a promise is being made (e.g., "I'll come to the meeting"). Another example of an implicit speech act would be a warning such as "Shoplifters will be prosecuted." Whether the sentence contains an explicit performative verb or not, the point is that speakers do perform an act through what they say. An utterance which has the significance of an act is termed an "illocutionary act." When speech act theorists describe the performing of such an illocutionary act, they refer to the "force" of the utterance, which might be to promise or to warn, as in the examples given above. From this derives the notion that utterances may have "illocutionary force" such that they are interpreted as specific kinds of acts. This kind of categorization of speech acts has been very useful to applied linguists in describing problems in communication which arise when language learners translate sentences having a specific illocutionary force in their first language into the target language, in which the interpretation of the utterance may be very different. That is, the words may translate, but the meaning or "force" of the utterance is often lost.

Communication problems involving the nontranslatability of the illocutionary force of an utterance are particularly noticeable in the use of what Searle (1975) has called "indirect speech acts." Briefly, an indirect speech act is one in which the form and function do not coincide. An obvious example is a request which is put in the form of a question, such as "Can you close the door?" which, in most varieties of English, functions as an "indirect request" but which, as we have seen in the previous chapter, may be interpreted in the target language as a simple request for information and therefore lose its illocutionary force as a request when it is translated.

Appealing as these categories are, they can, when we apply them to the analysis of everyday interaction, prove very difficult to use. As many investigators have noted, utterances frequently serve more than one function at the same time and are therefore not easily classified. Among speakers of middle-class American English, a compliment, for example, may well serve as a greeting or an expression of gratitude. In addition to the fact that utterances may have more than one function, it is also the case that a function such as warning may well take the form of several sentences or even of a lengthy discourse in the form of a story. Speech Act Theory thus attempts to capture all the possible functions of language by classifying the kinds of action that can be performed by speech. In so doing, it treats language as a chain of utterances which are usually defined in terms of speaker intentions and beliefs, rather than taking into account the interaction and negotiation inherent in conversation. Since speech is much more than a series of utterances, and since the interaction of the participants is crucial to our understanding of sociolinguistic patterns of behavior, much of the information most critical to sociolinguists as well as to the language teaching profession is left out of account in this framework of analysis. As Cicourel (1980) has pointed out, there are four major limitations of speech act theory, apart from its inability to account for data from other cultures. As he puts it:

> The criticism voiced by the anthropologist-sociologist is that speech act analysis, as carried out by philosophers and linguists, has been limited to simulated or brief fragments of exchanges. These materials are seldom contextualized in terms of a sociocultural setting or of some larger social activity or organizational or institutional framework. In asking how we can apply speech act theory to actual discourse, we must recognize additional issues. Some of these issues are often implied in speech act theory but are not examined explicitly.
>
> First, the fact that speech acts occur in complex social settings leads to serious difficulty in the application of speech act theory to actual utterances in discourse. More than one message can be communicated by an utterance. . . . A progressively developed sense of what is going on in the discourse from the point of view of the participants is not part of the theory.
>
> Second, because discourse occurs in particular situations that include a number of personal, biographical, social, and cultural conditions, utterances and actions, along with their paralinguistic and nonverbal elements, are embedded in the way participants presume typical meanings on the basis of the previously mentioned conditions. These conditions . . . are seldom identified in speech act theory.
>
> Third, speech act theory describes a number of idealized conditions, . . . but other elements contribute to the production of normal appearances, including the way participants work at and modify their own talk and seek to sustain an environment of objects that gives the impression of being "normal." (Cicourel 1980:9–10)

Related to the work of the speech act theorists are the philosophical notions concerning the organization of conversation, in particular those put forth by Grice (1975), who has proposed a set of principles which he has termed "conversational maxims." Briefly, Grice says that there exists a code of cooperative behavior which organizes the way interlocutors interpret each other's speech. Because speakers expect their interlocutors to share this code, they interpret what others say on the basis of the assumption that their conversational partners are following what Grice calls "The Cooperative Principle" (Grice 1975:45). The code or conversational behavior which supports the "cooperative principle" is given in terms of a set of "conversational maxims":

> Quantity: Make your contribution as informative as is required (for the current purposes of the exchange). Do not make your contribution more informative than is required.
> Quality: Be truthful. Do not say what you believe to be false. Do not say that for which you lack adequate evidence.
> Relation: Be relevant.
> Manner: Be brief and orderly. Avoid obscurity and ambiguity.

According to Grice, these maxims give interlocutors the ability to interpret each other's comments by means of "conversational implicatures," so that the speaker's implied meaning is what is attended to.

A major difficulty with Grice's conversational maxims and the notion of speakers' ability to make implicatures based on them is that they, like the work of Austin and Searle, are built on the unstated assumption that the principles underlying face-to-face interaction are universal.

In an article comparing Grice's description of conversational organization with what she found in Malagasy society, Keenan (1976) points out that in working out their concepts, the philosophers "probably reflect on conversational conduct as it operates in their own society. But they don't make this qualification explicit and, in fact, present their principles as universal in application" (Keenan 1976). On the basis of her own work and that of others in various different speech communities around the world, Keenan observes: "It is an empirical question as to whether in all societies and in all situations, independent observers agree on the conversational implicature of a given utterance, since the implicature depends on how the utterer is expected to behave with respect to conversational maxims, and these may vary situationally and cross-culturally" (Keenan 1976:68).

As she goes on to explain, the principle Grice puts forward as the maxim "Be informative" is not at all operative in Malagasy society, where new information is a rarity which gives its owner prestige and which he or she would be unlikely to part with simply because someone asked for it. Her point is that the principle that speakers will satisfy each other's informational needs is "not a basic norm."

Related to the reluctance of Malagasy speakers to give out information is another instance of the nonuniversality of Grice's maxims. In this case, the maxim involved is "Be relevant." Given the code of behavior described by Grice, it would be expected that a speaker who asks a question can expect the addressee to respond with an answer. For this reason, whatever the addressee says in response to the question will be interpreted as an answer—an example of the kind of assumption which Grice calls a conversational implicature. However, in some societies, questions are not necessarily followed by answers since answers are in no sense obligatory and may even be considered foolish if the addressee has not thought the matter through carefully, a process that may take considerable time, which may well be filled with conversation about completely unrelated topics. That this principle regarding lengthy time gaps between the asking and answering of questions operates among the Indians at the Warm Springs Reservation in Oregon has been well attested in the literature through the independent ethnographic investigations of both Virginia Hymes (1975) and Susan Philips (1976). As Hymes (1975) puts it:

> Unlike our norm of interaction, that at Warm Springs does not require that a question by one person be followed immediately by an answer or a promise of an answer from the addressee. It may be followed by an answer but may also be followed by silence or by an utterance that bears no relationship to the question. Then the answer to the question may follow as long as five to ten minutes

later. . . . The fact is that at Warm Springs there just seems to be no rule that a question demands immediate response. In fact, answering without time for sufficient thought is explicitly considered stupid, or heedless. (Hymes 1975:33)

These are but two examples of findings by linguistic anthropologists which provide empirical evidence that the conversational principles put forth by philosophers of language, based mainly on introspection regarding the behavior of middle-class speakers of English, are very far from universal.

Because these descriptions of how conversation is organized have not been thoroughly researched through the systematic observation of naturally occurring interaction, it is also the case that these principles do not even necessarily hold true for any known community of native speakers of English. That is, there are likely to be contexts in which each of the maxims put forth by Grice are not operative. An example of this lack of universality, even within the "model" society, is demonstrated when a maxim such as "Be informative" must be contradicted by anyone whose occupation or social role requires that confidences be kept. Still another example of the potential fallacies underlying these maxims has to do with the rules governing what English speakers call "white lies." As every competent native speaker of English knows, being "informative" can, in many circumstances, be antisocial in the extreme.

While the philosophical tradition of language analysis just described does not provide us with universal facts, it does define dimensions of language behavior which are open to testing and which can therefore help to point up contrasts and to throw light on the great diversity to be found in human interaction. Thus, despite the limitations of this work, much may be gained by a systematic empirical investigation of the dimensions and concepts discussed in this literature.

ETHNOMETHODOLOGY

The area of investigation known as ethnomethodology arises from sociology and is specifically associated with the work of a group of sociologists including Harold Garfinkel and his associates and students at the University of California at Berkeley. *Ethnomethodology* is, in fact, a cover term for a view of social organization and a theoretical and methodological approach toward investigating the activity of day-to-day interaction. Strongly influenced by the work of the sociological theorist Alfred Shutz, Garfinkel has a special interest in making visible and describing everyday events which normally go unnoticed because they are taken for granted. As Garfinkel himself puts it:

Almost alone among sociological theorists, the late Alfred Schutz, in a series of classical studies of the constitutive phenomenology of the world of everyday

life, described many of these seen but unnoticed background expectancies. He
called them the "attitude of daily life." He referred to their scenic attributions
as the "world known in common and taken for granted." Schutz' fundamental
work makes it possible to pursue further the tasks of clarifying their nature and
operation, of relating them to the processes of concerted actions, and assigning
them their place in an empirically imaginable society. (Garfinkel 1972:3)

The aim of ethnomethodological analysis is to uncover speakers' unconscious
cultural knowledge and the assumptions arising from it which lead to the way they
interpret and react to their experiences. What is of particular importance in this type
of analysis is the notion of interaction as a process in which speakers create the very
events they are engaged in. Not only is it necessary for cultural knowledge or rules
to be shared; people use this knowledge in constructing a social and communicative
environment for each other as they speak and respond to one another. That is,
speakers and addressees, by responding to one another's ways of speaking and
listening, are constantly creating what McDermott (1977:26) calls "environments
for each other." Constantly aware of one another's reactions, conversational partners interpret each other's meanings partly on the basis of shared cultural knowledge and partly on that of a fine-tuned ability to read and react to even the most
subtle verbal and nonverbal responses.

Using the metaphor of interaction as work, analysts working within the ethnomethodological framework examine the organization of conversation in order to
discover how speakers "accomplish" interaction. Conversations are transcribed,
using a very specific and carefully worked-out set of conventions for the transcription itself. The transcript then becomes the data for detailed analysis aimed at
uncovering the assumptions which speakers must share in order for what is said to
have coherence. Assumptions which appear to be regularly made by members of a
culture and which seem to make it possible for them to make sense of each other's
speech are analyzed in order to come to a more general understanding of how
conversation is organized (see, for example, Sacks et al. 1974, Goffman 1976).

An example of this sort of finding regarding conversational expectations is the
"adjacency pair" rule, which states that some kinds of utterances within a conversation can only be interpreted as responses to utterances which precede them. Thus it
is claimed that utterances may come in "pair parts" such as question/answer or
greeting/greeting, such that the parts are dependent upon one another for coherence.
The point of this kind of anlaysis is to identify regularities in conversational structure which permit speakers to interpret what is said. An utterance such as "yes,
that's a good idea" would make no sense unless it was understood as the second part
of a question/answer sequence. Another example of such sequencing rules has to do
with the principle of "turn-taking" in conversation. In the work of Sacks et al.
(1974) it is stated that a basic feature of conversation is that no more than one party
speaks at a time and that speakers take recurrent turns at talk, turns ordered sequen-
tially through a speaker selection "machinery." Transition points occur at the

completion of an utterance and are recognized through various verbal and nonverbal cues such as intonation and eye contact. Such turn transitions are seen as an achievement since conversational participants must orient themselves very closely in order to avoid simultaneous speech. Since the timing is very delicate, there are often very brief overlaps where one speaker begins a turn just as another is coming to the end of a turn.

While the work of the ethnomethodologists has led to fruitful and often significant findings, it has not gone unchallenged. The notion that members of a culture rely on their shared but unstated knowledge of their culture to interpret what is said has long been accepted, and the principle that intelligibility of an utterance is dependent on the way in which something is said as well as on the grammar and lexicon is a principle intrinsic to sociolinguistics. However, neither the methods of analysis nor such specific concepts as that of the adjacency pair are universally well regarded by scholars who study conversation from different perspectives. Coulthard (1977:92), for example, points out that the work of Sacks et al. produces many interesting insights into the workings of conversation, but the analytic methodology and categories employed remain so informal and imprecise that they are difficult for others to use in any practical way. Discourse analysts such as Brown and Yule (1983) say that the most we can learn from the notion of adjacency pairs is that what follows a question should be treated as an answer to that question and that we are, according to this formula, expected to assume that two formally unconnected utterances placed together form a coherent piece of discourse. Clearly this formula has only limited usefulness. As Philips (1976:81) has pointed out, answers do not necessarily follow questions in the American Indian society she studied in Warm Springs, Oregon. It is also the case that questions can be ignored or remain unanswered in conversations among middle-class white speakers of American English, and it is foolish to try to insist on a formula that requires all utterances following questions to be heard as answers. An example of the problematic nature of defining or determining such two-turn units as adjacency pairs is that many, if not most, conversations, even when limited to two participants, consist of far longer sequences during which the same topic is maintained over a considerable number of turns at talk by both participants. Compliment/response sequences, for example, are not, as ethnomethodologists might claim, easily reduced to adjacency pairs. Indeed, an important finding of the analysis (Wolfson 1983a) is that compliments are frequently used as conversation openers. For this reason, the sequence which follows the initial compliment can be very long indeed. Further, conversations are not necessarily restricted to two participants, and a topic may be discussed by several people, making the determination of adjacency pairs artificial at best. An example of the artificiality of trying to reduce such sequences into adjacency pairs comes from data collected in my ongoing study of compliment/response sequences (Wolfson in press). The situation is one in which a mother and her two daughters are involved in conversation with one another. While the first sequence could easily be seen as an adjacency pair, the reemergence of the topic and the entry of a third conversational participant, typical of spontaneous conversation, demonstrates the difficulty in attempting to analyze what follows into first and second pair parts:

A: That's a nice sweater, Mom.
B: Thanks.

and then, after some 20 minutes of unrelated talk:

A: That really is a nice sweater.
C: It really is very nice. Where'd you get it?
B: I got it at X in exchange for the red bag.
C: Oh, you got rid of the red bag!
B: Yeah, well, what else was I going to do with it?
C: I think you did exactly the right thing with it—that sweater is great.
A: It really is.
B: I like it too. I needed a new black sweater. But what makes it so great?
A: The neckline is really good on you . . .
C: And the weave is unusual and very elegant.
A: It fits well too.
C: Does it have shoulder pads? (feels sweater) Yes, but they look good.
A: They're not too big—they fit just right.
B: Well, that's what I thought. I plan to wear it with a lot of dresses and I think it'll be practical.
C: It will. It should go with most of your dresses.
B: That was the idea.
C: I'll have to look over at X too—I could use something like that.
B: They've got a good selection.

Thus, if we look at Sacks et al. (1974), we see that their aim is to identify the regularities of conversational structure by describing the ways in which participants take turns at speaking. They do this by describing two term units as the basic adjacency pair organization, and, as the above example shows, this is usually difficult to determine in actual conversation. The adjacency pair problem is, however, by no means the only one. It is, for example, a well-documented fact that participants in conversations do not always take turns. We know from studies of non-English-speaking societies that some have rules which do not include turn-taking at all (Reisman 1974, Philips 1976). In her article, Philips compares the way Warm Springs Indians regulate their talk with the way white middle-class Anglos do so. To begin with, Philips gives us a helpful definition of her use of the term *Anglos*:

> In using the term Anglos, I refer to those persons, usually of white middle class, who have participated in the taped interactions and experiments that are used as a data base by students of conversation in the U.S. and England. . . . all of these

sources involve activities familiar to persons of Anglo or white middle-class background, although clearly we need, where possible, to become more specific about just who is involved. (Philips 1976:82)

Philips then quotes and summarizes from Sacks et al. (1974:6), in which they propose a number of "facts" they believe to hold true for "conversation". As Philips points out: "No explicit claim of universality has been made for these features. At the same time, no effort has been made to identify the specific social groups or situations for which they might hold true" (Philips 1976:83).

With respect to white middle-class American society (or those whom Philips designates as Anglos), the turn-taking argument is no more convincing. In her well-known study of a Thanksgiving dinner conversation among Americans of different geographical and ethnic backgrounds (Tannen 1981, 1982) the author points out that ethnic Jews from New York use very different conversational strategies than do non-Jews from areas further west. One of the most salient differences found in this study is that New Yorkers of Jewish background very often speak simultaneously and that this conversational style is in no sense intended or interpreted within the group as interrupting, but is rather seen as normal cooperative interaction. The fact that the non-Jewish group interpreted this conversational strategy very differently, frequently misinterpreting what was going on, is an important finding regarding differences in speech behavior among the various subgroups that constitute what is often characterized as middle-class American society. More relevant to the issue at hand, however, is the evidence Tannen gives us of the lack of validity of the conversational sequencing rules put forth by Sacks et al. (1974), in which it is claimed that conversational order is maintained by a constraint that permits only one person at a time to take a turn at speaking. In a representative statement from Tannen's description of this phenomenon, she describes her findings as follows:

> An individual learns conversational strategies in previous interactional experience, but chooses certain and rejects other strategies made available in this way. In other words, the range of strategies familiar to a speaker is socially determined, but any individual's set of habitual strategies is unique within that range. For example, research has shown that New Yorkers of Jewish background often use overlap—that is simultaneous talk—in a cooperative way; many members of this group talk simultaneously in some settings without intending to interrupt. . . . This does not imply that all New Yorkers of Jewish background use overlap cooperatively. However, a speaker of this background is more likely to do so than someone raised in the Midwest. (Tannen 1982:218–219)

While Tannen has given us a very telling example of the nonuniversality of turn-taking behavior even among native speakers of American English, it could be argued that her findings reflect the conversational strategies of only a small and perhaps not fully integrated ethnic group and is therefore not truly representative of "mainstream" American society. Any argument of this nature, however, is rendered totally invalid by other, more broad-based investigations of the phenomenon of cooperative simultaneous talk to be found in the sociolinguistic literature.

The most important work in this area, with respect to both theory and methodology, is the research conducted by Edelsky (1981) in which she analyzes a number of small, informal committee meetings in which she had been taking part over a number of years. The physical setting was a large university in the Southwest, and the participants came from a variety of ethnic and geographical backgrounds. In the tape-recorded conversations that serve as the data for the study, Edelsky took the part of participant observer. Unlike many of the studies which make use of participant observation, however, Edelsky had been an integral part of the group long before she began her research. How much this had to do with the spontaneity of the data she was able to collect is difficult to judge, but it is certainly fair to assume that her role as a researcher was made much less obtrusive because she had been, and continued to be, a committee member well known to all the other participants in that capacity. In explaining her use of, and preference for, gathering her data through observation rather than elicitation, Edelsky makes an important methodological statement—that the study on which she reports reveals how a piece of sociolinguistic research was conducted when both variables and hypotheses were allowed to emerge from the data. Indeed, one of most unusual and valuable aspects of the paper in addition to the importance of the actual findings is that Edelsky deliberately describes her methods not only for gathering but for transcribing and analyzing the data upon which the findings rest, demonstrating that the actual means adopted have a critical bearing on the results obtained.

Edelsky thus explains that in transcribing conversational data she found that the interpretation of which participant had what she calls "the floor" was biased by the very way the lines were organized in the process of transcription. It should be mentioned that the amount and method of transcription used by the ethnomethodologists have come under criticism from other scholars, e.g., Owen (1980), who says quite specifically: "In our opinion, however, there remains a failure to appreciate the effects of translation from one medium (spontaneous talk) to another (transcription) and the concomitant decisions of an '-emic' nature that have to be made" (Owen 1980:6).

In her description of the difficulties associated with transcribing the data on "floors," Edelsky also demonstrates that in analyzing the data she was unable, in many cases, to determine which participant had the floor because a number of people were speaking at once. The implication of this difficulty is that it led to a major research finding: that to describe the data adequately, it was necessary to divide "floors" into two types, the F1 in which a single person spoke at length (which she named a 'holding-forth') and a second type of floor, designated an F2, in which several conversational participants spoke at the same time. In a description of the literature on the subject, Edelsky shows that the one-at-a-time character of conversation is the basis for the work on turn-taking by Goffman (1971), Sacks et al. (1974), sequencing in speech acts or events (Schegloff 1972), and work on interruptions (Zimmerman and West 1975). She explains the results of these analyses by pointing out that turn-taking was found in these studies because most of the data reported on speech between only two participants, or were based on very formalized group talk situations which cannot really be classified as conversations in the usual sense, e.g., service encounters, classroom lessons, therapy groups, and elicited talk between strangers in laboratory settings. As Edelsky explains, the kind of talk in such formalized situations is, because of the constraints of the speech situation, likely to work on a one-at-a-time basis. In contrast to the studies which have been based on the unquestioned assumption that people speak only in turns, Edelsky's data and her analysis of them demonstrate convincingly that simultaneous talk is very common in what native speakers of English would define as ordinary group conversations.

In a very enlightening discussion, Edelsky then goes on to explain that turns and floors, although often used interchangeably, are not necessarily the same. In describing the use of the term *turn*, she points out that these are usually defined by the researcher. That is, turns are defined on the basis of speaker exchange, leaving out of account the "turn-taker's intentions as part of the definition." In turning to the definition of the term *floor* she shows how confusion arises through ignoring the difference between the two terms. Thus, Sacks et al. (1974) claim that what is organized in conversation is turns at talk which are accompanied by cues for requesting the floor and giving it up. But because turns and floors are so often not kept separate as analytic units, there has been no investigation or even acknowledgment that it is possible, and indeed typical, for there to be more than one way of "having the floor" in group conversations.

To be specific, Edelsky defines floor as "the acknowledged what's-going-on within a psychological time/space. . . . What's going on can be the development of a topic or a function and it can be developed or controlled by one person at a time or simultaneously or in quick succession." For this reason it is possible to take a turn without having the floor and also to have the floor when you're not talking. What is of particular relevance to the entire issue of turn-taking and the having of floors in conversation is Edelsky's well-documented finding that more than one type of floor exists, and that it is quite typical of conversation to have a number of people engaged in discussing the same topic, talking and listening at the same time in what she calls the F2, or "collaboratively constructed floors."

Since the patterns of speech behavior which involve conversational control are variable and complex, and since this is an exceptionally delicate area in terms of the potential for miscommunication, it would be well for language learners to be given access to the information regarding the ways in which interlocutors collaborate to construct conversations. To allow language learners to believe that conversations are ordered in the "one person speaks at a time" fashion described in the ethnomethodological literature would be misleading at best and could open the way for unnecessary misunderstandings.

Thus we see that although the work of the ethnomethodologists has yielded interesting and important insights into speech behavior, it is clear that many of their claims regarding the organization of conversation cannot be substantiated. While the research paradigm is interesting and often productive, it is necessary to recognize that the research findings themselves are problematic and cannot be accepted without further study. The work of those such as Reisman and Philips in different societies, and the work of Tannen and of Edelsky on the conversational behavior of middle-class speakers of Amerian English, give ample evidence that this interesting approach still leaves many questions that remain to be answered.

THE NOTION OF FACE

In connection with rules of speaking and with linguistic etiquette generally, the work of Brown and Levinson (1978) in putting forth a universal theory of politeness has had considerable impact on the research of scholars within the field of TESOL. Basing their theory on data from several quite different cultures, these scholars have suggested a conceptual framework based on the notion of "face." According to their theory, two aspects of people's feelings are involved with "face." The first is the desire of the individual not to be imposed on—this the researchers call "negative face"—while the second, "positive face," is the desire of the individual to be liked and approved of. Thus, if we fail to compliment a friend on a new hairstyle, we offend her positive face, while we may offend her negative face by demanding to speak with her when she is otherwise occupied. In deciding how much to take another person's feelings into account, we have three factors to consider. First, people are usually more polite to others when they are of higher status or are perceived as being powerful; second, people are generally more polite to others who are socially distant; and third, we are usually more polite in relation to the gravity of the threat we are about to make to the other's face.

Politeness, then, is the manifestation, through speech, of respect for another's face. This is usually accomplished by showing that we have concern for the other even when we are in the very act of threatening his or her face. Positive politeness involves strategies that let the addressee know that he or she is liked and approved of. An example of positive politeness is the positive evaluation of an addressee's accomplishments, appearance, or other attributes, a form of speech behavior culturally defined by speakers of English as complimenting. Other possible ways to show positive politeness involve the use of signals to show the addressee that he or she is considered a friend or a member of the speaker's "in-group," showing similarity in viewpoints and aims, giving gifts, showing interest in the other, and being generally friendly and cooperative. Negative politeness, on the other hand, usually involves a show of deference and an assurance that the speaker does not wish to disturb or to interfere with the other's freedom. Apologies and other forms of remedial work, as well as such strategies as indirectness in making requests, further exemplify what is meant by negative politeness.

In contrast to a show of politeness is the sort of speech in which there is no attempt at all to take the feelings of the other person into account. Here the speaker simply makes a direct statement or request. In Brown and Levinson's terminology, such speech is called "bald on record," and whatever risk it involves in ignoring the addressee's "face wants," it gains in being clear and unambiguous. The motivation for speaking "bald on record" may be that there is an emergency, that the speaker is indifferent to the feelings of the addressee, or, indeed, a host of other possibilities.

Since Brown and Levinson assume that most relationships between people are relatively stable, they suggest that the most common reason for a change in level of politeness will have to do with the degree of threat to the other's face which is involved in the speech act. That is, if the speaker is about to ask a very minor favor, the level of politeness will not be great, but if he or she is about to threaten the other's face by asking for something which involves considerable effort, the level of politeness will reflect the importance of the request.

Apart from differences in the importance of the threat to the other's face, politeness levels are, say the authors, fairly constant in ongoing relationships. For this reason, the general level of politeness shown in a particular relationship is a good index of social closeness and degrees of relative power of the interlocutors.

By looking at politeness as a social strategy, it is postulated that cultural members will be able to judge who the speaker feels socially close to and who is respected or looked down on: Negative politeness is seen as a strategy of those who are in some way less powerful than the addressee, while positive politeness is a sign of social closeness. Thus it should be possible, by observing the strategies used, to get a good view not only of relations between individuals but, on a larger scale, of the way a particular society is structured.

Probably the most serious problem in applying Brown and Levinson's framework lies in ascertaining levels of politeness and their meaning in speech communities with which the investigator is not intimately familiar. Native speaker intuitions may present problems for the investigator in this sense, since one is apt to see behavior in the context of the cultural dimensions and expectations which form a part of one's world view.

Although there are undoubtedly some difficulties with this framework, it is a very useful contribution to the study of language in society. Nevertheless, the notion of positive and negative face has proved fruitful in many respects. It is quite possible that significant findings may result from further extensions of this model by different researchers to the contrastive investigation of ever larger numbers of disparate speech communities.

ELICITATION AS A METHOD OF SOCIOLINGUISTIC RESEARCH IN TESOL

While researchers in the field of TESOL have made use of some of the terms and concepts stemming from paradigms such as those described above, it is also the case that we have developed methods of our own which have not only proved fruitful for our own analyses but will undoubtedly make important theoretical and methodological contributions to the field of sociolinguistics.

A widely used and fruitful elicitation procedure is the Discourse Completion Test (DCT), originally developed by Blum-Kulka (1982) and used by such researchers as Olshtain and Cohen in their study of apologies in Hebrew and English, Beebe in her work on refusals in Japanese and English, and Eisenstein and Bodman in their investigation of expressions of gratitude among native and nonnative speakers of English. In most cases, the major aim of studies using this method of elicitation is to collect data which may be compared for the purpose of cross-linguistic study and also to investigate the sociolinguistic problems faced by second language learners. What these researchers wanted to know was whether the pragmatic or sociolinguistic rules of the first language were causing serious interference problems for second language learners.

Accordingly, these researchers have tested groups of speakers learning English, and, in order to have baseline data on native speaker norms by which to judge nonnative speaker performance, they have also tested groups of native speakers in their own first languages. Since their aim has been to collect the speech forms considered appropriate by society members, given speech acts as they occurred in spontaneous settings were frequently used as models in creating the elicitation instrument. That is, given the responses of a specific cultural group, researchers were able to establish the perceived norms of speech behavior for each of the groups they wished to study. In the study of apologies by Olshtain and Cohen, for example, the elicitation procedure involved working out a set of carefully contrived situations which represented violations of some rule of behavior and which would therefore be candidates for apologies. In this case, the major variables examined had to do with the gravity of the offense and the status of the addressee, two factors which they considered most relevant in the selection of appropriate apology form. These situations were read by the subjects, who were then asked to role-play or to write their responses. Thus, researchers in TESOL have done considerable work in developing procedures to get at native speaker norms, both through the use of role-plays and through the kind of written dialogues called discourse completion tests. In the latter procedure, subjects are given written questionnaires containing a series of situations, each followed by a dialogue in which one of the responses is left blank. The subject is asked to read the situation and the incomplete dialogue which follows, and then to complete it by writing in what he or she would say in the situation given. By analyzing the data thus elicited, it is possible to gain considerable information concerning the speech act forms regarded as most appropriate by members of a particular cultural group.

Discourse completion tests have become increasingly widespread in the collection of data on speech act realization both within and across language groups. Like all methods used in the collection of sociolinguistic data, they have disadvantages as well as advantages. One great advantage of this type of data collection is that it permits the researcher to control for specific variables of the situation, thus giving a coherence to the findings which may be very difficult to achieve otherwise. If, for example, the investigator wants to test the effect of the social status of the participants in a given speech act, it is possible to include this in the questionnaire descriptions, thus leading subjects to take this factor into account in their responses. Since all subjects are responding to the same situation, the factor in question is automatically addressed by all answers, though it may be differently weighted by different respondents. Another great advantage of elicited data, and one which cannot be ignored, is that they allow investigators to collect a considerable amount of data on a given type of speech behavior within a relatively short time. Not all speech acts occur with equal frequency, and some, which may provide valuable insight into cultural rules, may occur in situations which are inaccessible to the researcher. Even the collection of data on a speech act as commonly heard as apologies requires much less effort to accomplish through elicitation than by, for example, observation. Thus, even when investigators are aware of the problems inherent in the direct elicitation of sociolinguistic data, they may well consider that the values to be gained by this method are greater than the disadvantages. Olshtain and Cohen (1983) have confronted this issue very directly:

> As Manes and Wolfson (1981) state in their paper on the compliment formula,
> the best approach to collecting data about speech acts is the ethnographic
> approach—i.e., the collection of spontaneous speech in natural settings. From
> our perspective, however, there are disadvantages to collecting data in this way.
> Collecting a corpus of naturally occurring speech behavior takes considerable
> time. In addition, some speech acts, like apologies, occur less frequently and
> are more situation-dependent than others. Furthermore, we wanted to determine
> the selection and realization of semantic formulas in given discourse situations
> in order to produce archetypal sets for each given situation in each language.
> We therefore decided to set up a number of fixed discourse situations to use as a
> constant element in a series of studies. (Olshtain and Cohen 1983)

While it is true that the use of such questionnaires is a quick means of acquiring a large amount of data about a community's perceptions regarding correct speech behavior, it is necessary to recognize that the data collected in this way cannot be expected to give us all the information we need about the ways in which a speech act is performed in spontaneous interactions. In some respects, there is a high degree of convergence between subjects' responses to this sort of elicitation procedure and the actual behavior found to occur spontaneously, while in other respects, we must face the fact that the nature of the task will produce intrinsic differences. That is, it must always be recognized that responses elicited within a written frame are, by their very nature, not the same as spontaneous speech. On the one hand, the conventional rules for speech differ considerably from those for written communication, and this cannot fail to have an effect on the results obtained. On the other hand, the simple fact that writing an answer permits more time to plan and evaluate it than one normally has while participating in an ongoing interaction must also be taken into account when comparing the results of these two modes of responding to a given situation. Indeed, the method of eliciting written responses to predesigned dialogues has inherent underlying limitations which make it impossible to collect the kind of elaborated (and often negotiated) behavior which we typically find in naturally occurring interactions.

As both Beebe (1985), in her study of refusals, and Eisenstein and Bodman (1986), in their work on expressions of gratitude, have pointed out, an important distinguishing feature of the behavior they investigated was the elaboration of these speech acts in actual conversation. Not only were responses to situations calling for these acts often far longer than could be fit into the written form of the test dialogue, it was also the case that speakers often responded with series of refusals or thanks, constituting a sequence in which different formulas appeared, sometimes interrupted by narratives or by illustrative comments. In addition to lack of space mitigating against the likelihood or even the possibility of such sequences, a further point of dissimilarity with written responses is related to the absence of flexibility inherent in written dialogue elicitations. What has been found in a number of studies of spontaneous interaction, including the work reported by Eisenstein and Bodman (1986), is that in addition to sequences of forms which perform essentially the same semantic function, speakers will frequently make reference to the topic which has triggered a given speech act throughout a conversation, going through additional thanking routines, for example, long after the initial sequence has been completed. With respect to expressions of gratitude, Eisenstein and Bodman have reported that a topic often surfaces in conversations that may be far separated in time from the original act, calling forth renewed thanking routines.

If we wish to capture the true nature of culturally appropriate speech behavior, it is essential to describe these phenomena since, in some societies it is literally required that an act such as that of expressing gratitude be performed more than once and/or after a considerable interval of time has passed. Still another aspect of behavior associated with speech acts has to do with the nature of the interaction in which they are embedded. Frequently, the successful outcome of an act requires the active participation of both the speaker and the addressee in a sequence of act and response constituting an entire speech event which can only be regarded as a negotiation. Results of work by Wolfson (1981b) and Wolfson et al. (1983) on invitations has demonstrated that the vast majority of social commitments are reached not through a single speech act but through a sequence of acts that may involve considerable negotiation. Similarly, Eisenstein and Bodman (1986) have found that the successful thanking routine requires the active participation of both members of the interaction. As they point out in the introduction to their paper "May God Increase Your Bounty," "Expressing gratitude requires a complex interaction between interlocutors which is mutually developed. When a gift or a service is given, the giver and thanker engage in a delicately orchestrated conversation which continues until both participants are satisfied." Later in the same paper they state:

> In our current study, our initial analysis revealed that an adequate description of how gratitude is conveyed must encompass the entire speech event and focus not only on the the thanker but on the dynamic interaction between the giver and thanker. It was this interaction that accounted for the lengthy nature of the data alluded to earlier.

In expressing gratitude, we found that the giver is as active as the thanker. The giver provides comments and prompts throughout the speech act set. The giver also reacts to the thanker to help that person carry out the expression of gratitude satisfactorily. (Eisenstein and Bodman in press)

In her comparison of data on refusals elicited through Discourse Completion Tests with those collected by means of recording spontaneous telephone conversations, Beebe (1985) concludes by saying:

In this paper we argue that Discourse Completion Tests are a highly effective means of:
(1) gathering a large amount of data quickly;
(2) creating an initial classification of semantic formulas and strategies that will occur in natural speech;
(3) studying the stereotypical perceived requirements for a socially appropriate (though not always polite) response;
(4) gaining insight into social and psychological factors that are likely to affect speech act performance; and
(5) ascertaining the canonical shape of refusals, apologies, partings, etc. in the minds of the speakers of that language.
However, they are *not* natural speech and they do *not* accurately reflect natural speech or even unselfconscious, elicited speech with respect to:
(1) actual wording used in real interpersonal interaction;
(2) the range of formulas and strategies used (some, like avoidance, tend to get left out);
(3) the length of response or the number of turns it takes to fulfill the function;
(4) the depth of emotion that in turn qualitatively affects the tone, content, and form of linguistic performance;
(5) the number of repetitions and elaborations that occur; or
(6) the actual rate of occurrence of a speech act—e.g., whether or not someone would naturalistically refuse at all in a given situation. (Beebe 1985: 11).

Thus we see that while the type of elicitation procedures described here can be very useful in certain respects, they have serious limitations as well. While such data can be effectively used to complement those gathered through the collection of naturally occurring speech, it would be unwise to depend solely on such methods.

THE USE OF SPONTANEOUS SPEECH DATA IN RESEARCH IN TESOL

Given that elicitation has serious limitations and that much more needs to be known about the rules of speaking for groups whose dominant language is American English and, indeed, for as many speech communities as possible, in order for us to have a clearer idea of what communicative competence is all about, the question which continually arises is: How do we find out about them? Acceptance of the basic principle that patterns of speech behavior are below the level of native speaker consciousness leaves us with the initial question of where to begin. If the researchers are themselves native speakers of the language under study, they know that while they and others around them interact, they are following rules and patterns of behavior as unreflectingly as they put one foot in front of another when they walk down a street. But just as people would be hard pressed to describe just which muscles and reflexes are put into operation when they walk or talk or tie a shoelace, they have only the most casual notion of which rules and assumptions they operate with when they engage in talk. Yet it all seems so normal, and indeed so unremarkable, that even when concentrating on an interaction between two people, it seems very difficult to focus on any one aspect of a conversation in a way which would lead to an objective description.

In this respect, sociolinguists working within the field of second language learning, and specifically in TESOL, are in a particularly fortunate position. Constantly interacting with nonnative speakers who have very different sets of rules, we see our own sociolinguistic rules broken in dozens of different ways. And, while we are clearly not in a position to describe these rules objectively enough to teach them, we are perfectly competent to make intuitive judgments concerning the acceptability or the appropriateness of the speech behavior of others. When the others whose speech behavior we are judging are not native speakers, they are very likely to transfer rules of speaking from their own native languages in ways that are not at all appropriate to speakers of American English. This inappropriate speech behavior is a jolt to any native speaker; to a sociolinguistic researcher it may be seen in the nature of a gift in that it provides sudden insight into a rule whose existence may have passed unnoticed up to this point. What we have, then, is a sociolinguistic researcher who, having been socialized into conforming to the rules of speech behavior common to his or her speech community, is oblivious to their existence until they are broken. Thus, we are in the happy position of being able to learn from the mistakes of others.

Once it becomes clear that a rule is being broken, we have something on which to focus. Just as Borkin and Rinehart noticed that foreign students at the University of Michigan were using the phrases "Excuse me" and "I'm sorry" in inappropriate ways, we can see the same sort of thing happening not only with specific phrases or formulas but at all levels of sociolinguistic behavior. In some cases, as with compliments in American English, formulas exist without native speakers' being aware of them. But unless nonnative speakers had given compliments which the author saw as inappropriate, it is unlikely that such speech behavior would have been seen as a topic worthy of research at all.

Not all rules of speaking are equally amenable to sociolinguistic investigation. Worse, it is difficult to say in advance which will be the more difficult areas to study. In choosing a topic, especially for an initial try at this sort of work, it is well to limit oneself to a feature or topic, speech act or form, which occurs with some frequency. The other important consideration is that it be an aspect of speech behavior to which the researcher has access in daily interactions with native speakers. Here, a word of warning needs to be given. Within sociolinguistics it is well known that such factors as age, sex, socioeconomic status, educational background, ethnic group, and occupation are all potentially important factors in conditioning speech behavior. If research into sociolinguistic rules is undertaken in order to discover and describe native speaker patterns, it is important to sample the speech of as varied a group of native speakers as possible. Unless the aim of the study is to describe the rules of speaking which obtain in academic circles, it is inappropriate to use data collected within the academic community as the sole sample. As we all know, students are an accessible population, and the temptation to use them as subjects of study is difficult to overcome. Indeed, in all too many studies, this is the only population tested. This is unfortunate since it is impossible to know from such studies whether university students have the same rules for speech behavior as the rest of the population. Of course, if we are interested in describing the culture and ways of speaking of an American university, this is exactly the population to tap. Certainly, the results of such studies can offer very useful information to international students who plan to pursue their education in universities situated in English-speaking countries such as the United States. It is easy to imagine a class in English for Academic Purposes which included information on rules of speaking, told students how to respond when professors addressed them by their first names or gave them a compliment on their work, etc. However, not all learners of English will be interacting primarily with academics in universities, and it is therefore necessary to have a more balanced data base upon which to rest analyses of American English speech behavior. This means that researchers are responsible for going out of the university and into areas of the community which are frequented by people of a variety of ages, occupations and socioeconomic levels.

In our study of address forms to women in service encounters, for example (Wolfson and Manes 1980), we made it a point to observe speech behavior in places where we would be likely to find not only middle-class people but those from other social class backgrounds as well. In this regard, it should be pointed out that service encounters provide a rich source of data on speech behavior. They represent public speech among strangers in situations where both interlocutors have a role to play. Nearly all able-bodied adults are, at one time or another, involved in service encounters, and this makes them a useful site at which to collect samples of speech from a wide variety of speakers. Service encounters have the great virtue of occurring frequently, and, even more to the point, they are nearly always open to observation by the researcher.

Other research sites are waiting rooms, lobbies, hairdresser and barbershops, airports, train terminals, and, indeed, any place where people wait and while away their time by talking. Needless to say, the research site must be chosen to suit the topic being studied. If one were interested in studying greetings or good-byes in American English, one would look for occurrences of such speech acts in offices, at meetings and parties, and the like. There is nothing intrinsically wrong about collecting data in interactions among one's own friends and family. Indeed, as I have pointed out elsewhere (Wolfson 1976), the long-term participant observation which is made possible when the group whose speech is being studied is one's own is, for some purposes, the very best kind of data collection. This is particularly true if one is looking at a rather rare feature or at one which occurs only in the speech of minimal social distance. In the first instance, one would need to hear the same speaker in a range of speech situations and on a great number of occasions before deciding that he or she did or did not use a specific feature. In the second case, it is clearly not easy to study the speech of minimal social distance by observing strangers.

To come back to the choice of topic, researchers whose field is TESOL are, as has been pointed out, in an unusually good position in the sense that the inappropriate behavior of our students can lead us to focus on topics which would not otherwise have occurred to us to study. The analysis of compliments and of invitations in American English are examples of research inspired in just this way. The ongoing project on invitations in American English is itself a result of student complaints. In the case of invitations, foreign visitors to the United States mentioned frequently how insincere Americans were. According to numerous international students at the University of Pennsylvania, the Americans they met were constantly inviting them to spend time together socially and then never following up their invitations. This recurrent complaint, combined with the fact that international students clearly did have a hard time making friends with Americans, raised the important question of what sort of miscommunication was at the root of the problem. It is well known that Americans habitually make suggestions about social arrangements which, just as often as not, come to nothing. Yet this behavior is rarely regarded by cultural members as insincere, and certainly does not seem to impede American interlocutors from making friends and arranging social appointments with one another. What, then, was the problem? It seemed worth studying for several reasons. On the one hand, the topic had practical implications. If students learning English in the United States were having difficulty in making friends with native speakers, this would seriously reduce their opportunities for practice in using the language they were striving to learn. There is, of course, a great deal of controversy over the issue of whether or how much learners gain by engaging in unstructured communicative interactions with native speakers, but no one seriously doubts that using the target language is an aid to learning it. Clearly, the knowledge of how to further relationships with native speakers and, more specifically, to achieve social commitments would be a useful tool to foreign learners of English, if not a key to language acquisition itself. At a different level, it was recognized that a study of the ways in which Americans give and respond to invitations could well provide interesting insights into speech behavior and even social structure which would be valuable to native as well as nonnative speakers.

Thus, an important means by which our students' reactions can lead us to focus on research topics which will, in the end, help other nonnative speakers is to pay careful attention to the sort of comments (both negative and positive) that nonnative

speakers make about the ways in which Americans behave. Recently arrived foreigners are especially struck by the many differences between speech behavior in
the United States and that in their home communities. It frequently happens, especially if the teacher is sympathetic, that students will express amusement, pleasure,
anger, dismay, or a range of other emotions, all stemming from their initial surprise
at the way Americans behave in certain situations. As an example of this phenomenon, the study (which will be described in detail below) on telephone call behavior
in the United States compared with that in France (Godard 1977) was motivated by
just such a reaction.

In order to choose a topic for study, then, it is well for the researcher to be
particularly careful to note areas where miscommunication seems to be occurring.
There are, as has just been pointed out, two ways of getting at this information. The
first is to pay special attention to one's own (and other native speakers') reactions to
the speech behavior of nonnative speakers in their interactions with native speakers
of the target language. Where the nonnative speaker seems to be doing or saying
something which seems particularly inappropriate, it is useful to take careful field
notes about the situation and what was said by both parties to the interaction. This
very preliminary research must be done with great delicacy. The researcher must
pay special attention to the point where miscommunication seems to have occurred
and see whether it is an isolated instance or something which happens regularly. At
the same time, it is imperative to listen closely for comments by nonnative speakers
about their reactions to the speech behavior of members of the target language
speech community. People who have recently arrived in a foreign country are in a
much better position to point out the peculiarities of speech behavior in the host
community than are those who have been part of it for years or even months.
Adaptation takes place quickly, and stereotypes (often negative, as has been pointed
out) can deaden reactions to everyday occurrences.

Once a topic has been chosen, it is necessary to collect data concerning the
phenomenon in question. There are several important methodological considerations which must be kept in mind when data are being gathered. First and most
obvious is the reminder that it is unwise to make people self-conscious by letting
them know that one is paying special attention to their speech behavior. For this
reason, it is necessary to be discreet. Depending on what topic one has decided to
focus on, one may collect data by audiorecording or by simply writing down
relevant parts of interactions that may be overheard. The only major limitation on
writing, which is by far the simpler procedure, is that the interaction one wishes to
study may be too long and/or complicated to be written down accurately. If one is
collecting data on compliments or on forms of address, for example, the exchanges
will often be so short that there is no difficulty at all in using a simple pencil-and-
paper technique. Not all compliment exchanges are brief, however, and even such
seemingly superficial events as leave-taking may evolve into long and intricate
negotiations which cannot be captured unless they are recorded. One cardinal principle is that researchers must never try to write down what they have heard *after* it
has happened. The human memory is short when it comes to the recollection of

exact wording, and researchers too often hear what they expect to hear. If it is impossible to take careful written notes or to audiotape, it is best to simply make notes on the gist of the interaction and its outcome for use in evaluating future data and to wait for the next opportunity to collect the exact wording of examples.

Since large numbers of examples are needed for a thorough analysis of any sociolinguistic pattern, and since it is also necessary to have examples representative of as large a range of speakers and speech situations as possible, it is often a very good idea to have several researchers collect data on the same speech act. The point here is that no one investigator is in a position to observe or to participate in the variety of situations which need to be sampled in order to analyze how rules of speaking work. In this regard, it must be remembered that speech behavior is not static, but dynamic. Thus, the same speaker will vary his or her behavior to suit the context of the total situation, and this includes the social identity of the interlocutor(s). A middle-class female researcher, for example, will typically have no difficulty in collecting data on the ways in which other middle-class females give compliments to one another. Similarly, she should have little problem in gathering data on how speakers of a range of different backgrounds compliment those with whom she is socially identified—other middle-class women. On the other hand, if the same researcher wants to know how compliments are given to members of groups with which she is not identified, she may have very serious problems indeed. She cannot, by definition, participate in all-male interactions, and although she may observe them, her presence must be recognized as a factor in the speech situation which may have an influence on the very forms she is attempting to study. This is true not only of sex differences but of all the factors which make up the researcher's social identity. Obviously, we cannot hope to collect data which will represent the speech of every possible type of dyad or conversational group within a speech community, but we must do our best to sample a range of interlocutors and, most important, to be aware of the inherent bias caused by the presence of the researcher in any group other than his or her own.

Still another very effective method of gaining access to data for sociolinguistic analysis is that reported by Schmidt (1983) in which his personal friendship with one subject gave him access to a great deal of data, both tape-recorded, in day-to-day social interactions, and observational. In addition, Schmidt had available to him 18 one-hour tape recordings concerning business and daily activities which Wes (the subject) himself recorded while in Japan and mailed to the United States. The recordings have two great virtues. One is that they were made by the subject himself for the purpose of communicating important information. That is, they were not gathered as part of an experimental task. The second is that they were made during six separate trips to Japan over the space of a three-year residence in the United States. It was therefore possible for Schmidt to trace the development of his subject's linguistic ability in English over an extended period. As Schmidt himself says of these data: "One of the major advantages of these tapes is that they were not recorded for the purposes of linguistic analysis and consist of authentic, meaningful, and often important material, both professional and personal. A major disadvantage for the present analysis is that they are monologues. . . An additional source of data used in the analysis has been extensive but irregular field notes gathered by me over the entire period of observation, June 1978 to June 1981."

Making use of material taped for reasons having nothing to do with sociolinguistic analysis may be extremely fruitful. The videotapes used by West (1985) in her study of gender-related interruptions among physicians and patients is a good example of this approach. Since the tapes were made for the purpose of instructing young doctors in how to conduct medical interviews, West's use of them for the purposes of her own analysis was quite independent. Another useful point to be taken from Schmidt's work is that one may do very well to make use of the data to which one has greatest access—that is, the speech of one's own friends and family. Indeed, some of the very best information about language use may be obtained in just this way. In my own study of the conversational historical present tense in American English narrative (Wolfson 1976, 1978a, 1979a, 1982a,b) much of the most interesting data as well as a great many important insights came from the speech of those people with whom I was in closest and most frequent contact. In this case, it would not have been adequate to collect only those narratives told by people I knew well. Yet with respect to level of information about background of interlocutors and of interactional patterns generally, nothing could have been better.

CONCLUSION

The foregoing account of methods currently in use in the anlaysis of sociolinguistic rules within the field of TESOL is intended as a guide to understanding the work that has so far been done. It is also hoped that the description provided here will help those interested in pursuing research in sociolinguistics and TESOL to gain insight into the advantages and disadvantages of the various methods so far attempted, and, perhaps, to develop additional ways of collecting and analyzing sociolinguistic data.

A brief survey of some of the concepts and findings which have served to inform much of the recent discussion and research in sociolinguistics and TESOL cannot be expected to give the reader a full picture of the methodological and theoretical issues involved in the study of speech behavior. Nevertheless, it is hoped that this short introduction will provide a useful background to a description of the sociolinguistic studies which have provided us with information relevant to the teaching and learning of English.

4

The Sociolinguistic Behavior of English Speakers

INTRODUCTION

As we have pointed out earlier, analyses of sociolinguistic usage in American English are desperately needed in order that materials developers and language teachers have concrete, empirically based information upon which to plan instruction. Although it is true that much research remains to be done in this area, a fruitful beginning has been made. It is the purpose of this chapter to describe such studies of sociolinguistic behavior, with particular emphasis on those which have sought to provide the TESOL profession with analyses of rules of speaking in native English-speaking communities. Thus, the following discussion is intended as a survey of empirical analyses of speech behavior, especially (though by no means exclusively) those which have focused on the needs of the TESOL profession.

FORMS OF ADDRESS

One of the earliest sociolinguistic studies of speech behavior among speakers of American English concerns the way people in this society address one another. Perhaps because forms of address are frequent and easily observed, and because they have long been considered a very salient indicator of status relationships, they have received considerable attention in the scholarly literature. Indeed, so voluminous is this literature that an extensive bibliography exclusively concerned with personal address usage has been gathered and published (Philipsen and Huspek 1985). The significance of work on personal address forms is elegantly described by the authors:

> Personal address is a sociolinguistic subject par excellence. In every language and society, every time one person speaks to another, there is created a host of options centering around whether and how persons will be addressed, named,

and described. The choices speakers make in such situations, and their meanings to those who interpret them, are systematic, not random. Such systematicity in language behavior, whether of use or interpretation, is universal, although what elements comprise the personal address system and what rules govern its deployment, vary across contexts. And such variation in structure is, according to the extant empirical literature, correlated with social ends and social contexts of language use. From this view, personal address is a systematic, variable, and social phenomenon, and these features of it make it a sociolinguistic variable of fundamental importance. (Philipsen and Huspek 1985:94)

As Ervin-Tripp (1969) has pointed out, there are differences even in the way different social groups in the United States use forms of address. For speakers in the West Coast academic community of which she is a member, the title "Doctor" is always followed by the last name of the addressee. Lower-status occupational groups, however, often use such titles as "Doctor" without last name as address forms. Unlike the situation involving pronoun selection in Sweden described earlier (Paulston 1976), however, this differing pattern in address forms does not lead to miscommunication. Sociolinguistic rules are subject to considerable variation with respect to region and social class. In some cases, the variation is great enough to cause miscommunication and in others it merely serves as a marker of social or regional difference. Thus, Wolfson and Manes (1978) report that the address form *ma'am* has different meanings in the southern part of the United States than it has elsewhere. In the South, the term *ma'am* is often used as a substitute for the formula "I beg your pardon?" or "Pardon?" in asking someone to repeat what she has said or to explain something. The contrast in the use of the two forms is exemplified in the following conversations:

1.   A: Could you tell me how late you're open this evening?
     B: Ma'am?
     A: Could you tell me how late you're open this evening?
     B: Until six.
2.   A: You're not open on Sundays?
     B: Pardon?
     A: You're not open on Sundays?
     B: No.

In addition, it was found that the phrase "Yes, ma'am" is often used instead of "You're welcome" as a response to "Thank you." Examples of the two forms in use will show the contrast:

3.   A: Could you tell me how late you're open this evening?
     B: Until nine.
     A: Thank you very much.
     B: Yes, ma'am.

4. A: Could you tell me how late you're open this evening?
   B: Until five-thirty.
   A: Thank you very much.
   B: You're welcome.

Not only is the form *ma'am* given different meanings in the South, it is also used in very different social contexts than elsewhere in the country. In the Northeast, for example, *ma'am* was found to occur between strangers and, to a lesser extent, from lower- to upper-status speakers. In the South, however, it was found that the term *ma'am* is used not only to strangers but also to acquaintances and even intimates. Thus, graduate students at the University of Virginia were heard to be addressed as *ma'am* by their male professors, female colleagues were given this address form by their male colleagues, and husbands were even heard to use this term to their own wives. While it is unlikely that women from other parts of the country would become offended if they were addressed as *ma'am* in situations where they were unaccustomed to it, it is possible that southern women would misunderstand the absence of this form where they were used to expecting it, and would therefore regard nonsouthern speakers as rude or lacking in respect for women.

A noteworthy phenomenon concerning address forms among speakers of American English, however, is the way in which strangers in public situations address unknown women by terms of endearment (Wolfson and Manes 1978). In an ethnographic investigation of the forms of address used to women in service encounters (e.g., address by gas station attendants, waiters and waitresses, salesclerks), it was observed that women in American society are often addressed with a good deal less respect than are men. The findings of this study will be described in detail in the chapter concerned with issues of language and gender, but it is worth noting here that such usage is one of the many ways in which forms of address play a part in both expressing and perpetuating inequality between the sexes in American society.

Like the use of second person pronouns in Swedish as investigated by Paulston (1976), the rules governing the choice of whether to address another person by first name only, rather than by title and last name, is very much in transition the United States. In one of the earliest sociolinguistic studies of American English, Brown and Ford (1961) suggested a model of the reciprocal and nonreciprocal patterns governing the way middle-class Americans address one another. Interested in general usage rather than in the somewhat differing patterns that might be found in separate subgroups in the society, Brown and Ford gathered their data through the observation of spontaneous interactions among men and women of different occupational status in work-related environments. They found that most pairs of speakers (or dyads) follow what is called a reciprocal pattern. That is, both interlocutors use first name to each other or both use title and last name to each other. In analyzing the data they collected, they found that the great majority of dyads use mutual first name in addressing each other, while mutual title and last name (TLN) is reserved for addressing new acquaintances, when it occurs at all. In addition to the reciprocal patterns of mutual first name (FN) and mutual title and last name (TLN), Brown and Ford also discuss a nonreciprocal pattern in which one member of the dyad uses FN to the other but is addressed by TLN. According to the model put forth by Brown and Ford, and in an earlier work by Brown and Gilman (1960), the two major dimensions which condition the choice of address terms are power, here usually realized in the form of social status, and solidarity, in terms of degree of social distance. Thus, the terms used to interlocutors who stand higher in social or occupational rank than the speaker are manifestations of deference and are not reciprocated, while the very same terms used reciprocally by speakers who share approximately the same status are expressions of social distance and formality. By the same token, the address terms used in a nonreciprocal fashion by superiors to subordinates are expressions of power, while these identical terms, when used reciprocally by social or occupational equals, express lack of distance or formality. As Brown puts it: "The linguistic form that is used to an inferior in a dyad of unequal status is, in dyads of equal status used mutually by intimates. . . . the form used to a superior in a dyad of unequal status is, in dyads of equal status, used mutually by strangers" (R. Brown 1965:92).

This model has proved to be extraordinarily powerful as a means of analyzing address forms not only in English but in a number of other languages as well. The principle upon which it rests appears to be quite widespread in European languages and may therefore be a familiar one to many learners of English. Since learning to use forms of address appropriately in a new speech community is often intimidating, the model described here should be extremely useful in giving students a helpful set of guidelines. As Brown and Ford are careful to point out, however, it sometimes happens that even competent native speakers are unsure about what to call each other. This is particularly common when relationships between people change as they become better acquainted. The usual rule or sociolinguistic principle given by Brown and his associates is that the person who is of higher status initiates a switch from more to less formal address forms. In cases where the younger person or the one who has lesser status is uncertain whether to reciprocate first name, an option in American English is to avoid using any form of address at all. This, in Brown and Ford's terminology, is called "no-naming" and is a great deal more common than one might suspect. As long as it is not necessary to call someone from a distance in order to attract that person's attention, it is perfectly possible in English to interact with others for years without ever actually calling them by name. This alternative to making a definite choice of address form is a particularly convenient fact for learners of English to know about, since language learners are often uncertain of appropriate usage in different types of speech situations. Because it is usually not possible to avoid expressing status and social distance in their native languages, learners of English will be unlikely to realize that this possibility exists in English unless this is explained to them.

Another important aspect of address form rules which must be taught to nonnative speakers is how titles combine with last names. Ervin-Tripp (1969) gives a very clear description of the rules for American English:

A priest, physician, dentist, or judge may be addressed by title alone, but a plain citizen or an academic person may not. In the latter cases, if the name is unknown, there is no address form (or zero, 0) available and we simply no-name the addressee. The parentheses below refer to optional elements, the bracketed elements to social selectional categories.

[Cardinal]:	Your Excellency
[U.S. President]:	Mr. President
[Priest]:	Father (+ LN)
[Nun]:	Sister (+ religious name)
[Physician]:	Doctor (+ LN)
[Ph.D., Ed.D.]:	Doctor (+ LN)
[Professor]:	(Professor + LN)
[Adult], etc.:	(Mister + LN)
	(Mrs. + LN)
	(Miss + LN)

Whenever the parenthetical items cannot be fully realized, as when the last name (LN) is unknown, and there is no lone title, the addressee is no-named by a set of rules of the form as follows: Father + Ø = Father, Professor + Ø = Ø, Mister + Ø = Ø, etc. An older male addressee may be called "sir," if deference is intended, as an optional extra marking. (Ervin-Tripp, 1969)

While the model which Brown and Ford proposed, and other scholars such as Ervin-Tripp have elaborated, still exists in American English, the frequencies with which the forms are now used has been changing in the direction of ever-increasing use of first names between strangers and between people of asymmetrical age and status. It is now not uncommon to hear employees first-naming their bosses, students their professors, young people their seniors. Another rather striking change has been taking place in the frequency with which strangers introduce themselves by first name alone. It has been noticed that service personnel in stores, car agencies, restaurants, and similar places now often identify themselves to clients and customers by giving only their first names. While such usage undoubtedly varies with geographical area and social class, the movement away from TLN and toward FN appears to be widespread in the United States. That this is a relatively new development in American speech may be seen by the fact that older sales personnel in department stores, for example, still tend to identify themselves to customers by TLN when the need for identification arises at all.

In a study of this phenomenon, Katherine French (1981) examined the way in which service personnel, often total strangers to their customers, not only introduce themselves by first name but request that they be so addressed. According to French, the reasons for this usage given by interviewees were that the use of first name was friendlier, that it simplified the interaction since last names are often difficult to understand or remember, and that such usage provides the employee with anonymity. When, because of the nature of the service encounter, the employee has access to the first name of the customer, it often happens that first names are used reciprocally by both participants to the interaction. In these cases, it would appear that the intention is to deliberately avoid any manifestation of differences in social status.

Since nonnative speakers (and even English speakers from other parts of the world) often express surprise at the wide distribution of reciprocal first naming in American society, it is worth noting here that the factors governing the selection of FN as opposed to TLN in American English seem to be closely related to those which condition the choice of pronoun in those European languages which retain a distinction between the familiar and formal second person singular pronouns. These are usually referred to as informal "T" and formal "V." As Brown and Gilman (1960) and others (e.g., Paulston 1976) have pointed out in their analyses of the usage of these forms, they are closely related to two dimensions: power and solidarity. The use of the formal V form by both members of a dyad implies that they are of approximately equal status but that they lack what Brown and Gilman call solidarity. Because this model of how terms of address are selected is so powerful, it is worth our while to make the principle behind it as clear as possible. The major point to be emphasized is that formal address terms are reciprocally exchanged where neither member of the pair has power over the other, but there is also nothing in their relationship or their backgrounds which would lead to a feeling of familiarity, or of membership in the same group. Where people do share occupation, social background, membership in same political organization, in addition to age and sex, the likelihood of their exchanging the mutual informal T increases with the number of attributes shared. Strangers of equal status exchange V, while intimates exchange T. The dimension of solidarity implies that the closer the relationship between two people, the more likely they are to exchange T. What has just been described are symmetrical relationships in which forms of address are reciprocal, just as mutual FN is in American English. The dimension of power, on the other hand, causes speakers to use V to those of superior status while the speakers are addressed with T. The use of nonreciprocal V is an acknowledgment by the speaker that the addressee is older, wealthier, better born (e.g., of the nobility), or in a more highly respected occupation. The nonreciprocal use of T thus implies that the speaker has some sort of power over the addressee.

As Brown and Gilman point out, however, in recent years in these languages the dimension of solidarity has been steadily winning out over that of power, so that it is more and more common for people to exchange mutual or reciprocal forms of address. This is the same principle that seems to be at work in the use of FN and TLN in American English. Even between adults and children, mutual FN is increasingly accepted. What is interesting, however, is that role relationships continue to be expressed and even created by the use of asymmetrical address forms. Thus, many physicians in the United States make a point of asserting power by first-naming their patients, while insisting on being addressed by TLN. It is interesting that patients who regard themselves as being socially equal often resent this usage and attempt to redefine the relationship by demanding reciprocal TLN or by first-naming the physician in return. A systematic study of the ways in which speakers of American English attempt to negotiate their relationships through naming practices would no doubt shed light both on present-day social structure and on the interpersonal manipulation of power.

While, in European languages, speakers unconsciously choose pronouns or address forms so as to reflect status relationships, many non-European languages have many more subtle distinctions than the ones so far discussed. Asian languages in particular are known for the complexity of their formality-marking devices. An example comes from the work of Clifford Geertz (1973), who says: "In Javanese it is nearly impossible to say anything without indicating the social relationship between the speaker and the listener in terms of status and familiarity. Status is determined by many things—wealth, descent, education, occupation, age, kinship, and nationality, among others, but the important point is that the choice of linguistic forms as well as speech style is in every case determined by the relative status (or familiarity) of the conversers."

That a similar situation exists in Japanese is well known. The difficulties which this presents to learners is frequently mentioned in the literature. O'Neill (1966), for example, says that "an understanding of respect language is as necessary to a student of Japanese as a slide-rule to an engineer, for it is involved in any exchange of Japanese between one person and another, including the simplest phrases of greeting etc."

To summarize, the concept behind the use of appropriate forms of address is not difficult for language learners to grasp, since all languages make use of some kind of address forms, and many languages are much more complex than English with regard to respect forms. Indeed, it has been pointed out (e.g., Ferguson 1976, Brown and Levinson 1978) that politeness may itself be a universal feature of language. Ferguson further suggests the likelihood that all languages make use of precoded routines or what he calls "politeness formulas," which speakers are required to utter in certain situations. As Coulmas (1981a) observes:

> . . . a great deal of communicative activity consists of enacting routines making use of prefabricated linguistic units in a well known and generally accepted manner. We greet and bid farewell to one another, introduce ourselves and others, apologize and express gratitude, buy groceries and order meals, exchange wishes, make requests, ask for advice or information, report on what we did, and announce what we are about to do, etc. As similar speech situations recur, speakers make use of similar and sometimes identical expressions, which have proved to be functionally appropriate. . . . In every society there are standardized communication situations in which its members react in an auto-

matic manner. Routines reflect, in a sense, a conception of a social system, and their importance for socialization as well as secondary acculturation is quite obvious, because routines are tools which individuals employ in order to relate to others in an accepted way.

APOLOGIES

Erving Goffman, whose recent work has focused on the everyday behavior of the American middle classes, has observed that in our society these linguistic formulas serve to create and maintain what he calls "the public order" (Goffman 1971). An example of how the public order is served by linguistic means is what Goffman calls "the remedial interchange," in which speakers attempt to remedy potentially unpleasant social situations by offering an explanation or an apology. Interested more in describing patterns of social interaction than in working out the rules for the use of specific formulas, Goffman himself does not go into detail about the forms themselves or their distribution. He has, nevertheless, inspired other scholars to gather and analyze data on the way speakers of English give apologies.

Owen (1980) chose to examine apologies because, as she says, Goffman's work is "rich in the suggestions it offers for further research, but is in need of more explicit empirical support than that provided by Goffman himself." Basing her analysis on actually occurring speech, Owen reports that the primary remedial move (PRM) is the central move in a remedial interchange (RI). These vary, however, from "ritual to substantive." The most frequent means of expressing a PRM in English is, Owen finds, to include the key word *sorry* in the utterance. The remedial interchange, which Owen takes as the basic unit of analysis, can only be completed when the recipient of an apology responds to it. Assuming that the recipient of a PRM wishes to give a positive response, he or she can either acknowledge the remedial utterance as adequate or indicate that it was unnecessary. As Owen points out, both acceptance and minimalization usually are accomplished by means of a similar formula: "The forms used for these two types of responses are very similar to each other: OK is the form used exclusively in our corpus for acknowledgements, whereas '{that's/it's} OK' or even just 'OK' functions as an acceptance" (Owen 1980:98). In addition to the formulas given, responses to apologies may include thanks to the offender for any attempts that have been made to remedy the offense. In some cases, however, the apology is not accepted and a response is withheld, implying that the apology is being rejected.

Recognizing that a cross-cultural comparison of apologies is fraught with difficulties, Owen nevertheless suggests that strategies for repairing an offense may be used as guidelines in such studies. Basing her analysis of cross-cultural patterns on the work of Brown and Levinson (1978), which will be discussed in some detail below, Owen suggests that if we focus on the imbalance created by an offense, we may be able to predict strategies for primary remedial moves that have cross-cultural application. Although Owen points out that the major moves are ritual, she recognizes that the degree to which they are actually ritualized in a given society will vary. Separating the possible strategies for initiating a repair into three major categories, she lists four nonsubstantive (ritual) strategies, one semisubstantive strategy, and two substantive strategies. The nonsubstantive or ritual strategies include (1) asserting imbalance or showing deference, (2) asserting that an offense has occurred, (3) expressing an attitude toward the offense, and (4) requesting the restoration of balance. What Owen classifies as a semisubstantive move is that of giving an account. This is separate from the others, presumably because, as has been found for English, native speakers do not equate an account with an actual apology (Wolfson et al. in press.). Owen's third category, which she labels substantive, consists of two possible moves: (1) repair the damage, and (2) provide compensation. These last strategies are, of course, nonlinguistic, but may be used along with one of the strategies mentioned above. As Owen points out:

> The extent to which either ritual or substantive remedies are considered appropriate in a particular case will depend on features of the offense (e.g. is the damage suffered by the victim of a kind it is possible to repair?) and on cultural criteria; it is quite conceivable that in some cultures only substantive remedies will be acceptable. Thus, if we found what appeared to be a culture without any linguistic remedial expressions, we should not conclude that no remedial activity is engaged in, since such activity might be non-linguistic. (Owen 1980:170)

As we will see below, many of Owen's suggestions for a cross-linguistic study of apologies have been used independently by a number of researchers working on a large international research program, the Cross-Cultural Speech Act Realization Project (CCSARP). Before we describe this study in detail, however, it will be useful to those specifically concerned with the teaching of English to have more background concerning the studies on apologies which have specific relevance to TESOL. It should be pointed out that most of these have focused on the ways in which apologies are expressed by native speakers of American English.

Borkin and Reinhart (1978), for example, have done a very useful analysis of two formulaic expressions associated with apologies *excuse me* and *I'm sorry*. In investigating the distribution of the two forms, Borkin and Reinhart point out that *I'm sorry*, although usually referred to as an expression of apology in English, is not necessarily used to apologize at all. Basically, it is an expression of regret or dismay "about a state of affairs viewed or portrayed as unfortunate." For this reason it is perfectly appropriate for English speakers to say, "I'm sorry," even when no injury or potential injury has been done. Thus, *I'm sorry* is used to express regret when refusing an invitation even though no social norm has been violated. Again, when we hear of a friend's misfortune, we commiserate by saying how sorry we are to learn of the problem or difficulty or loss. The form *excuse me*, on the other hand, was found to be used exclusively to "remedy a past or immediately forthcoming breach of etiquette" on the part of the speaker. Thus, in conversation with friends one says, "Excuse me," when one interrupts another's turn at talk whether the interruption was deliberate (to answer the telephone, for example) or inadvertent. Borkin and Reinhart recognize that there is an area of overlap in the use of these two forms, and that both *excuse me* and *I'm sorry* may be used as remedies. Nevertheless, they hold that the difference between the two forms is basically a semantic one:

> *Excuse me* is more appropriate in remedial exchanges when the speaker's main concern is about a rule violation on his or her part, while *I'm sorry* is used in remedial interchanges when the speaker's main concern is about a violation of another person's rights or damage to another person's feelings; in other words, the basic concern behind *excuse me* is "I have broken or am in danger of breaking a social rule, " and the basic concern behind *I'm sorry* is "You are or you may be hurt." Even in situations in which either of the two forms might be used to perform the same remedial function, we feel that *excuse me* primarily expresses the speaker's relationship to a rule or a set of rules, while *I'm sorry* primarily expresses the speaker's relation to another person.

The accuracy of Borkin and Reinhart's analysis has been corroborated by Fraser (1981), who, along with two of his graduate students at Boston University, collected "several hundred examples of apologizing through personal experience, participant observation, responses of role playing, and from reports provided by friends and colleagues." In analyzing the various strategies used in apologizing, Fraser found, as did Owen, that in cases where social norms were broken, people often followed their formulaic apologies with "some account which sought to provide an explanation or excuse for why the infraction happened in the first place." Where the apology was for an act which resulted in injury or some sort of serious inconvenience, people tended to offer some form of redress instead of simply accounting for their action. In looking at the effect of the situation on choice of apology form, he found that "the more formal the situation, the longer and more elaborate the apology." It is interesting that in situations which he defined as formal, Fraser collected examples of speakers saying, "I apologize" or even, "Please accept my apologies for . . . ," two forms which Borkin and Reinhart did not consider in their study at all, thus limiting their analysis to the basic formulas which nonnative speakers are most in need of learning. Indeed, Fraser makes it clear that in public places and interactions between strangers, *Excuse me* and *I'm sorry* are heard in the majority of cases. It is interesting, however, and probably useful for the learner to know, that there is a negative correlation between intimacy and elaborate apologies. Thus, Fraser mentions husbands and wives reporting "apologies frequently taking the form of 'Oops,' 'No good,' 'I'm an idiot' and the like, where the utterance does not even specifically refer to the act in question. . . ." In addition to intimacy, Fraser looked at sex differences and found that there was no distinction to be made in the way men and women apologize, in spite of popular beliefs to the contrary.

In order to investigate how and to what extent first language norms interfere with second language learners' ability to conform to the norms of the target language community, Cohen and Olshtain (1981), Olshtain and Cohen (1983), Olshtain (1983) have compared native and nonnative responses in both Hebrew and English to a variety of situations that included an offense of some type. As we will see in more detail in the chapter dealing with sociolinguistic or pragmatic transfer, the data were collected by means of a carefully controlled elicitation procedure in which subjects are asked to read and then role-play their reactions to a variety of situations. Each "offense" was graded in terms of severity of the violation and the relative social status of their interlocutors. Their findings show, as do those of Owen (1980), that native speakers' choices of apology forms are highly patterned. According to the Olshtain and Cohen analysis, the major strategies used to express an apology are the following: (1) expression of apology (formulaic) = I'm sorry, (2) expression of responsibility = It was my fault. Either of these two strategies could stand alone as an apology, but in addition it was found that three other strategies often occur in conjunction with them, depending on the speaker's evaluation of the severity of the offense and also on the social distance and/or the status of the "victim." Thus, speakers may employ the following additional three strategies intended to make amends for the offense, or use one or both of the first two along with any or all of the following: (3) explanation, (4) offer of repair, (5) promise of forebearance.

As in Owen (1980), the analysis provided by Olshtain and Cohen makes it clear that these are regularly invoked strategies. While Owen suggested the possibility of cross-cultural comparisons, Olshtain and Cohen, in gathering baseline data for their study of sociolinguistic transfer, conducted several important studies in which they actually made comparisons, based on data elicited by means of discourse completion questionnaires, from two different groups of native speakers: Hebrew-speaking Israelis and native speakers of American English. One of the findings of this study which will be of particular interest to English instructors is that in their own native language, speakers of American English apologized much more frequently than did Hebrew-speaking Israelis. Indeed, in a further study in which she compared both of these groups with native speakers of Russian, Olshtain (1983) was able to establish that among the three groups, the use of apologies, in terms of both frequency and distribution, was the most frequent among the native speakers of American English.

Studies such as those conducted by Olshtain and Cohen are extremely valuable in language teaching since they not only throw light on the strategies in use among a given group but also provide information about the situations in which specific types of apologies are deemed appropriate by native speakers. By taking such information and applying it to the comparison of responses to the same situations by language learners, researchers can gain insight into the ways in which the sociolinguistic rules of the target language group are interpreted and the degree to which native language patterns are transferred.

In an elaboration of the term *speech act,* Olshtain and Cohen (1983) have proposed the notion of the "speech act set," which would include the major semantic formulas used to accomplish a specific speech function. As Olshtain and Cohen (1983) explain:

> We would like to suggest that our goal be the description of the maximal potential set of semantic formulas for each act. Therefore, a "speech act set" would consist of the major semantic formulas, any one of which could suffice as an "emic" minimal element to represent the particular speech act. A combination of some of the formulas or all of them is also possible. Research will have to concern itself with the reasons why sometimes speakers prefer one formula and at other times another. This differential preference will need to be examined as it relates to the particular discourse situation within which the speech act is performed.
>
> Apology, then, has a speech act set which will consist of a number of semantic formulas. The question now arises as to how we can arrive at the description of the complete speech act set. We must first accept the fact that this is an idealized goal which requires considerable research of an ethnographic and sociolinguistic nature. (Olshtain and Cohen 1983:21)

In their most recent work, Olshtain and Cohen (1987) have reported on an experiment in which they set out to test the degree to which the speech act of apologizing in English could be taught to a group of advanced adult speakers of Hebrew. In this investigation, Olshtain and Cohen based their research questions on a somewhat earlier study by Olshtain, in which she discovered a high degree of convergence in the apology strategy selection of native speakers of four groups: Hebrew, American English, Canadian French, and Australian English. What differences did exist had to do with the selection of substrategies in the sense that the nonnatives tended to intensify their apology expressions considerably more than did the natives, and that the distribution of these intensifiers differed significantly from that manifested in the use of native speakers. Emotional interjections, on the other hand, were found to be typical in the usage of native speakers, while the nonnatives tended to avoid them, with the result that their apologies sounded more formulaic and less sincere.

The three research questions which Olshtain and Cohen (1987) sought to answer were these: (1) How much work on speech behavior is needed at the advanced level of English language teaching? (2) Is it possible to develop language activities that will focus learners' attention on such "complex speech act behavior"? (3) What changes in such behavior can be expected to result from explicit teaching of this nature? To investigate these questions, preteaching questionnaires were given to native English speakers and their results compared with responses to the same instrument produced by the Hebrew-speaking language learners, materials and lessons geared to the specific problems of the learners were developed and taught in three consecutive lessons of 20 minutes each, the details of the three lessons were recorded, and the learners were then given a postteaching questionnaire. The results of this innovative study show that in the posttest, the subjects used apology strategies which were much more similar and therefore acceptable to native speakers, and there was a qualitative difference in the degree to which learners accommodated toward native speaker behavior. One aspect of this difference had to do with utterance length, an aspect of learner behavior earlier studied by Blum-Kulka and Olshtain (1985), who suggest that when learners are uncertain about how to say what they mean in the target language, they tend to say much more than is appropriate, thus unintentionally failing to express their intended meanings. Similarly, Olshtain and Cohen (1987) found that "in the post data most students had become more confident in the use of apology strategies and their utterances became shorter and more matched to the native norm."

The Olshtain and Cohen (1987) study just described is of particular relevance to TESOL since it is, to my knowledge, the first research report of the results of a direct application of sociolinguistic findings to the instruction of learners of English. While there is some controversy over whether and to what extent such applications *should* be made, no one would dispute the fact that it is important to have empirical findings as to whether these applications *can* be made. The results obtained by Olshtain and Cohen, therefore, provide an important indication concerning what may be accomplished along these lines. While these findings shed light on an area which has so far received very little attention, a word of caution should be introduced at this point. Put simply, it should be recognized that although the languages of the groups which provided baseline native speaker data were indeed different in terms of genetic origin, the speakers of these languages were, for the most part, from the same ethnic group and shared a common heritage. Studies of the speech behavior of different subgroups within the United States (e.g., Tannen 1981, 1982) have demonstrated that the rules of speaking are very different across ethnic groups and that, long after a language has been lost to an immigrant group, traces remain not only in phonology and syntax but also in sociolinguistic patterns. As Blum-Kulka et al. (in press) puts it: "Tannen's work shows that even Greek-Americans who no longer speak Greek retain Greek cultural norms for indirectness and risk being misunderstood by the more direct Americans" (Blum-Kulka et al. in press:8).

Given this situation, it is not surprising to find a high degree of convergence resulting from a comparison of groups which speak different languages but share the same ethnic background. Such convergence in sociolinguistic behavior would be far more unexpected if the groups in question were historically as well as geographically and linguistically unrelated. The fact that such convergence was found to exist even before Olshtain and Cohen began their instruction should not be seen as a shortcoming of the study, which loses nothing in importance because of this. Indeed, the research conducted by Olshtain and Cohen is very valuable both in itself and as a needed starting point for similar investigations among different cultural groups. The issue of sociolinguistic transfer among different language groups whose members share a common ethnic identity will be discussed in greater detail in a later chapter since this is a question which needs to be dealt with openly in all work concerning cross-cultural communication.

From the point of view of sociolinguistic description, one of the most interesting aspects of investigations into apologies is that they cannot help but shed light on other rules of speaking. By collecting and analyzing data on apologies in a particular speech community, we coincidentally collect data on when and under what circumstances remedies are felt to be called for. Since some of these will be related to violations of other sociolinguistic rules, we are made aware that such rules exist. These rules, like others involving speech behavior, are otherwise difficult to isolate. For this reason, cross-cultural studies of apologies like the ones reported by Olshtain and Cohen not only are intrinsically useful but also shed light upon many other aspects of speech behavior.

REQUESTS

The most comprehensive sociolinguistic investigation of requests in American English is that of Ervin-Tripp (1976), in which she divides her treatment of the speech function known as the directive into three major sections, each corresponding to one of the research questions she poses. The questions Ervin-Tripp raises are as follows: (1) What is the empirical distribution of formal variants across social features, or can we predict the form of a directive from the social features of its context? (2) How might the variants be recognized as directives given the social contexts in which they actually occur? (3) Are variants of directives simply a function of politeness?

Ervin-Tripp separates directives or requests into six categories:

1. *Needs statements,* which she finds are used by superiors in work settings and to superiors in age in family settings.
2. *Imperatives,* which are most frequent within a family or when used downwards in rank or among equals. The use of the word *please* marks age or rank differences, is used more by females, and occurs among peers when the request is outside the scope of the addressee's normal obligations. Imperatives often cooccur with slang and with casual pronunciation, especially if the interlocutors are "blue-collar workers."
3. *Imbedded imperatives,* such as "could you . . . ," are used to superiors in rank and age, when the task is especially difficult, and when the speaker is the beneficiary of the request.
4. *Permission directives* are infrequent and used most when the activity requested includes action by the addressee. They are used to superiors in rank in the workplace as well as in the family and are the most elaborated of all directives.
5. *Nonexplicit question directives* tend to state a condition that would make compliance difficult or impossible and thus give the addressee an escape route. The probability of noncompliance with this sort of request is very strong. In wording, nonexplicit question directives tend to be ambiguous and frequently make use of negative tag questions, which, in turn, usually elicit negative responses. This category of request is used to superiors in

rank and/or age and when both physical and interpersonal distance are greater.

6. *Hints* go furthest in leaving the addressee's options open and are used generally within closed networks when shared knowledge between the participants is greatest, familiarity or solidarity between interlocutors is greater, and when the task requested is most "special."

In examining the explanations Ervin-Tripp gives for her six categories of directives, it appears that a number of social factors were found to condition the form of the directives in a more indirect or less explicit direction: greater rank, age, social status, physical distance, tension, and specialness of the request in terms of the addressee's usual obligations to the speaker. At the same time, requests were also less direct when there was less likelihood that they could be met, when less solidarity, compatibility, and familiarity between interlocutors existed, and when there was a lack of shared territoriality. The two other social factors that were found to influence the request in terms of less directness were the presence of a third person of higher rank and the situation in which the speaker would be the beneficiary of the action requested.

Ervin-Tripp found that if the form of the request is inappropriate to the context, the directive may not be interpreted as a directive at all. She gives the example of a foreign student who is unable to communicate a request because the choice of pronoun is inappropriate to the status of her addressee. Further, listeners bring cultural knowledge to their interactions, and this normally includes an awareness of what goods and services they will be expected to supply in a given interaction. Thus, a declarative or an interrogative will be interpreted as a directive if the action or activity designated is a forbidden one.

From Ervin-Tripp's point of view, the distribution of request forms cannot be attributed to politeness alone. For example, "polite" forms, when used inappropriately, are not interpreted as polite. Rather, they are either misinterpreted completely or are heard as sarcasm, joking, or even rudeness. When polite forms are misused among native speakers, it is assumed that rudeness or intentional distancing is intended.

As we will see in detail in the chapter concerned with sociolinguistic transfer, a great deal of research has been conducted by Blum-Kulka (1982, 1983a) on request behavior in Israeli Hebrew as it compares with that of both Canadian and American speakers of English. In addition, Blum-Kulka et al. (1985) have investigated requests in Hebrew on its own terms. Blum-Kulka's studies demonstrate that the most important factors conditioning request forms are the degree of social distance and power that exist between interlocutors, but that these major variables interact with other factors of the social context in which requests occur. As with the American speakers studied by Ervin-Tripp, Blum-Kulka et al. found that the degree to which requests are made indirect varies with the relative power of the addressee, so that the least direct requests are made to those in the most socially dominant positions. Clearly, cultural differences must be taken into consideration, although many of the results described by Blum-Kulka et al. for Israeli Hebrew were similar in some respects to those found by Ervin-Tripp for speakers of American English. That is, in both cases, the directness of request forms covaries with increased familiarity. In Israeli Hebrew, however, the degree of directness in request forms was less influenced by social distance than by the purpose of the request, and by the age and power of the addressee relative to that of the speaker. Unlike the American findings, those for Israeli Hebrew showed social distance between the interlocutors to have relatively little influence in choice of request form. The research findings from Israeli Hebrew, while not immediately relevant to TESOL (except, of course, where the learners have Hebrew as their first language), raise questions critical to the descriptive analysis of speech behavior, especially in terms of cross-cultural comparisons. As Blum-Kulka et al. (in press) puts it:

> Many of the issues involved in this type of research still need further investigation; it is not at all clear for example whether we know how to differentiate between relevant and non-relevant situational factors that affect speech production, or whether the relevant factors, if established, actually affect linguistic behavior in similar ways across different cultures. Or, to add another difficulty, do we know whether degrees of illocutionary clarity ("indirectness"), which determine length of processing for the hearer, play a similar role in different situations across cultures? (Blum-Kulka et al. in press:7)

In contrast to the differences in request behavior between Hebrew and English speakers found by Blum-Kulka, a comparison of requesting strategies used by Spanish and English speakers (Fraser et al. 1980) suggests that, of the two groups, it is the English speakers who are more direct and less deferential. As the researchers report, the results of the three experiments they carried out demonstrate the following: "When degrees of deference of the learner's requesting strategies in English and Spanish are compared, we find that most of the time, the corresponding English request was less deferential than the Spanish one for the same situation" (Fraser et al. 1980: 85). Clearly, the English speakers, who appear more than appropriately polite to Israelis, will be judged very differently by Spanish speakers, who may well tend to see them as lacking in this very attribute.

Data for the investigation were collected through a series of role-playing situations. In addition to their interest in the extent to which nativelike strategies were carried over into speech in the target language, the questions the researchers sought to answer had to do with the degree to which requesting strategies differed between groups and which factors of the situation would most influence the choice of request form. Fraser et al. hypothesized that the age, sex, and status of the addressee would prove to be the most important variables, and therefore they designed the eight situations they used to elicit data in such a way as to control specifically for these factors. As their findings indicate, age did indeed prove important as a conditioning factor for both groups, with greater deference shown to older addressees. A significant difference along these lines between the two groups was pointed up, however.

That is, where age and status interacted such that an addressee was both older and of lower status than the speaker:

> . . . requests made by English speakers to older addressees and considered to be highly deferent were equally divided between high and low-status addressees. For them, higher status and older age were often seen as one combined attribute, and the change to lower status of an older addressee did not seem to alter the level of deference accorded to him. On the other hand, the highly deferent Spanish requests made to older addressees were addressed most often to addressees who were also of higher status; a much smaller proportion were put to addressees of lower status who were also older. It seems that the Spanish speakers were more sensitive than the English speakers to social status as a separate attribute of the hearer, distinct from age. (Fraser et al. 1980:85)

The findings of this study thus provide the sociolinguist with a perspective on American behavior that differs considerably from those found by investigators who have focused on other cultural groups, thus pointing up the extreme variability and complexity in the forces which constrain such superficially straightforward speech behavior as that of making requests.

THE TELEPHONE

In another such study, Godard (1977) looks at the differing rules for the giving of apologies in telephone call beginnings in the United States and France. Although Godard agrees with Schegloff (1972) that the ringing of the telephone and the "hello" of the answer together constitute a summons–response sequence, she points out that there is a sharp difference in the way the two societies regard the speech event of telephoning, and that these differing values cause speakers to follow different sets of rules. Telephone calls in the United States may begin with the caller offering an apology for disturbing the answerer, especially if the call is made during mealtime or late in the evening. In France, however, it is required that all telephone calls begin with an apology for disturbing the answerer. In addition, French callers are expected to begin the call by checking that they have reached the right number, identifying themselves, and then chatting with whoever has answered the telephone if this person is known to them. Only after some conversation may callers indicate their wish to speak with the person they have actually called to speak to. In contrast, callers in the United States apologize only when they feel they have called at an inappropriate time; they often ask for the intended addressee without identifying themselves or conversing with the answerer, even when that person is known; and they behave, in general, as though the person who has answered the telephone is an extension of the instrument itself. Godard gives examples of situations that occurred when she was residing in the United States and was shocked by the way Americans behaved on the telephone. In some cases, when she followed French rules in making calls and attempted to converse with acquaintances who answered the telephone, they would ask whom she wanted to speak with, and then would hand the phone over directly without allowing her to continue. On other occasions, she answered the telephone, heard the voice of an acquaintance, and was surprised and hurt when the caller, instead of greeting and conversing with her, simply asked for someone else.

Schegloff's (1972) analysis of the way telephone call beginnings are sequenced points out that, in the United States, the ring of the telephone is heard as a summons and that the person who answers it must always be the first to say hello. It is then up to the caller to introduce the first topic of the conversation, which proceeds as an a-b-a-b-a-b sequence. In discussing the forms used for self-identification, Schegloff makes the point that in telephone conversations, it is customary to frame one's name by saying "This is _____," a form never used in face-to-face interaction except when introducing a third party. In contrast, the frame "I am _____," which frequently occurs in face-to-face interaction, is never used on the telephone. The frame "My name is _____" may be used in both speech situations. This little rule, as insignificant as it may seem, is extremely important to the learner of English, who might, if not shown how the two frames work, use the wrong one and thereby be misunderstood. The difficulty with the analysis as given by Schegloff is that although it seems clear that he is correct in saying that "This is _____" is a very common frame for self-identification on the telephone, observational data indicate that the frame "I am _____," like "My name is _____," functions as a means of self-introduction and may be used both on the telephone and in face-to-face interactions when the caller or speaker is unknown to his or her interlocutor. The frame "I am _____," when used in telephone calls, is usually given the further frame "You don't know me but . . ." and serves not only to introduce the speaker but also to lead into the reason for the call.

The rules for self-identification in telephone call openings are, of course, quite variable across cultures. Schmidt (1975), in a comparison of telephone call beginnings in Cairo, examined three interactions between dyads of Egyptians, Americans, and Germans and found that, of these, only the German answerer identified himself without being asked to do so. American callers tended to verify that they had reached the right party by saying that party's name with a rising question intonation. Egyptians, on the other hand, seemed to be unwilling to be the first to be identified. Thus, they would counter one another's greetings and demands for identification until they were able to guess each other's identity. Schmidt found that it was sometimes necessary for speakers to take a dozen or more turns at talk before the identification was satisfactorily made. Westerners living in Egypt found this behavior strange, and even offensive, since their own rules, which they take for granted, are very different. The fact that German speakers were found to be the only ones to identify themselves without being requested to do so raises the question of whether there is a more general European rule for telephone call openings which cuts across specific individual languages in such a way that it may be considered an areal feature (Neustupny 1971).

Schmidt's comments on the reactions of Westerners to Egyptian telephone customs coincide well with Godard's findings. Both cases exemplify the fact that sociolinguistic rules are not usually open to conscious reflection. What this means is that speakers tend to be unaware that such rules exist at all, and it is only when their sociolinguistic expectations are disappointed that speakers are shocked into realizing that rules exist. In speaking of the differences in telephone call beginnings in France and the United States, Godard (1977) makes this point: "As a foreigner who has lived in the United States for only a few months, I have been made conscious of some differences in the speech behavior related to telephone calls: I have sometimes been amused. . . . What does this mean? Simply that I am not fully a member of the community in which I am at the moment residing" (Godard 1977).

In a recent article by Clark and French (1981), telephone good-byes are analyzed. The authors say that the uses of *good-bye* in urban American telephone conversations can be looked at from the point of view of belonging to a particular part of a unit of conversation which they, following Schegloff and Sacks (1973), call the "closing section." This is the last part of the telephone conversation and serves to permit caller and callee to agree that there are no further topics to be raised, that their relationship will continue, and to exchange good-byes. What Clark and French wish to make clear is that the leave-taking subsection of the closing section of a telephone conversation is independent of the rest of the material in the closing section, and that when it is absent, there will be no exchange of good-byes. Using the results of three experiments as data, Clark and French show that when people call a switchboard for information or, indeed, make any sort of routine inquiry on the telephone, they do not ordinarily end their conversations with a *good-bye* exchange but rather use a *thank you, you're welcome* routine. What is interesting about the study is that the authors, through observation of the results of operator errors, found that when any sort of personal information is exchanged, such as an account of an error or an apology on the part of an operator, the likelihood of the conversation's ending with a good-bye exchange increased dramatically. Apparently, people feel the need to include a leave-taking section of a conversation if they have begun to be acquainted with one another. As Clark and French remark:

> The *goodbye* exchange isn't simply a device for terminating telephone calls, as is often assumed. If it were, there would be no explanation for why it is used more often the more acquainted the caller and operator become. Rather, it signals the presence of, and it completes, the leavetaking subsection of the closing section of the conversation. . . . The more general lesson here is that the meaning of *goodbye* inheres in use, and its use is tied to certain socially and culturally defined routines. . . . Its meaning cannot be described for isolated utterances, or even for isolated exchanges of *goodbye*. It can only be described in relation to the larger routines of which *goodbye* is a part.

Telephone behavior, with its culture-specific rules for openings and closings, is, of course, not the only speech behavior open to misunderstanding by the native or nonnative speaker. We will examine studies specifically aimed at analyzing miscommunication in detail in a later chapter.

DISAPPROVAL

Like compliments, expressions of disapproval are heavily value-laden and must be expected to vary cross-culturally both in form and in content. D'Amico-Reisner (1983), in her analysis of adult-to-adult scolding in American English, focuses mainly on the linguistic form which these expressions take. Using an ethnographic approach, D'Amico-Reisner tape-recorded everyday conversations to discover where and how adults in our society reprimand one another. In analyzing her data, she found that these expressions could be either "dressed" or "undressed," the undressed taking the form of imperatives while the dressed have the surface structure of interrogatives and declaratives. Thus, any surface form can express disapproval, but the undressed forms are more direct. Dressed disapproval may take the form of interrogatives; here we have two categories—the RQ, or rhetorical question, and the REQ, or response-expected question. RQs typically begin with the word *what*, but no answer is expected ("What are you, some kind of nut?"), whereas REQs, which D'Amico-Reisner finds to be more common among intimates, may begin with a variety of other question words ("Why did you eat that cheese?" or "What are you doing with my water?"). Declaratives may also be used to express disapproval ("These things have been ready for two weeks"), and D'Amico-Reisner finds that although the most dressed disapprovals take this form, the message can nonetheless be conveyed with severity.

In a later and more comprehensive analysis of disapproval exchanges, D'Amico-Reisner (1985) distinguished two types of disapproval exchanges (D) which she calls direct and indirect D. These categories are described in the following way:

> Direct D and indirect D were distinguished on the basis of the ways in which addressee and referent person markers related to a speaker I : With direct D, addressee and referent were one and the same second person(s) singular or plural and referent occurred as third person(s) singular or plural . . . less immediate distinctions between direct D and indirect D were revealed by surface patterns of initiating moves and addressee response options, both of which suggested differences in the strategic orientations of the speakers in the two types of D. (D'Amico-Reisner 1985:215)

In terms of the rules of speaking which constrain the use of D, D'Amico-Reisner found that both direct and indirect D occurred most frequently among speakers who were intimates and more or less equal with respect to social status. When direct D occurred between nonintimates, however, they were nearly always between strangers in service encounters. Speakers who were equal in status but neither intimates nor strangers seldom participated in direct expressions of disapproval. Setting was found to have an important conditioning effect on the use of D, and especially of direct D. The most frequently issued direct expressions of disapproval were found to occur in private settings; the only other setting where the frequency of direct D was at all significant was, as mentioned, in service encounters with employees who had, in one way or another, been responsible for disappointing the expectations of the customer. Indirect D, on the other hand, appears to be motivated by a desire to establish greater solidarity between interlocutors and was frequently found to occur in public settings other than service encounters. What D'Amico-Reisner demonstrates in this study of disapproval exchanges is that D is a very common speech activity in the everyday speech of adults who are intimate status equals. Since it seems to work to establish what D'Amico-Reisner calls "behavioral expectations" and "boundaries of interaction," it serves to promote solidarity. This is an interesting finding in light of the fact that D is a form of speech behavior that is often carefully avoided in more traditional cultures. Keenan (1974), for example, makes it clear that in the Malagasy-speaking culture she studied, expressions of disapproval are to be carefully avoided. In other cultures, proverbs and other forms of indirect expressions are regularly used as a means of avoiding the risk of even the most indirect spontaneous expression of disapproval. Thus, this study of patterns of D among native speakers of American English should be of particular importance in providing curriculum developers and instructors in the field of TESOL with the empirical facts necessary to explain the way in which this form of speech behavior works in American society. Language learners need to know how to interpret the expressions of disapproval they hear, and they need to have the information which will enable them to express their own concerns appropriately within the context of the target culture. This is an area which has potential for serious misunderstandings to arise, and it is only through the application of analyses such as that presented by D'Amico-Reisner that we can be in a position to avoid unnecessary negative reactions.

Related to expressions of disapproval is the speech act of complaining. While some work has been done in this area for American English, published analyses of empirical studies are as yet unavailable. Work done on complaining by native speakers and learners of Israeli Hebrew has been reported by Olshtain and Weinbach (1986). A brief description of the findings of this study, based on elicited data from discourse completion tests (Blum-Kulka 1982), indicate that on the basis of a scale of "the severity of the complaint," five major categories may be defined. The authors summarize their findings as follows:

> The possible realization for each of the strategies according to the level of severity might be something like the following:
>
> A. *below the level of reproach* "No harm done, let's meet some other time."
> B. *disapproval* "It's a shame that we have to work faster now."
> C. *complaint* "You are always late for these meetings and now we have less time to do the job."
> D. *accusation and warning* "Next time don't expect me to sit here waiting for you."
> E. *threat* "If we don't finish the job today I'll have to discuss it with the boss."

Olshtain and Weinbach (1986) found that both native and nonnative speaking populations make use of all the strategies mentioned but that the differences between them "lie in the overall preference of the learners for the softer end of the scale while native speakers are more severe in their complaints." With respect to the parameters of social distance and status, it was found that among Hebrew speakers, social distance had little or no effect on the choice of complaint strategy. On the other hand, the social obligations of participants toward one another (especially when these are explicit) and the degree of frustration felt by the speaker both play an important role in the selection of the complaint strategy selected by the speaker.

REFUSALS

Several major investigations into the speech act of refusing have been conducted by Beebe (1985, Beebe et al.1985, Beebe and Takahashi 1987). Since much of this work has had to do with the issue of pragmatic transfer in the speech of Japanese learners of American English, a detailed description of Beebe's work will be reported in the chapter which deals specifically with miscommunication, and will therefore not be repeated in this section. However, since Beebe's findings concerning the speech behavior of middle-class Americans in this regard have great relevance to our understanding of rules of speaking in American English, we will discuss this aspect of her work here.

Beebe et al. (1985) collected data from 60 subjects, divided into three groups: native speakers of Japanese speaking in Japanese (JJs), native speakers of American English speaking in English (AEs), and native speakers of Japanese speaking in English (JEs). Although the aim of the study was to discover whether the refusals given by the JEs were closer to those of the JJs or to those of speakers of the target language, the AEs, the fact that Beebe et al. made a careful investigation of the behavior of speakers of American English is of particular value in our review of the sociolinguistic information available concerning what is, after all, a major target population for TESOL.

The design of the study used both ethnographic data and responses to a Discourse Completion Test or DCT (Blum-Kulka 1982). The DCT, a written questionnaire, contained 12 situations or dialogues, each with a blank in which only a refusal would be appropriate. The refusals studied were divided into four categories: refusals to (1) requests, (2) invitations, (3) offers, and (4) suggestions. The social factors deemed most likely to condition the form refusals would take were built into the design of the questionnaire, so that refusals had to be made to interlocutors of higher, lower, and equal status. Examples of types of semantic formulas found in the data on refusals are apologies/regrets, excuses, direct "no"s, suggestions of alternatives, and statements of philosophy.

The findings of the study demonstrate that Japanese learners of English manifest sociolinguistic transfer in refusals by the sequencing of formulas for refusing, the actual frequency in use of formulas, and their specific content. Not surprisingly, in view of the extreme differences in the cultural backgrounds of the groups studied, it was found that the Japanese learners of English used strategies of refusal which resembled those of the Japanese speaking in Japanese and differed from those of the native speakers of American English speaking in English. One significant finding was that the status of the addressee is a much stronger conditioning factor in the speech of Japanese speaking both in English and in their native language. An example of the influence of status in the behavior of the Japanese is that they, unlike English speaking Americans, did not apologize or express regret in responses to those of lower position. Additional evidence of status-related differences is manifested in the Japanese responses to invitations from higher- as opposed to lower-status interlocutors. In contrast, Americans in these situations make a distinction along the lines of social distance by responding in a brief and unelaborated fashion to both higher- and lower-status unequals while offering much longer and more detailed responses to peers, corroborating the Bulge theory put forth by Wolfson (1981b, 1986, in press), which will be discussed in detail in a later chapter. Additional evidence of the differential effects of status upon the two groups is that, compared with the American English speakers, both the learner and native speakers of Japanese apologized with greater frequency to addressees of higher than lower status.

In their analysis of strategies for refusing, Beebe et al. (1985) classify refusals into those which are direct and those which are indirect. Direct refusals such as "I refuse" or "no" were, as mentioned earlier, found to be used by Americans mainly in response to intimates and status unequals or strangers. Indirect refusals, used by Americans primarily to acquaintances of equal status, included three major strategies which were usually found to be used in sequence at the beginning of a refusal. These were (1) an expression of positive opinion such as "I'd like to," (2) an expression of regret such as "I'm sorry," and (3) an excuse, reason, or explanation such as "My children will be home that night" or "I have a headache." Other strategies included a statement expressing a wish to be able to comply with the request, the statement of an alternative, a condition for future or past acceptance (e.g., "If you had asked me earlier . . .), a promise of future acceptance (e.g., "I'll do it next time"), a statement of principle (e.g., "I never do business with friends"), a statement of philosophy (e.g., "One can't be too careful"), an attempt to dissuade the interlocutor, a criticism of the request, a request for empathy, a statement letting the interlocutor off the hook (e.g., "Don't worry about it"), self-defense (e.g., "I'm doing my best"), an unspecific or indefinite reply, a display of lack of enthusiasm, and verbal or nonverbal avoidance such as silence or a topic switch, a hedge, or a joke (Beebe et al. 1985).

The rigorous and detailed analysis of refusal patterns provided by Beebe et al. will undoubtedly prove of extreme value to the field of TESOL, giving teachers, materials developers, and students ample information on the ways in which native speakers of American English handle the often difficult problems posed by the need to refuse.

THE EXPRESSION OF GRATITUDE

The expression of gratitude has been investigated both across cultural groups and among speakers of American English. The most comprehensive studies in this area have been conducted by Eisenstein and Bodman (1986, in press). The description of the research on cross-cultural problems concerning the speech act of thanking will be discussed in the chapter dealing specifically with miscommunication and transfer. Here we will focus on the research findings that pertain specifically to the way gratitude is expressed and responded to by speakers of American English.

An important finding regarding the thanking sequence is that the expression of gratitude requires that both the thanker and the giver interact together to create a mutually satisfactory speech event. Thanking routines studied ethnographically were thus discovered to be much longer than originally found in the data from oral and written questionnaires, with extensive and dynamic interaction between the participants a critical aspect of socially appropriate speech behavior. The length of the thanking routine was also found to be influenced significantly by the degree to which the thanker felt indebted. Thus, as Eisenstein and Bodman (in press) report, "the greater the indebtedness incurred by the gift, service or favor, the more profuse were the thanks that followed its receipt." It is also noteworthy that the researchers found thanks to be repeated long after the event which engendered it. Thus, they say:

> It should be noted that thanking is not necessarily over after the end of the first thanking episode. We have collected a number of examples of "re-entry of thanks" . . . a re-entry of thanks occurred when a woman welcomed her friend and her small child at the door one cold January day:
> Friend 1: I've got the heat on. I hope the house isn't too cold.
> Friend 2: I don't think it will be. I've got a sweater on. (opening her coat) See? It's the one you gave me! I wear it all the time. It's my favorite.
> What is remarkable is that this took place more than a year after the gift was given. (Eisenstein and Bodman in press)

From the point of view of native speaker strategies, the investigators found that in order to express thanks adequately, native speakers of American English seemed to need to use formulas which involved from two to five different functions of speech. To begin with, speakers often expressed surprise at the offering and then followed their statements with actual thanking formulas (e.g., "Thanks"; "Thank you so much"). After the actual formulaic expression, it is typical to find another statement, this time expressing pleasure (e.g., "That's great!"). An additional speech act, that of complimenting the giver (e.g., "You're wonderful") is also frequently employed as part of the sequence of thanking, and, finally, it is common for the recipient to employ a further strategy, that of expressing a desire to continue the relationship or to repay the favor. Other strategies which occur frequently fall into the category called a "ritual refusal" by the researchers. As they put it: "When the gift, service, or favor is first offered, the receiver often chooses to appear reluctant or overwhelmed and proffers a gentle refusal." Many of these ritual refusals are formulaic in nature (e.g., "Oh, I couldn't" or "You shouldn't have!"), and although Eisenstein and Bodman do not report on them in detail, it would be interesting to investigate the extent to which all the strategies they described are precoded with respect both to syntax and semantics.

Ethnographic research into expressions of gratitude conducted by Rubin (1983) indicates that at least some of these expressions are quite distinctive. In addition to reporting that the expression "thank you" was regularly used to serve functions, such as opening or closing an interaction, which had nothing to do with gratitude, she also finds (as do Wolfson 1983a and Eisenstein and Bodman in press) that other speech acts, such as compliments, may be used to perform a thanking function. Rubin comments that gratitude is an important area for study, especially among speakers of American English since they, more than members of many other cultural groups, regard thanking as a social necessity. This, she asserts, is manifested by the fact that this social act is one of the earliest taught to children in American society. To contrast American norms with those of India, Rubin cites Apte (1974), who points out that among family members "there is no room for verbal gratitude because it is assumed that role performance is obligatory on the part of the individual, and because acts of assistance are accepted in the spirit of mutual cooperation without words."

It is interesting that the most unusual expressions of gratitude collected by Rubin and her students all had a religious undertone. Such expressions as "God bless you" and "Bless your heart, honey" may indeed verge on the formulaic in some speech communities. However, it is difficult to imagine that the words "I'll recommend you to the Lord" could be anything but original. Indeed, the fact that Rubin was able to collect such a form provides excellent evidence of the range of unexpected findings which may result from use of an ethnographic approach to the collection of data.

In a research report in 1985, Dorolyn Smith analyzed more than 400 responses to expressions of thanks used by native and nonnative speakers of English. Through observation of responses occurring in a range of natural settings, the author found that the most common native speaker responses were silence, "mhm," "you're welcome," and "thank you." Nonnative speakers responded with silence, "okay," and "you're welcome." While nonnative speakers did not use the "mhm" response, native speakers used "okay" only very infrequently. The factor which seemed to have the most influence on response selection was the nature of the act leading to the expression of gratitude. In eliciting data on responses to thanks, the author composed dialogues based on differing situations involving both native and nonnative speakers. The purpose of the elicitation was to collect acceptability judgments by both groups. As might be predicted from their observed behavior, native speakers found "mhm" more acceptable than did nonnative speakers, while nonnative speakers judged silence more favorably than did native speakers.

That sex differences may influence the frequency with which thanks are given is suggested by a laboratory study conducted by Grief and Gleason (1980) in which young girls and boys, accompanied by equal numbers of mothers and fathers, were placed in a position where it would have been appropriate for them not only to thank the research assistant but also to produce greetings and farewells. Berko-Gleason (1987) describes their results as follows:

> We did not find differences in the ways boys and girls were treated; both sexes were encouraged (actually urged) to say thank you when given a gift and, to a lesser degree, to say "Hi" and "Good-bye" as well. There were large differences in the mothers' and fathers' own politeness behavior, however: The mothers were much more likely to say thank you to the assistant when their child was given a gift than the fathers were. . . . If parents provide models for their same-sex children, we would, therefore, expect to see in the emerging language of the little girls more conventional expressions of politeness than in the speech of boys. (Berko-Gleason 1987:196–197).

The finding that women were more likely to thank than men under laboratory conditions may prove quite significant in future studies of the rules for the expression of gratitude. Clearly, more studies of this seemingly superficial speech act are needed so that we may gain deeper insights into the rules and constraints that condition it, as well as a broader knowledge of the range of forms that are involved. The work done so far has provided us with valuable and unexpected information, whetting our appetites for an even fuller picture of the way speakers of American English express and respond to thanks.

GREETINGS

A laboratory study of greetings was conducted by Krivonos and Knapp (1975) to discover the most frequent verbal and nonverbal behavior associated with them and to investigate whether these behaviors varied according to relationship between interlocutors. All 64 subjects were college-age men who were asked to fill out forms giving information concerning their "scale of acquaintance" with respect to all other participants in the study. With this information in hand, the authors were able to divide their subjects into 16 pairs of acquaintances and 16 pairs of strangers. Each pair then participated in a task designed to elicit a greeting by one of the members of the pair. All greetings collected in this way were videotaped and transcribed.

The most common nonverbal greetings were found to be head gestures, mutual glances, and smiles. Typical verbal greetings involved topic initiation, verbal salutes, and references to the interlocutor. The only nonverbal difference between acquaintances and strangers was that more smiling occurred when participants were acquainted. Differences between the two sets of subjects manifested themselves in the fact that verbal greetings were more common among acquaintances than among strangers. While Krivonos and Knapp regard greetings as "ritualized behavior," the authors point out that their results could have been specific to the situation in which they conducted their study.

That this may indeed be the case is suggested by a preliminary study of nonformulaic greetings conducted by Marsha Wesler as part of a seminar project conducted at the University of Pennsylvania. Basing her findings on an ethnographically oriented study of her own speech community, Wesler (1984) discovered that in interactions among status equals who were well acquainted, conversations were typically initiated not by a formulaic greeting but by a comment or question related to information shared by the participants. While the study was preliminary in nature, a considerable amount of data was collected and analyzed, leading to a strong indication that social distance and amount of shared knowledge about one another's lives have a strong influence on the frequency with which nonformulaic greetings are used. The investigation of the ways in which members of American speech communities go about the social act of greeting one another is of particular interest to TESOL, since many of the forms actually in use differ considerably from community norms regarding this form of speech behavior and are therefore not likely to be represented in descriptions of greeting routines normally taught to language learners. If language learners are to be able to interpret such forms, it will be necessary to investigate this aspect of speech behavior more thoroughly in order to provide information which may be incorporated usefully into teaching materials.

PARTINGS

In a study on leave-takings, Knapp et al. (1973) investigated the verbal and nonverbal behaviors associated with this speech event in American society in order to (a) describe them and (b) learn whether these vary with the status and relationship of participants to the interaction. The study was conducted in a laboratory setting and included 80 pairs of acquaintances—40 pairs who were unequal in status and forty who were of equal status. In each situation, one of the members of the pair interviewed the other, and the leave-taking at the end of the conversation was videotaped and transcribed for anlaysis. The nonverbal behaviors Knapp et al. found to be most associated with leave-taking were breaking eye contact, leaning toward the door, and leaning forward. With respect to verbal behavior, the findings were more significant in that differences in status between participants was demonstrated to have an effect on what strategies they tended to adopt. Thus, it was found that reinforcement of the relationship occurred among status equals but not among unequals, while such acts as making professional inquiries played a part in the behavior of participants of unequal status but not among peers.

In contrast to the laboratory study conducted by Knapp et al. (1973), an investigation of the linguistic forms used in spontaneous leave-taking situations was carried out by Schmandt (1985). Here, data were gathered from 180 conversations in a variety of settings: between co-workers in the workplace and outside it, between members of a household at home, and between guests at parties and receptions. Schmandt's findings indicated that the most significant variable conditioning the form of the leave-takings was the participants' expectations about future contact. Age and sex were found not to be significant factors. Intimates (close friends and family members) were found to make more statements involving specific intentions for future contact than were nonintimates. With respect to nonverbal behavior, intimates tended to include hugging as part of the leave-taking.

Different aspects of parting routines were also studied in my sociolinguistics seminar in 1984. The findings of this work on partings done by Kipers, Williams, Rabinowitz, and Kaplan provide additional evidence that speakers behave in markedly different ways with those who occupy fixed positions in their social world and those with whom their relationships are less settled. As Kipers (1983) put it:

> Where there is no framework of social contact in place to assure casual friends
> and acquaintances that a future meeting will take place, partings reflect concern
> over the survival of the relationship. Mean number of turns in these partings was
> the highest of any group in this study. Individual utterances were notably longer
> too. . . . The lengthy negotiations over future meeting time reassure both
> participants that even though they may not designate a definite time when they
> will see one another again, they both value the relationship enough to want it to
> continue. (Kipers 1983)

While all partings share certain basic features, our analysis supports that of Knapp et al. (1973) and of Schmandt (1985) in demonstrating that shared knowledge of social distance and mutual certainty of future meeting are the important factors conditioning the form of the parting sequence. As Williams says:

> Where one or another or both of these factors is shared by the participants,
> interactions will exhibit certain predictable characteristics. Pre-partings will be
> absent as will lengthy negotiations as to when the parties will meet again.
> Parting signals and "goodbye" and its variants will occur in only a minority of
> cases. Conversely, when knowledge of both social distance and time of future
> meeting are absent, partings diverge from this pattern. (Williams 1983)

In her 1986 study of service encounter closings, Kipers collected 102 instances of naturally occurring interactions in a variety of settings: "retail stores, gas stations, doctor's and dentist's offices, etc." She found that the topics discussed during these interactions was almost entirely limited to those having to do with the transaction itself, and that it was the service receiver who usually initiated this form of closing, especially when the service provider was not busy and seemed inclined to continue the interaction. As Kipers (1986) describes her findings:

> In summary, the rules of speaking that govern initiation of and response to
> closings in service encounters differ from those that prevail in other closing
> situations. The factors that affect these rules are the context of the service
> encounter itself and the cooperation of the parties involved through mutual
> understanding of the rights and obligations inherent in their respective roles
> within the service encounter situation. The often complex interdependence of

these factors sometimes made it difficult to pinpoint the controlling element or combination of elements with any great degree of certainty. Further, more narrowly focused study is needed in order to better understand the influence of each specific factor or combination of factors in any given situation. (Kipers 1986:1–13)

CONCLUSION

The cross-cultural studies described above, as well as those which are discussed throughout the first part of this book, demonstrate that speech communities typically manifest quite different styles of interaction at the sociolinguistic or pragmatic level. Although this fact has long been acknowledged, the possibility of the existence of higher-level conditioning factors that operate universally is still open to question. Although some frameworks for analysis have been proposed and preliminary investigations carried out, it is still the case that relatively few empirical studies have been conducted for the express purpose of contrasting specific types of speech behavior across cultural groups. Much has been written about the need for such contrastive analyses of sociolinguistic rules, not only for the purpose of language teaching but for the information they could contribute to the field of intercultural communication generally. It is clear that only by extending and expanding on what is currently known can we hope to resolve the claims made for and against the potential universality of the factors that condition speech behavior.

In view of the findings of Beebe et al. (1985) regarding the extreme status sensitivity of Japanese subjects, for example, the results reported by Fraser et al. (1980) concerning the behavior of Spanish speakers leads to some interesting questions. From the point of view of cross-cultural comparisons, a study which investigated the ways in which Spanish and Japanese speakers respond in the context of varying status relationships might well give us subtle and important insights not only into the differences and similarities of the two groups but, perhaps more important from a theoretical point of view, into the ways in which status differences may work to condition speech behavior. Since there are large and growing Japanese communities living in many of the Spanish-speaking countries of Latin America, such an investigation is quite feasible and might well provide a valuable topic of research to sociolinguists who have access to such settings. Indeed, research findings such as those of Beebe et al. and of Fraser, Scarcella, and Walters, all conducted within the context of applied linguistics, point up the degree to which sociolinguistic theory may be influenced by applied research. Thus, it has become increasingly obvious that scholars within the field known as applied linguistics have done much more than "apply" the theories, methods, and findings of the so-called parent discipline. As much of the work undertaken demonstrates, investigators within the areas of language teaching and intercultural communication have made discoveries and invented techniques for study which go far beyond mere applications of the work of others, and which have much to contribute to the study of language behavior generally.

It should be clear from the foregoing that the studies described in this chapter represent only an incomplete sample of the range of speech behavior which constitutes the sociolinguistic aspect of what has come to be known as communicative competence. As we have pointed out earlier, sociolinguistics is a relatively new field and much empirical work remains to be done. We need to add to our knowledge about the vast amount of speech behavior as yet unstudied and to further analyze the details and complexity of the sociolinguistic behavior so far investigated.

As the reader will have noticed, the studies described above do not fall easily into any sort of systematic pattern. Scholars have worked on various facets of speech behavior independently or in small groups, choosing to focus on topics and areas which seemed most relevant to them within the context of their overall interests. For this reason, it has not been possible to develop a coherent framework in which these studies could be described. Reports of sociolinguistic investigations deal with topics on a variety of levels and of numerous types, representative of the enormous range of the work to be found in this new and growing literature.

In spite of the quantity of research which remains to be done, it is still not possible in a book of this length to provide an exhaustive account of all that has so far been learned regarding the socially conditioned speech patterns of native speakers of English. Choices have had to be made, and these were guided, insofar as possible, by the relevance of the research to the field of TESOL. Therefore, although no claim is made with respect to comprehensiveness, it is nevertheless hoped that this survey will provide research findings and insights that will prove useful to practitioners within the field of TESOL who need concrete, empirically based information concerning the results of the sociolinguistic research most pertinent to their work. The findings described here are thus intended to serve as a background for the designing of authentic classroom materials, as well as for teachers and learners of English who, if they are to work toward developing communicative competence in the target language, must have access to as much knowledge of what this comprises as possible.

CHAPTER
5

An In-Depth Analysis of Speech Behavior

INTRODUCTION

Now that we have reviewed some of the major sociolinguistic studies pertinent to the description of the rules of speaking among middle-class Americans, we need to look into the question of what can be gained from such investigations. The major point we will be making in this chapter is that such descriptions have a great deal more to offer than information about surface forms, however useful this might be. Thus, in this chapter we will focus on the deeper aspects of the kinds of studies summarized in the last chapter by giving in-depth descriptive analyses of two speech acts: compliments and invitations. Through looking at these studies, we will demonstrate some of the ways in which the study of rules of speaking can not only give us new information about forms and formulas but also provide insights into the norms and values of a speech community. In the chapter to follow, we will show how this material, and other analyses of the same type which were discussed in Chapter 2, can provide information about the interaction process and the situations in which interlocutors negotiate their relationships with one another. In addition, a theory will be put forth concerning overall patterns of interaction within a general middle-class American speech community.

In our discussion, we will continue to use Hymes's terminology, which describes a speech act as the minimal unit of speech that has rules in terms both of where and when they may occur and of what their specific features are. As we have seen, many of these are culturally named acts, such as complaining, apologizing, commanding, advising, scolding, and so on. As we have also seen, some speech acts such as greeting, thanking, and saying good-bye, have at least some rules which are explicitly taught, while others may well have rules or patterns of which native speakers are only partly, and sometimes not at all, aware. In most cases, native speakers are able, if asked, to give forms which they, as members of their speech communities, believe to be the proper ones for carrying out specific speech acts. These forms may or may not be the ones which are used most frequently, or, in fact, at all, in actual speech. What native speakers are even less capable of doing, however, is describing the actual rules for the *use* of these forms and of others which are used to carry out the speech act in question. As we have shown, rules of speaking are often noticed by sociolinguists when they are accidentally broken by a child or a nonnative speaker, or when nonnative speakers comment on them. In cases such as these, the sociolinguistic investigator will begin to collect examples and examine them to see what their features are and what factors seem to be conditioning their use. Thus, once a pattern has been shown to exist, it can be analyzed and described, and the insights gained may be made available to the scholarly community and applied by materials writers, by teachers, and, ultimately, by language learners themselves.

SPEECH BEHAVIOR—SURFACE FORMS AND THE REFLECTION OF CULTURAL VALUES: THE INVESTIGATION OF COMPLIMENTS

To begin with, a speech act or act sequence, whether it be apologizing, thanking, scolding, complimenting, inviting, greeting or parting, or even the telling of a performed story, has important cultural information embedded in it. At the most superficial level, as we have seen, sociolinguistic data, collected systematically and analyzed objectively, can yield information as to what specific formulas and routines are in use in a particular speech community, as well as their patterns of frequency and appropriateness in different speech situations.

An example of the sort of information to be gained by an examination of the surface structure of a speech act is the work on how compliments function in the speech of middle-class native speakers of American English (Pomerantz 1978, Wolfson 1978b, Manes and Wolfson 1981, Wolfson and Manes 1980, Wolfson 1981a, b, Manes 1983, Wolfson 1983b, Knapp et al. 1984, Daikuhara 1986). In their study of compliments, Manes and Wolfson showed that in American English, compliments are so highly patterned that they may be regarded as formulas. That is, although it is not explicitly recognized by native speakers, compliments tend to have clearly definable forms, just as do greetings, apologies or expressions of gratitude.

The analysis of compliments given in Manes and Wolfson (1981) and in Wolfson and Manes (1980) is based on a corpus of well over twelve hundred examples collected in a great variety of everyday speech situations. An ethnographic approach toward the collection of these data made possible a sampling of the speech behavior of men and women of different ages and a wide variety of occupational, educational, and ethnic backgrounds. Thus, the data include compliments given and received by jewelers, hairdressers, clergymen, doctors, and salesclerks. In addition, careful attention was paid to the relationships of the interlocutors, with data collected from such dyads as employers and employees, landlords and tenants, professors and students, classmates, friends, co-workers, and family members. The topics of the compliments collected include personal attributes and possessions, children, pets, accomplishments, and changes in appearance.

Analysis of the syntax of all the compliments collected reveals a regularity not hitherto suspected. Well over 50 percent of all the compliments in the corpus make use of a single syntactic pattern:

1. NP is/looks (really) ADJ (e.g., "Your blouse is beautiful")

Two other syntactic patterns,

2. I (really) like/love NP (e.g., "I like your car")
3. PRO is (really) (a) ADJ NP (e.g., "That's a nice wall hanging")

account for an additional 16.1 percent and 14.9 percent of the data, respectively. As Manes and Wolfson (1981:120-121) say:

> Thus only three patterns are necessary to describe fully 85% of the data. Indeed, only nine patterns occur with any regularity and these account for 97.2% of our data. In addition to the three major patterns already described, we find the following six:
>
> 4. You V (a) (really) ADJ NP. (3.3%) (e.g., "You did a good job.")
> 5. You V (NP) (really) ADV. (2.7%) (e.g., "You really handled that situation well.")
> 6. You have (a) ADJ NP! (2.4%) (e.g., "You have such beautiful hair")
> 7. What (a) ADJ NP! (1.6%) (e.g., "What a lovely baby you have!")
> 8. ADJ NP! (1.6%) (e.g., "Nice game!")
> 9. Isn't NP ADJ! (1.0%) (e.g., "Isn't your ring beautiful!")
>
> No pattern other than those listed above occurs more than twice in our data.

Since nine patterns suffice to account for virtually all of the data and only three patterns account for 85 percent of it, we must conclude that what we have here is a syntactic formula. When we turn to an analysis of the semantic composition of compliments, we see that in this respect as well, compliments exhibit a striking regularity. In order to see just how formulaic the choice of lexical item is, it is necessary to recognize first that compliments fall into two major categories, the adjectival and the verbal, depending on the term which carries the positive evaluation. Of these categories, it is the adjectival which predominates overwhelmingly. What is of interest here is that although the range of semantically positive adjectives is enormous and although some 75 different adjectives occurred in the data, the great majority of adjectival compliments make use of only five different adjectives: *nice, good, beautiful, pretty,* and *great,* with all the rest occurring only once or twice. If we consider the extremely wide privileges of occurrence of these five adjectives (as opposed to such topic specific adjectives as *curly*), it is not surprising that they should prove so frequent. Indeed, the two most commonly used adjectives, *nice* and *good,* are so vague and general that they are equally appropriate when referring to such diverse subjects as hair (e.g., "That's a good haircut"), clothing ("That sweater looks good"), ability ("He's a good actor"), and accomplishments of all sorts (e.g., "Nice shot!" or "Your lecture was good"). That is, because *nice* and *good* lack specificity, they are usable with almost any subject. In present-day American English, the adjective *beautiful* is rapidly approaching the same status. The fact that *pretty* is used more than *great,* which is the more general adjective, seems to reflect the greater than equal number of compliments directed at women in this society.

Of compliments which make use of verbs to carry the positive semantic evaluation, the overwhelming majority have either *like* or *love,* and these two verbs can be applied to virtually any topic from kittens and ice cream to sports, clothing, jewelry, and people. Again, relatively weak semantic load favors frequency; 86 percent of all compliments which rely on a verb for their positive evaluation make use of either *like* or *love.*

Although 96 percent of the data consist of compliments which use semantically positive adjectives and verbs, a few do rely on an adverb, usually *well,* to express the positive evaluation, and an additional few depend on a noun (e.g., "You're just a whiz at sewing"). It is clear, however, that in American English there is an overwhelming tendency for speakers to choose from one of only five adjectives and two verbs to express their positive evaluations. As Manes and Wolfson (1981:123) point out:

> The combination of a restricted semantic set and an even more restricted set of syntactic structures makes it clear that what we are dealing with here is not simply a matter of frequency. Rather, we are forced to recognize that *compliments are formulas,* as much so as thanks and greetings. The speech act of complimenting is, in fact, characterized by the formulaic nature of its syntactic and semantic composition. Compliments are not merely sentences which remark on a particularly attractive item or attribute; they are highly structured formulas which can be adapted with minimal effort to a wide variety of situations in which a favorable comment is required or desired. By substituting the correct noun phrase, "I really like NP" or "NP looks nice" can be appropriately applied to haircuts, homemade bread, shirts, new cars or a job well done.

The compliment formulas found in this analysis will look very familiar to native speakers. However, there is nothing intuitively obvious about the formulas themselves. Native speakers, even those who helped to collect the data, were shocked when the corpus was analyzed and we discovered that the way in which Americans give verbal expression to our approval and appreciation of one another's appearance and accomplishments is largely prepatterned. However, the tendency among middle-class Americans interviewed was to regard compliments as sincere or insincere based on whether or not the compliments were given using recognizable formulas. Thus, most people felt that if the speaker was sincere, the compliment would somehow be original, rather than precoded. The easiest way to demonstrate to native, or, indeed, to nonnative speakers, that sincerity has very little to do with the form or wording of the compliment is to ask them to write down the compliments they hear Americans give to one another, paying close attention to what they say. When even a small amount of such data is collected, it quickly becomes obvious that the vast majority of compliments given by speakers of American English are indeed formulas.

For language learners, teachers, and materials writers, there should be little difficulty in applying the findings described above. The formulaic nature of compliments should, indeed, make this topic particularly amenable to explicit presentation. It should also be pointed out that because compliments are expressions of approval, they necessarily contain valuable information concerning the underlying cultural assumptions of speakers. The occurrence of large numbers of compliments with the same referents allows us to see what is valued by the speech community.

With respect to topic, compliments seem to fall naturally into two general categories: those which focus on appearance and/or possessions, and those which have to do with ability and/or accomplishments. The first category is at once the most simple and the most difficult to characterize. In addition to compliments on apparel, hairstyle, and jewelry, it is not at all unusual for Americans to compliment one another on such seemingly personal matters as weight loss. Being slim has strong positive value among mainstream speakers of American English, and the adjective *thin* (e.g., "You look thin") is interpreted as complimentary in itself in this society. That this is very definitely not the case for speakers from other societies around the world is often a cause of some confusion, and even insult, when nonnative speakers are the recipients of such remarks. Favorable comments on the attractiveness of one's children, pets, and even husbands, boyfriends, wives, or girlfriends seem to fall within this same category, as do compliments on cars and houses.

The second category of compliments, that which has to do with ability or accomplishment (e.g., "You're so efficient!" or "Nice job!"), seem on the surface to be rather straightforward. It is only when we take sex as an independent sociolinguistic variable and look at the kinds of compliments women receive and what this reflects about our society that the line between the two categories seems to break down. We will discuss this finding further in the chapter which deals with language and sex.

We have relatively little information regarding ways in which nonnative speakers experience difficulties regarding the rules for the giving and the interpreting of compliments in American English. We do know that one very important problem area is that of knowing which kinds of compliments are appropriate in which speech situations. Here the issue has to do with both the role and the relative status of the participants in the interaction, as these interact with the topic of the compliment. In this respect, compliments on appearance and possessions appear to be more generally acceptable than those which involve a judgment of another's ability. Almost anyone in our society feels free to offer a compliment on an item of jewelry or on a car, for example, and it is not unusual for a waitress or a cashier who is a total stranger to a customer to comment favorably on a possession such as a ring or a pin, especially when the recipient of the compliment is a female (which is most often the case).

The situation with regard to comments on ability, however, is very different. Although it is frequently assumed that people in a lower-status position use compliments for the purpose of ingratiating themselves and gaining favorable treatment, the data suggest that the reverse is true. That is, it is the person in the higher position, especially in a continuing relationship, who regularly uses compliments as positive reinforcement. When we consider the implications of complimenting another on ability, it is not difficult to see why this should be the case. An ability/performance compliment is a serious judgment, and the person who makes it must be seen as a competent judge. In situations of unequal status, especially those which are work-related, the competence to judge goes hand in hand with superior skill or knowledge. Further, there appears to be an implicit rule against expressing judgments about one's superiors, at least directly. Just exactly the opposite rule applies when status is reversed; the speaker of higher status is expected, and even required, to judge the work of subordinates.

By far the greatest number of compliments involve interlocutors of equal status. Interestingly enough, however, intimacy does not favor frequency of complimenting. Indeed, among family members and housemates we found relatively few compliments. Those which we did find often served to soften a scolding or to replace thanks. It is noteworthy, for example, that there appears to be a constraint against thanking someone with whom you share a house (family or not) for performing a service which benefits all. A husband does not normally thank his wife for cooking (though in these days of working wives, it may well be that a wife does thank her husband for performing this service); a housemate does not normally thank another for marketing or cleaning or taking out the trash. What people do instead in these cases is to offer a compliment as a sign of appreciation.

By far the greatest number of appearance/possession compliments are given and received by acquaintances, colleagues, and casual friends. And although it would be misleading to suggest that compliments are actually required in American society, it is nevertheless the case that they are strongly expected in some speech situations. It is useful for nonnative speakers to know, for example, that the quality of newness is so highly valued in this society that a compliment is appropriate whenever an acquaintance is seen with something new, whether it is a car, a new article of clothing, or a haircut. The fact that the new appearance may be due to an alteration (such as a new hairstyle or the loss of weight) as well as to a purchase leads us to conclude that the true importance of the comment lies in the speaker's having noticed a change, thereby proving that he or she considers the addressee worthy of attention.

In her study of compliment responses, Pomerantz (1978) takes note of a different sort of cultural value at work in the compliment/response sequence. Thus, although the preferred behavior (according to informants' stated norms) is for the recipient of a compliment to accept it with what Pomerantz calls an appreciation (thanks), this conflicts with another norm, or what she calls "the self-praise avoidance" constraint. For this reason, she says, it frequently happens that speakers will downgrade the compliment by praising the same referent in weaker terms or by shifting the credit away from themselves. This shift is an important technique, occurring rather frequently in the Manes and Wolfson corpus as well. Thus, Pomerantz gives the example:

F: This is beautiful.
K: . . . 'N that nice.
R: Yah. It really is.
K: It wove itself. Once it was set up.

and from the Manes and Wolfson corpus, we have:

S: This is beautiful. I've been admiring it since I came in.
A: It's from Israel.

and:

S: Boy, that's nice work. I don't know how you do it.
A: It's easy when you have good tools.

or:

S: That's a pretty sweater.
A: My mother gave it to me.

Another very frequent response to a compliment is to return it. Pomerantz points out that this is most frequent in "openings and closings of interactions." For example, in an opening:

S: Yr lookin good.
A: Great, S'r you.

On the other hand, Pomerantz also points out that thanks, or what she terms appreciations, are usually used to respond to compliments "when the parties are asymmetrically related to the referents of the compliments"—that is, when compliments cannot be exchanged because the referent is a belonging, attribute, or accomplishment of the addressee and the speaker has no equivalent object on which a compliment can be focused.

From the point of view of the language learner, it is important to know that simple appreciations are virtually always appropriate as compliment responses but that what Pomerantz calls "the self-praise avoidance" constraint will often lead the addressee of a compliment to downgrade it or to shift credit or even to disagree with the speaker, although this last is much less frequent and usually restricted to interactions between intimates. From ethnographic observation and interviewing of foreign students residing in the United States, we know that not only are compliments less frequent in most other societies but also the responses considered appropriate are somewhat different. This is especially connected to the issue of disagreeing with the compliment, and even vigorously denying its truth.

Clearly, the status and the relationship between speaker and addressee is a critical factor in the selection of a response type. From the Wolfson and Manes data it appears that the self-praise avoidance solutions discussed by Pomerantz are used primarily with intimates or with casual friends in this society, situations in which the relationship between speaker and addressee is symmetrical. In speech situations in which compliments are given by persons of higher status than the addressee, the safest and most appropriate response is a simple "thank you."

Another significant finding, mentioned by Wolfson (1978b) and elaborated by Manes (1983), is that in downgrading compliments, responses by speakers of American English rarely deny that the recipient has the quality mentioned. Rather, another quality, also deeply valued by the culture, is downgraded or denied, saving addressees from directly contradicting speakers and at the same time giving them the opportunity to make little of the attribute or object being praised. Thus, when speakers are complimented on an attractive article of clothing, they will not usually deny that the article is attractive or even suggest that it might be less attractive than the speaker has said. Rather, they will downgrade the compliment by invoking a value other than attractiveness—for example, newness or costliness—and, by responding that the article is either old or that it was bought for very little money (e.g., "I got it on sale"), indicate that the object is less valuable than might be thought. In this respect, compliment responses in American English are rather different from those which are appropriate in some other speech communities where the very quality being complimented may be denied. In response to a compliment on the beauty of a house, therefore, an American might say, "Well, we would have liked to have a bigger one" or "We wish the neighborhood were quieter," but Americans would be very unlikely to suggest that the speaker was wrong and that the house was not beautiful at all.

In discussing both giving and responding to compliments, it is important to stress that the findings presented here relate specifically to middle-class speakers of American English. The patterns described here, like all other sociolinguistic patterns, must be expected to vary across speech communities. We should not expect the specific formulas or frequencies with which various ones are used by speakers of American English to be matched precisely by those used, for example, by British speakers, though it has been observed that a very similar set of formulas does exist for them. What counts as a compliment will differ from society to society, making interpretation of speaker intentions extremely difficult at times. Even where societies have rather similar value systems, differences will occur, and it is here that the most serious misunderstandings are likely to be found. Thus, some of the comments that speakers of American English regularly accept as compliments could seem very insulting to someone who understood the words but not the rules for interpreting them. For example, we have compliments in which the speaker, in saying that the addressee looks unusually well, implies that the reverse is usually the case. Thus, two men meet at an elevator and one says to the other, "Hey, what's the occasion? You look really nice today." Or two friends meet and one greets the other by exclaiming, "Wow! Linda! What did you do to your hair? I almost didn't recognize you. It looks great."

Indeed, this sort of compliment, immediately recognizable to any native speaker of American English by its intonational contour, has more than once been perceived as a serious insult by a nonnative speaker who was unfamiliar with the meaning of the intonation and who could only interpret the words by their literal meaning.

The frequency and distribution of compliments given by speakers of American English are, as we have said, open to misinterpretation. In American society, compliments occur in a very wide variety of situations and are quite frequent even among strangers. It is not uncommon to hear nonnative speakers remark on what is perceived as excessive use of compliments, or comment on their seeming insincerity, especially when they express approval of something not held in particular esteem by their own native speech communities.

Thus we see that not only can an in-depth study of a speech act yield information concerning its patterns and appropriate usage, but, as in the case of compliments, some of the richest insights into cultural values can be gained by analysis of the judgments people express. If we look at the compliments speakers give, we discover what values are made explicit through the expression of admiration and approval. For example, when we see that again and again, in the data collected by observation of middle-class native speakers of standard American English, compliments are given on objects that are new, and even on appearance that has changed, we can say with some evidence from actual speech behavior that Americans seem to value newness. When we see, in one compliment after another, that speakers of American English compliment one another on looking thin or on losing weight, it is not difficult to come to the conclusion that Americans, unlike many other cultural groups, regard thinness as a positive attribute. If we look at a large range of compliments collected from naturally occurring speech, we see that what is common to all is that in one form or another, compliments are directed toward achievement. As we have seen, the manifestation of achievement may reside in the ability or the good taste or the wherewithal to effect positive change in one's appearance or to purchase new items. In other cases, it may have to do with the kind of family or friends one has or with a particular act well done. We could go on and on listing the cultural assumptions implicit in the compliments which have been collected from the spontaneous speech of native speakers of American English and, indeed, Manes (1983) has given a detailed account of just this means by which values are reflected. The point here is that by looking at what is complimented, we can come to some reasonable conclusions as to what is valued in the society in question. What is important for the purposes of this argument is that all this information, so valuable to nonnative speakers, is embedded in the speech acts themselves.

THE UNRECOGNIZED NEED FOR
NEGOTIATION: A LOOK AT INVITATIONS

The lack of recognition by native speakers of their own speech patterns is particularly obvious when we begin to deal with situations in which social negotiation is the key to successful interaction.

A case in point is a study of invitations as they are given by speakers of middle-class American English (Wolfson 1979b, Wolfson et al. 1983). The knowledge of how to give, interpret, and respond to invitations is an aspect of communicative competence which is critical to those who wish to interact socially. This is particularly important to nonnative speakers who are learning English as a foreign language in the host speech community. As Hatch (1978) has pointed out, the language learner is most likely to do best when given frequent opportunities to interact with native speakers. In order for any but the most formal or superficial interactions to take place, social arrangements of one sort or another need to be made somehow, and, among middle-class Americans, the extending of invitations is a principle means of accomplishing this. Since, as we have already pointed out, speech communities around the world vary greatly with regard to the rules which constrain speech behavior, it is clear that nonnative speakers cannot hope to interact effectively in the target language speech community unless they learn its rules. In this case, the rules for the appropriate management of invitations are, like so many other aspects of communicative competence, well below the level of conscious awareness of speakers. Thus, the only way that the rules for giving and responding to invitations among speakers of American English can be analyzed and made available to language learners is through empirically based descriptive analysis.

The data upon which the study of invitations was based were collected through participant observation of everyday interactions among a great variety of native speakers. Not only were invitations and responses recorded, but as much information as possible was gathered concerning the age, gender, occupation, and, perhaps most important, relationship of the interlocutors involved in these invitation exchanges. Since relationship of interlocutors has been shown in study after study to be so critical to what is said and how it is said and responded to, it will be useful to digress slightly in order to elaborate on this point. What is meant by relationship is very complex, and not always open to casual observation—a good reason for including, as much as possible, examples of the speech behavior of those with whom one has some knowledge or acquaintance. In my own research, I have found it most useful to begin by viewing the relationship of interlocutors on a continuum of social distance from intimates to strangers. Clearly, this is only a beginning and can be refined to the degree necessary. What, for example, constitutes intimacy? Membership in a nuclear family is one possible feature, but even here we are faced with the undeniable fact that the relationship between husband and wife is very different from that between parent and child or between siblings. Close friendship falls at the intimate end of the continuum in that there is a minimum of social distance in such relationships. Still, it is important to see the social distance continuum in terms of ranges and not of discrete points. It must also be recognized that social distance is merely a cover term and that there are many features that interact with it, such as age, sex, ethnic background, and relative status. People who are in asymmetrical status relationships with one another may be viewed as being within the minimum range of the social distance continuum, and, at the extreme end, we have people who may interact with one another in service encounters and such but who are, in fact, complete strangers.

With this picture of varying degrees of social distance in mind, we can now return to the findings regarding the way invitations are managed among middle-class speakers of American English.

According to popular wisdom, social commitments are normally arrived at through unambiguous invitations. Our operational definition of such a speech act is that it contains reference to time and/or mention of place or activity, and, most important, a request for a response. A simple example would be the following:

DO YOU WANT	TO HAVE LUNCH	TOMORROW?
(request for response)	(activity)	(time)

According to our data, the request for response can come before or after the mention of time or activity. As with most conversational interaction, it is also true that context frequently substitutes for words in giving some of the information to be communicated. This, combined with the fact that the request for response can be signaled by question intonation alone, makes it possible for speakers to utter invitations which are no longer than a single word and yet be perfectly understood.

In the data, an example occurs in which, as part of a leave-taking sequence, a woman said to a close friend, "Saturday?" Since it was well known to both participants in this interaction that this single utterance referred to the fact that the two women and their husbands were in the habit of spending most Saturday evenings together, the single-word question was enough to convey the speaker's wish to confirm a date for the following Saturday. In this case, the context and the shared knowledge of the interlocutors, as well as the question intonation, supplied the information which words might otherwise have done. Among intimates, where a great deal of contextual knowledge is shared, single utterances such as the one given above, are not at all uncommon. To the nonnative speaker, or even to the native speaker who has only intuitions and norms of usage to refer to, such truncated invitations may, on the surface, seem hardly to qualify as speech acts; yet they contain all the information necessary to perform the function intended and must therefore be seen as a minimal invitation form.

Another such example occurs in our data in a situation where a friend and colleague of the addressee opened the door to her office at noon one day, leaned into the room to make eye contact with her, and asked "Lunch?" As in the first case of this type exemplified above, the interlocutors in this exchange are friends who frequently interact socially. Nevertheless, the question must be interpreted as an invitation because it is not the case that these two people always do eat together at noon or that they had had previous plans to do so that day.

What has been given above so far are obviously minimal forms. What is particularly significant about invitations, however, is that, contrary to the stated norms of native speakers, the sort of unambiguous invitations which we have defined and illustrated are not the most common form in which invitations occur in the actual usage of middle-class Americans. This finding is especially important from the point of view of the ability of nonnative speakers to interpret what they hear as an invitation. Here it is critical to be aware that fewer than one-third of all the invitations in the data collected by Wolfson et al. (1983) were of this minimal type. What we found instead was that the vast majority of social engagements are arrived at by a process of negotiation whereby the interlocutors move step by step, turn by turn, until a social commitment has been reached. The linguistic material which constitutes the beginning or opening of such a sequence, a statement or question that we have termed *the lead*, may be seen as a definable discourse segment. The lead is the question or comment which signals the addressee that an invitation will follow if he or she makes the appropriate responses. If we characterize them by function, leads are of three types. The first type of lead is the most obvious in terms of letting the addressee know what can be expected to follow. This beginning to a sequence clearly functions to establish the *availability* of the addressee. Here the speaker may either utter a question/statement which is meant to elicit the desired information, such as (1) "Are you doing anything on the 28th?" Or, a question can be posed which seeks specific information about an addressee's availability at a particular time, such as (2) "What are you doing Saturday night?" (3) "What's your schedule tomorrow?"

The second type of lead is much less obviously the beginning of an invitation sequence; it may be described or labeled *expressive* because it is intended to convey the feelings of speakers without any specific commitment. (4) "I'd really like to have a chance to sit down and talk with you" or (5) "It's really horrible that we never see each other" or (6) "You know, X, we're gonna have to get together for lunch one of these days." This second type of lead is so vague that most native speakers would hesitate to characterize it as a lead at all. Nevertheless, this type of expressive lead is extremely common and, as we will see, is very likely to begin a sequence which will end with a definite invitation being worked out.

The third and final type of lead, referred to as the *past tie,* is related to some shared knowledge of a past attempt to negotiate a social arrangement by the participants in the interaction or by someone closely associated who is not present at the moment of speaking: (7) "Did we decide on anything specific?" or (8) "Are we going to have lunch still?" In this way, it is possible for interlocutors to refer to some previous discussion which did not end in a completed invitation, while still leaving the matter open for further negotiation and a possible refusal by the addressee.

Of the three types of invitation leads we have just illustrated, the type we have labeled *expressive* (those sharing speaker feelings with the addressee and hinting at a social engagement in a rather vague way) are much more numerous than our intuitions had led us to expect. Of these, the pattern which occurred most frequently in the data was the following: I'd (really) like/love to VP (e.g., "I'd really like to make a date with you to have lunch and talk things over"). An example of the way this pattern is followed by a negotiation which turns into a successful social commitment is the following:

> s: I'd really like to make a date with you to have lunch and talk things over.
> A: Fine, when are you free?
> s: How about Monday?
> A: I'm trying not to come in on Monday. I'm free on Thursday.
> s: Okay, but it has to be after one.
> A: Okay with me. I don't teach on Thursday.
> s: One-fifteen?
> A: Fine. I'll write it down.
> s: Good. We have a lot to catch up on.

Whether it falls into the category of expressive leads or is used to determine availability, to refer to a past tie, or simply to reaffirm a relationship by suggesting a future meeting, a lead will normally contain at least one of the components of an unambiguous invitation—reference to time and/or mention of place or activity, and a request for a response. Thus, the lead may mention only time, as in many of the availability leads, or there may be mention of a place or of an activity, however indefinite:

"Did you know that A's is having a big sale right now?"

"I'm going to call Paula and Don and we'll all get together at my house, okay?"

"You should come down on a Thursday before your class."

"I'd like you to come out here and spend the day with us soon. Bring your bathing suit and we'll have lunch outside."

As we saw in the example given above of a fully and successfully negotiated sequence, interlocutors will very frequently move turn by turn to complete the set of components necessary to produce a full invitation. In this way, leads and the set of responses and counter-responses which follow them are linked by discourse rules such that together they form what any native speaker would unambiguously identify as an invitation. Some examples of the completion of a lead into a full invitation are the following:

> s: Will you finish your exam tonight?
> A: I'd like to. I think I will.
> s: Have you seen "The Competition?"

    A: No, I haven't.
    s: We should go.

or:

    s: We should get together. Why don't we get together sometime this
       week?
    A: Yeah, I'd like to, but I don't know . . .
    s: Why don't we get together at O'Hara's or somewhere on Thursday
       night?

Unambiguous invitations are not necessarily preceded by leads. What is of particular interest in the study of invitations as part of American speech behavior, however, is that not only may invitations occur with leads but leads may occur without invitations. That is, it is perfectly possible, and, indeed, quite frequent, to find that speakers express the desirability and even the necessity of arranging a social commitment. These expressions, however, are not necessarily followed by the conclusion of the arrangements under discussion, and it is a moot point as to whether such commitments were ever intended to be completed. Some of these leads without invitations have become so commonly used that they have gained the status of formulas. They are immediately recognizable to the native speaker by the following features: (1) Time is always left indefinite. (2) A response is not required. There is no yes/no question. (3) A modal auxiliary such as "must" or "should" or "have to" is almost always used.

The cues that allow native speakers to recognize leads which are unlikely to continue to the point of fulfillment are time expressions like "soon," "one day," or "sometime," and any of the indefinite phrases beginning with "when" (e.g., "Let's have lunch together when things settle down"). These often appear to the native speaker in the light of a polite brush-off, a way of expressing interest in continuing the relationship without making any definite commitment for a future meeting. However, as we will see, this is not necessarily so. Other cues of this sort are the very words and phrases that a learner might reasonably expect to carry the most illocutionary force: words like *definitely* (e.g., "Let's definitely get together") serve as further indications to the communicatively competent native speaker that the lead may well *not* be followed up.

In order to appreciate the role of the lead in middle-class American social interaction, it must be understood by the nonnative speaker that most urban Americans belong not to one social group or network whose members interact constantly in the neighborhood, on the job, at church functions, and in places of amusement, but rather to a series of such groups, each connected with certain aspects of their lives. These groups are frequently nonoverlapping, so that the individual tends to interact with a great variety of people, many of whom do not themselves come into contact or even know of each other's existence. It often happens that an individual, for one reason or another, moves into or out of some of these groups. It is very difficult to keep up with old friends and acquaintances, however much one might wish to do so. It often happens, however, that a situation arises in which people who have lost touch with one another are brought together. Friends and relatives may meet by chance at parties, stores, or even on street corners. It is usual for a conversation to ensue, and often a nostalgic wish for a renewal of the relationship is aroused and expressed. Neither participant regards this sort of expression as a binding invitation for a firm future commitment, although interlocutors may go to considerable trouble to compare their schedules as a preliminary to fixing an actual date. Here we come very close to the negotiation which could lead to a true social commitment, but in the end, none is made. An example of this sort of aborted attempt follows:

s: It's really horrible that we never see each other.
a: I know. We have to try to arrange something.
s: How about dinner? Why don't we go out to dinner together?
a: That's a good idea.
s: What days are good for you and Joe?
a: Weekends are best.
s: Oh, weekends are bad for us. Don't you ever go out to dinner during the week?
a: Well, we do, but we usually don't make plans till the last minute. Joe gets home late a lot and I never know what his schedule is going to be.
s: Okay, well, look, why don't you call me when you want to go out. Any week night is good.
a: Okay, I will.
s: Really! Don't forget.
a: Okay, I won't. I'll call you.

Thus, it often happens that a lead, though seemingly (and very probably actually) welcomed by the addressee, never develops beyond the talking stage. Just as frequently, however, such a social overture does indeed lead to a firm plan for a social engagement. The sincerity with which such negotiations are pursued may obscure the inconclusive outcome of the interaction and lead a nonnative speaker to suppose that an actual invitation has been given and thus, by analogy, to categorize all tentative expressions of this sort as invitations. Misunderstandings are inevitable. It is, for this reason, essential that nonnative speakers learning English in order to use it with native speakers in the United States learn that in this society, a speaker who suggests a social meeting without including a specific time is simply making a first move in a negotiation which may never go further than the talking stage. If the addressee wishes to respond to such an opening in a way which will lead to a firm commitment, he or she must learn to become an active participant in the actual construction of the invitation. Leaving it all to the first speaker will most often result in no commitment being reached.

One very important insight to be gained from the findings concerning the way native speakers of American English go about working out their social commitments is that in choosing to negotiate their future social arrangements, they are spared the necessity of exposing themselves to possible rejection. Thus, the fact that social arrangements in this society are so frequently arrived at through the active participation of both interlocutors may lead to some important revelations. Far from being insincere or unfriendly, it might well be the case that many Americans, however informal and seemingly open their interactional style, are in reality quite hesitant to put themselves in a position to be refused. An invitation is, after all, a request for another's time and, very often, for a closer social relationship. If Americans so often prefer to arrive at a social arrangement through the mutual effort of a negotiation, this may well say something extremely revealing about Americans.

CONCLUSION

The aim of the research presented in this chapter has been to uncover and describe patterns of speech behavior in American English which are a part of the communicative competence of every native speaker. In the next chapter, we will look at the implications of such findings for a deeper understanding of the dynamics of social interaction and the implications of such findings to students who wish to be able not only to speak grammatically but to interpret what they hear and to interact effectively with members of mainstream American society.

CHAPTER
6

Speech Behavior and Social Dynamics

INTRODUCTION

The purpose of this chapter is twofold. First, I will discuss ways in which the study of rules of speaking can provide information about the interaction process and the situations in which interlocutors negotiate their relationships with one another. Second, I will put forth a theory of my own concerning the way interaction is patterned within the general middle-class American speech community.

The choice of looking at speech behavior in the researcher's own speech community should be understood to be purposeful and critical to the analysis. As Schneider (1968:vi) points out in the preface to his book on American kinship, the insights one has into one's native language and into the behavior within one's own speech community permits a level of analysis which is far deeper than that which can be reached in other field sites:

> There is another reason why the study of kinship in America is especially important to Americans and that is that as Americans, this is a society and a culture which we know well. We speak the language fluently, we know the customs, and we have observed the natives in their daily lives. Indeed, we *are* the natives. Hence we are in an especially good position to keep the facts and the theory in their most productive relationship. We can monitor the interplay between fact and theory where American kinship is concerned in ways that are simply impossible in the ordinary course of anthropological work. When we read about kinship in some society foreign to our own we have only the facts which the author chooses to present to us, and we usually have no independent source of knowledge against which we can check his facts. . . . By the same token of course we are able to achieve a degree of control over a large body of data which many anthropological fieldworkers hardly approach, even after one or two years in the field. Hence the quality of the data we control is considerably greater, and the grounds for evaluating the fit between fact and theory is correspondingly greater. (Schneider 1968: iv)

The issue of evaluation by other researchers, who are themselves members of the speech community under analysis, is of great importance here. Much of what the researcher brings to light about the speech behavior of the community in question and what it reflects about the value system and the social structure of that community, may be new in the sense that it has not been noticed or subjected to critical analysis from the perspective of the social scientist. Nevertheless, once an analysis of one's own group has been made, it is open to the evaluation of other social scientists who may also be members of the same community and who therefore have the means of examining and evaluating what has been analyzed through their own observations and intuitions.

One further issue concerning the choice of studying the behavior of middle-class speakers of American English needs to be examined here. This is that the unit of analysis which I refer to as "middle-class speakers of American English" is necessarily circular. As mentioned earlier, in my opinion, the most useful definition of speech community is that given by Hymes (1972b): "Tentatively, a speech community is defined as a community sharing rules for the conduct and interpretation of speech, and rules for the interpretation of at least one linguistic variety. Both conditions are necessary."

A major point to be remembered is that not all speakers of a language do share the same rules of speaking, and therefore, not all may be said to belong to the same speech community. In defining and using the analytical unit which we call a speech community, we have pointed out the need to recognize that speakers of a single language often constitute many different speech communities, each with their own norms and rules of speaking. Where speech community may be said to correspond to geographical area, this fact is relatively easy to deal with. The English-speaking world, for example, is made up of a large number of speech communities, composed of both native and nonnative speakers. Even where boundaries may be said to coincide with territory which is politically or geographically or even socially defined, the situation is extremely complex. Nevertheless, it is possible to say, without doing too much violence to the facts or to the feelings of those being spoken of, that the British and the Australians differ sharply from the Americans in many aspects of linguistic usage although all three nations have English as their dominant language. Further, people who have lived in more than one English-speaking country, or who have interacted extensively with people from other English-speaking nations, know that pronunciation, grammar, and lexicon are not the only features that differentiate one set of speakers from another. Norms and values differ and so too do rules of speaking. Even within political and geographic boundaries, it is typical to have a great variety of smaller social groupings, and these are much less easy to define. For this reason, as was pointed out earlier, it is unrealistic to speak of investigating the rules of speaking for English, or indeed, most other languages. Depending on the group studied, the rules are likely to vary. This, of course, leads to some extremely difficult questions. If a speech community is to be defined by shared rules, and if these rules are largely unanalyzed and also, very importantly, unavailable to the conscious knowledge of native speakers, where do we begin? Even where we notice patterns of usage, how can we tell how far they extend? The most straightforward answer is to focus on groups which have some sort of pre-

existing definition apart from speech behavior. A group which shares a particular
territorial space and whose members interact frequently has been called a primary
network. It may reasonably be expected that rules of speaking will be shared within
such a group (see Milroy 1980, for example) since interaction is maximal, and
people often function in many different roles vis-à-vis one another (on the job, at
church, in the neighborhood, etc.). If, however, our concern is to describe the
speech behavior or rules of speaking which obtain across such subgroups and which
have a wide enough frame of reference to be useful to such applications as language
teaching and learning, then we are faced with an inescapable circularity in the
definition of our object of study. That is, a speech community is defined as a group
which shares rules for the use and interpretation of speech, but there may be no
predefined feature external to speech which can be used as a criterion of membership. Furthermore, when the language under consideration is, like English, that of a
number of complex, highly industrialized societies, each composed of a great
number of subgroups, the notion of speech community must be used at a level of
abstraction which ignores many subtle distinctions.

For this reason, in our discussions of the usage of middle-class speakers of
American English, we are forced, for heuristic purposes, to treat them as a speech
community. That is, we must, if we wish to make the kinds of generalizations
which could be useful to language learners, do our best to investigate what the
various subgroups in this category have in common. This does not mean that we
wish to ignore differences in norms and values and speech behavior which stem
from, for example, regional or ethnic identities, but rather that we will take such
distinctions into account as factors in the analysis. In this respect, it is extremely
useful to see what Goffman says in the preface to his book, *Relations in Public :*

> So the problem is not merely that of having to make statements about groups
> and communities without sufficient data, but that of not knowing very much
> about the identity and boundaries of the groupings about which there are insuffi-
> cient data. I employ the term "our" but do so knowing that in regard to small
> behaviors the "our" cannot be conventionally or conveniently specified. I can
> with least lack of confidence make assertions about my "own" cultural group,
> the one with which I have had the most first-hand experience, but I do not know
> what to call this grouping, what its full span or distribution is, how far back it
> goes in time, nor how these dimensions might have to be changed, according to
> the particular bit of familiar behavior under question. (Goffman 1971)

Keeping these reservations in mind, it is the purpose of this chapter to attempt
to cast light on the speech behavior of the present-day American urban middle class,
and what this behavior reflects about the structure of this society. As always, I draw
heavily upon Hymes's theoretical position for inspiration and encouragement. In
undertaking the analysis to be described below, it is important to recognize that
Hymes himself sees this aspect of sociolinguistic work as central to the entire
endeavor. As he himself puts it: "The most novel and difficult contribution of

sociolinguistic description must be to identify the rules, patterns, purposes, and consequences of language use, and to account for their interrelations. In doing so it will not only discover structural relations among sociolinguistic components, but disclose new relationships among features of the linguistic code itself" (Hymes 1974a:75).

SPEECH BEHAVIOR AND NEGOTIATION OF ROLES

An important way in which sociocultural insights may be gained through the study of rules of speaking is to focus on the way the social identities of interlocutors vis-à-vis one another condition what is said. Here it is useful to take two different, though overlapping perspectives. On the one hand, by looking to see who has the right or the obligation to invite, compliment, or scold, and who has the obligation to greet, thank, or apologize, we can learn a great deal about how the society is structured.

On the other hand, if we examine the relationship of speech act form, or degree of elaboration used, to the identity of the interlocutors, we can often get at something much more subtle and difficult to characterize—the social strategies people in a given speech community use to accomplish their purposes—to gain cooperation, to form friendships, and to keep their world running smoothly.

When we look first at the way what is said reflects cultural values, it is immediately apparent that not all speech acts are equally informative. The most useful in this regard are, like compliments, thanks and apologies, of a type that involve a specific topic and that make an implicit or explicit judgment. Speakers compliment one another on belongings or appearance or performance; they thank or apologize for an action. The topics of these speech acts are not necessarily stated explicitly, but they must at least be understood so that they can be inferred from the context. At the other end of the speech act spectrum, we have greetings and partings, which are spoken specifically to mark beginnings and ends, openings and closings of encounters, and which do not necessarily contain evidence of cultural values in themselves. Between the two, we have invitations, which, like greetings, focus on social interaction in and of itself. Because they have to do with planning and commitment to specific activities, invitations do often give us information about the kinds of social events that different groups within the community are likely to participate in, and even about which kinds of activities are planned as opposed to spontaneous or taken for granted.

In some speech communities, for example, it is normal practice for friends, family, and neighbors (who may, in fact, be the same people) to visit or even to turn up for a meal or a weekend or several weeks' stay without any announcement at all and certainly with no explicit invitation. That is, in such communities, it is part of the obligations of people in certain role relationships to extend hospitality to one another for any length of time and under virtually any circumstances (Ayorinde

Dada, personal communication). In other speech communities, specifically large complex urban communities, even a short visit to the home of another member of the family or to a close friend requires an invitation or, at the minimum, a telephoned self-invitation. Clearly, the kinds of invitations which the researcher might collect in two such different speech communities would be very different in kind and in distribution.

If we use this same body of data and focus on the social identities of participants, rather different insights are likely to emerge. In this respect, speech acts of all types appear to be equally informative. Thus, if we are interested in analyzing what the rights, obligations, and privileges of speakers are vis-à-vis one another, or of who engages in which speech acts with whom and in which situations, we can probably learn as much from studying greetings, partings, and invitations as we can from analyzing thanks, apologies, and compliments. And most revealing of all, if we examine the forms people use spontaneously with different interlocutors, we frequently find that the degree of elaboration corresponds not only to speakers' roles and expectations but also to the manipulation of roles and to the formation or reaffirmation of relationships.

A female customer in a busy department store, for example, may, in order to gain the attention and service of a saleswoman, step out of her role as customer and engage in a friendly chat, signaling solidarity of age and sex, and the difficulties they share as working mothers.

THE BULGE: A THEORY OF SOCIAL INTERACTION

A case in point is a consistent finding of mine that there is a qualitative difference between the speech behavior which middle-class Americans use to intimates, status unequals, and strangers on the one hand, and to nonintimates, status-equal friends, co-workers, and acquaintances on the other. I call this theory the *Bulge* (Wolfson 1986, 1988), because of the way the frequencies of certain types of speech behavior plot out on a diagram, with the two extremes showing very similar patterns, as opposed to the middle section, which displays a characteristic bulge. That is, when we examine the ways in which different speech acts are realized in actual everyday speech, and when we compare these behaviors in terms of the social relationships of the interlocutors, we find again and again that the two extremes of social distance—minimum and maximum—seem to call forth very similar behavior, while relationships which are more toward the center show marked differences.

On the face of it, this may seem strange and even counterintuitive. What do intimates, status unequals, and strangers have in common that nonintimates, status-equal friends, co-workers, and acquaintances do not share, and what does the last-mentioned group have in common with the first? Why should strangers and status unequals behave to one another in ways that resemble the interaction found among intimates, but which is in sharp contrast to that found to occur in the speech of the second group, which includes peers. The explanation lies, very simply, in the relative certainty of the first relationships in contrast to the instability of the second. Put in other terms, the more status and social distance are seen as fixed, the easier it is for speakers to know what to expect of one another. In a complex urban society in which speakers may belong to a variety of nonoverlapping networks, relationships among speakers are often uncertain. On the other hand, these relationships are dynamic, and open to negotiation. There is freedom here but not security. The emergent and relatively insecure nature of such relationships is reflected in the care people take to signal solidarity (Brown and Gilman 1960) and to avoid confrontation (D'Amico-Reisner 1985).

For example, although compliments are exchanged between intimates and between total strangers, the great majority (the Bulge) occur, as was pointed out in Chapter 3, in interactions between speakers who are neither. This is a question of frequencies and not of absolutes. Compliments do, of course, occur in interactions between interlocutors who are intimates, status unequals, or even strangers. In fact, compliments on performance are often very important in the relationship of boss to employee or teacher to student (see Wolfson 1983a). Where the compliment has to do with appearance, sex is the major variable, overriding status in virtually all cases. This in itself is a revealing finding since it relates directly to the position of women in American society and touches on sociocultural expectations of a very different sort (Wolfson 1984). We will discuss this finding regarding the way sex interacts with the rules for the giving of compliments in the chapter which deals specifically with the issue of language and gender. For the purposes of this discussion, we will draw on analyses of data from several English-speaking communities to show that the social dynamics of complimenting behavior may interact with gender in critical ways. Although the question of sex-related differences is still under investigation, we can say with considerable confidence that of all compliments, no matter what else may be true of them, the great majority occur between status equals among whom the potential for lessening of social distance exists.

The data on invitations is even more striking in this regard. With respect to this speech act, we have described in Chapter 3 how the data collected from spontaneous interactions fell into two categories (Wolfson 1981b; Wolfson et al. 1983). The first consisted of unambiguous, complete invitations giving time, place, or activity and a request for response. These unambiguous invitations occurred most frequently between intimates and between status unequals—the two sets of interlocutors whose relationships with the speaker were at the extremes of social distance. The second category of invitations consisted of ambiguous or incomplete references to the possibility of future social commitments. Once a large body of data had been collected, it was possible to recognize these so-called invitations as "leads." Utterances such as "We really must get together sometime" or "Let's have lunch together soon" are typical examples. But in order for a social commitment to result from a lead, it was nearly always the case that both parties to the interaction took part in negotiating the arrangement. And what was particularly significant about these leads was that they occurred between status-equal nonintimates—that is, between speakers whose relationships are most open to redefinition. As was explained earlier, the data showed that inequality of status favors unambiguous invitations and disfavors attempts at negotiation, and that the same is true of intimacy. What inequality of status and intimacy have in common is that in both situations, interlocutors know exactly where they stand with one another. In contrast, speakers whose relationship is more ambiguous tend to avoid direct invitations, with their inherent risk of rejection, and instead negotiate with one another in a mutual back-and-forth progression which, if successful, will lead to a social commitment. To illustrate the difference between the two types of interactions, we have some additional examples. Again we will use the convention established earlier in which the speaker is labeled "S" and the addressee is called "A":

1. The unambiguous invitation:
    s: Do you want to have lunch tomorrow?
    a: Okay, as long as I'm back by one-thirty.
2. The negotiated social arrangement:
    s: You doing anything exciting this weekend?
    a: No, I'll be around the pool here.
    s: Okay, I'll see you.
    a: Maybe we'll barbeque one night.
    s: Okay, that's a nice idea. I'm tied up Sunday night.
    a: All right. We'll keep it loose.
S begins to walk away and then turns and walks back, saying:
    s: We're supposed to do something with Helen tomorrow night. Want to do something with us?
    a: Okay. Let us know.

During the time I was working on the analysis of invitations, I was struck by the fact that Americans seemed, from my observations, hesitant to put themselves in a position to be refused and therefore prefer to arrive at a social arrangement through the mutual effort of a negotiation (Wolfson 1981b).

Since the publication of this early work on invitations, studies of other speech acts have uncovered similar patterns. Thus, the findings of work on I did in a seminar on the speech sequence of partings with Pam Kipers, Jessica Williams, Josephine Rabinowitz, and Marsha Kaplan provided, in some respects, even stronger evidence that speakers behave in markedly different ways with those who occupy fixed positions in their social world, and those with whom their relationships are open to redefinition. As Kipers (1983) put it:

Where there is no framework of social contact in place to assure casual friends and acquaintances that a future meeting will take place, partings reflect concern over the survival of the relationship. Mean number of turns in these partings was the highest of any group in this study. Individual utterances were notably longer too . . . the lengthy negotiations over future meeting time reassure both participants that even though they may not designate a definite time when they will see one another again, they both value the relationship enough to want it to continue.

While all partings share certain basic features, our analysis indicated that shared knowledge of social distance and mutual certainty of future meeting are the important conditioning factors. In the report on her part of the research, Williams (1983) says:

> Where one or another or both of these factors is shared by the participants, interactions will exhibit certain predictable characteristics. Pre-partings will be absent as will lengthy negotiations as to when the parties will meet again. Parting signals and "goodbye" and its variants will occur in only a minority of cases. Conversely, when knowledge of both social distance and time of future meeting are absent, partings diverge from this pattern.

Similarly, D'Amico-Reisner (1983, 1985), in her study of expressions of disapproval, found that among native speakers of American English direct disapproval was expressed almost exclusively to intimates or to strangers in service encounters. When disapproval was expressed to nonintimates, only very indirect forms were used. As D'Amico-Reisner (1985) puts it: "When exchange types are considered with respect to social distance, the data reveal generally low non-intimate participation in disapproval exchanges." In analyzing the grammatical forms which function to express disapproval, D'Amico-Reisner found that two of the most frequent syntactic patterns, imperatives and rhetorical questions, are never used by nonintimates. The two patterns chosen for use to nonintimates by the speakers she studied are declarative sentences and the response-expected question. Even these patterns, however, are used significantly less often by nonintimate interlocutors, with only 28 percent of the declaratives and 25 percent of the response-expected questions uttered in "disapproval exchanges" between people who were not on intimate terms. D'Amico-Reisner then goes on to say that "all but 7% of the declaratives in non-intimate exchanges and 9% of the response-expected questions in non-intimate exchanges were issued during service encounters." What this means is that 94 percent of all the disapproval exchanges among nonintimates were found to occur between strangers. Thus, the pattern described above, in which intimates and strangers (or people at the extreme ends of the social distance continuum) tend to behave similarly in contrast to the verbal behavior of those who occupy the middle range of the social spectrum, exactly follows the theory described above. Put differently, one could say that interlocutors who are in the Bulge almost never voice their disapproval of one another overtly. As D'Amico-Reisner says:

> The latter finding suggests that direct D (disapproval expression) is an activity of evaluation that most frequently involves speakers and addressees who are either intimates or strangers. Consistent with Wolfson's "Bulge Theory,"

which accounts for the behavioral similarity of individuals at opposite ends of
the social distance continuum . . . , these findings imply that interlocutors
engage most frequently in direct D where concern for risk of rejection and/or
(concern for) risk of damage to one's presentation of self is low. Even more
important is the fact that individuals in the bulge, or in the center of the social
distance continuum, do not participate frequently in direct D whether the potential for confrontation exists or not. (D'Amico-Reisner 1985:218)

Thus we see that a systematic analysis of constraints on the social identity of
participants in disapproval exchanges yields additional support for the theory of
social interaction put forth here.

If the expression of disapproval is relatively rare among speakers within the
social category which I have labeled the Bulge, the same cannot be said for expressions of gratitude. Indeed, as researchers into first language acquisition (e.g., Grief
and Gleason 1980) have pointed out, thanking routines are among the earliest that
young English-speaking children are explicitly taught. Given the nature of this
routine and the importance placed on it, it is noteworthy that Eisenstein and Bodman (1986) in their description of expressions of gratitude used by native speakers
of American English, comment that they found the language patterns used in interactions between status unequals to be the same as those used between status equals.
However, they point out: "What was different in the formal setting was that there
were few uses of expressing surprise and complimenting. . . . in expressing gratitude, it may be that formality is conveyed by what is not said as well as through
specially marked lexical items." That is, they found that the thanks were restrained,
or unelaborated, in situations where the interlocutors were of unequal status, while
expressions of gratitude among friends contained not only the formulaic thanks but
also considerable elaboration. As they state in their conclusion: "Shorter thanking
episodes sometimes reflected greater social distance between interlocutors."

In the description of her ethnographic research into the speech act of refusals as
they function among speakers of American English, Beebe (1985:4) is explicit in
reporting that her own findings give strong evidence of the Bulge theory: "Our
ethnographically collected data appears to follow Wolfson's hypothesis. Strangers
are brief. If they want to say no, they do so. Real intimates are also brief. It is
friends and other acquaintances who are most likely to get involved in long negotiations with multiple repetitions, extensive elaborations, and a wide variety of semantic formulas."

Evidence for the validity of the Bulge theory described here has recently
emerged in the work of three separate investigators, all working independently on
the speech behavior associated with compliments. In my own most recent work, I
have, in conjunction with the members of two of my classes at the University of
Pennsylvania, been engaged in collecting and analyzing data not only on the speech
act of complimenting but on the speech sequence which includes the responses to
compliments as well. One of the classes, that concerned with language and gender,

has focused on possible sex-related differences in complimenting behavior, while the other, concerned with cross-cultural variation in language behavior, has been working on differences in complimenting behavior across cultural groups. While Manes (1983) has reported on some of our earliest findings regarding compliment responses, and our original work certainly included the collection of responses along with the compliments that initiated them, it is only since 1985 that I myself began to focus specifically on the entire complimenting sequence as a speech event which might yield new and important insights into the underlying motivation of this aspect of speech behavior. My findings, while as yet incomplete, clearly indicate that the compliment/response sequence is a negotiated one in which two or more participants are involved in an often elaborated exchange. In the earliest of our joint reports on compliments (Manes and Wolfson 1981, Wolfson and Manes 1980), we suggested that the function of the act was to create or reaffirm solidarity. My own most recent work, as well as that of others (Herbert 1986a, Holmes 1987), has verified this hypothesis and provided additional results which add considerable depth and breadth to it. In my own analysis, I have found that elaborated responses occur in the speech of both intimate and status-unequal females, but that the great majority of lengthy sequences are to be found in conversations among status-equal acquaintances. Since the Bulge theory is my own, it might be expected that I would unconsciously find evidence to support it. The fact that my students collected and analyzed their own data, finding very much the same patterns, provides some safeguard against this possibility, particularly since they were working in independent groups and did not report their findings to me until they were complete. However, it is always possible that some inadvertent comment of mine might have influenced them, and their results cannot therefore be seen as evidence totally unrelated to my own work. For this reason, it is particularly noteworthy that researchers who had had no contact with me, apart from their knowledge of my early published work, have reported findings which lend strong support to the Bulge theory I have put forward here, both by converging and by diverging with my analysis of complimenting behavior among speakers of American English.

Thus, Herbert (1986a) reports on his analysis of a corpus of 1062 compliment responses, both spontaneous and experimental, collected at the State University of New York at Binghamton. In a systematic investigation of the responses given by the native speakers of American English sampled, Herbert focused on the frequency of occurrence with which compliments were and were not accepted by addressees. His findings are striking in that speakers were "almost twice as likely to respond with some response other than ACCEPTANCE" (Herbert 1986a:80). As Herbert points out, this finding disagrees with the societal norm requiring that compliments be accepted with thanks. Herbert also raises two interesting questions concerning (1) the degree to which the student population he sampled is actually representative of the behavior of members of American society, and (2), which is perhaps even more significant, whether native speakers of other varieties of English follow similar behavior patterns. While Herbert does not claim to be in a position to answer the first question, he provides us with good evidence regarding the second. To quote him:

> With regard to the second question, however, certain data suggest that the pattern reported here may be uniquely American. That is, varieties of English differ from one another not only in phonology, syntax, and lexicon, but also in PRAGMATICS, that is in the ways in which speakers use the linguistic reper- toire available to them. Such differences have crucial importance for learners of English and for speakers of other varieties of English; both groups, operating with other norms, are liable to misinterpret and be misinterpreted in the Ameri- can context.
>
> In a study similar to this one conducted among a comparable university population in South Africa, a sharply different distributional profile emerged. . . . Briefly, ACCEPTANCES . . . accounted for fully seventy-six percent of the South African responses. That is, in place of the approximately one-in-three likelihood of receiving an ACCEPTANCE response from an American speaker, the likelihood is three-in-four among English-speaking South Africans. . . Similarly, an ongoing investigation of response-type frequency among British university students suggests that their pattern of usage approximates that ob- served in South Africa. . . . To what factors can one attribute this difference in pattern usage? Why are American speakers less likely to accept a compliment than speakers of South African or British English? . . . I suggest that Americans accept compliments less often than other English speakers due to the dominant value profile of American culture, which rests upon the notions of democratic idealism and human equality. (Herbert 1986a:82)

In a later paper (Herbert and Straight in press) the authors posit an explanation for this phenomenon, pointing out that social stratification and inequality are intrin- sic to South African ideology. Thus, the paucity of compliments given by South Africans in contrast to the frequency with which they occur in the speech of Americans, along with the fact that Americans tend to reject and the South Africans to accept compliments, has to do with the social systems in which the two groups interact. They point out that Americans give compliments frequently because they are attempting to establish solidarity in a social context in which their own status is uncertain. For the same reason, Americans tend not to accept the compliments they receive, thus further working toward the building of solidarity by stressing equality with their interlocutors. South Africans, in contrast, function in a society in which solidarity with status equals is assumed, and they have no need to make use of compliment negotiations to establish what they already have—certainty as to their relationships with one another. Thus, the analysis put forward by Herbert (1986) and by Herbert and Straight (in press) fits neatly within the framework of the Bulge theory, supporting it through their evidence and their explanation of why Americans and South Africans differ so sharply in their behavior regarding compliment/ response sequences.

In her report of compliment/response behavior in New Zealand, Holmes (in press) reports that "it is relatively rarely that New Zealanders overtly reject compliments." Holmes's ethnographic study, which includes a corpus of 484 New Zealand compliment/response sequences, yields many significant findings. Although she does not discuss the underlying ideology which may lead to this speech behavior from the same point of view as that addressed by Herbert (1986a) or by Herbert and Straight (in press), it is very possible that New Zealand society, like that in the United States, is sufficiently lacking in stratification to cause speakers to behave in similar ways for similar reasons. Indeed, Holmes's findings are so highly convergent with my own on virtually every level that it is difficult to know how else to account for her findings. With respect to the frequency of occurrence of compliments among speakers of different social positions, for example, Holmes says: "The New Zealand data used in this analysis consists predominantly of compliments between status-equals. . . . It is clear that compliments between equals are by far the most frequent in the New Zealand community sampled (79%). This finding is supported by Wolfson's data" (Holmes in press:11). While Holmes finds that compliments between status unequals occur both "upwards" and "downwards," she also points out that those which are given to someone of higher position were most likely when the speakers knew each other well or when the complimenter was older and therefore more confident. This finding diverges slightly from my own earlier analysis, but since these compliments among status unequals both in the United States and in New Zealand represent only a minority of both sets of data, and since my own analysis is in need of updating and refinement based on more current samples and further analysis, it may well be that even in this respect the similarities are greater than originally believed. This area clearly needs further work.

From the point of view of the theory under consideration, the most significant point to be taken from Holmes's study is the clear finding that most New Zealand compliments occur within what I have called the Bulge, thus lending further independent support to this analysis.

It should be mentioned in passing that while I, along with my students in the course in language and gender at the University of Pennsylvania, have continued to investigate sex-related differences in compliment/response behavior, both Herbert (in press) and Holmes (in press) have conducted independent studies along the same lines. What is most impressive about the findings and the analyses reported to date is the high degree of convergence in all three studies. That is, it is clear from all three reports not only that women give and receive more compliments than men do, but also that their responses indicate that this speech activity functions differently among men and women, with women making far greater use of such compliment/response strategies to create and reaffirm solidarity. The fact that all three studies indicate similar patterns among women as opposed to men may well lead to some significant refinements of the Bulge theory reflecting the status-related social strategies of women. This is an area which demands further attention since it goes to the heart of the entire issue of speech behavior and social dynamics.

Thus, the findings from the ethnographic studies discussed above all converge in revealing a qualitative difference between the speech behavior which middle-class Americans use with intimates, status unequals, and strangers on the one hand, and with nonintimates, status-equal friends, co-workers, and acquaintances on the other. With respect to the frequency with which a particular speech act or sequence occurs, the degree of elaboration used in performing it, and the amount of negotiation which occurs between interlocutors, the two extremes of social distance show very similar patterns, as opposed to the middle section, which displays a characteristic bulge. Although all the studies so far examined are based on relatively large samples of data, it could still be argued that the numbers of examples collected were still too small to be representative. What is particularly significant, therefore, is that if we take the coded results from the CCSARP questionnaire described earlier, and arrange them along a scale of social distance, we find the same pattern emerging. If we plot out the feature of apologies which has, in this study, been designated "explanation or account," we see the characteristic Bulge found through ethnographic research. At the two extremes of social distance, less than 40 percent of the subjects did not include an explanation in their responses. In contrast, approximately 70 percent did not make use of explanations when the situation involved interaction between interlocutors who were in the middle of the social distance continuum. See Figure 1 for an example of the typical Bulge pattern.

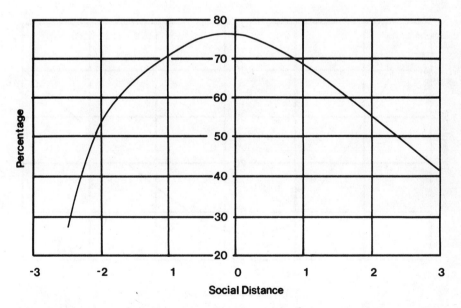

Figure 1. Percentage of respondents not including an explanation in their response to "apology" situations versus the social distance between the participants. (*Source:* Wolfson, Marmor, and Jones 1985.)

A second explanation of the way in which the Bulge is reflected by the CCSARP data may be seen by an examination of the feature designated "taking on responsibility," as shown in Figure 2. Here we see that 90 percent of those at the extremes of social distance did not take on any responsibility in their responses, whereas only 60 percent of these in the middle of the continuum did not express some sort of responsibility.

The inverse relationship between the features "explanation" and "responsibility" shown in both figures above seems at first glance to be counterintuitive. Why should a situation that elicits the taking on of responsibility not also elicit a similar proportion of explanations for the "offense?" This seeming paradox can be understood only if we recognize that for native speakers of American English, explanations do not necessarily constitute apologies.

There is, then, evidence for the Bulge pattern I have described here, not only in my own analyses but also in a considerable number of studies by other scholars. The fact that this convergence has been found not only in analyses of investigators who, like Beebe, were familiar with this aspect of my work but also in the findings of those who were unaware of the existence of the Bulge theory is, I think, very striking. It follows from this that previous research must be examined to see if there is evidence of the Bulge in the work of earlier scholars.

The fact that urban middle-class Americans live in a complex and open society means that individuals are not members of a single network in which their own

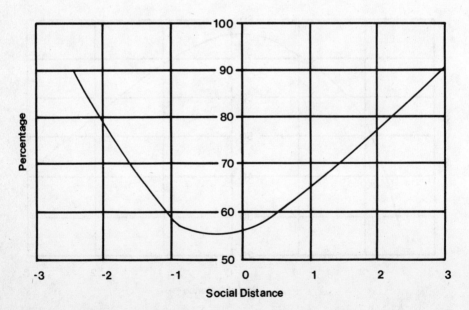

Figure 2. Percentage of respondents not taking any responsibility in their response to "apology" situation versus the social distance between participants in the dialogue. (*Source:* Wolfson, Marmor, and Jones 1985.)

place is well defined, but rather belong to a number of networks, both overlapping and nonoverlapping, in which they must continually negotiate their roles and relationships with one another. The importance of the Bulge theory lies in what it tells us about how the very openness and potential for mobility of American middle-class society is reflected in our everyday speech behavior. The fact that very similar findings have emerged in research on complimenting behavior in New Zealand (Holmes in press), as well as the report of very different behavior patterns among native speakers of South African English (Herbert and Straight in press) provides additional evidence for the analysis presented here.

CONCLUSION

Thus we see that a major contribution to the study of speech acts and sequences is that by examining them in the context in which they occur, we are able to analyze patterns of social behavior. This in-depth work serves to demonstrate a great deal about the social structure of the society and about the dynamics of social interaction which prevail within it. Clearly, this is critical information for language learners. It is enormously valuable for nonnative speakers of English, as consumers of literature and films as well as all sorts of productions disseminated by the mass media of English-speaking countries, to understand and to be able to interpret how social interaction operates.

As Daikuhara (1986) has said in reporting on the findings of her study of compliment/response sequences in Japanese: "The analysis of a corpus of 115 examples of compliments has shown that there are both similarities and differences between Japanese and American compliments. . . . This may result in serious communicative interference if the interlocutor interprets such conduct as an insult according to his/her own rules" (Daikuhara 1986:128–129).

The sort of research described here provides important insights into American culture which could prove invaluable to language learners who are living, even temporarily, in the United States. Once an overall picture of the dynamics of social interaction is gained, it will be much easier for nonnative speakers of English to interact effectively with members of the host community. Having seen the importance of negotiating personal relationships, learners will be able to avoid many of the frustrations of attempting to get along in a new culture. The end result of gaining such insights into the way speakers of the new language behave is that learners are given the ability to interpret what is meant by what is said to them and, just as important, will gain control over the way in which they present themselves to others.

CHAPTER 7

Miscommunication

INTRODUCTION

The scientific study of communication and miscommunication across cultures is a relatively new area of research and one that holds much promise both in terms of language learning and, more generally, in terms of intercultural communication. The fact that there is great variability across cultures with respect to sociolinguistic norms and behavior patterns has already been described in detail. Through numerous examples of culturally based misunderstandings between interlocutors from different backgrounds, we have seen that sociolinguistic variability provides fertile ground for miscommunication. It is the aim of this chapter to demonstrate that the roots of such socioculturally based miscommunication can be investigated empirically so that we may come to understand how such problems develop and where solutions to them may best be found.

In surveying the scientific investigation of sociolinguistic miscommunication, we will examine two major lines of inquiry, both relatively new and both of central concern to applied linguistics. First, we will look at the research into what has come to be known as sociolinguistic or pragmatic transfer. Here we will be discussing studies which specifically aim to investigate the sociolinguistic behavior of language learners when interacting in the target language. In general, such studies focus on a specific aspect of the speakers' communicative competence, and very often on the use of a single speech act or routine. By comparing the learners' behavior in this regard with that of native speakers of both the first language and the target language, it is possible to ascertain the extent to which patterns and rules from the first language may be influencing the students' acquisition of communicative competence in the language they are learning. Closely related to the sociolinguistic study of learners' errors is the cross-cultural comparison of speech patterns. Inspired by the possibility of avoiding the pitfalls that result in learners' miscommunication by predicting problems before they arise, investigators compare native speaker responses to identical speech situations in a variety of languages. The aim of such comparisons is to produce contrastive analyses at the sociolinguistic or pragmatic level, thus providing a basis for determining which areas are most vulnerable to miscommunication and should therefore be focussed upon.

The second line of inquiry to be examined here is that known as interactional sociolinguistics (IS). Making use of videotapes to capture a tremendous richness of interactional detail, researchers in this area employ microethnography in their rigorous and elegant analyses of videotaped encounters between interlocutors. Given the recognition that it is now a commonplace in modern industrialized societies for individuals from quite different sociocultural backgrounds to have the occasion and even the necessity to interact, and that these interactions are often fraught with tension, if not outright hostility, the aim of interactional sociolinguistics is to isolate the differences in behavioral patterns which lead to miscommunication.

SOCIOLINGUISTIC/PRAGMATIC TRANSFER

The use of rules of speaking from one's own native speech community when interacting with members of the host speech community or simply when speaking or writing in a second language is known as sociolinguistic or pragmatic transfer. The phenomenon, variously referred to as *interference* or *transfer,* was early recognized by such researchers into bilingualism as Uriel Weinreich (1953), who says: "Those instances of deviation from the norms of either language which occur in the speech of bilinguals as a result of their familiarity with more than one language, i.e. as a result of language contact, will be referred to as INTERFERENCE phenomena. It is these phenomena of speech, and their impact on the norms of either language exposed to contact, that invite the interest of the linguist" (Weinreich 1953:1).

The term *transfer,* which we will use here, has been taken from psycholinguistic studies of linguistic transfer which occurs during language learning, and has gained wide currency in recent years through the research of applied linguists who have focused on just this phenomenon. In this section, we will examine in detail some of the most recent of the empirical studies of sociolinguistic (or what is often termed pragmatic) transfer.

PRAGMATIC TRANSFER AMONG IMMIGRANTS
IN AUSTRALIA

Michael Clyne (1977, 1979, 1982) has long been interested in the effects of language contact on immigrant groups in Australia. For example, Clyne (1982), in his discussion of immigrant language patterns, mentions that immigrants to Australia often adopt the Australian custom of addressing colleagues and acquaintances by their first names. If these people are also part of one's own ethnic group, and if under certain circumstances or in certain domains it is still the habit to speak the ethnic language with these interlocutors, a dilemma arises since it is difficult or impossible to change to a more formal address form in the ethnic language. For this reason, Clyne says, there is a tendency for first names to be used far more often in ethnic circles in Australia than in similar situations in the country of origin. This, he says, sometimes leads Australian immigrants to use the familiar form of the second person pronoun in their ethnic language when such usage would not be acceptable in the country of origin. Some people, he says, "avoid this by switching to English."

Another example of transfer among immigrants is given by Clyne (1982:105) when he says, "An English pragmatic rule that has penetrated German discourse in Australia is '*Ja, danke*' or even '*Danke*' ('Yes, thank you'; 'thank you'; cf. Standard German *Bitte* or *Ja, bitte*, 'please', 'yes, please') as a positive reply to an offer. (Ger. *Danke* is a negative reply.)"

As Clyne has amply demonstrated, examples such as these abound, and most people who have studied immigrant languages as well as individual language learners could supply many stories of individual cases where transfer of a sociolinguistic nature has taken place.

In his analyses of language contact between immigrant groups and native Australians, Clyne (1977) has demonstrated that pragmatic transfer or the transfer of rules of speaking occurs very similarly to the transfer of phonological, semantic, and syntactic rules and that such transfer can have a major effect on the interactions of interlocutors.

In constructing a framework for the analysis of pragmatic transfer, Clyne makes a distinction between transfer that leads to what he labels "communication breakdown" or (CB) and "communication conflict" or (CC). In the first, communication breakdown, the speaker's intention is not understood by the addressee, while in communication conflict, such a misunderstanding can lead to actual friction between the interlocutors. As Clyne puts it:

> Both CB and CC can often be attributed to cross-cultural (interlingual or dialectal), social (sociolectal) or individual (ideolectal) differences in communication competence rules, e.g. different rules for the realization of particular speech acts. CB is also caused by transference (interference) at the phonological, lexico-semantic or syntactic level or by the absence of a contextual knowledge necessary for the comprehension of the communicative intention, and CC by non-linguistic factors, by images and prejudices concerning the speaker and his culture, nation or society or by authoritarian personality. CC is, however, manifested through language. (Clyne 1977:130)

In order to test out his framework empirically, Clyne (1977) conducted an experiment in the form of a questionnaire administered to 60 German and Austrian immigrants to Australia and to an Australian control group. The questions were designed to test the subjects' responses to rules which, from observational evidence and the self-report of immigrants from these countries, appeared to be different in German and in Australian English. Following this experiment, a similar questionnaire was administered to groups of immigrants from Italy and from Greece as well as to yet another Australian control group. All the questionnaires were translated into the subjects' first language so that they had access to both the English and the version in their native language. In addition, Clyne controlled for the possible influence of the interviewer's background by having the questionnaire administered to the Greek and Italian immigrants by a member of the subjects' own ethnic community.

The results of Clyne's investigation indicate that most of the immigrants had accepted Australian rules of sociolinguistic behavior. He concludes that it is not so much the specific rules of speech acts that the immigrants had difficulty learning, but rather the more general ones. This was especially true for the Greeks and Germans in contrast to the Italians. In a later paper describing these results, Clyne (1979) points out that there is most potential for communication conflict in situations "where the rule threatens the dignity of the individual—i.e. on three types of issue: power, trust, and solidarity. Either the power structure is upset by a more 'egalitarian' routine or a power structure is specially stressed. At the solidarity level, friendship/mateship is threatened or a lack or sympathy is shown" (Clyne 1979:33).

Given the results of his own work in this area, Clyne argues that "far more research of a contrastive nature should be undertaken into communicative competence rules and they should be taught in English as a second language classes."

THE STUDY OF TRANSFER IN APOLOGIES

In order to investigate how and to what extent first language norms interfere with second language learners' ability to conform to the norms of the target language community, studies by Cohen and Olshtain (1981), Olshtain and Cohen (1983, 1987), and Olshtain (1983) compared native and nonnative responses in Hebrew and English to a variety of situations that included an offense of some type. The data were collected by means of a controlled elicitation procedure in which subjects are asked to read and then role-play or write their reactions to eight "apology" situations. The written elicitation instrument, known as a discourse completion test (DCT) which is now widely used, consisted of "scripted dialogues" intended to represent situations differing along specific social and situational dimensions. The dialogues are introduced by a brief description which gives the context in which the dialogue is supposed to occur and specifies the conditioning factors considered most relevant. Since it was hypothesized that the type of violation would interact with the social identity of the interlocutors in the choice of remedial strategy adopted, each situation contained an "offense" which was graded in terms of severity of the violation and the relative social status of the interlocutors. The subjects in this first study were 44 college students—12 native English speakers (to provide data on native English-speaking patterns of apologizing) and 32 native Hebrew speakers (12 to give baseline data for Hebrew native language apologies and the other 20 to give nonnative responses in English).

Cohen and Olshtain (1981) demonstrated that native speakers' choices of apology forms are highly patterned. In contrast to more recent findings, nonnative speakers were found to deviate from native speaker norms not only as a result of transfer but also because their proficiency in their second language was inadequate to express the appropriate degree of regret. Work on sociolinguistic or pragmatic transfer is still in its infancy and therefore we do not have sufficient information on this aspect of transfer among learners from different cultural backgrounds and in different learning contexts to explain the differences in the findings concerning the relationship of learner proficiency and sociolinguistic transfer in the pioneering work reported by Cohen and Olshtain (1981) and by Takahashi and Beebe (1987). While some of the difference may be due to the different tasks subjects were asked to perform, it appears even more likely that the contrast in findings has to do with the extreme differences between the learner and target language populations in terms of sociocultural background. Although there are certainly differences in sociolinguistic behavior among them, there can be little argument that Americans and Israelis share many more cultural characteristics than do Americans and Japanese. Further, as we will discuss at greater length below, it is also the case that Americans learning Hebrew in Israel tend to be from ethnic Jewish backgrounds, thus sharing with Israelis of East European descent a common cultural heritage from which both groups have only recently been separated.

In spite of their shared heritage, it is nevertheless the case that both Americans and Israelis have each adopted many new and different sociocultural values and behaviors. Thus, in their comparison of written role-played responses, Cohen and Olshtain found that their sample of Hebrew-speaking Israeli learners of English were less likely to accept responsibility for an offense or to make offers for damages they might have caused, and that the overall level of intensity with which they made their apologies was less than that of the control group of native American speakers of English.

In a separate study, Olshtain (1983) made use of the same elicitation procedure to collect data on the apology performance of two sets of learners of Hebrew as a second language, one whose native language was English and the other Russian. The total number of subjects in the Olshtain (1983) study was 36. In order to provide baseline data on the sociolinguistic behavior of native speakers using their own first languages, Olshtain elicited data from 12 native speakers of English speaking in English, and 12 native speakers of Russian speaking in Russian. The learner groups in this study consisted of 13 native speakers of English studying Hebrew, and 14 native speakers of Russian learning Hebrew. The objective of the study was to "describe the nonnative deviations within an area of sociocultural appropriateness and thus tap the learner's pragmatic competence as a significant element of their overall communicative competence." Again focusing on the speech act of giving apologies, Olshtain points out that these are

> triggered by specific behavior or discourse situations that need to be defined beyond one sociocultural context, as well as within each such context. Insulting someone, or physically hurting another person unintentionally, seem to be universally accepted situations which call for an apology, yet different degrees of severity of the action, or different circumstances related to the behavior which results in the need to apologize, might call for different types of apologies

and different intensities of such apologies in different cultures. In studying language transfer problems, we need to focus our descriptions of speech acts on cross-linguistic and language-specific features, as well as on situation-specific information.

One new element of the Olshtain (1983) study was to try to find out how the subjects perceived the universality of the need to apologize in given situations. For this information, Olshtain not only tabulated the results to the elicitation responses but also interviewed each subject, asking two questions: (1) "Do you think that speakers of Hebrew apologize more or less than speakers of your native language?" and (2) "Do you feel that a native speaker of Hebrew might apologize differently from a speaker of your language for any of the eight situations?"

When the subjects said that people apologize differently in different languages, Olshtain took that to mean that they saw speech acts in language-specific terms. Conversely, when subjects insisted that the apology had to do with the situation only, and that people should apologize similarly no matter what language they were speaking, Olshtain took that as evidence of a view of apologies as universal speech acts.

Thus, in her 1983 study, Olshtain had two objectives. The first was to discover the extent and type of transfer in the speech act of apologies of both English- and Russian-speaking learners of Hebrew. The second objective was to try to learn whether learners' perceptions of "language universality or specificity affects actual performance."

With respect to native speaker baseline data, Olshtain found that the "highest degree of apology overall was in English, somewhat lower in Russian, and the lowest in Hebrew." In view of the results for learners' behavior, it is noteworthy that when Olshtain interviewed her subjects in order to learn whether they saw the act of apologizing as one which differed from language to language, she discovered that English speakers perceived less need to apologize in Hebrew than in English. The Russian-speaking subjects, on the other hand, maintained that apologies have to do with feeling responsibility for a violation and that this motivation should remain unchanged no matter what language one happened to be speaking. This finding is of particular interest when we consider that Russian speakers also apologize more than do Hebrew speakers, while English speakers express the greatest degree of responsibility of the three groups. One wonders whether native speakers of Russian, perceiving apologizing as a universal behavior pattern, are more likely to make negative judgments when Hebrew speakers break their norms, even though the transaction occurs in Hebrew rather than in Russian.

True to their perceptions, results showed that "English speakers apologized considerably less in Hebrew than they did in English," showing that these learners had acquired some of the sociolinguistic rules for Hebrew. As Olshtain says,

. . . speakers of English were found to have a "language-specific" perception concerning the apology speech act in general and this situation in particular, as they claimed that "Hebrew speakers apologize considerably less than do English speakers." They did not find it necessary, therefore, to express an apology as often in Hebrew as they would in English. . . . Speakers of Russian, on the other hand were found to have a more universal perception of the apology act and maintained almost the same level of frequency of semantic formulas in Russian and Hebrew. (Olshtain and Cohen 1983:28)

Thus, the overall results of this study of transfer in the use of apologies in Hebrew show very different patterns for speakers of Russian and for speakers of Hebrew. The English-speaking group, who saw spoken Hebrew as requiring less apologizing, did in fact decrease their use of apologies when speaking in Hebrew. They nevertheless apologized considerably more than native speakers of Hebrew did in the same situations and therefore can be said to have exhibited transfer. The Russian speakers, true to their perceptions of the universal nature of the responsibility to apologize, did so far more often when speaking Hebrew than did native speakers of the target language, thus also exhibiting considerable transfer.

The most exciting aspect of the study carried out by Olshtain (1983:246) and summarized above is that she not only investigated whether transfer in apologizing existed, but, by comparing groups of language learners from two different sociocultural backgrounds, she was able to demonstrate that cultural norms regarding proper behavior have a direct bearing on the extent to which a particular group shows a tendency to transfer rules from their native language. That is, she shows not only that language proficiency affects transfer but that a general philosophical outlook has a direct bearing on the issue. As Olshtain (1983) puts it: "The present study also points to the fact that the tendency to transfer features from L1 to L2 may depend on the learner's perception with regard to the assignment of language specificity or language universality to the speech act under consideration. It is the latter which may induce a higher tendency toward transfer."

The Olshtain (1983) study of transfer in apologies thus adds a new and important dimension to the field. An in-depth study of this type which attempts to account for the motivation behind sociolinguistic behavior is impressive in and of itself for the information it can provide us with respect to the attitudes and probable behavior of various groups of language learners. It is also exactly this sort of background information that we, as applied linguists, need to have. The insights provided by studies such as this one will be invaluable in preparing curriculum materials for different language groups, in working toward guiding language learners in their efforts to interpret the meaning of native speaker behavior, and in helping them to achieve the ability to interact effectively with members of the target language speech community.

THE STUDY OF TRANSFER IN REFUSALS

Beebe et al. (1985, in press) report on a systematic study which investigates the evidence for sociolinguistic or pragmatic transfer in the English of native speakers of Japanese. In the study, the authors collected data from 60 subjects, divided into three groups: Native speakers of Japanese speaking in Japanese (JJs), native speakers of American English speaking in English (AEs), and native speakers of Japanese speaking in English (JEs). The aim of the study was to discover whether the refusals given by the third group (the JEs) corresponded more closely with those of the JJs or with speakers of the target language, the AEs. The design of the study used both ethnographic data and responses to a discourse completion test, a written role-playing questionnaire consisting of 12 situations. Each situation contained a blank in which only a refusal would fit. The investigators further divided their questionnaire on refusals into four categories: refusals to (1) requests, (2) invitations, (3) offers, and (4) suggestions. In each case, the questionnaire was designed so that one refusal had to be made to someone of higher status, one to someone of lower status, and one to a status equal. Evidence of transfer was defined as similarity in any of these situations to native Japanese (JJ) formulas and dissimilarity to the formulas used by native speakers of English (AEs). Formulas were defined in semantic terms. Examples of types of semantic formulas found in the data on refusals are apologies/regrets, excuses, direct "no"s, suggestions of alternatives and statements of philosophy.

The findings of the study show clear indication of transfer in three areas: the order in which semantic formulas for refusing were used, the frequency of semantic formulas, and the content of semantic formulas. Grammatical accuracy was not examined for the purpose of this study since what was of interest here was the sociolinguistic behavior of the subjects.

With respect to refusals to requests, the Japanese speaking in English resembled the Japanese speaking in Japanese and differed from the native speakers of American English speaking in English. A most critical finding here, with respect to sociolinguistic rules, is that in terms of order of formulas, the Japanese speaking in English "omitted apology/regret when they were higher status than the requester." The influence of status, as we will see, is very strong in the speech of Japanese whether speaking English or their native tongue. Another finding concerning transfer in refusals to requests is that JEs apologized about twice as often as the Americans in the sample. Again, Beebe et al. found that "Japanese subjects (JJs and JEs) were particularly sensitive to high vs. low status . . . whereas AEs were sensitive to status equals vs. status equals. It is probable that JEs were transferring into English a sensitivity to status that exists in Japanese."

Additional evidence of this difference in sensitivity to status comes in the results gathered on the refusal of invitations. Here again, Beebe et al. say: "Japanese seem more inclined to make different responses to high and low status interlocutors, whereas Americans in these situations seem to react similarly to status unequals of both types (higher and lower), but to give different responses to equal acquaintances." This finding regarding choice of formula depending on the status of the interlocutor is particularly well exemplified in the results for refusals of invitations. As Beebe et al. put it: "Just as they did with requests, JEs and JJs generally omitted expression of apology/regret when they, the refuser, were higher in status than the person who was inviting them." They then go on to say:

It appears that Japanese subjects reacted differently to higher status versus lower status position. Americans ordered formulas in virtually the same way with status unequals of both types. They changed their order of semantic formulas when refusing a status equal friend. This AE pattern is similar to one noted by Wolfson . . . in which Americans make a distinction between an interlocutor who is familiar and one who is either an intimate or a stranger. Wolfson notes that exchanges with familiar interlocutors (e.g., friends and acquaintances) are longer and involve more negotiation than those between two intimates or two strangers. (Beebe et al. in press)

When it comes to refusing offers and suggestions, the data show sociolinguistic transfer both in the content and in the status sensitivity shown by JJs and JEs. Americans did not suggest alternatives when refusing an offer or a suggestion, but Japanese did. No group suggested alternatives to an equal, but Japanese subjects did suggest alternatives to status unequals, especially if they had higher status. In their refusals of offers from someone of lower status, all respondents gave essentially the same semantic formula, but the JEs resembled their native JJ counterparts in adding two additional semantic formulas—a statement of philosophy (e.g., "Things break anyway"; "This kind of thing happens") and then a suggested future alternative (e.g., "Be more careful from now on").

In sum, then, Beebe et al. found sociolinguistic transfer in the order, the frequency, and the content of the semantic formulas that Japanese speakers of English used in making refusals. In their analysis of the content of the semantic formulas used by the three groups, they found that "there is pragmatic transfer in the content of several formulas, the most interesting being excuses, statements of principle, and statements of philosophy." As they point out, refusals, like other speech acts, reflect fundamental cultural values, and for this reason nonnative speakers are likely to engage in sociocultural transfer in just those speech acts, like refusals, that involve delicate interpersonal negotiation.

In a recent paper, Takahashi and Beebe (1987) focus on the tone and content of refusals by Japanese learners of English in comparison with that of native Americans. Based on the written refusals of 80 subjects, their study examines pragmatic transfer as a function of both context (ESL vs. EFL situations) and level of language proficiency. In this carefully designed study, 40 of the subjects are native speakers, half of them Japanese responding in Japanese, and half Americans responding in English. In addition to the baseline data, refusals were elicited from 40 Japanese students of English, half studying EFL (English as a foreign language) in Japan and half studying ESL (English as a second language) in the United States. Within both categories of learners, half were at graduate school level and half at undergraduate level, thus reflecting what Takahashi and Beebe call their "approximate level of proficiency."

Hypothesizing that at the pragmatic level transfer increases rather than decreases with proficiency, Takahashi and Beebe explain their position on the grounds that "the lower proficiency students do not have the fluency in the target language to give reign to pragmatic transfer phenomena." As we have just seen, their previous study (Beebe et al. 1985, in press) showed that pragmatic transfer among Japanese leaders manifested itself in the frequency, order, and what they call "intrinsic content and tone of semantic formulas used in ESL refusals." Compared with the American English speakers, both the learner and native speaker groups of Japanese apologized more often with addressees of higher status than they did with those of lower status. Another difference found was that the Japanese excuses were much more vague than those given by Americans, and their philosophical tone had the effect of making them sound more formal.

In the 1987 study, Takahashi and Beebe asked their subjects to fill out a discourse completion test (DCT), which contained 12 situations, each with a blank space where only a refusal would fit. In addition to using four "stimulus types" to elicit refusals to invitations, offers, suggestions, and requests, each group involved a refusal to an addressee of higher, lower, and equal status.

With respect to their hypotheses, Takahashi and Beebe found evidence of pragmatic transfer among both EFL and ESL students at both the lower and higher proficiency levels. Further, they found that transfer from Japanese rules of speaking was more common in the EFL group than it was among the ESL students. The findings for the last of their four hypotheses—namely, that greater amount of transfer will correlate with greater proficiency—was not definitely supported by their data, although they argue that the evidence points in that direction.

To sum up the evidence so far, it seems clear that Beebe and her colleagues have provided the field with ample demonstration that pragmatic transfer exists both among students of English studying in the host speech community and among those for whom it is a foreign language being learned in their own country. Further, they have given good reason to believe that, unlike other types of transfer, pragmatic transfer may well increase with learners' ability to express themselves in their new language.

It is essential to recognize that linguistic fluency in a foreign language, even when it has reached the point of near mastery, can often prove to be a disadvantage from the point of view of native speaker judgments. Foreigners in English-speaking countries who have a reasonable command of English and who understand and can make themselves understood without great difficulty, are unconsciously assumed to be equally knowledgable regarding the sociolinguistic rules of the community. Since linguistic competence is an aspect of communicative competence, people who have one are expected to have the other and are therefore held responsible for sociolinguistic violations in a way which those with less ability to communicate would not be. Furthermore, the fluent speaker in an English-speaking environment is likely to interact more with native speakers and therefore has more opportunities to err and in more ways. As Beebe et al. (1985, in press) point out, this situation seems to be somewhat different from what Taylor (1974) found for linguistic transfer versus overgeneralization. In analyzing learners' linguistic errors, Taylor found that those of beginning students were most likely to arise from a process of interference or transfer, wherein learners, ignorant of the rules of the target language, make use of the patterns they do know, those of their native language. In contrast, more advanced students, having learned (but not mastered) the very different syntactic rules of the target language, may well err by applying their newly learned pattern to cases where it is not grammatical because of some irregularity or constraint in the target language which they have not yet learned. This sort of error, common also to children acquiring their first language, is known as overgeneralization. Children or nonnative speakers who say, "she runned," for example, are showing that they have learned to form the past tense in English and that they are capable of analogizing. They are also demonstrating that they have not yet learned that the verb *run* has an irregular past tense formed by substituting a vowel rather than adding *-ed*. The ability to analogize is, of course, fundamental to learning, and in the great majority of cases the addition of the past tense marker /ed/ will have exactly the effect the learner wants to produce. Most grammatical patterns, however, have some irregularities, and analogies or generalizations will always be inappropriate in some cases. Overgeneralization is part of the process of language acquisition, a process which cannot occur until the learner has acquired some patterns upon which to base analogies. The difference between what Taylor found for linguistic transfer and overgeneralization by second language learners and what seems to be the case for sociolinguistic behavior is that while linguistic transfer correlates negatively with advanced proficiency, the reverse is the case for sociolinguistic or pragmatic rules. As Beebe argues, the more fluent the speaker, the more the potential for inappropriate speech behavior.

THE STUDY OF TRANSFER IN REQUESTS

In order to investigate the pragmatics of interlanguage used by language learners and to examine it for evidence of transfer, Blum-Kulka (1982, 1983a) conducted a study at York University in Canada. Focusing her study on requests, Blum-Kulka began by comparing the relevant sociolinguistic rules among speakers of English and of Hebrew. As the subject of her study of the speech behavior of language learners, Blum-Kulka investigated the use of directives or requests among native speakers of Canadian English who were learning Hebrew. Concerned with testing the claims of sociolinguistic or pragmatic universality put forth by such scholars as Searle (1965, 1975), Gordon and Lakoff (1975), and Fraser (1978), Blum-Kulka designed a study to compare the speech act performance in making requests of second language learners of Hebrew with that of native speakers of both Hebrew and English. Using a discourse completion test as her elicitation instrument, Blum-Kulka collected baseline data from native speakers of Hebrew and from native speakers of Canadian English and compared the responses from both native speaker groups with those of native speakers of Canadian English who were learning Hebrew as a second language. On the basis of the data collected and analyzed for this study, Blum-Kulka found that although certain forms could be translated word for word from one language to the other, the meaning or illocutionary force of the utterance was very often lost. As Blum-Kulka says: "From a second language learner's point of view, though, the difference in the linguistic realization of this strategy (between Hebrew and English) can have serious consequences; learners' attempts to formulate a 'willingness' question in Hebrew by using the verb *roce* ('want'—probably echoing the English 'would like to') results in a phrase that fails to carry the illocutionary force of a request" (Blum-Kulka 1983a:40).

A striking finding of this study is that again and again in her data, Blum-Kulka finds examples where learners have made direct translations from their native language (Canadian English) and thus ended by using forms for requests that either were ambiguous or simply did not carry the meaning of a request in Hebrew. As she explains it: "None of the native speakers of Hebrew used this form for making a request. This difference in usage suggests that the learners transferred the forms from English, without realizing the depletion in illocutionary force that occurred through translation" (Blum-Kulka 1983a:51).

It is important to note, however, that Blum-Kulka found some cases in which sociolinguistic rules seemed to be shared across the two cultures she was studying, so that learners were able to get their meanings across by applying their own native speaker rules in translation. Her interpretation of this finding is that the similarities and differences in speech act realization (or actual forms used) can be explained by seeing the rules that condition the performance and interpretation of speech acts across languages "on a continuum from the cross-culturally shared, possibly universal rules to the language-and-culture specific ones." This, she says, explains why some of the forms used by second language learners are appropriate both socially and linguistically while others miss in one way or the other, and sometimes in both. Thus, according to Blum-Kulka, the performance of second language learners comes closest to native speaker usage when the rules are shared across the two cultures. When the rules are language- and culture-specific, the most deviation from native speaker usage occurs. Since only two language groups were studied, however, and since the likelihood is great that both the Hebrew speakers and the Hebrew learners, though of different nationalities, were members of the same ethnic group whose recent immigrant backgrounds were very often identical, it is a bit difficult to accept this as an argument for universality of sociolinguistic rules. Israel has, after all, been a Jewish homeland for only a few decades, and the most socially and linguistically influential group have been the descendants of Eastern European Jewish emigrants. Similarly, the great majority of Canadian Jews are descendants of immigrants from Eastern Europe. As is well attested in the literature (see for example, Zborowski and Herzog 1952), the cultural patterns of Jews from this area were remarkably cohesive. As Mead (1952:23) says in the preface to the book *Life Is with People: The Culture of the Shtetl:* "Despite countless local variations, the Jews of Eastern Europe had one culture, possessing the characteristics that mark a culture: a language, a religion, a set of values, a specific constellation of social mechanisms and institutions, and the feeling of its members that they belong to one group." For the most part, only two or at most three generations separate the two groups studied by Blum-Kulka in terms of recent cultural background, and for this reason it may be expected that a considerable number of shared sociocultural norms continue to exist. Obviously, this does not mean that the sociolinguistic rules of the two groups under study will be identical, but it would be surprising if at least some of them did not continue to be shared. It is for this reason that the groups under investigation seem a poor choice for the investigation of the possibility of universality of pragmatic or sociolinguistic rules. Differences certainly exist, owing to the language shifts and the very dissimilar cultural experiences of the two groups during the decades since they both migrated and became members of quite different societies. Still, one would expect to find some similarities in sociocultural behavior, and this makes it difficult to argue strongly for or against sociolinguistic universality based solely on this study.

   One of Blum-Kulka's most important findings is that with respect to sociolinguistic rules, or what she calls "target language acceptability norms," native speakers of Hebrew were found to be far more direct in their requests than were their English-speaking counterparts. For this reason, it was not surprising to find that the learners of Hebrew who were first language speakers of Canadian English often failed to convey their intended meanings because they chose forms which were too indirect to be interpreted by Hebrew speakers as requests. In an example, Blum-Kulka says: "In attempting to formulate a request from a subordinate, some learners used the Hebrew equivalent of "is it possible to notify the teachers." . . . the strategy fails to carry the illocutionary force of a request in this context in Hebrew." This issue of directness is particularly worthy of attention, since, as Katriel (1986) has pointed out so eloquently, "talking straight," or using what is called *dugri* speech, is highly valued in Israeli culture and is, indeed, a manifestation of the recently constructed Israeli cultural ethos. As Katriel explains it, *dugri* speech is marked and set off from other behavior in that it is used on specific occasions or in specific ways, known to and recognizable to everyone in the speech community. What Blum-Kulka's findings show, regarding the greater directness in the everyday speech of Israeli speakers of Hebrew in contrast with the relatively indirect style of the Canadians, is that there has been a diffusion from *dugri* speech into general sociolinguistic usage, causing Israelis to tend toward a direct style of speech in all sorts of situations. Canadians, on the other hand, tend to follow the model British-influenced cultural pattern of indirectness. If this tendency to be direct, which Blum-Kulka has found throughout her Hebrew data on request forms, is indeed a general one for Israeli society, this would be an important factor in guiding learners of Hebrew to achieve communicative competence in the target language, in terms of both interpreting what is said to them and making themselves understood. Since it is also very likely that this direct style of speech is transferred by Hebrew speakers learning English, it may also account for the well-known fact that Israelis are often negatively stereotyped as being rude and abrupt when they are interacting in English-speaking communities.

   With respect to Blum-Kulka's research question regarding the claim mentioned above that pragmatic or sociolinguistic rules are universal, her findings indicate that although there are some rules that *do* seem to be less language- and culture-specific than others (perhaps for the reasons of common ancestry mentioned above), one of the major problems confronted by English-speaking learners of Hebrew has to do very specifically with the inappropriate transfer of sociolinguistic rules. Indeed, Blum-Kulka is very specific in arguing against the universalist hypothesis, saying: "Contrary to such claims, I would like to argue that the nature of the interdependence among pragmatic, linguistic, and social factors that determine speech-act realization varies from one language to another, and that as a result, second language learners often fail to realize their speech acts in the target language both in terms of *effectiveness* (getting their meaning across) and in terms of social appropriateness" (Blum-Kulka 1983a:38).

An important conclusion which Blum-Kulka draws from her investigation of transfer in the speech act of requesting is that language learners seem to develop what she calls "an interlanguage of speech act performance," a system that differs from both native and target language usage. Transfer of rules from the learners' native language to the target language often results in violations of norms of appropriateness. On the basis of the differences she found between the speech act performance of native speakers both of English and of Hebrew, Blum-Kulka argues that a nonuniversalistic approach to the analysis of sociolinguistic behavior is the only realistic one.

An even more recent finding regarding transfer in request behavior arises from an analysis of the CCSARP data mentioned earlier. As we have pointed out, the CCSARP design was based on a two-way comparison of native and nonnative language use in a variety of languages. Thus, a great deal of data on interlanguage pragmatics phenomena was gathered. One very significant phenomenon uncovered from the analysis of these data is that it is the learners and not the native speakers who are most verbose in carrying out specific speech acts. Thus, Blum-Kulka and Olshtain (1986) found that learners' utterances were regularly characterized by being much longer than those of native speakers. As Blum-Kulka et al. (in press) put it:

> This trend is manifested by the use of supportive moves; learners of Hebrew, regardless of linguistic background, tend to embed their requests in lengthy explanations and justifications, which in turn create undesirable effects of inappropriate use. House and Kasper . . . report the same trend for Danish and German learners of English, confirming the finding that verbosity seems to be definitely a language learning specific phenomenon. (Blum-Kulka et al. in press.)

It is noteworthy that language learners, lacking sufficient proficiency in the target language to perform requests in a fluent, nativelike manner, should so consistently choose to compensate for their difficulties by adding a great deal of unnecessary and inappropriate information. This finding about how learners attempt and fail to present themselves favorably provides us with an extremely useful insight into the pragmatics of interlanguage, substantiating Blum-Kulka's earlier (1983a) argument that second language learners "seem to develop an interlanguage of speech act performance" which is different from the sociolinguistic behavior of both first and second language native speakers.

PRAGMATIC TRANSFER IN THE EXPRESSION OF GRATITUDE

In a paper called "I Very Appreciate," Eisenstein and Bodman (1986) investigated pragmatic transfer in the speech act of expressing gratitude. As a beginning to their collection of baseline data, Eisenstein and Bodman gathered spontaneous data in which native speakers of English used formulaic expressions containing such semantic items as "appreciate" and "thank," carefully separating out those examples which had functions other than the expression of gratitude. Making use of the spontaneous data, the investigators then prepared a questionnaire incorporating 25 situations in which gratitude had been expressed. This questionnaire was then presented in written form to subjects who were asked to respond in writing by indicating what they would say if they had been in a similar situation. Following the administration of the questionnaires, informal interviews were held with both native and nonnative subjects.

What is particularly impressive about the Eisenstein and Bodman study is that their 67 nonnative speaking subjects represented 15 different language backgrounds. In order to compare the data from these language learners with baseline native speaker data, Eisenstein and Bodman gave their revised questionnaire to 56 native speakers of English who came from a wide variety of socioeconomic backgrounds and geographical areas within the United States and who represented an age span from 12 to 82 years old.

In analyzing the questionnaire data elicited from native speakers, Eisenstein and Bodman found that in spite of some individual differences, the native speakers produced highly formulaic responses. As they put it: "Another item of interest in the native data was the abundant appearance of routines and the almost ritualistic inclusion of certain semantic information. Although a wide variety of responses were theoretically possible, the native speakers were remarkably consistent in their choice of language—almost as if there were a finite number of options from which selected—a mutually shared script" (Eisenstein and Bodman 1986:15).

In contrast to the native speaker data, the nonnative speakers of English performed very differently. Their productions of expressions of gratitude were highly dissimilar from the routines used by the English-speaking Americans. According to Eisenstein and Bodman, the nonnative responses were similar to nativelike behavior only 30 percent of the time; the other 70 percent showed difficulties not only with syntax and lexicon but with the very formulas or conventionalized routines and expressions which were so strikingly typical of the data collected from native speakers.

In an extension to the original study of expressions of gratitude, Eisenstein and Bodman (in press) examined more fully the differences in the ways in which this function is expressed in English and in a variety of other languages. Using data gathered from spontaneous role-plays and from naturally occurring conversations, they sought to determine the extent to which their earlier questionnaire data reflected spoken language. What they found is that in American English, thanking is a mutually developed or negotiated speech act in which the addressee is as active as the person expressing gratitude. With respect to transfer, they found, as did Beebe and her colleagues, that advanced-level learners have considerable difficulty in attempting to perform what are, for native speakers, formulaic speech routines.

A critical finding regarding cross-cultural differences in the use of linguistic resources is that although speakers of American English used highly conventionalized formulas in their expressions of gratitude and in their responses to such expressions as well, there are relatively few fixed expressions which do not explicitly mention gratitude. In contrast, Eisenstein and Bodman found that there were many "fixed sayings which express ritualized wisdom" in the data from their Arabic-, Farsi-, and Punjabi-speaking informants. For example, Eisenstein and Bodman say that "when receiving a loan, these informants used expressions like 'May God increase your bounty'; 'May God grant you a long life'; 'You are a blessing to us from God'; (Eisenstein and Bodman in press). Although these ritualized expressions were very common in the data, the researchers found that there were few instances of these in spontaneous role-plays performed by advanced-level nonnative speakers. Rather, they found that these students evinced considerable awkwardness, with many hesitations and pauses. They attribute this behavior to the students' lack of knowledge of the relevant expressions of gratitude in American English and, even more importantly, the realization on the part of the learners that they must avoid transferring expressions of gratitude literally from their own first languages.

Eisenstein and Bodman's findings concerning both the existence and the non-transfer of precoded ritualized phrases used by Arabic and Iranian students coincide exactly with those of Wolfson (1981a) in the study of complimenting behavior among these groups. In this study, it was found that when spontaneously occurring native speaker data were gathered from conversations in Arabic and in Farsi, a large number of proverbs and other ritualized expressions, not transferred into the English used by these same speakers, were a common feature of conversational interactions containing compliments. As is pointed out in the article, entitled "Compliments in Cross-Cultural Perspective" (Wolfson 1981a):

> Compliments collected by Iranian and Arabic speakers exemplify this point particularly well. In a conversation between two Jordanian women, for instance, one says about still a third woman:

     s: X is a nice girl and beautiful.

Her friend, in order to express the view that the speaker is even more beautiful, responds with a proverb:

     A: Where is the soil compared with the star?

In complimenting her friend's child, an Arabic speaker says:

     s: She is like the moon and she has beautiful eyes.

And from an exchange between two Iranian friends, we have the following:

     s: Your shoes are very nice.
     A: It is your eyes which can see them which are nice.

While an Iranian boy says to his mother:

     s: It was delicious, Mom. I hope your hands never have pain.
     A: I'm glad you like it. (Wolfson 1981a:119-120)

Thus we see that sociolinguistic expressions may be realized not only in formulaic expressions like those used by native speakers of American English, but as ritualized precoded proverbs or expressions which may well be uninterpretable cross-culturally since some of the values and attitudes they express are so different from one society to another. It is especially impressive that in spite of their difficulty in making use of the formulaic expressions which commonly serve sociolinguistic functions in American English, advanced learners have been found to avoid direct translation or transfer of the corresponding responses from their own first languages.

INTERACTIONAL SOCIOLINGUISTICS

Another very important line of research, which relates to the study of sociolinguistic behavior and to transfer, is that known as Interactional Sociolinguistics (IS). Regarding the context in which speakers interact as something emergent that is created by the participants moment by moment through the process of interaction itself, investigators attempt to identify the cues by which people signal to one another and interpret what is happening. By means of videotapes, researchers gather data on face-to-face interaction and then analyze them in detail.

From the point of view of TESOL, what is particularly valuable about this work is that much of it has to do with communication breakdown or the failure of a speaker to accomplish a goal owing to miscommunication, usually across ethnic group boundaries. Although both participants in an interaction may be fluent speakers of English, they often come from very different backgrounds (a West Indian who has settled in Britian, for example, interacting with a mainstream speaker of British English), and although they may think that they are speaking the same language, analysis demonstrates that rules for speech behavior and its interpretation are not necessarily shared. Expectations as to rights and obligations may be very different. With regard to interpretation of what is going on in the interaction, participants make use of what Gumperz (1982a) calls *contextualization cues*. These are groups of features of the speech looked at from many different levels: lexical, intonational or prosodic, syntactic, and nonverbal. It is the shift from expected behavior that constitutes the cues. A wide range of behavior, including posture, facial expression, and intonation, as well as the use of a formal address term where an informal one is expected or vice versa, can act as cues, carrying meanings that are interpreted and responded to as part of the interaction process.

One of the major motivations of scholars working in this framework is to try to understand how miscommunication occurs, and, by providing these insights, to learn how it may best be avoided. This is an increasingly important question, since modern urban industrialized societies require that people interact, very often with total strangers, across ethnic group boundaries. That is, the populations of most large industrialized urban areas are extremely diverse. Added to this, the ever-increasing bureaucracy of our society makes it necessary for individuals to interact in institutional settings with people who are usually strangers to them and who very often come from quite different ethnic group backgrounds. As Gumperz says in his introduction to *Discourse Strategies* (1982a):

> Because it makes no assumptions about sharedness of rules or evaluative norms, the interpretive approach to conversation is particularly revealing in modern urbanized societies where social boundaries are diffuse, where intensive communication with speakers of differing backgrounds is the rule rather than the exception, and signalling conventions may vary from situation to situation. Much of the work . . . concentrates on encounters involving participants who, while speaking the same language, nevertheless show significant differences in background knowledge and must overcome or take account of the communicative symbols which signal these differences to maintain conversational engagement. (Gumperz 1982a:6)

Thus, in order to go through the educational system, to get and keep a job, to receive a variety of social services, health care, and the like, it is necessary for members of different groups to interact. The success or failure of such interactions depends to a large extent on the ability of the participants to avoid misunderstandings based on different sets of sociocultural assumptions and behavior patterns and thus to communicate with one another effectively.

In analyzing face-to-face interaction, scholars who work in this tradition (e.g., Gumperz 1982a, 1982b, Erickson and Shultz 1982) focus on what Erickson and Shultz have labeled *gatekeeping encounters*. That is, they identify situations which are examples of points in an individual's life where there is a juncture of some type, and someone else, usually a stranger, has the power to make decisions that will affect one's future in terms of, for example, socioeconomic mobility, health care, and the legal system. In each of these cases, it is the face-to-face encounter between the person seeking a particular goal and the person who has the discretionary authority regarding what sort of special treatment will be accorded the goal-seeker that will decide the outcome. Thus, important decisions which will have serious consequences for the lives of individuals are made on the basis of nonrecurring, present-moment, face-to-face interactions between strangers who are often from different ethnic backgrounds. The gatekeeper, or interviewer, must depend heavily on the interaction itself to make judgments about the interviewee, and these judgments or diagnoses have institutional force. In creating a context for one another through their interaction, the participants in these encounters must rely on their sociocultural knowledge, making use of communication patterns and interpretations which they have internalized as members of their own specific groups.

At the same time, Interactional Sociolinguistics holds that it is how people make use of these patterns that counts. From this point of view, individuals who are communicatively competent will improvise on the patterns they know, constantly responding to one another and creating an environment for one another to react to. That is, the context is never static, but always emergent. People constantly work at interaction using their communicative resources to accomplish their ends.

In the work of both Gumperz and Erickson, as well as of their students, an important motive is the attempt not only to understand how individual communication and miscommunication arises but also to investigate how these interactional processes reproduce and reinforce macrolevel patterns within a society.

In their book, *The Counselor as Gatekeeper: Social Interactions in Interviews,* Erickson and Schultz (1982) demonstrate how communication is organized. On the basis of their own studies of face-to-face encounters, and the work of others, they explain how people give each other clues as to what is going on during the emerging interaction. Thus, what the student does in the counseling session depends on how the counselor behaves, and what the counselor does is a response to how the student behaves. Together, the two participants work to create an "environment" for one another. Because college counseling is the means by which people are selected to move into a particular area of education and hence occupational opportunity, these "gatekeeping" encounters have outcomes that may well be critical to students' future lives. The "counselor as gatekeeper" has the authority to channel students into or away from certain career paths. The outcome of these sessions is in large part affected by how well the participants are able to communicate. Since members of different backgrounds are brought together in these encounters, cultural differences may well cause miscommunication.

In investigating college counseling sessions, Erickson and Shultz were looking for instances of miscommunication caused by differences in behaviors and expectations of members of different backgrounds. What they found was that while these differences do exist, and may have an important effect on the way students are treated by counselors, there are other means by which the participants in such interactions may establish other types of comembership based on commonality of experiences or interests which can cut across such ethnic group divisions. This is an extremely important finding since, by implication, it points to ways in which nonnative speakers may learn to elicit help and cooperation from native speaking interlocutors in spite of differences in sociolinguistic patterns.

A particularly poignant example of the way in which miscommunication across ethnic group lines both effects specific outcomes for individuals and leads to the reinforcement of prejudice and discrimination is given by Chick (1985) in his analysis of encounters between white South African professors and Zulu students at a South African university. Choosing situations in which students' examination results are gone over by their professors, Chick contrasts the interactions between white professors with white students, and white professors with black students who are fluent second language speakers of English. In his analysis, Chick makes use of Gumperz's framework to show how members of the two groups differ in their interpretation of one another's intentions, and in the professors' evaluations of the students' motives and abilities. As Chick says:

> I argue that asynchrony arising from a mismatch of contextualization conventions, can have serious consequences for persons from groups which do not enjoy power in South Africa (e.g., Blacks, women, immigrants). Their ability to improve their socio-economic positions depends vitally on successful communication with persons belonging to the dominant group (white males) who occupy most "gatekeeping" positions (e.g., job interviewers, examiners, educational and career counsellors etc.). Such people have the power to decide who is to get opportunities and a greater share of the help, goods and services a society has to offer. Where their abilities are misjudged as a consequence of miscommunication, members of powerless groups fare badly in attempts to advance themselves. Moreover, the negative cultural stereotypes generated by repeated intercultural communication failures, further reduce the effectiveness because, even when contextualization conventions do not cause problems, they predispose people to selectively perceive whatever reinforces the stereotypes and ignore what does not. Once generated, these stereotypes are often passed on from generation to generation without needing to be constantly reinforced by discrimination, and by providing a justification or rationalization for discrimination, contribute to forces which maintain the social barriers and power differential between groups, which made it difficult, in the first place, for people to learn the contextualization conventions of other groups.

TESOL AND THE STUDY OF MISCOMMUNICATION ACROSS CULTURES

As has been demonstrated throughout this chapter, the area of pragmatic failure, transfer, and sociolinguistic miscommunication is of critical importance to everyone concerned with understanding and solving the problems having to do with intercultural communication. In this respect, it is clear that both lines of inquiry, that into pragmatic transfer of specific sociolinguistic rules and that known as interactional sociolinguistics, have great importance to the field of TESOL.

In the past several years the issue of pragmatic transfer has been increasingly recognized as a critical one for researchers into second language acquisition. Given the intrinsic interest of the subject and, more crucially, its importance for materials writers and instructors as well as for language learners themselves, scholars in the field of applied linguistics have begun to focus more and more attention on sociolinguistic or pragmatic transfer, with the result that many more systematic empirical studies of this phenomenon are being contributed to the literature.

With respect to the microanalysis of face-to-face interaction between members of different ethnic groups living in the same society, the implications for the teaching of sociocultural rules are equally inescapable. Chick (1984) makes explicit the important link between the information gathered by this sort of fine-tuned analysis and its application to TESOL. From the point of view of communicative language teaching, he points out, these analyses can provide insights to teachers that will make them much more deeply aware of the subtleties involved in becoming communicatively competent in a second language. With this knowledge, language learners can be guided in developing "interpretive strategies for negotiating, together with other interlocutors, the contexts for their talk, and for using this contextual information to infer the functional and social meaning of what is being said." Methods to accomplish this aim would include "task-based activities in which learners are required to use language to overcome an information gap or solve a problem, and in which both the motivation for success and the yardstick for success are to be found in the situation itself."

As a significant side note to Chick's discussion of the methods best suited to help language learners to acquire communicative competence, it should be pointed out that researchers in the United States, have been testing just these sorts of task-based activities, and that findings and recommendations show strong convergence. Coming at the problem of how best to facilitate language learning in classrooms, second language acquisition researchers such as Pica (1983, 1985a,b), Pica and Doughty (in press), and Pica et al. (1986, 1987) have designed and carried out a great deal of research in which language learners are required to engage in a task which requires cooperation through communication on the part of each of the students. Pica (1985a) concludes that: "What seems essential is the combination of group interaction and a task with a built-in information gap which places demands on students to convey and receive meaningful messages in the second language rather than simply inviting them to do so."

Thus, it appears that the empirical investigation of pragmatic transfer and related work in interactional sociolinguistics have a great deal to contribute to our understanding of why and how communication breaks down, and how the larger social consequences of such repeated breakdowns takes place. Finally, we are led to means by which, as applied linguists, curriculum writers, and instructors of English to nonnative speakers, we can apply this information in concrete ways. Clearly, this area of work is still in its infancy. Much more research into specific areas of pragmatic transfer are needed, and means for the dissemination and use of this knowledge must be worked out. Considerable progress has already been made; there is every reason to expect that this work will burgeon rapidly so that we will soon have at our disposal much more desperately needed information concerning the ways in which sociolinguistic miscommunication is manifested.

CHAPTER
8

Language and Sex

INTRODUCTION

An increasingly important area of sociolinguistic work which has great potential relevance for TESOL is that which is usually categorized under the heading of language and sex. The research that has been going on in this area deserves to be reported in a book of this sort for two reasons. The first reason has to do with language teaching directly; that is, as specialists in language teaching, we need to be aware of findings concerning the differences between men's and women's speech so that we will not teach inappropriate forms to our students. The fact that the studies which have resulted in the findings to be reported in this chapter were conducted in order to discover what, if any, differences exist in the speech of men and women, and how speech to men and women may differ, is very important to the field of TESOL. If there are differences, we need to know what they are so that we can incorporate this information into our teaching and our curriculum materials. The fact that sexism is already inadvertently woven into much of the materials in use in ESL classrooms is another facet of the same issue, though it has more to do with what we teach our students about the target culture than how we teach them to express themselves. The second reason we need to know as much as possible about this area of sociolinguistic work is that research on speech patterns of men and women who are native speakers of American English constitutes an important source of information regarding rules of speaking in these communities. We have seen again and again in earlier chapters how much we can learn about sociocultural values by studying the speech patterns that manifest them. Sex has clearly been shown to be a sociolinguistic variable, and in order to fully understand sociolinguistic rules, we must take into account what is known about the way speech behavior is constrained by it.

Research into language and sex may be said to fall into two major categories. The first has to do with sexism in language or the ways in which speakers (and writers) demonstrate their different cultural attitudes toward men and women. The second major category concerns possible or alleged differences in the actual speech of men and women. As research into both these areas has progressed in recent years, however, it is becoming more and more apparent that there are important connections between them. Since most work on language and sex has tended to focus on one of the two areas mentioned, we will in this chapter maintain the

162

conventional distinction while recognizing that the lines between them are sometimes blurred.

Both areas of research, that into sexism in language and that which concerns
differences in the speech of men and women, are relatively new. Like so much of
the work covered in this book, research into language and sex did not really begin in
a systematic or serious way until the early 1970s. This is not to suggest that no one
before had ever noticed or made mention of sex-related differences in speech. Such
differences have always been a source of fascination, especially with respect to the
ways in which these manifested themselves in non-Western societies, and for centuries travelers, missionaries, and scholars have reported on what they regarded as
unusual and exotic. It is significant, however, that there was until very recently no
scientific investigation of gender-related differences among speakers of European
languages. Apparently, this sort of research was inhibited by an unquestioning
acceptance of existing stereotypes. The reasoning seems to have been that since
everyone already knew what the differences were between men's and women's
speech in their own societies, there was no point in investigating them. Folk wisdom about language took for granted that men's language was "the language" and
that insofar as women might speak differently, their speech must be considered
deviant. In his treatise *Language: Its Nature, Development, and Origin*, Otto Jespersen (1922) devotes an entire chapter to "The Woman." Here he discusses
accounts of differences between men's and women's speech in exotic (non-Western) societies. Many of these differences he attributes to taboos on what women
may say. Thus, in describing the Bantu people of Africa, he says:

> With the Zulus a wife is not allowed to mention the name of her father-in-law
> and of his brothers, and if a similar word or even a similar syllable occurs in the
> ordinary language, she must substitute something else of a similar meaning. In
> the royal family the difficulty of understanding the women's language is further
> increased by the woman's being forbidden to mention the names of her hus-
> band, his father and grandfather as well as his brothers. If one of these names
> means something like "the son of the bull," each of these words has to be
> avoided and all kinds of paraphrases have to be used. (Jespersen 1922:239)

Jespersen then goes on to describe the speech of women in western European
societies, particularly English. Although he gives very little evidence to support his
description of women's speech, Jespersen does not hesitate to assert that women are
prone to use euphemistic words and paraphrases in order to avoid "coarse" language, and to use less extensive and much more conservative vocabularies than
men. In describing the way women speak, Jespersen goes on to say that women use
more emotionally loaded adverbs and adjectives (especially intensifiers like *so* and
such), employ less complicated sentence structure, and have a tendency to express
themselves in partial or unfinished sentences. Jespersen says that women think and
read more quickly than men do and therefore fly from subject to subject. However,
this rapidity is not attributed to greater intellect. Rather, it is explained that men are

slower because they are more thorough in evaluating what they say and read, and have more background information to bring to this evaluation than women, who simply accept every statement "immediately and without inspection to fill the vacant chambers of the mind. . ." (Jespersen 1922:252).

It was not until the current women's movement that these and other largely unsubstantiated generalizations began to be questioned. The area of research currently subsumed under the heading of language and sex took hold quickly and has expanded and extended into many disciplines in addition to linguistics. Scholars trained in anthropology, folklore, psychology, child development, education, sociology, speech communication, history and literature have brought their skills to research in this field, so that a considerable literature has developed over the past 15 years. The fact that scholars from a variety of disciplines have engaged in research into language and sex has led not only to a great many exciting results but also to more and more questions as researchers have come to grips with the complexity of the problem.

One of the most provocative of the present-day scholars to deal with the issue of language and sex, both in terms of sexism in language and in terms of differences between the speech of men and women, is Robin Lakoff. In an article which appeared in *Language in Society* in 1973, Lakoff argued that language gives expression to cultural assumptions and for this reason it both reflects and reinforces the social order. What was especially important about this argument was that she chose to illustrate the point by giving examples of the ways in which women in our society are shown to have inferior status both by the way they are spoken about and by the way they themselves speak. Thus, Lakoff claimed that while men's language is assertive, adult, and direct, women's language is immature, nonassertive, and hyperpolite. Although Lakoff based her description of women's language entirely on her own intuitions and casual observations, her discussion of such characteristics was very valuable. On the one hand, because she based her analysis on her own native speaker intuition, she inadvertently characterized for us the stereotypes common in mainstream American society. On the other hand, Lakoff's claims about women's language, based as they were on introspection, challenged other scholars to design and carry out empirical studies to test them. In this sense, Lakoff (1973) may well be seen as a forerunner of recent research into language and gender in Western societies. Lakoff's original description covers both the phenomena of sexism in language and of putative differences in the speech of women and men. In the pages to follow, we will examine both these areas.

SEXISM IN LANGUAGE

It is important to recognize that in English there are no categorical grammatical differences which depend upon the gender of the speaker or the addressee. Since the linguistic system of English makes no such gender-based distinctions, any differences which are found can be explained only by examining social norms or expectations. Sexism in language is not truly systemic in English but is rather a reflection of the social attitudes of speakers, both male and female. In the current literature on language and gender, the investigation into sexism in language takes as its central theme the fact that females are either excluded from mention in English (the "he/man" problem) or given disparaging treatment not accorded to men. Both the exclusion and the semantic inequality which exist in English have been extensively studied. With respect to grammatical usage, the "he/man" issue has received particular emphasis, both in terms of its theoretical implications and in terms of the effect of this usage on speakers. As P. M. Smith (1985:48) puts it: "Of all the referential asymmetries that pertain to the female-male domain, none has attracted more attention and controversy than the practice of using nouns and pronouns that are marked for masculinity (*man, mankind, he, him, his*) when referring to people in a general sense, and to individuals of unknown or indefinite sex." Thus, the use of the singular pronouns *he* and *him* or the generic use of *man* to refer to all humans irrespective of sex is commonly cited to demonstrate how the English language works to make the male seem to be the representative of the human species and his speech to be the standard. This usage, it is felt, has a damaging effect on the way females are taught to view themselves. There is some dispute over whether the generic use of *he/man* is, in fact, interpreted as generic by those who hear or read these pronouns, and a considerable number of experiments have provided evidence that the so-called generic *he* is by no means always understood to include both sexes, even where it is clearly meant to do so.

In one such study, Mackay and Fulkerson (1979) asked students to indicate whether or not they thought that sentences which had sex-related nouns (e.g., *aunt*) or pronouns (*her*, referring to the noun *housekeeper*) or the generic *he* (e.g. "he is not safe from dogs") could be understood to refer to females. The results showed that where students were given sex-linked nouns or pronouns, they almost never had problems understanding whether a male or a female was being referred to. On the other hand, where the sentences contained the generic *he*, problems in comprehension occurred in 87 percent of the cases. What is particularly noteworthy about this finding is that the sentences given used the generic *he* in reference to nouns which are culturally linked with females, such as *model* and *secretary,* as well as with either those linked with males or those which could have been read as neutral. That is, the sex-linked meaning of the noun to which the generic pronoun referred did not seem to have much influence on the way the pronoun was interpreted. The point of Mackay and Fulkerson's research findings is that the pronoun *he* is nearly always interpreted as referring to a male, even when the context of the sentence would otherwise lead people to recognize that a female was being referred to.

Some of the best known research into the "he/man" problem has been carried out by Martyna (1978, 1980, 1983). An example of her investigation into actual interpretations of the generic term is an experiment she conducted (Martyna 1980) in which she gave subjects sentences with one of three generic pronouns (*he, they,* and *he* or *she*). Each sentence was followed by a picture of either a male or a female, and the subjects were asked to judge whether the picture was appropriately matched to the sentence. The underlying question was that if the pronoun *he* is truly interpreted in its generic sense, then pictures of females should be seen as appropriately related to sentences which contained the generic pronoun *he*. If, on the other hand, the pronoun *he* is ambiguous or sex-exclusive in the minds of those who hear or read it, sentences which contain the pronoun *he* will often be judged inappropriate. The results of Martyna's study showed that 20 percent of the subjects felt that a female picture did *not* match a sentence which contained a generic *he*. In a second experiment, Martyna presented subjects with the sentence and the picture at the same time, and in this case some 40 percent reported that the female picture was inappropriate. In still another study, subjects were asked to give names to each of 10 hypothetical people. Four of these were referred to as either *he* or *they*, or *he* and *she*. It was found that when the pronoun used was *he*, more male names were chosen than when it was *they* or *he and she*. Furthermore, male subjects chose many more male names than did female subjects. As Martyna says, "Although women are unwilling to use the generic masculine to refer to themselves, they seem to make a special effort to draw generic interpretation from 'he' and 'man,' for to do otherwise means self-exclusion" (Martyna 1980:75).

There are many English speakers who regard the "he/man" problem as trivial, but it is worth considering and letting students of the language know not only that for many others the use of the singular pronoun *he* as a generic is extremely irritating and often confusing, but also that it has been known to lead to some rather painfully amusing situations. Illustrations of the awkwardness of using the generic *he* abound in the literature. When Dr. S. I. Hayakawa was asked about his stand on abortion, for example, he replied, "I believe it's strictly a matter between the patient and his doctor," a comment which may be grammatically correct from a prescriptive standpoint but seems a bit shaky from the biological point of view. An equally ridiculous quotation comes from the General Assembly of the State of Connecticut: "At least twenty-four hours before any abortion is performed in the state, the person who is to have such abortion shall receive counselling . . . concerning his decision to have such abortion."

These quotations may seem funny, but it is not particularly amusing to recognize the following, as does Graham (1973:62): "If a woman is swept off a ship into the water, the cry is 'man overboard!' If she is is killed by a hit and run driver, the charge is 'manslaughter.' If she is injured on the job, the coverage is 'workman's compensation.' But when she arrives at a threshold marked 'men only,' she knows the admonition is not intended to bar animals or plants or inanimate objects. It is meant for her."

Quite a number of books on language and gender have included discussions, descriptions, and theoretical positions on the use of the prescriptive masculine pronouns used to refer to sex-indefinite nouns. Spender (1980) states that the prescriptive grammarians' insistence on the use of *he* to refer to both males and females is one of the ways in which men have made use of language to codify male supremacy. Through the use of the masculine forms *he, him, man,* and *mankind,* females have been excluded from consideration as members of the human species.

The ambiguity resulting from this usage is amply demonstrated by Miller and Swift (1976):

> The "generic man" trap . . . operates through every kind of medium whenever the human species is being talked about. Writing in a national magazine, the psychoanalyst Erick Fromm described man's "vital interests" as "life, food, access to females, etc." One may be saddened but not surprised at the statement "man is the only primate that commits rape." Although, as commonly understood, it can apply to only half the human population, it is nevertheless semantically acceptable. But, "man, being a mammal, breast-feeds his young" is taken as a joke. (Miller and Swift 1976:23)

The fact that even young children are taught to understand the word *man* as referring to the male of the species is also brought out by Miller and Swift, who say:

> A word means what it means not because of what dictionaries say about it, but because most speakers of the language use it with a certain meaning in mind and expect others to use it with the same meaning. If Billy, at age three or four, were to see the "Avon lady" coming up the front walk and say to his mother "Here comes a man," she would correct him. If at nursery school he were asked to draw a picture of a man and he drew a figure that appeared to be a woman, he might well be carted off to a psychiatrist.

Studies of the way in which young children interpret the word *man* have been conducted by scholars such as Alleen Pace Nilsen (1977), who found that most children of both sexes interpreted *man* in sentences such as "Around the world man is happy" to refer to males and not to females. No one knows exactly how this exclusionary usage affects children's views of themselves, but both pediatricians and child psychologists have gone on record as saying that the practice is a form of discrimination which could cause enormous harm. Alma Graham makes the point particularly clear when she says: "If you have a group half of whose members are A's and half of whose members are B's and if you call the group C, then A's and B's may be equal members of group C. But if you call the group A, there is no way that B's can be equal to A's within it. The A's will always be the rule and the B's will always be the exception—the subgroup, the subspecies, the outsiders" (Graham, cited in Miller and Swift 1976:29).

Other writers, such as Frank and Anshen (1983), hold that in spite of prescriptive dictates regarding the use of *he* and *him*, the choice of pronoun in actual use will depend heavily on the sex roles of the referents, as defined by the culture in question. Thus, when referring to a nurse or a schoolteacher of unknown sex, speakers will normally use the pronoun *she*, while *he* is much more generally used to refer to doctors and professors. Be that as it may, and it is probably accurate with respect to sex-specific use in everyday conversation, the fact remains that the "he/man" problem does lead to endless confusion, ambiguity, and a strong sense of exclusion for women. It is impossible to judge how much this is a cause and how much an effect of discrimination against women in our society. What is important is that as long as it continues to be used in this way, women will both be seen and see themselves as not quite equal to the males of the species.

Another very significant aspect of sexism in language concerns the terms of address and reference used to and about men and women. Studies by Kramer (1975) and by McConnell-Ginet (1978) found that women in general American society had at their disposal a much smaller repertoire of address forms than did men. That is, while men seem to be free to address other men, especially those whose occupations involve driving taxis or bartending, by use of such terms as *Buddy* or *Mac*, social rules for women preclude such usages. Both authors comment that women are frequently addressed by terms of endearment even in situations where the speaker is a total stranger or a nonintimate with whom the female addressee is not in a position to reciprocate such terms.

With respect to the use of names as terms of address and reference, the literature is somewhat less clear. R. B. Rubin (1981), in a study of terms of address for male and female professors, found that female professors, especially those in the 26 to 33 age group, were addressed by first name much more often than their male colleagues. Since Rubin's data show female students using familiar terms more often than male students, it is unclear whether the motivation for this more familiar address pattern has to do with women students' greater sense of solidarity with young female professors or with their perceptions of more equal status with female professors than with male.

In a study which included both observation and interviews, students in my sociolinguistics class were asked to gather data on the way male and female professors were referred to by secretaries and other lower-level staff in a large northeastern university. Several departments were investigated, and it was found that, by and large, both females and younger male faculty were referred to by first name, while older male faculty nearly always received title and last name. The one exception was a department in which there was an explicit convention stating that all professors would be addressed and referred to by first name. Where secretaries did use first name for women while reserving title and last name for male faculty, this usage appeared to be a manifestation of a combination of female solidarity with a sense that female professors were in lower-status positions than their male colleagues, even where age and rank were similar. Examples of actual address and reference forms used in everyday interaction suggest that a perception of lower status for female faculty is the stronger reason. The fact that such usage was pervasive and largely unconscious is evidenced by several examples:

1. When two faculty members of approximately the same age and status, one a male and the other a female, arrived for an appointment with a senior administrator, the receptionist announced their presence through the intercom, saying, "Dr. X, Mary and Dr. Smith are here to see you."
2. One middle-aged female secretary in the dean's office was asked how she addressed male and female professors. She said, "I always call female professors Dr. X—because I'm so proud of you girls."

3. An invitation to a reception given by the president of the university for newly tenured faculty was sent to a female professor who had recently been awarded tenure. The invitation was addressed to Mrs. John Smith. The fact that John Smith had not been awarded tenure and was not, indeed, involved in academics at all was irrelevant here, as was the more important fact that the woman whose achievement was being celebrated was not even accorded her own name or rank.

In her (1977) book *Body Politics,* Nancy Henley points out that many features of male/female interaction which are commonly attributed to feelings of friendliness or solidarity are, in fact, heavily loaded with connotations of male dominance over females. A good example of this is the nonreciprocal way in which terms of endearment are used in many English-speaking societies. As McConnell-Ginet says, "Men receive endearments only from intimate women while women receive them from everybody" (McConnell-Ginet 1978:32).

What is particularly remarkable about this observation regarding address forms used by speakers of general American English is the way in which strangers in public situations address unknown women by terms of endearment (Wolfson and Manes 1978). In an ethnographic investigation of the forms of address used to women in service encounters (e.g., address by gas station attendants, waiters and waitresses, salesclerks), it was observed that women in American society are often addressed with a good deal less respect than are men. Approximately one thousand naturally occurring interactions were observed and recorded in which women of various occupations, ages, and social backgrounds were addressed by men and women of equally diverse backgrounds. Although learners of English are usually taught that where names are unknown, the forms *miss* or *ma'am* and *sir* are used in English, this was found not to hold true in many situations. Observations of Americans interacting spontaneously with one another in public places revealed that women whose names are not known to the speaker are usually addressed in one of three ways: by the respect form *ma'am,* by no address form at all (zero form), or by a so-called term of endearment such as *dear, hon,* or even *sweetheart* or *doll.* The first two of these address types, the respect form and the zero form, are used in parallel ways to both men and women. That is, both sexes may be addressed by the appropriate form, *ma'am* or *sir,* and both may be addressed without any term at all. The third address type, the term of endearment, is used to males only infrequently in service encounters, and then usually only by older women to much younger men. We recorded no cases of men using these forms to other men, although it has been suggested that such usage may well occur in some places. In contrast, it was found that women are very frequently addressed with endearment terms both by men and by other women. Series of interactions were recorded in which one woman after another was addressed by a salesclerk as *hon* or *dear,* while men in the same line, asking for service from the same clerk, were regularly addressed as *sir.* There were no instances of the reverse occurring.

Thus it seems that women in American society (no matter what their age or social status) are frequently addressed by what many would consider an intimate form, often by men much younger than they. It is rare that any but very young men are given such treatment, and then only by much older women. Although it is not clear exactly how far this usage extends, it was recorded throughout the Northeast, in the South, in several midwestern cities, and in major cities on the west coast.

What is especially noteworthy about the use of terms of endearment to women in service encounters is that their use is, apparently, nonreciprocal. What this means is that, unlike forms of this type used to intimates, the person who is addressed by a term of endearment by a stranger does not use it in return. Although we have some cases in the data where the term of endearment was used by a customer to a salesclerk instead of the other way around, we have no instances in which a person so addressed reciprocated by using the same or a similar term when responding to her interlocutor. According to the analytic model first put forth by Brown and Gilman (1960) and Brown and Ford (1961), nonreciprocal address forms, in English and other languages, carry with them the implication that the addressee is somehow subordinate to the speaker. An example is the extreme freedom with which adults—strangers as well as friends and relatives—address children by terms of endearment, while children, no matter what their relationship with an adult, may never use these terms as address forms. The fact that women are addressed publicly by nonreciprocal terms of endearment, no matter what their age or status, may be seen as a sign that females are generally held in less respect than are males in American society. It should be pointed out in this context that although the usage described here is fairly widespread, it is nevertheless a source of extreme irritation to many women.

For this reason, although learners need to know that such forms are in use so that they will not be confused by being addressed in this way, they would be well advised not to use such forms themselves. Lest this seem to be gratuitous advice, it should be mentioned that learners do very often incorporate terms of this type into unanalyzed chunks acquired by copying the speech of native speakers. Thus, it is not uncommon to observe a beginning learner of English address his or her interlocutor by a term of endearment in a service encounter. An example of this phenomenon occurred when, at the conclusion of a service interaction, a young Asian man who appeared to be at the very beginning stages of English acquisition was heard to say to a woman who had just purchased some vegetables from him: "Have good day, dear." Clearly, the speaker had no idea that he was using an address form that was not part of the salutation. On several other occasions, restaurant waiters who appeared to have very little control of English were overheard to include a term of endearment in their request for an order.

While the use of nonreciprocal terms of endearment to women in service encounters has been well documented, there are other, similar uses of endearment terms which have not yet been investigated systematically. One of the most salient of these is the use of endearment terms by males to female friends or colleagues. Going back to Henley's (1977) observation that many aspects of male/female interaction which appear to be manifestations of friendliness or solidarity are in fact demonstrations of male dominance, it would be instructive to note here that the nonreciprocal use of any form of address is suspect precisely on the grounds that the person who receives it cannot return it unless she or he deliberately breaks the social conventions in order to make a point. The fact that many males regularly use terms of endearment to female colleagues, for example, is a clear message of dominance and power since the man is well aware (at however unconscious a level) that the woman who has been so addressed is not free to reciprocate by addressing him similarly. The same rule holds for the nonreciprocal use of terms of endearment by males to female friends.

The study of differential terms of address and reference for women and men of the "same" occupational status and the investigation of terms of endearment to women in service encounters (Wolfson and Manes 1978, 1980) are, then, only a few manifestations of the uninvited and often unwanted intimacies that women are forced to accept. Terms of address and reference are, however unconsciously used, rather transparent and easily noticed. What is not so obvious is a more general tendency among speakers of American English to show less respect or deference to women through the frequency and type of speech acts considered appropriate to address to them. Two examples of this phenomenon were discovered during the investigation of complimenting behavior (Wolfson and Manes 1980, Wolfson 1983a) and a class research project concerning cross-cultural attitudes toward inappropriate questions.

With respect to the work on inappropriate questions, it was discovered that in both the ethnographic observation and the interview data, there were almost no examples of what the researchers or their subjects judged inappropriate questions. A particularly remarkable point arising from the analysis of the interview data is that questions that might have been reported as inappropriate in the sense of being too personal were often not reported by women because, it was speculated, women may be so accustomed to having their privacy invaded in this way that they do not notice such questions or judge them as particularly inappropriate. It was found, on the other hand, that men, especially older, native English-speaking men, were virtually unapproachable and received almost no questions which the investigators considered inappropriate. As one of the reports stated: "Our ethnographic data reinforced the tendency that we noticed in our interview data: males receive less 'inappropriate' questions than females. In fact, the ethnographic data revealed only one 'inappropriate' question directed toward a male" (Dalsheim et al. 1986:5).

With respect to the study of compliments, a great deal has already been said in an earlier chapter, and I will restrict my comments here specifically to the differences in both type and distribution of compliments received by the two sexes. To begin with, one of the functions of compliments as used by speakers of American English is to encourage or reinforce desired behavior. In the original analysis, it appeared that there were two separate topic categories of compliments—those having to do with appearance and those having to do with accomplishment. However, if we take desired behavior to include performance not only in the sense of a job well done but also in the sense of acting out a socially accepted role, then it appears that nearly all compliments are social judgments of performance.

If this is true, it provides an explanation for some sex-linked aspects of complimenting which had not previously been clear.

One such problem has to do with the interaction of topic of compliment with the status and the sex of the addressee. That is, the effect of status as a variable was very strong when the sex of the addressee was male. Upper-status males rarely received compliments, and these were nearly never associated with appearance. That there are few ability/performance compliments to higher-status males is easily explained since it is the person in the position of authority who has the right to encourage, guide, and judge the behavior of subordinates. Since males are usually in either equal or higher positions than women in the workplace, it is not surprising that the great majority of such compliments are addressed to women. With respect to compliments of the appearance/possession type, women are again the recipients of the great majority of compliments. In this case, however, the status of the woman seems to have little if any effect, since she can be complimented on her appearance by virtually anyone. This is not true for men. In fact, in spite of many efforts to collect samples of compliments addressed to men, it remains true that they are rare. Further, the constraints on compliments of the appearance type to men who are older or of higher status than the speaker are very great.

What is the explanation for the distinction between women and men as addressees of compliments? If we move away from topic distinction and accept the view that all compliments are, at some level, a means of expressing approval or encouragement of socially accepted role behavior, then the matter becomes quite clear. Women in American society are expected to make themselves as attractive as possible and to be interested in clothing, jewelry, hairstyles, and all forms of adornment, as well as in matters related to home and children. For a woman to look attractive is one aspect of acting out a socially conditioned role and thus must be seen as performance. These role expectations are not at all changed by the woman's professional status. Seen in this light, it is clear why women, whatever their status, are frequent recipients of compliments having to do with their female role. If we take note of the deference accorded to high-status males which places a strong constraint on "personal" comments by subordinates or, indeed, by strangers, and compare this with the absence of any such constraints on speech to women of similar status, we see that no matter what professional level a woman may attain, she is still treated like a woman.

In order to illustrate how this pattern is acted out in everyday situations, we have a number of examples. In the first, a female professor upon walking into an office to speak with a male colleague, is greeted by his secretary who says, "Hi. Cute outfit!" and in another situation, we have a senior professional woman walking in the hallway of her office building and being greeted by a much lower-ranking female staff member who says, "Those are some beautiful shoes you're wearing." Personal comments relating to women's physical dimensions are also quite common: "Join us for dessert. With your figure, you don't have to worry about the calories."

If females who have reached a certain degree of status have little protection against such personal comments, females in positions subordinate to males have none at all. Typical of the kind of "compliments" that come their way is the following, said to a secretary by her boss: "You look so pretty when you smile. You should do it more often." There are no examples of male subordinates being spoken to in this way. It is only when we regard attractive appearance in the light of socially approved performance that we can make any sense of behavior which must otherwise be considered very odd indeed. Two examples, very different from one another, fit into this category. The first, like the one above, has to do with a woman's smile. In this case, however, the setting was a small restaurant where a group of women were eating. Involved in their own conversation, they were amazed when a completely strange man, middle class and middle-aged, stopped at their table on his way out of the restaurant and addressed one of the women with this comment: "I've been watching you all through lunch. You have a beautiful smile. It lights up the whole room." And with that, the man walked out, never to be seen again.

The second example is, in a sense, even more peculiar, since the interlocutors were colleagues, the setting was a university building in which both worked, and the behavior violated an unwritten rule that only in case of emergency may a professor be interrupted while lecturing to a class. As it happened, the class was a large one, the door was open, and much to the surprise of the professor and her class, a male colleague walking past the door caught sight of her and walked right in. Coming up close to her and interrupting her in the middle of a sentence, he said, "Can I whisper in your ear? I didn't have a chance to tell you this morning how lovely you look!" It is, of course, unimaginable that any male professor could be treated in a similar way, just as it is unimaginable that a woman would walk up to a strange man in a restaurant and compliment him on his smile. If we are to make sense of these and other, similar examples, we have no recourse but to recognize that women, because of their role in the social order, are seen as appropriate recipients of all manner of intimacies and social judgments in the form of compliments.

With respect to the foregoing discussions on differences in the way men and women are treated in terms of forms of address, personal questions, and compliments on appearance, Lakoff's (1973) argument that speaking like a lady keeps a lady in her place seems to miss the point. What we see in these analyses of speech behavior to women is that the way a woman is spoken to is, no matter what her status, a subtle and powerful way of perpetuating her subordinate role in society.

Another area of research having to do with sexism in language, and one which may, in some respects, be of even more interest to those interested in language teaching, is that concerned with what has been termed the semantic derogation of women. Bosmajian (1974), in *The Language of Oppression*, discusses the fact that language serves both to reflect and to perpetuate society's beliefs. The fact that the word *female* is attached before a word describing a profession (e.g., "female judge," "female doctor") is seen as belittling to women and particularly harmful to girls growing up in an English-speaking society. If these young girls are given the impression that it is normally men who occupy positions of high status, it will be more difficult for them to identify with such careers themselves. Lakoff (1973) argues that the need to identify a female professional by indicating overtly that she *is* a female is only part of the problem. Certainly, this usage demonstrates that apart from some culturally defined "women's professions," such as elementary school teaching and nursing, it is assumed that males occupy most of the professional positions in English-speaking societies. This, however, is only part of the story. The use of the word *lady* rather than *woman*, Lakoff says, is in itself derogatory, in the sense that it implies a certain lack of importance or seriousness.

The point that males are regarded as the standard is particularly well put by Spender (1980), who says: "Masculinity is the unmarked form: the assumption is that the world is male unless proven otherwise. Femininity is the marked form; it is the proof of otherwise." (Spender 1980:20). Worse, says Stanley (1977a,b), it is not only that the English vocabulary is heavily oriented toward males, it is also the case that the semantic items specifically identified with females carry the connotation of being of less value than their male counterparts. For this reason, Stanley says that women have less semantic space in English and that what they do have is mainly negative.

Perhaps the ugliest aspect of this problem is the existence of a great many more negative words for females in the English language than there are for males. That many of these began as designations for the same state, role, or condition as their male counterpart words, and that it is only the words denoting females which have taken on negative meanings, has been one of the major pieces of evidence to demonstrate the low esteem in which females are held in English-speaking societies. The fact that the word *queen*, for example, has a negative connotation, and one which is, moreover bound up with sex in a disapproving way, is good evidence for this phenomenon when it is compared with its counterpart, *king*, which is used only to mean the crowned head of a nation or, metaphorically, a particularly fine male leader, as found in expressions such as "a king of industry" or even "the king of beggars." The fact that the words *dame, mistress*, and *madam* have all taken on negative sexual meanings, while *sir, master*, and *mister* have none, is further evidence of the way in which speakers of the English language have given connotations of indignity to words referring to females while treating their male counterparts with respect. When we look at such pairs as *hound* and *bitch*, we see that not even words which refer to animals are exempt from negative sexist overtones.

Indeed, a look at the metaphoric use of animal names to refer to human subjects is instructive. Clearly, it is not the case that animal terms are never used to denote males. Men and women may be described as pigs, dogs, chickens, snakes, skunks, and turkeys. It is worth noticing, however, that to call a woman a pig or a dog implies that she is unattractive sexually. No such connotation applies to males. On the other hand, to call a man a tiger implies that he is aggressive, a valued masculine attribute, and to call him a bear implies merely that he is large. Only two animal terms, wolf and goat, carry negative sexual connotations for men, and in

both cases they imply excessive and usually aggressive sexual drive, another attribute which is not regarded as altogether negative by most English speakers. In
comparison, nearly all of the animal metaphors used to describe only women, and
there are many, have negative overtones related to the sex of the referent. Thus,
women are called chicks, birds, and kittens when they are young and attractive, but
they are called cows, dogs, pigs, and even horses when they are not. There is no
male equivalent of these terms, since they denote male judgments of women, while
the pejorative terms used for men such as *wolf* and *goat* indicate not that the man is
unattractive to women but that he is an attacker and user of women—an active
rather than a passive role. The only non-sex-related animal metaphor used exclusively about women is *cat*, which connotes a spiteful, gossiping woman. There is
no male equivalent.

What is particularly distressing about the semantic derogation of woman is that
it clearly appears to be part of a historical process whereby words which once were
positive or neutral and often used to refer to members of either sex have taken on
negative sexual connotations and are now used exclusively about women. As
Spender (1980:22–23) explains it:

> Words such as biddy and tart have shifted dramatically in meaning since they
> were first used positively as terms of endearment. Tart meant a small pie or
> pastry and its first metaphorical application was as a term of affection and
> warmth. Not surprisingly in a society where women are evaluated as sexual
> objects, the meaning shifted to that of a young woman who was sexually
> desirable, and then—of course—to a woman of careless morals. Finally and
> currently it refers to women of the street. . . .
>
> The semantic rule which has been responsible for the manifestation of
> sexism in the language can be simply stated; there are two fundamental catego-
> ries, male and minus male. To be linked with male is to be linked to a range of
> meanings which are positive and good; to be linked to minus male is to be linked
> to the absence of those qualities, that is, to be decidedly negative and usually
> sexually debased.

Still another manifestation of this semantic rule is that it is nearly always an
insult to use a female word when referring to a male, while the reverse is not at all
the case. Thus, to call a woman by a term usually associated with males is sometimes intended as a compliment (e.g., "She has as much courage as any man here",
or even "She's a good man to have on the team"), sometimes as neutral (e.g.,
"She's a bachelor girl"), but very rarely as an insult. In contrast, to call a man by a
term associated with women is nearly always an affront. Thus, while it is acceptable
to refer to a woman as a bachelor, calling a man a spinster or an old maid implies
that he is nervous and prissy and, worst of all insults, unmanly. It is important for
second language learners to be made aware that this is the case. As Schulz
(1975:65) says: "If you speak of a woman as being a warlock, you may be corrected; if you say a man is a witch, he is presumed to have a vile temper. Or call a

woman an old man and you have simply made an error of identification. Call a man an old woman or a granny and you have insulted him.''

GENDER-RELATED LANGUAGE DIFFERENCES

As we mentioned earlier, Lakoff (1973) was one of the early articles to deal with the issue of differences in men's and women's speech. Basing her claims entirely on introspection, Lakoff describes and discusses six major characteristics of what she calls women's speech.

1. *Lexical choice:* Certain words are, according to Lakoff, used almost exclusively by women. These include the less common color terms such as *mauve* and *chartreuse*. In addition, Lakoff claims that women use "empty" adjectives such as *divine* and *cute*. These adjectives are said to be not only meaningless but also devoid of any connotation of power if contrasted with "men's adjectives," such as *great* and *terrific*.

Although it is not my purpose to evaluate each of Lakoff's claims here, I would like to draw the reader's attention back to the study of complimenting behavior among speakers of American English (Wolfson and Manes 1980), in which it was clearly demonstrated that one of the five most common adjectives used by men and women alike is *great*. It would also be instructive in this context to point out that the adjective *cute* was found to occur about equally in the speech of both men and women, and that the adjective *divine* did not occur at all in our data. In going through the claims made by Lakoff regarding women's speech, it is important to keep in mind that these are based on introspection and not on empirical findings. Because the claims she put forth were so provocative, including a host of negative stereotypes, Lakoff's work has given rise to a considerable number of studies intended to test these claims by examining men's and women's speech empirically. Many of these studies will be discussed below.

2. *Question intonation in statements*: Lakoff's second claim is that women show nonassertive behavior by using question intonation in conjunction with declarative sentences. That is, rather than making direct statements, they make suggestions or request agreement from their addressee(s). Lakoff says that in answer to a question like "When will dinner be ready?" women will respond not with a statement but with a question intonation response, such as "Oh, about eight o'clock?"

3. *Hedges:* Along with the use of question intonation for statements goes the frequent use of tag questions and hedges. With respect to tag questions, Lakoff's argument is that women, rather than making straightforward statements, request the agreement of their addressee by adding a tag question (e.g., "He's a nice guy, isn't he?"). In speaking of hedges, Lakoff includes all modifiers which serve to make a statement less than an assertion. Thus, the use of the word *kind* in a sentence like "It's kind of hot in here," or the expression *sort of* in a sentence like "I'd sort of like to see that movie" would be counted as a hedge.

It will be immediately apparent to teachers of English that tag questions serve many more functions than that of requesting agreement from an addressee. Depending on the intonation of the utterance, a tag question can serve just as easily as a threat or an expression of anger. An example of a tag question used as a threat might be "So you think you can get away with that, do you?" and an expression of anger might easily carry a tag as illustrated by the following: "You didn't write that report, did you?" or, to a child, "You've torn your coat, haven't you?"

4. *Emphatic modifiers and intonational emphasis:* The claim here is that women use the modifiers *so*, *such*, and *very* to emphasize their utterances much more frequently than men do and that they combine this usage with an intensity of intonation out of proportion with the topic of the phrase. Expressions like "It's *so* beautiful!" are seen as feminine.

5. *Hypercorrect grammar and pronunciation:* According to Lakoff, women tend to use more formal syntax than men, to use forms of pronunciation which are closer to the prestige norm, and in general to speak more formally than men do in similar situations.

There is some empirical evidence for this claim from early sociolinguistic studies. Both Labov (1966) and Trudgill (1972) found more extreme style shifting toward the "prestige norm" in women's speech. Indeed, one of Labov's major hypotheses is that the linguistic insecurity of lower-middle-class women leads to sound change. Of all groups studied, the lower-middle-class speakers showed the greatest tendency to use prestige forms in careful speech, and when sex was isolated as a variable, it was found that females demonstrated the most hypercorrection. Labov's point was that since children are usually cared for by women, and since the majority of schoolteachers at the elementary school level tend to be middle-class women, children are very likely to be exposed to hypercorrect forms and to acquire them. Labov also notes that in addition to the overt norms held by both sexes in the New York speech community, there are also covert norms which place a high value on the tough talk of working-class men, equating it with masculinity. Indeed, Nader (1968) made this very point when she challenged the notion that linguistic borrowing always goes in one direction. While both Labov and Nader mention the propensity of middle-class men to borrow from the pronunciation, syntax, and lexicon of men lower than they on the social scale, neither discusses the reasons behind the greater formality found in women's speech. Trudgill, however, finding a similar pattern in his study of Norwich speech, speculates that women may use more prestige forms than men do because, lacking an occupational identity of their own outside the home, they are more likely than men to be judged by how they present themselves rather than by what they do, and speech is very much a part of self-presentation.

Thus, Lakoff's claim that women's speech is more formal does receive support from sociolinguistic studies of the correlational type. However, it should be noted that the data upon which these analyses of women's speech styles were based came from sociolinguistic interviews conducted by upper-middle-class male academics who, by virtue of sex and occupation as well as in their capacity as interviewers, were in a dominant position vis-à-vis their women subjects. Although neither Labov nor Trudgill took the attributes (e.g., sex) of the addressee/interviewer into account in their studies, there is good reason to believe that such factors are quite significant (Wolfson 1976). The female subjects studied might have spoken very differently, even in formal interview tasks, if the interviewer had been a woman. As Labov was quick to note in his study of the speech of male black teenagers in Harlem (Labov et al. 1968), the ethnic identity of the interviewer can pose a very serious research bias. In this case, he made use of black fieldworkers to collect the data. Unfortunately, neither Labov nor his followers applied this reasoning to the factor of sex. For these reasons, the validity of these sociolinguistic studies regarding women's speech cannot be accepted without further study.

6. *Superpolite forms:* Women are said to frame requests and other sorts of utterances with excessively polite forms such as "Would you please open the window, if you don't mind."

The fact that Lakoff's description of women's speech was based on her own intuitions presented a challenge to researchers to design empirical studies in order to test out what had been said. As it happens, these studies have not necessarily substantiated the assertions regarding women's speech made by Lakoff. Indeed, many popular beliefs about differences between the sexes in terms of their use of language are simply not borne out by the data at all. In a few cases, research findings contradict the stereotypes completely.

Crosby and Nyquist (1977) did a series of empirical studies in which they tested out Lakoff's categorization of women's language, or what they call "female register." What they found was that sex differences in speech were due to role differentiation. Basing their hypotheses on Lakoff's description of features of women's language, they predicted that these features would be more apparent in the speech of women, but, citing her argument that these features are an expression of inferior status, they also predicted that the relative status of speaker and addressee would have an effect on the use of female register. By investigating the way both men and women spoke to police personnel, for example, they were able to show that both sexes used speech forms which have been characterized as belonging to the female register. For this reason, the female register is characterized in Crosby and Nyquist's study not as women's speech but as client speech.

A still more recent test of Lakoff's claims regarding differences in the speech of men and women is described in the report of a study conducted by O'Barr and Atkins (1980). In their article the authors report on a study of sex-related speech patterns found in a courtroom situation. In many ways, the hypothesis tested in this study is similar to that investigated by Crosby and Nyquist, since both sets of studies seek to discover how the role and status of the speaker will affect the extent to which the features Lakoff identifies will actually occur.

Noting that trial practice manuals written by successful trial lawyers often had special sections describing the differences in behavior between male and female witnesses, and frequently gave advice concerning how the lawyer should treat female witnesses, O'Barr and Atkins became intrigued with the question of how male and female witnesses actually did behave in court. Over a 30-month period, the researchers sampled the speech of some 150 male and female witnesses. In analyzing these data, O'Barr and Atkins (1980:104) were able to provide empirical evidence to demonstrate that the features characterized as women's language by Lakoff are neither limited to women nor characteristic of the speech of all women. Rather, they found, those features originally isolated by Lakoff were directly linked to the position of the speaker in the context of the courtroom situation. Where status was low, both men and women were found to use a high percentage of features associated with women's speech, while both men and women who had high status (e.g., expert witnesses whose professional knowledge was being called on) were found to make very little use of them. Thus, the higher the status of the individual speaker, the more "powerful" their language. Given these findings, O'Barr and Atkins suggest that what Lakoff has termed "women's language" would be more appropriately termed "powerless language." In their view, the association of such "powerless" features as hedging, using superpolite forms, and the like, with the speech of women has to do with the fact that many more women than men in our society occupy powerless positions:

> Further, we would suggest that the tendency for more women to speak power-less language and for men to speak less of it is due, at least in part, to the greater tendency of women to occupy relatively powerless social positions. What we have observed is a reflection in their speech behavior of their social status. Similarly, for men, a greater tendency to use the more powerful variant may be linked to the fact that men much more often tend to occupy relatively powerful positions in society.

Related to Lakoff's suggestion that the way women speak is both cause and effect of their inferior position, O'Barr and Atkins found that speakers who used "powerless language" were judged as less convincing, less intelligent, less competent, and less trustworthy. The researchers made use of a matched guise test in which male and female actors were tape-recorded as they played the parts of witnesses, each giving two samples of testimony, in one case using "women's features" and in the other omitting them. These tape recordings were then played for subjects who acted the part of the jury and were asked to rate the witnesses on the attributes mentioned above. The results showed that women who did not use these features were heard as much more convincing than those who did. This is an important finding since it provides us with strong empirical evidence that the use of the features in question can have serious social consequences.

The previously mentioned study by Brouwer et al.(1979) also investigated the speech forms used by men and women in a specific situation. In this case, the setting was the Central Station in Amsterdam, and the interactions recorded in-volved two ticket sellers, one male and one female. By tape-recording customers as they requested tickets and information of the two clerks, Brouwer et al. were able to test for specific features of speech which they had hypothesized were typical of female speech. The results were something of a surprise to the investigators. Not only did Brouwer et al. find that features considered to be part of women's language occurred in the speech of both the men and the women customers, they also discovered that both the male and the female customers used these features to the male ticket seller but not to the female. That is, both men and women customers were much more polite and nonassertive with the male ticket seller, and both were more direct and less polite in dealing with the woman. Clearly, sex of addressee was an important sociolinguistic variable.

Another stereotype associated with women's use of language has to do with the issue of verbosity. Women are generally believed to talk a great deal more than men do, and there are many proverbs and folk sayings in languages all over the world which attest to this widespread belief. It is perhaps precisely because the belief in women's volubility is so general that it has attracted the attention of a number of researchers interested in sex differences in language. The studies which have been designed to test, in a systematic way, the comparative amount of talk produced by men and women have not confirmed the stereotype of the talkative woman.

Strodtbeck and Mann (1956), for example, found that in jury deliberations men contributed almost four-fifths of the talk. Eakins and Eakins (1976) analyzed seven tape-recorded faculty meetings and found that men took more turns at talk, spoke longer when they had a turn, and did most of the interrupting. Edelsky (1981) also tape-recorded a series of mixed-sex faculty meetings. However, in examining the shifts in the conduct of the participants during these meetings, Edelsky noticed two different types of "floors." In the first (F1), a single speaker held the floor. Edelsky calls this type of behavior "holding forths." The second type of floor identified by Edelsky (F2) is constructed as a joint, often overlapping production in which several people are involved at once, there is much building on one another's topics, and a great deal of joking and laughter occurs. Edelsky found that women took equal part in jointly developed floors but that in the "holding-forth" floors, men talked more than women did (Edelsky 1981).

Thus, not only have there been no results showing that women speak more than men do, there have been a number which indicate the exact reverse to be the case.

In one such study, Swacker (1975) had 17 men and 17 women each speak into a tape recorder for as long as they felt it would take them to describe a particular line drawing by Dürer. Since socioeconomic status and age of the subjects were held constant, and the task was identical for all, sex was the major variable correlated with speech. The results of this experiment showed that men spoke much more than women in a comparable experimental situation. One man was so verbose, in fact, that he continued talking for 30 minutes after the tape had run out.

In analyzing her data, Swacker also noticed that the women subjects were, as Lakoff had claimed, much more apt to use hedges and to express uncertainty. The men, on the other hand, were given to making positive statements in which not a hint of doubt was shown. The amusing (if painful) aspect of this phenomenon was the discovery that in spite of their hedging, the women were usually quite accurate in reporting, for example, the number of books on a shelf, while the men, in spite of their assertiveness and lack of hesitation, were found to be much less accurate in their descriptions.

Related to the notion that women speak more than men do, a notion for which no evidence could be found, is the idea that women do a lot of interrupting. Again, research results reveal that the reverse is true. In mixed-sex conversations studied by Zimmerman and West (1975), it was found that almost all (96 percent) interruptions were made by males. Men, it turned out, interrupt women far more than women interrupt men or than men interrupt other men, or than women interrupt women. The data for this study came primarily from tape recordings of spontaneous speech. In further studies, West has investigated male/female interruption patterns in a laboratory setting and in doctor–patient interactions. In all studies reported on, males are shown to do most of the interrupting, and those they interrupt are nearly always females.

In a particularly revealing article called "When the Doctor Is a Lady," West (1984) made use of videotaped medical interviews to study interrupting patterns. It was found that male doctors interrupt their female patients far more than they do their male patients, and, even more striking, male patients interrupt female doctors far more than they are interrupted. This finding led West to conclude that sex rather than occupation was the superordinate status, so that whatever occupational status a woman might achieve, she would still be treated first and foremost as a woman.

But if men do most of the talking and almost all of the interrupting, why is it that women are stereotyped as the verbose sex? Spender (1980) has an explanation for this seeming contradiction:

> The concept of women as the talkative sex involves a comparison: they must talk too much against some sort of standard or yardstick and we have erroneously assumed that the measurement of women as talkers is in comparison to men. But this appears not to be the case. The talkativeness of women has been gauged in comparison not with men but with *silence*. Women have not been judged on the grounds of whether they talk more than men, but on whether they talk more than silent women . . . when women are supposed to be quiet, a talkative woman is one who talks at all. (Spender 1980:42)

When we look at the claim that women use tag questions and question intonation for statements as a way of being less assertive in their speech and of hedging, we find that the research literature contains mixed results. DuBois and Crouch (1975), for example, in analyzing tape recordings of an academic conference, found that almost all the tag questions were used by men. As already pointed out, tag questions can have more than one function, and it is therefore not surprising that research results are mixed. P. Fishman (1978a,b), in her analysis of the interaction of heterosexual couples in their own homes, found that women used more than twice as many tag questions as men did. Clearly, the function of tag questions needs to be subcategorized, so that we can make more sense of these findings. The Fishman study (1978) makes it clear that although women were using tag questions at a much greater rate than men were, this was only part of the story. The findings indicate that women use more questions of all sorts and that these are used as attention-getters and ways of introducing conversational topics, not as hedges. It is Fishman's thesis that women do most of the interactional work of supporting conversation, while men reap the benefits of this support but do not return it. The women in Fishman's study tried more often to introduce topics, but they had far less success in getting conversations going. Men, on the other hand, tried much less often and almost never failed. As Fishman (1983) puts it:

> The failure of the women's attempts at interaction is not due to anything inher-
> ent in their talk, but to the failure of the men to respond, to do interactional
> work. The success of the men's attempts is due to the women doing interaction-
> al work in response to remarks by the men. . . . As with work in its usual sense,
> there appears to be a division of labor in conversation. The people who do the
> routine maintenance work, the women, are not the same people who either
> control or benefit from the process. (Fishman 1983:98–99)

With respect to question intonation, the research results are also somewhat mixed. Edelsky (1978), for example, found that women did not, as Lakoff (1973) had claimed, use question intonation in declarative statements, but McConnell-Ginet (1978, 1983) found that they did. In a study of questions asked by men and women in audiences at an academic meeting, Swacker (1976) found that the types of questions asked were very different. Women, she found, tended to ask clarification questions, while men, who did far more of the questioning, began with long introductions which had the effect of making them the center of attention, and of raising issues which had very little to do with the subject at hand. Thus, men took twice the amount of time to ask their questions than women did and asked questions five times more often.

These studies represent only a small part of the work that has been carried out in the investigation into the beliefs and reality concerning differences in men's and women's speech. Despite the fact that the stereotypes which make up common wisdom concerning the way women speak have been found to be largely unsupported by empirical research, it is important to recognize that these beliefs have meaning of their own and influence the amount of power, status, and control that men and women have available to them in the general American society.

IMPLICATIONS FOR SECOND LANGUAGE TEACHING

Having had a look at some of the issues and findings connected with the subject of language and sex, we are now in a position to ask where all this leads us with regard to the teaching of English to nonnative speakers. With respect to sexism, the message is clear enough. Nonnative speakers need to know which terms to avoid and which are acceptable, and the teacher, whether male or female, can serve as an excellent model and guide here. As newcomers to American society, nonnative speakers should be made aware of the controversy concerning issues of sexism in language. Such forms as *Ms* and *Chair* need to be taught and discussed. Students need to learn that society is changing in its view of women and that many of these changes are manifested in nonsexist language use. Obviously, nonnative speakers from other cultures will have their own sets of values regarding men's and women's speech as well as other aspects of social behavior. It is not the right or the obligation of teachers to try to change these cultural values; rather, what is needed is that students learn the importance of this issue in American culture and the ways in which it is manifested in language.

With respect to such issues as the "he/man" problem, it is important that instructors point out the implications of the usage described above. Teachers of English need to be aware that an alternative does exist and that it is not necessary to perpetuate sexist usage by teaching it to new speakers of the language. As Bodine (1975a) has pointed out, the use of singular *they* is not only quite common in spoken standard English but has a long history of use in the language. Until the nineteenth century, grammarians had said nothing against this usage. It was only during the period of prescriptive zeal that grammarians began to make vehement objections to the use of *they* for sex-indeterminate reference. Although it is now considered grammatically incorrect by many, taught as they were from rigidly prescriptive grammar books, ESL teachers and materials writers need to know and teach the actual linguistic facts concerning this usage. Students should be told openly that in spite of what prescriptive grammar books say, the use of *they* as a singular pronoun is quite common in actual spoken standard English. They need to be given examples so that when they hear sentences like "Someone left their coat on the chair," they will recognize this as perfectly acceptable English. Indeed, linguists like Bodine (1975a) have argued very convincingly that although vigorous efforts have been made to eradicate the use of singular *they* in the last two centuries, it has been remarkably resistant in terms of the everyday, unreflecting use of speakers. For this reason alone, it is important to explain this usage to learners of English as a second or foreign language.

Equally important is the teacher's obligation to describe other ways to avoid sexism in pronoun usage which have become increasingly popular in the last several years. One possibility is to use plural forms wherever possible. Thus, instead of saying or writing, "the student . . . he," one can very easily say "students . . . they." Yet another way of avoiding this problem is to write "he or she" or simply "s/he." For reference, it is increasingly common to see and hear such usage as "him or her," rather than simply "him," as was the custom only a decade ago. Both the use of the plural form in order to avoid the generic *he*, and the use of *s/he* are especially helpful when guiding students in advanced forms of composition.

With respect to sexism in curriculum materials, we have had ample evidence that language perpetuates the stereotyping of women. Alma Graham (1973) describes a computer search through children's textbooks in which it was discovered that most of the people children read about in school are male. Thus, it was found that in the textbooks written for children, sons outnumber daughters two to one. Further, fathers have sons four times as often as they have daughters, and almost all firstborn children are male. There are almost no aunts or nieces. To complete the picture, the males are always presented as doing the work of the world, while the females are passive and nearly always appear in their role relationships to males rather than as separate individuals.

Sexism in textbooks is, unfortunately not limited to materials prepared for children. Textbooks written for adult second language learners of English are, as Hartman and Judd (1978) have demonstrated, replete with sexist overtones. An examination of a representative sample of ESL texts revealed that women are no more visible in these materials than in those written for children: "In 'Steps to Composition' . . . the ratio of male to female referents was found to be 63% to 3%. 'On Speaking Terms' . . . showed 64% to 36%; and 'English Sentence Structure' . . . yielded 73% to 27%" (Hartman and Judd 1978:385). One of the ways in which language learners are introduced to the cultural values held by native speakers is through readings and instructional materials used in the classroom. For this reason, ESL materials writers are in a particularly sensitive position with respect to their portrayal of different groups within the society. For the most part, this aspect of materials writing is dealt with very responsibly indeed. We do not find negative or belittling attitudes toward ethnic or racial groups expressed in ESL textbooks. Unfortunately, however, the taboo against demeaning minority groups does not extend to the treatment of women. On the contrary, Hartman and Judd (1978) found that jokes and slurs on women were painfully frequent. What is particularly striking is the way women are stereotyped as homemakers and mothers. Some of the examples of sexism in ESL textbooks are so appalling that they are actually funny. An example given by Hartman and Judd comes from Alt and Kirkland 1973:2:

> Written exercises further the dichotomy between the roles of boys and girls. One example so blatant as to be humorous, was found in a series of sentences using linking verbs with noun complements. All the sentences except the one in question deal with inherent properties of the subject noun. For example:

> > Dogs are animals.
> > Tadpoles become frogs.

> Yet, there in the midst of these immutable truths is the amazing juxtaposition:

> > Boys become men.
> > Girls become housewives. (Hartman and Judd 1978:387)

Given that well over half the ESL teachers in the United States are women, it is clear that this is not only insulting but untrue. Hartman and Judd (1978) have done the TESOL profession an important service by taking a strong stand on this matter of sexism in ESL materials.

Teachers and curriculm writers need to be aware of sexist language usage and also of sexist bias in the materials they select for use in the classroom. The monitoring of classroom materials for bias toward sexism as well as racism and other linguistic manifestations of prejudice is very much the responsibility of teachers and administrators.

When it comes to differences between the speech patterns of men and women, however, we are confronted with a very different situation. While, as we have seen, many of the stereotypes associated with women's speech have been empirically proved false, there do remain some differences, and, to the extent that we have information regarding these differences, they should be explained. Here, it seems to me, we have two rather different points to consider. On the one hand, it is an important aspect of language learning to be given insight into what the stereotypes are and what the evidence is. It will be useful for language learners to know, for example, that in spite of the almost universal belief that women are more talkative, not one shred of evidence exists to support this notion, while there is a great deal of empirical evidence to show that in general American society at least, it is the males who do the most talking in mixed-sex situations. While it is necessary for students to know the facts, it is critical that such discussions be open and honest concerning the underlying social factors which are responsible for the stereotypes. Much as we would like students to learn to avoid sexist usage themselves, it would be misleading to gloss over the biases that are known to exist and the ways in which they manifest themselves in the way English speakers behave.

The second, and perhaps most delicate point to be considered in this regard is the question of how to balance instruction in nonsexist usage with the need for language learners to learn to use appropriately sex-linked forms of speech. Since male speech, for example, has long been regarded as the norm, not enough research has been done to make it possible to describe what may be legitimate differences. From this point of view, it appears that the only alternative open to us is to give language learners exposure to both male and female models so that they can acquire gender-appropriate speech behavior by observation and emulation.

Since English classes for nonnative speakers held in English-speaking countries are not normally homogeneous with respect to sex, the problem of how to provide adequate input is a difficult one. As long as we assume that at least some sex differences in language are, in fact, genuine, neither male nor female teachers can hope to serve as perfect models for all their students. Indeed, it is for this very reason that a double standard is often applied in the hiring of ESL teachers. That is, in many programs, there has long been a de facto (and usually unmentioned) affirmative action campaign in favor of male teachers. In TESOL, as in much of the teaching profession, women far outnumber men except in administrative positions and in upper-level academic jobs. That is, the majority of the actual ESL classroom teachers in English-speaking countries tend to be women. And, since it is usually considered to be important for students to be exposed to both male and female native speakers, it often happens that male applicants for ESL teaching positions are given preference in hiring. If it is the case that there are genuine differences in the way men and women speak, this sort of reverse discrimination can be defended on the grounds that male students need male speech models if they are to acquire sociolinguistically appropriate behavior in the target language. If, on the other hand, it turns out that the speech behavior generally attributed to women is, as O'Barr and Atkins (1980) maintain, a function of relative social status, then the argument for hiring male teachers because they are speakers of the "male register" cannot be supported. Female ESL instructors have the same professional status as their male counterparts and should, if the theory holds, use approximately the same level of "powerful language" in their classroom speech behavior. This is, of course, a testable hypothesis. A comparison of the features of speech of male and female ESL instructors *in class* would be of extreme interest. Of course, such factors as age, socioeconomic background, and, above all, amount of experience would all have to be taken into account. The results of such a study would, I believe, give us a picture of the way men and women speak when they are in control of a speech situation. Given their relative status in society as a whole, there are not many similar situations in which men and women are in positions of power in identical situations. For this reason, such a study would be a valuable addition to the literature on language and sex, as well as providing us with important information about sex-related differences (or lack thereof) in ESL classroom interaction.

The question of whether women teachers can serve as adequate sociolinguistic models for male students is probably a vacuous one if the teaching and learning are going on in the country where the target language is spoken, since learners of both sexes will almost certainly have many opportunities to interact with native speakers of both sexes. Where the language teaching is taking place in the student's own country, the situation is much less clear. Teachers are sometimes native speakers, often not. In many parts of the world, the classes are segregated by sex and males are unlikely to be taught by females, or females by males. Furthermore, since interactions with native speakers are apt to be limited, one would not expect that gender-related differences in speech behavior would have much effect. Indeed, of all the aspects of speech behavior, that which has to do with socialization into sex roles is probably least likely to change when a new language is acquired. Again, this is a testable hypothesis and one which researchers in the area of second language acquisition might well find worthy of investigation.

CONCLUSION

From the point of view of the study of speech behavior in American society, it seems clear that sex as a sociolinguistic variable must be taken much more seriously than it has been so far. The analysis of speech acts gives us some insight into the forms native speakers use and the rules for their use, but unless sex of speaker and addressee is investigated seriously and systematically, we are likely to obscure some of the most important sociocultural patterns of speech behavior among native speakers of English and, therefore, to produce descriptions that are lacking critical information regarding rules of speaking needed by nonnative speakers.

In terms of the general issue of second language acquisition, much more needs to be known about male and female speech behavior than is currently available in the literature before realistic evaluations can be made concerning the role of male and female teachers as models of sex-appropriate sociolinguistic behavior. For these reasons, it appears that the field of language and gender research has several important links to the field of TESOL. It is to be hoped that scholars interested in both areas will take this need for further information as a challenge to begin investigations into a field that has, until now, received far too little attention.

CHAPTER 9

Social Class Variation in English–Speaking Communities

VARIATION BY SOCIAL CLASS, REGION, AND STYLE

Although people often tend to think of a language as if it were a single system, a very little reflection will allow us to see that although we all share our language(s) with countless others and are able to communicate with relative ease with people from many geographic areas, it is nevertheless the case that speech varies considerably from region to region. The study of regional differences in speech, called dialectology, has been one of the major traditions in linguistics. It is only since the 1960s, however, that many scholars have begun to pay serious attention to other dimensions of linguistic variation. Since sociolinguistics is the study of language behavior as part of social behavior, and since language use is influenced not only by the speech situation but according to the social as well as the regional background of both speaker and audience, the study of social class variation soon became a dominant area within this new field. During the 1970s, interest in the relationship between language forms and social meaning led many people to regard the entire field of sociolinguists solely as the study of variation in language.

Clearly, there are many areas of sociolinguistic concern besides social class differences in speech, but it is also the case that it is part of the communicative competence of the native speaker to recognize differences in social class based on speech behavior. For this reason, it is important for language learners to have some familiarity with the ways in which social class is manifested in speech. For the teacher of English as a foreign or second language, it is even more important to be well informed about the research into social class variation in English. In general, teachers who are native speakers of English will hardly need to be reminded of those nonstandard grammatical features which are so well known that they have become stereotypes, or even of those features of pronunciation which are generally recognized to be "lower-class" features over a wide area of the United States. This is only the beginning of the story, however, since social class differences in speech intersect with regional differences in such a way that features which are used by the prestige group in one region may well be regarded as markers of low socioeconomic status in another. A particularly well known example of this phenomenon is the pronunciation of the (r) sound after the ends of words. In England, and in the Boston area of the United States, (r)-less speech is part of the pronunciation pattern of the prestige group. Once this was true for New York City as well. At present, however, the exact reverse is true. For this reason, studies which seek to investigate social class variation must focus on specific dialect areas or even speech communities.

In addition to regional and social class differences, a third extremely important dimension of language variation is that which comes under the label of style. In many ways this is the most critical of all, since stylistic variation intersects with social class differences such that speakers speak differently depending on the social identity of their interlocutor(s) as well as on the speech situation in which they happen to find themselves. What is important in the study of style is that no one who is communicatively competent speaks the same way all the time. While the social class and educational background of speakers will have a strong influence on speech patterns for everyone and in every situation, it is still the case that part of the communicative competence of every native speaker is the ability to alter patterns of speech behavior to suit the situation, including the identity of those who are listening. We shift styles to indicate varying degrees of social distance, for example, such that we do not normally speak the same way to intimates as we do to strangers. The speech event in which one is participating also has a very strong influence on the patterns (or style) of speech used. The same person, for example, may, in a casual conversation over lunch, be addressed in a style which indicates little social distance. An hour later, involved in a professional meeting with others in attendance, the same interlocutors may use a far more formal style. On the other hand, individuals engaged in one specific speech event, that of telling a personal narrative, for example, may well use very different styles when engaging in conversation with a close friend than they would use with someone who is a distant acquaintance or, indeed, a total stranger (Wolfson 1976, 1978a). The background of the speaker is thus only one of the variables which must be taken into account when studying stylistic variation. That most early sociolinguistic studies failed to take these factors into account is probably due in large part to the fact that they grew out of the tradition of dialectology, wherein regional background, age, and education of the speakers themselves were seen as the key variables in speech differences, and little or no attention was paid to stylistic variation.

THE DEPARTMENT STORE STUDY

Certainly, the most original and influential of the early research in the area of sociolinguistic variation was that carried out by William Labov (1966). Combining his expertise in linguistics with rigorous survey methods drawn from the social sciences, and principally from the field of sociology, Labov's early work created a model for the study of social dialectology which completely revolutionized the field and which was in great part responsible for the development of sociolinguistics as a separate subfield of linguistics.

One of Labov's earliest and best known investigations into social class differences in speech behavior was a short but extremely well designed study which focused on the pronunciation of department store clerks in three New York City stores. So famous has this study become that it is now known simply as "the department store study." A brief description of this research will provide an introduction to the kind of work for which Labov was to become famous.

Labov hypothesized that New Yorkers' pronunciation of postvocalic and final /r/ is a reflection of social class differences and, more particularly, that New Yorkers share norms about speech which cause them to use the prestigious /r/ pronunciation much more frequently when they are conscious of their speech than when they are not. In order to put this to the test, Labov chose three New York department stores, Klein's (which, during the period of the study catered to the lower classes), Macy's (which is middle class), and Saks Fifth Avenue (which caters to the upper middle class). Making the assumption that the speech of the clerks would be representative of the social class of the customers, Labov followed a very ingenious plan to elicit first a casual and then a careful speech style from them. Since the words *fourth floor* contain the (r) sound in the two positions of interest, and since all these stores had fourth floors, Labov went to one after another of them asking clerks to tell him the location of a department which he knew was on the fourth floor. Thus, if the directory said that the shoe department was on the fourth floor, Labov would go from counter to counter, clerk to clerk, asking where he could find the shoe department. Busy and preoccupied, the clerks would give a quick and un-self-conscious response in which the frequency of (r) pronunciation was relatively low. Labov would pretend not to have heard or understood and would ask for a repetition of the information. This time the clerk would make a conscious effort to be clear or careful about pronunciation, and the frequency of (r) use would rise dramatically. In this way, Labov was able to show that the clerks at Saks used more (r) in their casual pronunciation than did the clerks at either of the other two stores. The clerks at Macy's, in fact, were closer in frequency (or lack thereof) to those at Klein's than to those at Saks. However, in their more careful pronunciation, the clerks at Macy's used a greater frequency of (r) than did the clerks at Saks in their most careful speech. The fact that all shifted to more (r) usage when speaking more carefully was seen as support for Labov's hypothesis that New Yorkers share norms of speaking.

THE NEW YORK CITY STUDY

The Department Story Study just described was, in fact, a preliminary investigation, conducted in 1962 and designed to test some of the ideas Labov planned to examine much more fully in his doctoral dissertation in linguistics at Columbia

University. Indeed, this pilot study was incorporated into the dissertation itself. One of the earliest major studies which attempted to investigate style shifting and to correlate this with differences not only in the regional but also in the social class background of speakers, Labov's groundbreaking dissertation was entitled *The Social Stratification of English in New York City* (Labov 1966). While very much in the tradition of dialectology, this was, nevertheless, a pioneering effort at a large-scale sociolinguistic analysis of a speech community. In investigating the speech behavior of New Yorkers, Labov set out to test several hypotheses. To begin with, he defined the entire city as a speech community on the basis that its speakers shared norms for the evaluation of speech. That is, although New York City speech itself was heterogeneous, Labov hypothesized that speakers would prove to be united in their attitudes toward the forms used in their community. Basing his analysis on the principle that all speakers have available to them a range of styles, Labov set out to test two major hypotheses: (1) that the more careful their speech, the greater the frequency with which speakers will attempt to use the forms regarded as prestigious by the community, and (2) that depending on their social class backgrounds, speakers have differential control over the frequency with which they are able to produce prestige forms. In order to test these ideas, Labov focused his study on a section of New York City called the Lower East Side. Some years previously, a sociological study had been made of this area in which a sample of community members had been assigned to nine social classes on the basis of the income, occupation, and educational level of the head of each household. Using the results of this earlier study, Labov set about interviewing a subset of people from the original sample. The interviews were tape-recorded in the homes of the subjects and were carefully designed to test Labov's hypotheses by eliciting a series of different "styles" of speech from each subject.

ATTENTION TO SPEECH

Equating formality of style with attention to speech, Labov categorized five "speech styles" to correspond with the set of tasks which he had designed. Noting that the interview itself constituted a formal speech situation in which speakers would be likely to monitor their speech, he classified the speech they produced in response to his question as "careful style." Then, on the assumption that subjects would pay even closer attention to their pronunciation while reading aloud, he tape-recorded them as they read a connected text, and classified this as "reading style." Still further along the dimension of attention directed toward speech was a task in which Labov had each subject read lists of words; this was classified as "word list style." And, to get at the most careful speech style of all, Labov designed special word lists, in the form of minimal pairs, in which one member of each pair contained, for example, a postvocalic or final (r) to test one of his variables. These pairs of words, if read in the (r)-less dialect characteristic of New York speech, would rhyme. If, on the other hand, subjects were careful to pronounce the (r) variable, there would be a distinction in pronunciation between the two words of the pair. This "style" was classified as the most careful of all since speakers' attention would tend to be drawn to the pronunciation of the very feature under study, and, according to Labov's hypothesis, this awareness would cause them to attempt to pronounce in a way which most closely resembled the community norm for prestige speech. In other words, Labov expected speakers to be particularly sensitive to their pronunciaton of variables which the entire community recognizes as being socially stigmatized. In order to get at the style of speech in which least attention is paid to features of pronunciation, Labov designed a means of eliciting the style he termed "casual speech" in which he asked his subjects questions concerning dramatic events in their own lives. An example of a question which was intended to elicit "casual speech" was "Have you ever been in danger of death?" If subjects answered in the affirmative, the interviewer immediately followed up by asking them to tell the story of what had happened. The idea here was that the subjects would become so involved in recounting this dramatic event that they would forget, for the moment, to monitor their speech as they normally would in an interview situation with a stranger, and would therefore pay the least attention to their speech. Ranging the five interview tasks along the dimension of amount of attention to speech, Labov (1966) was able to define five separate "styles": (A) Casual Style, (B) Careful Style, (C) Reading Style, (D) Word List Style, and (D') Minimal Pair Style.

FREQUENCY

The five variables which Labov chose to study, all stereotypical features of New York City speech, were the prevocalic and final (r) already mentioned, the vowels (oh) and (eh), and the consonants (th) and (dh). An important aspect of Labov's general hypothesis about the way in which these features are socially stratified has to do with frequency—that is, that the social class background of the speaker would be manifested not by the absolute or categorical presence or absence of the feature but rather by the frequency of its occurrence. Thus, according to Labov, the speech of upper-middle-class members of the New York City speech community would be marked not by the total absence of the stereotyped features under investigation but rather by their low frequency of occurrence in their speech. Further, and most important, Labov hypothesized that speakers of all social classes would vary their speech behavior depending on the formality of the situation. For this reason, Labov hypothesized that the prestige pronunciation of the variables he was investigating would occur more frequently in formal contexts, while the socially stigmatized variant would be more frequently found in casual contexts, and that this would be true for speakers of all social backgrounds.

HYPERCORRECTION

The results of Labov's survey were of vital importance for several reasons. His hypotheses were confirmed in that speakers of all social classes were found to use lower frequencies of the prestige variable in the contexts which Labov had defined as casual speech and greater frequencies of these same variables in the contexts defined as careful. Thus, although there was a great difference in the absolute frequency of (r) usage between lower-working-class speech and that of the upper middle class, both groups had considerably lower (r) scores in "casual style" than in any of the more formal contexts. Put another way, all social groups in Labov's sample showed their awareness of community norms in that for each group there was a considerably higher frequency of usage of prestige variables in formal contexts. The most unexpected and revealing finding, however, was that it was the members of the second ranking social group, those defined as "lower middle class," who used the highest frequency of prestige forms in their most "careful style." Thus, although speakers in this group had very low frequencies of (r) in their "casual style," they showed such a dramatic increase in the use of the prestigious (r) in their "word list style" that they far surpassed the frequencies found for the highest class. Labov used the term *hypercorrection* to describe the way people in the second highest status group overshot the mark in their attempt to imitate the speech of the highest group. In explaining his use of the term, Labov (1966:88) says: "The lower middle class speakers go beyond the highest status group in their tendency to use the forms considered correct and appropriate for formal styles".

It should be pointed out here that overcorrection or hypercorrection is a phenomenon well known in linguistics wherein speakers, in an attempt to emulate the speech habits of those they admire, overgeneralize a particular feature such that they use it in positions where it does not occur in the speech of the model group. As Hall (1964:361) puts it:

> People are also often likely to misunderstand the social extent and acceptability of such a later innovation in the regional dialect on which the standard language is based. The supposedly "vulgar" pronunciation written "boid," "hoid," etc., is normal in all of New York City and wide areas on the Eastern seaboard, and I have heard it from such obviously acceptable speakers as heads of departments in Hunter College and Princeton University. . . . Then, the speakers of nonacceptable regional or social dialects try (as is natural) to acquire more acceptable speech patterns. But neither they nor their critics have the requisite linguistic training to analyze the situation objectively and accurately, and all the nonstandard speaker has to go by is a blanket condemnation—often based on misunderstandings . . . of some particular feature of his speech. The cockney who has been told he must not "drop his aitches" comes to the conclusion that he ought to put an /h-/ at the beginning of every word where he pronounces only a vowel; since he has been condemned for saying "'Arry,", "'Erbert," "'Ounslow" for standard Harry, Herbert, Hounslow, he puts in an /h-/ in such words as Anna, Alice, or Ealing, and makes them into Hanna, Halice, Healing. This process is known as overcorrection or hyper-urbanism.

SUBJECTIVE REACTION TESTS

A vital aspect of Labov's research was that he checked the speech actually produced by members of the New York City community against questionnaires and subjective reaction tests administered to the same set of subjects, in which they were asked to evaluate their own and others' speech. Following the technique first designed and used by Wallace Lambert et al. in 1960 to test subjects' evaluations to linguistic behavior, Labov devised a test which would focus on the specific variables which he was investigating. Tape recordings were played to subjects who were asked to rate the speech heard on a scale of occupational suitability. The texts read were carefully organized so that subjects' reactions to the variables under study were tested. It was found that subjects were quite as sensitive to the social prestige of the variables in their evaluations of others as they had been in their own speech production. Indeed, Labov found a general pattern in which "those who show the greatest use of a stigmatized feature in casual speech, show the greatest sensitivity to this feature in subjective reactions" (Labov 1966:92).

Although similar patterns emerged for all variables tested, it is noteworthy that in the case of (r), the lower middle class showed even more sensitivity than did the upper middle class; a sensitivity matched by their clear tendency to hypercorrect this very feature in their most formal style. It is essential to note that speakers were quite regular in their evaluations of other speakers, although when questioned, they proved quite unable to identify the specific linguistic criteria on which they were basing their evaluations. Thus, again we see an example of the fact that native speakers have the communicative competence to judge whether or not speech is accurate or appropriate, but that this does not include the ability to describe what it is they know.

LINGUISTIC INSECURITY

In order to find out how New York speakers evaluated their own speech, Labov gave subjects a list of "socially diagnostic" pairs of words (e.g., [often] versus [ofn], or [ve:z] versus [va:z]) and asked them to say which of the two they thought was correct and then which of the two they themselves used. The number of items for which subjects said they used a form which they did not consider correct was then labeled those subjects' index of linguistic insecurity. Two impressive findings emerged. One was that lower-middle-class speakers had by far the highest indexes of linguistic insecurity, and the second was that subjects were very inaccurate in reporting their own speech habits and tended to give answers which reflected their beliefs about what they should say, rather than their observed performance.

Having investigated speech variation along the dimensions of social class and contextual style, Labov went on to suggest that language change is motivated by the linguistic insecurity of the lower middle class, which leads members of this group to hypercorrect features which are judged by the community to carry prestige, and is thus responsible for spreading these usages. As Labov put it: "Since r-pronunciation has been adopted as the norm for the most careful type of communication, it has perhaps become appropriate for many types of interaction between parent and child. Hypercorrection is certainly strongest in women—and it may be that the lower middle class mother, and the grade school teacher, are prime agents in the acceleration of this type of change" (Labov 1966:101).

THEORETICAL FOUNDATIONS

Because Labov's work has been of profound importance to the field of sociolinguistics, it should, to be appreciated properly, be seen in the context of the tradition from which it comes. Labov was the student of Uriel Weinreich, a great scholar whose work was deeply involved with dialect geography, language contact, and language change. Weinreich died tragically of leukemia while still a young man. His last work, "Empirical Foundations for a Theory of Language Change" (1968), written with two of his former students, William Labov and Marvin Hertzog, makes a strong case for the need to base a theory of language change on data gathered through actual fieldwork involving the collection of sociolinguistic data. This is not to suggest that Weinreich or Labov were in any sense breaking from traditional linguistic theory in their suggestion that language change is, to some extent, caused by the efforts of lower-class speakers to imitate the speech of those whom they admire. As Bloomfield (1933:403) put it: "The most powerful force of all in fluctuation works quite outside the linguist's reach: the speaker favors the forms which he has heard from certain other speakers who, for some reason of prestige, influence his habits of speech."

A NEW THEORY OF LANGUAGE CHANGE

The difference between the theory of language change put forth by Weinreich et al. and that of earlier scholars has to do with the fact that previous theories had regarded linguistic variation as random and accidental rather than as part of a structured whole. The individual was seen as having a single system, and any deviations from it could be ignored in description since they were irrelevant to the basic structure of the language. The problem, say Weinreich et al., is that if variation is ignored, the resulting description is a nonexistent construct, and actual speech, which is full of variation, is inexplicable within the very framework designed to explain it. From the point of view of linguistic change, the study of a perfect, idealized system devoid of variation is counterproductive, since it is only through the study of variation that linguistic change can be understood. If variations are regarded as random imperfections, an acceptance of them would contradict the very idea of language as a truly structured system. But since the object of the study has been the language of the individual, variations could not be explained as anything but random. However, say Weinreich et al., this conflict between variation and system is both unnecessary and inaccurate. If language is viewed within its social context, it can be seen that variation is governed by rules and is thus a part of linguistic structure. Language, say Weinreich et al., is heterogeneous, and any attempt to write a grammar without accounting for this all-important fact must fall far short of reality. A description which does account for variability and heterogeneity in an orderly fashion must be a description of the language not of an isolated speaker but of an entire speech community. Such a description will, necessarily, be very complex, but it is only when the sociolinguistic facts are understood that language change can be properly understood and adequately described.

If, however, language is divorced from its social context, the origin of linguistic change must be seen as having only linguistic causes. Although many such explanations have been put forth, none have accounted for all the facts. Thus, although it is possible to explain a change as having arisen from an unconscious desire on the part of the speaker for ease of articulation, this does not explain why such a change did not occur earlier in the history of the language or why the same change has not taken place in the speech of different dialects or, even more to the point, why a sound has changed only to reappear in the same language at a later date.

The theory that sound change arises out of a need to prevent homonymy is also considered and found to be contrary to fact since merger does continue to create large numbers of homonyms, no matter how confusing the consequences may prove to be. As Labov's New York City study shows, the dropping of postvocalic /r/ has resulted in a large set of homonyms on the order of bared/bad, but the fact that these homonyms now exist "show[s] that there are motivating forces in linguistic change which ride roughshod over any tendency to preserve cognitive distinctions" (Weinreich et al. 1968).

One of the serious paradoxes which the authors find in theoretical discussions of sound change is that although most linguists recognize that language change is a continuous process resulting from the contact between speakers of differing dialects, no reasonable account of how such change takes place has ever been provided. A true explanation of the mechanism of language change, say Weinreich et al., must be based on sociolinguistic findings which show that variant systems coexist within the speech community as a whole and, more importantly, within the repertoire of each individual speaker. When language is seen as an orderly heterogeneous system in which the choice between linguistic variables serves social and stylistic functions, the gradual favoring of one form over another can be seen as a process based on sociolinguistic factors. If speakers naturally have a number of dialects (e.g., stylistic, social) within their repertoire, and they switch back and forth depending on the situation they are in, they can easily transfer a feature of one style or dialect into that of another, and eventually they may generalize this feature and use it in all their styles. In Labov's New York City study of (r) usage, it was found that lower-middle-class speakers, whose casual speech is almost completely (r)-less, have an (r)-pronouncing dialect constantly available to them. They can and do make use of it in formal contexts because it is already part of their competence and can be picked up from within their own repertoire. This model of change, the authors argue, is more realistic than that of dialect borrowing since style switching is part of everyday speech behavior, while dialect borrowing is "in principle, a momentary and accidental event."

A CRITIQUE OF THE THEORY

Although there is undeniably a great deal that is both important and useful in this work, it could be said that the authors overstate the originality of their argument. The implications of sociolinguistic study for the understanding of language change are certainly very provocative. However, it should be made clear that historical linguists have probably always been aware of the heterogeneous nature of language and that it has been the necessity of first analyzing and describing the basic system, not blind ignorance, which has kept scholars from dealing with variation within it. It should also be remembered that the nature of the data available to historical linguists is almost never such that a complete analysis of stylistic or socioexpressive variables is possible. Skillful use of information gleaned from contemporary commentaries about language use and from poetry can contribute greatly to our knowledge of dialect differences and of linguistic changes which were occurring at the time under study, but such data are usually far too fragmentary to provide the overall sociolinguistic picture which would be required to make the sort of analysis suggested by Weinreich et al. As for the authors' explanation of linguistic change as a switch in frequency between dialects which already coexist within the linguistic competence of the individual speaker, this theory is a new and insightful way of describing an important phenomenon, and one that was certainly not unknown to earlier scholars of language change. The traditional historical linguistic explanation of borrowing as a means of language change has always taken hypercorrection into account. Social pressure has long been recognized as the motivating force behind the borrowing of upper-class or prestige speech forms by lower-class or dominated peoples. Labov's concept of change caused by pressures from above, or the more or less conscious effort of people to copy the speech habits of those in power, is not really much different from the borrowing that has always been known to exist between social class and/or regional dialects. The main difference between the two theories seems to be that the concept of internalized dialects coexisting in the speech of each individual makes it unnecessary to assume borrowing from a source completely outside the competence of the speaker. In this sense, the theory put forth by Weinreich et al., in which the major point is the explanation of linguistic change as a gradual change in frequency between dialect features which are already a part of the linguistic competence of the individual, may well be closer to the empirical facts.

URBAN LANGUAGE STUDIES

The influence of Labov's work on current sociolinguistic research cannot be underestimated. Although dialectologists have traditionally collected samples of actual speech upon which to base their analyses, and anthropologists have always gone into the field to gather their data, it was Labov who first combined the traditions of dialectology with techniques of large-scale sociological surveys in order to investigate social class differences in an urban speech community. Many researchers have adopted Labov's techniques, and a number of urban language surveys modeled on Labov's study of New York City have been carried out. Indeed, so prevalent did this sort of work become that for many people the term *sociolinguistics* became identified with Labov and the study of the way speech variation is correlated with the social class background of members of a (usually urban) community. Thus, in 1967, Shuy et al. carried out a study in Detroit in which large-scale survey techniques and individual interviews with a large sample of the urban population were used in order to correlate linguistic and social variables. The Detroit Dialect Study investigated grammatical as well as phonological variables. Again, the emphasis was on using sociologically valid procedures for selecting subjects for the sample. These subjects were then interviewed individually, and careful notes and tape recordings were taken of their pronunciation of certain features and of their use of specific grammatical patterns. As in Labov's New York City study, a regular feature of every interview was an attempt to elicit some form of narrative from the subject. In Labov's interviews, subjects had been asked about personal experiences and, specifically, whether they had ever been in danger of death. This question was intended to direct the attention of the subjects away from the interview situation and cause them to become so involved in the vivid narration of a dramatic moment in their lives that they would speak in their most "casual style" or vernacular. As we have already noted, Labov classified narratives elicited in response to questions of this nature as "casual speech" in his isolation of contextual styles. Shuy et al. (1968:28) were more modest in their assessment of the speech behavior they were able to record. As Wolfram (1969b) puts it: "It seemed to be a good sample of the speech used by children to adults and adults to respected strangers. Rarely can it be considered in-group speech" (Wolfram 1969b:17). Given the research findings resulting from Labov's New York City study and the fact that Shuy et al. modeled their study on many of the same working principles, it is not surprising that the Detroit study found social status to be the single most important variable correlating with linguistic differences. Further, it was found that the most clear-cut linguistic boundary is that between the lower middle and upper working classes.

THE NORWICH STUDY

Other large-scale urban studies of socially stratified varieties of English have utilized or attempted to utilize Labov's methodology. The work of Peter Trudgill (1971, 1972) in Norwich is a good example. The fact that Trudgill is a native of the town he studied is noteworthy. Not only was he able to conduct his interviews in the accent of the speech community he was studying, but he was in possession of a considerable amount of insider's knowledge about the social structure of the town. Taking advantage of his knowledge about Norwich, Trudgill chose four areas to represent different types of housing and social status. A total of 50 adult subjects and 10 children were randomly chosen from these areas. Trudgill used Labov's method of structuring his interviews to include a variety of tasks designed to elicit different speech styles. That is, although most of the interview speech was of the formal type usually associated with the speech used to strangers, Trudgill followed Labov in having his subjects read both passages and word lists, on the assumption that these tasks would cause speakers to pay closer attention to their speech production. Like Labov, Trudgill equates attention to speech with formality, and the inclusion of reading passages was intended to elicit the most formal style of the speakers in the sample. In addition, Trudgill followed Labov in classifying all personal narratives, along with speech directed to family members in the presence of the interviewer (but not defined as part of the interview proper), as "casual speech." The linguistic variables were selected, like Labov's, from what was already known about social class variation in the speech community under study. Trudgill's results confirmed his hypothesis that certain forms (e.g., the variable (-ing) are used more often by upper-class speakers than by members of the lower classes. It is significant, in view of Wolfram's analysis of invariant (-s) in the nonstandard Black English of Detroit, that in Norwich, too, a clear correlation between social class and use of (-s) was found. As in the Black English vernacular of Detroit, the lower classes are much more likely not to have third person -s in their speech than are members of the middle classes.

One finding of Trudgill's Norwich study was, however, unexpected. This was that speakers differed not only in the frequencies with which they used certain socially marked features but also in their very patterns of style shifting, depending on their social class background. That is, middle-class speakers showed the most extreme style shifting between formal interview style and the speech categorized as casual. Working-class speakers, on the other hand, made the most noticeable style shift between the speech of the formal interview and the speech they produced while reading. But why should working-class people be less concerned with monitoring their speech in a formal interview situation than they are when they are asked to read aloud? This rather mysterious finding is clearly explained when we examine the investigations and discoveries made by Milroy and Milroy (1977)—a study which uncovers some revealing and unexpected results.

PROGRESS IN BELFAST

In 1975, Leslie and James Milroy carried out a sociolinguistic investigation of speech behavior in three working-class communities in Belfast, Northern Ireland (Milroy and Milroy 1977, L. Milroy 1980). From the beginning, L. Milroy, the major fieldworker, combined ethnographic methods (cf. Hymes 1962, Blom and Gumperz 1972) with interview techniques. Thus, for example, a considerable amount of ethnographic data was collected, and several exploratory interviews in comparable working-class areas were carried out prior to the actual fieldwork. The most important difference between the work of the Milroys and that of Labov and his earlier followers, is that the unit of investigation in all three communities was the "network" (cf. Milroy and Milroy 1977:24) and not the individual. The Milroys pointed out that the working-class groups they studied were locally separate and that people belonging to them had a strong sense of where the boundaries of their area began and ended. Group members identified themselves as such, and residence within a specific locale was the major factor. In addition, such groupings were, the Milroys found, composed of what they called "dense networks." That is, they were characterized by a high degree of "multiplexity": "The networks in all these areas tended, in varying degrees, to multiplexity and density. In Ballymacarret, where multiplexity and density scores were highest, neighbours were usually kinsmen and workmates, attended the same church and enjoyed themselves at the same clubs."

In addition, individuals who are members of dense networks, have friends outside them who are then considered friends of friends by their own group. Making use of this situation, L. Milroy was able to establish a role for herself as a friend of a friend in each of the communities she studied. Visiting patterns in these communities are such that friends are free to drop into one another's homes without prior arrangements and without in any way disrupting the domestic activities of the family. As Milroy and Milroy (1977) put it:

> A state of open talk is maintained during which people have the right but not the obligation to speak. These interactional norms associated with the domestic setting proved very advantageous for this research. During recording sessions, people commonly walked into the house, were briefly introduced (e.g., "that's my brother") with no corresponding introduction of the fieldworker or any indication that the proceedings were being recorded. Often the new arrival would join in the chat, allowing the fieldworker to yield the floor to him and retreat to the edges of the group. She was often able to remain unidentified to several participants for a considerable period before conversation moved round to the topic of herself and her interests. (Milroy and Milroy 1977:34)

READING AND SPEAKING

In analyzing their data, the Milroys attempted to categorize the speech they had collected into five styles, following Labov's New York City model. They found, however, that while they were able to identify two speech styles, interview style (IS) and spontaneous style (SS), they were unable to apply the rest of Labov's model. Three of Labov's five "styles" involved reading, and since the written channel (cf. Hymes 1972b) has quite different meanings in different societies, the Milroys found that they could not place reading and conversational styles along the same stylistic continuum. Interpreting their findings through the perspective of the ethnography of speaking, the authors point out: "The written channel seems to us to be evaluated quite differently in working class Belfast and to function differently from the manner implied by Labov's 1966 model." Obviously, literacy has very different meanings and uses in lower-class Belfast than in middle-class New York. In some cases, the subjects were illiterate. In others, they made it clear to the fieldworker that they regarded reading fiction aloud as culturally strange—something they simply never did. Indeed, Milroy and Milroy point out that "it is quite arguable that in the reading passage people paid more attention to speech than in the word list." Apparently because of their cultural evaluation of the act of reading aloud, and perhaps also because of the greater ease in reading short words, subjects in Belfast tended to read the word lists more fluently than the connected text. If we consider the Norwich findings that working class subjects tended to make the most marked style shifts between formal interview speech and reading style, in the light of the findings of the Milroys that reading is evaluated differently among lower-class speakers in Belfast than it seems to be among the middle-class speakers in Labov's New York City study, we see that it is quite possible that the lower-class speakers in Norwich may have been having much the same reactions as those found to exist in Belfast. It seems perfectly reasonable that people who are insecure about their reading proficiency would pay much closer attention to their performance on a reading task (especially one which they know is being tape-recorded) than they would when simply being asked to speak. In addition, it does not appear that any attempt was made to discover whether, in fact, reading aloud is differently valued among lower- and middle-class people in Norwich, or, indeed, among the different social and ethnic groups which were studied in other areas. The fact that the Milroys took an ethnographic perspective in their study enabled them to make sense of a result which might otherwise have seemed paradoxical.

METHODOLOGY

It should be clear, by this point, that research methodology has serious and important implications for the field of sociolinguistics. In earlier discussions of sociolinguistic methodology (Wolfson 1976, 1986) I have pointed out that the approaches toward the gathering of oral data for linguistic analysis may be roughly classified into two types: *observation* and *elicitation*. Within the category of elicitation, which will be discussed first, we can include all techniques which directly involve the subjects' awareness that what they say is being studied by an investigator. This category will include such widely differing techniques as the elicitation of linguistic data from a single informant during many months or even years of work sessions, from numerous subjects during one or more work sessions, or, as in the sociolinguistic studies of the 1960s and 1970s, from a large number of subjects in single interviews. Introspection, or the elicitation of linguistic data by consultation with one's own intuitions, also falls into this category.

Clearly, there are important differences among the techniques just mentioned, both with respect to the role of the subject and with regard to the researcher's assumptions about the subject's consciousness of his or her role. They have in common that they are subject to the linguistic truism that awareness of oneself as an object of study may endanger the validity of the data. Descriptive linguists have recognized this problem from the first, and it has been mentioned in numerous handbooks. What has not usually been mentioned is that the traditional method of descriptive linguists who gather their data by eliciting linguistic material from native-speaking informants is, in principle, not much different from introspection. The use of an informant (or even several informants) must, by definition, involve the use of native speaker intuition. The fact that the intuitions being elicited are those of someone other than the linguist does not alter the fact that it is intuitive data which are being collected, and not speech as it actually occurs in everyday use.

Sociolinguists, because they are interested in finding out how people speak in different situations, have been especially conscious of the methodological problems inherent in their work. Labov, one of the first to emphasize the need for empirical data on everyday speech (or what he calls "the vernacular"), speaks of "the observer's paradox" (Labov 1970b:47). What he means is that we, as sociolinguists, need to have data on how people speak when they are not conscious of being observed. As a means of solving this paradox, Labov advocates asking subjects questions which will divert their attention from the interview situation, causing them to become so involved in *what* they are saying that they forget *how* they are saying it. Since Labov equates formality of style with amount of attention paid to speech, he maintains that this technique can often elicit what he classifies as "casual speech." Labov also suggests that the interviewer make use of any speech produced by the subject before and after the actual interview, and especially during any breaks or interruptions which may occur during the interview. Frequently, for example, if a subject is being interviewed in his or her own home, other family members are present and interrupt to ask questions and the like. Also, it sometimes happens that the telephone will ring during an interview and that the subject will be forced to break away for a time. Since the subject believes that the researcher is interested only in the answers to interview questions and in the specific interview tasks, his or her speech outside the framework of the interview may well be much more relaxed and un-self-conscious. This is exactly the kind of style shifting which is of interest to the sociolinguist, and the casual style or vernacular which may be tape-recorded in this way is the style which is of greatest interest since it is most likely to be consistent and is the most difficult to collect on tape.

Milroy and Milroy (1977) and Milroy (1980) have also commented on the usefulness of their subjects' ignorance of being tape-recorded. Although they have been heavily influenced by Hymes' concept of ethnography of speaking, they nevertheless attempted to incorporate into their study some of the elicitation techniques developed by Labov for use in survey interviews. Through a combination of observation and elicitation, Milroy and Milroy quickly recognized that in order to collect what they term spontaneous speech (or SS), it was best to have the fieldworker (L. Milroy) make herself as inconspicuous as possible. In addition, they found it very helpful that many of their subjects were unclear about when they were being tape recorded. As Milroy (1980) points out in a description of her fieldwork in the Clonard section of Belfast: "Martin Convery had clearly told the young men (his sons and their friends) that conversations would be tape-recorded; however, although no deceit was used on my part, they appeared to have an extremely unclear perception of how much of the proceedings were in fact being recorded" (Milroy 1980:57). Milroy goes on to explain that once the actual interview tasks, such as the reading of word lists, had been completed, they seemed to assume that the interview was over and went on talking, telling stories, and teasing one another without making any objection to the fact that the tape recorder was still in use.

Labov (1966, 1972) also describes the advantages of collecting samples of everyday speech from subjects who were unaware that they were being tape-recorded:

> Interruptions of the interview by telephone calls sometimes produce unusually good opportunities to study casual speech. In one interview, the telephone interrupted the proceedings at the very middle. The informant, Dolly R., had just returned from a summer spent in North Carolina, and one of her cousins was anxious for news of the family. I left the room with her nephew, and continued to talk to him quietly in another room; for twenty minutes, the informant discussed the latest events in a very informal style, and we thus obtained an excellent recording of the most spontaneous kind of speech. The contrast is so sharp that most listeners cannot believe it is the same person talking. (Labov 1972:89)

Although the speech sample described above was collected by Labov during a break in the framework of a sociolinguistic interview, it is exactly the sort of data that one might expect to gather through the type of fieldwork which we have categorized as *observation*. Under this second heading, observation, we have the tradition of qualitative research in which spontaneous speech behavior is studied in its natural context. Within the category of observation we have ethnographic field-work, which may or may not involve the researcher. When the investigator is involved, the approach is known as participant observation. The ethnographic approach toward the collection of data has its origins in anthropology, and many of the scholars who collect data in this way are anthropologists who are concerned with the description of speech behavior of groups of which they themselves are not members. Ethnographic fieldwork is not, however, limited to the study of groups foreign to the researcher. Increasingly, anthropologists and linguists have been turning to the investigation of speech behavior among speakers of their own languages, and, very often, among groups of which they are members. This focus gives participant observation new meaning, since the researcher is often not distinguishable from the group being studied and it is possible to observe everyday behavior without being noticed and without causing self-consciousness on the part of those being observed. Indeed, Labov (1966) has termed this sort of fieldwork anonymous observation and has used it most effectively.

Unlike the more quantitative tradition in which speech is elicited in various ways, and hypotheses and variables are usually defined before the data are gathered, the qualitative paradigm associated with observation assumes that hypotheses will emerge from the data as they are collected, and that the relevant factors will become apparent as the analysis proceeds. What the researcher does is observe and collect examples of naturally occurring speech in its usual social context. The aim of the researcher is to intervene as little as possible during the data collection and to try to understand what is going on from the perspective of the participants in the interaction. That is, whether or not the researcher is a participant in the event being recorded, he or she keeps in the background and does not guide the other participants. The most salient aspect of the observational approach to data collection is that it seeks to study speech behavior within the social context in which it normally occurs. As we have seen, the early studies of social class variation in language relied almost entirely upon the sociolinguistic interview and upon the random sampling of large populations. Recently, however, more and more researchers have been turning to an observational approach in their investigations of sociolinguistic variation. Although there is much to be gained by the approaches to sociolinguistic investigation which have been subsumed under the category of elicitation, it has become increasingly apparent that many insights into social variation in language use would be lost without the perceptions brought to bear on the subject through the use of observation. Because this tradition of research avoids setting up hypotheses in advance of investigation and assumes that these will emerge as data are collected and analyzed, it is always likely that one will discover conditioning factors that are unexpected and would not have been intuitively obvious.

In contrast to the experimental models in which data are elicited, the researcher using an observational approach toward the collection of data often finds it most useful to behave as a participant observer in a wide range of interactions with those speakers who have been singled out for study. The method chosen by Milroy (1980) of creating a role for herself in the community is a good example of the way in which such data can be collected. In this respect, researchers who are also practitioners of TESOL are in a particularly good position. As experts in this area, they have only to offer their services in tutoring a family to be welcomed into the homes of nonnative speakers who are seeking to learn English. By making use of their expertise in helping their informants to improve their language skills, the TESOL researcher provides a concrete service which is very much to the advantage of the people whose linguistic production is under study. Indeed, this kind of research/ teaching agreement between investigator and subject represents the epitome of reciprocity in fieldwork. Since tape recorders are a normal part of teaching equipment, subjects in this sort of situation are much less likely to be disturbed by their presence. Indeed, it is perfectly reasonable for the researcher to request permission to tape record the subjects both in order to better diagnose their linguistic problems and, by analyzing such data, to be in a position to help others in a similar position. There is no question that research into second language production, variation, and acquisition is much needed and that the results of such studies, when disseminated to other researchers, will benefit not only the original participants in the investigation but also large numbers of others involved in the learning and teaching of English. This approach toward data gathering is based on the assumption, common in the tradition of qualitative research, that those who contribute data to scientific studies have a right to benefit from them insofar as this is possible. Put differently, it is generally accepted that researchers who engage in participant observation have an obligation to share what they learn with the population under study. The ethical perspective of this attitude toward the collection of second language data is so reasonable, and, indeed, so honest and fair, that fieldworkers should have no difficulty in gaining the consent of the language learners with whom they wish to work.

With respect to the analysis of social and stylistic variation in second language acquisition, much can be gained by a thoughtful combination of observation with the more traditional elicitation procedures. While some work has certainly been done in the area of the investigation of style shifting within the interlanguage of learners of English (see Tarone 1979), this has mainly followed the methodological lead of Labov in its focus on experimental tasks. Indeed, Tarone has made a point of arguing that Labov's model for the study of style and style shifting in a speaker's first language should be transferred to research in second language variation. Her point is that the most stable variety of interlanguage is that which represents the least formal or careful style. For this reason, Tarone suggests that a more complete picture of interlanguage can be gained only if researchers are able to study the learner's vernacular. She points out that a considerable amount of research in second language acquisition has been done without taking account of variables such as topic and speech situation, which may well be conditioning factors which interact with the style of speech chosen by the learner. She argues very convincingly that since second language acquisition researchers have not taken account of the potential significance of these sociolinguistic factors, their data are often collected in a range of different speech situations, greatly reducing their value in terms of comparability. While it is certainly true that the best way of comparing interlanguage speech styles would be to make use of comparable samples, it may, for reasons that will be discussed below, be impossible to investigate the everyday interactional variety of learners by means of Labov's model of collecting what he defines as "casual speech" (Long, personal communication). If we agree with Tarone that our aim should be to collect data on the everyday speech of a specific community, whether they be native or nonnative speakers, then our best approach would seem to be to gather data in the settings in which the speech we wish to study usually occurs. A series of carefully controlled observational studies might well prove to be a way of collecting comparable studies. One solution would be if the researcher were to offer language lessons to a family, as was suggested above, and could then tape-record different styles of speech which occurred spontaneously in the course of day-to-day interaction in a variety of sites. At present, the foregoing amounts to no more than a suggestion for looking at sociolinguistic variation among learners of English. Clearly, much more thought and effort needs to be put into designing and carrying out such studies so that we may reach a clearer understanding of the patterns of style switching among language learners. The only reservation we must keep in mind when designing such studies is that there are a number of pitfalls to be avoided in applying traditional methods of research into variation along the lines of social class and style.

METHODOLOGICAL PROBLEMS AND ALTERNATIVES

There have been a number of critical evaluations of sociolinguistic research in the last several years. With respect to research into social variation in language use which relies on survey interviews for its data, several serious drawbacks have been pointed out. One is that by developing hypotheses about linguistic features which correlate with social variation and then testing for just those, investigators make it very difficult for themselves to uncover social class differences in speech which are not part of the original hypothesis. And since the hypotheses regarding social class features are usually based to some degree on community stereotypes, survey interviews which test for the frequency and distribution of only these features make it almost impossible for us to gain new information about less intuitively obvious ways in which language might be socially stratified. Other criticisms of this method of gathering data have to do with the failure to recognize that the interview itself is a speech event in some societies (though not in others) and that the speech behavior of both the researcher and the informant are constrained by the norms of behavior that condition the conduct of interviews in a given society. In New York City, for example, people are relatively sophisticated about interviews, having seen and heard them on television and radio and perhaps even having taken part in various telephone or face-to-face surveys. Having agreed to participate in an interview, people will tend to try to follow the rules by cooperating and answering the questions put to them. This may lead them to behave in ways which are very different from their day-to-day style of speech. When it is careful speech that we are studying, this is not a serious problem. However, in attempting to collect casual speech, questions like Labov's "Have you ever been in danger of death?" do put interviewees on the spot, as Labov himself points out in describing the elicitation procedure after a question of this type has been asked: "If the informant answers yes, the interviewer pauses for one or two seconds, and then asks, 'What happened?' As the informant begins to reply, he is under some compulsion to show that there was a very real danger of his being killed; he stands in a very poor light if it appears that there was no actual danger. Often he becomes involved in the narration to the extent that he appears to be re-living the critical moment, and signs of emotional tension appear" (Labov 1966:107).

However, the constraints of the interview situation may have a very different result. As I have pointed out elsewhere (Wolfson 1976), the compulsion to answer the question to the interviewer's satisfaction may cause informants to report events in ways which are quite self-conscious and very different from the involved, excited, casual style the researcher was attempting to elicit. This is because the interview situation is contrived and formal, making it very different from the speech situations in which people usually tell dramatic stories about their personal lives. For this reason, we cannot assume that a narrative elicited as part of a series of questions in an interview will be told as it would have been if it had been part of a conversation between the informant and someone he or she had chosen as a conversational partner.

Another very serious problem with sociolinguistic studies of the correlational type first used so effectively by Labov is that the means by which he and others who have followed his model have used to identify differences in styles have been based on the dimension which he calls "attention to speech." This approach to defining speech style has been so widely accepted as to become axiomatic. As Labov himself puts it: "Styles can be ranged along a single dimension, measured by the amount of attention paid to speech" (Labov 1972:208). The idea here, as we have mentioned above, is that the more attention speakers pay to how they speak, the more formal their speech style will be. Although many sociolinguists have accepted this view of style, others (e.g., Milroy and Milroy 1977, Wolfson 1976, Bell 1984) have pointed out there is little or no empirical validation for the correlation of "attention to speech" with style. As Rickford (1979) demonstrates, it is possible for attention to speech to increase rather than decrease as speakers shift to what is considered less formal speech, as he found in his investigations of speakers switching to basilectal Creole, the variety most distant from standard English.

It is important to recognize that the study of so human an aspect of behavior as speaking can never be totally precise. Even a carefully planned experiment must, because the subjects are human, contain some unknown variables. The relationship between speaker and addressee, subject and investigator, is one of the most difficult to control for. In his study of social class variation in speech, the first of the large urban dialect studies, Labov (1966) used a random sample representative of nine different socioeconomic groupings. Each subject was asked the same questions and given the same words and texts to read. Yet, as has been pointed out above, the research design had a serious flaw in that it assumed that each subject would react to the interviewer in the same way, in spite of differences in age, sex, and status. In other words, because the interviewer was a constant, his social identity was not taken into consideration. Since people make accommodations in their speech depending on the identity of the interlocutor (Giles et al. 1973, Beebe 1977, Beebe and Giles 1984), and since the interviewer is clearly a socially defined interlocutor, subjects can be expected to alter their speech to respond differently to different addressees, even in an interview (Wolfson 1976) . Thus, although the interview questions and tasks seem to be the same for all subjects, the differential power and solidarity relationships between subjects and interviewer may make for very different sets of responses. The methodological problem, then, is the failure of sociolinguistic survey interviews to take into account the social identity of the interviewer vis-à-vis the informant. Whether or not, for example, the interviewer shares with the informant such personal attributes as age and sex will have a serious effect on the chances of the interview producing speech samples which even resemble casual speech. When we add such important social attributes as relative occupational status, amount of education, dialect, or speech variety, we see that the success of the interview in terms of obtaining samples of what Labov calls the vernacular may be strongly influenced by the degree to which such factors are shared. This point is made in Wolfson 1976:

> . . . studies which attempt to correlate particular speech forms with the age, sex and social background of stratified samples of speakers cannot make use of interviewing as a technique for data collecting without controlling for the relationship between speaker and interviewer. Whether it is possible to control for this factor in a large-scale statistical survey is a question which has so far not been faced. There is, in fact, no real justification for using interviews to collect data for use in any kind of systematic comparison of speakers without controlling for all the other factors in the speech situation. (Wolfson 1976:198)

In her work on Thai/Chinese code switching, Beebe (1977, 1980, 1981) provides us with an empirical demonstration of the necessity of taking the identity of the listener into consideration when doing sociolinguistic investigations. In her study of ethnically marked phonological variation, she found that the ethnic background of the addressee had a very marked effect on the pronunciation pattern of subjects. In discussing her findings in relation to the work of Labov and other sociolinguists who have followed in his path, Beebe says:

> The significance of these data lies not only in demonstrating how important the role of the listener is in the code selection process. The data alert sociolinguists to the need for greater control and finer differentiation of environmental factors in their linguistic experiments. The findings demonstrate that linguists must discontinue the accepted practice of defining speech style in terms of the listener. The listener is a significant variable independent of speech style since speech varies predictably when someone is speaking in the same room on the same day about the same topics in the same order using the same speech style, but with two different listeners on the two occasions. (Beebe 1977:338)

In close relation to the issues mentioned above, it is important to point out that a rather different model has been put forth to account for style shifting. This model, arising from the field of social psychology and specifically from the research of Howard Giles and his associates (Giles and Powesland 1975, Giles and Smith 1979), proposes that speakers vary their speech style in an effort to accommodate to their addressee(s) and thereby win their approval. Called Accommodation Theory, this model has generated a large number of experiments which demonstrate that speakers may converge with their addressee(s) in such features as accent in an effort to show themselves similar or, alternatively, may maintain their own way of speaking or even, if they wish to dissociate themselves from their addressee(s), show a pattern of divergence from the speech of those with whom they are interacting. Thus, it has been repeatedly demonstrated that sociolinguistic variables will usually show sensitivity to the identity of the addressee and, by extension, to the audience as well (Bell 1984).

As forerunners in the application of Accommodation Theory to research into second language variation, Beebe (1980, 1981) and Beebe and Giles (1984) have demonstrated the important insights which may be gained by means of this approach. As Beebe and Giles (1984) point out: "it is the tension between limitations in ability to converge toward a native-speaking interlocutor and motivation to converge that makes second-language data unique. . ." (Beebe and Giles 1984:23). Thus, as Beebe has shown, Accommodation Theory can be very useful to TESOL, and to research into second language acquisition in particular, in that it gives us another means of explaining variation in second language production. In applying Accommodation Theory to second language data, Beebe and Zuengler (1983) propose: "When searching to explain our second language variation data, we see the need for SLA researchers to broaden their horizons. In the future, SLA researchers will have to extend their models to incorporate social psychological dynamics, or they will have to work on revising what Giles has already done if they are to account for variable performance data. We suggest both" (Beebe and Zuengler 1983:212).

Clearly, there is a great deal more to be learned about social and stylistic variation in language use, both by first and second language speakers. The potential offered by newer methodological models such as Accommodation Theory, along with carefully designed ways of combining the best features of both classical elicitation and observational models of research, provides continued hope that many of the problems so far brought to light will be solved so that we may come to a deeper understanding of the ways in which sociolinguistic variation is manifested.

CONCLUSION

Given the complexity of the problem, it is unlikely that we will find a perfect methodology for all sociolinguistic work. What we can do is choose the research framework which seems best suited to the particular problem we want to study, adapt it where necessary to fit our needs, and make very sure that we do not forget the limitations of the design we have chosen.

No one method is appropriate for all sociolinguistic research. Rather, the investigator must choose the method best suited to the problem. If a survey is intended, then obviously it is necessary to use survey techniques, including the most rigorous selection of a sample population. If the aim of the research is to gather a body of data concerning native speaker norms, then elicitation procedures may well be ideal. Close analysis of specific discourse features may rest on data collected from a large sample or a relatively small one.

What is essential is to recognize that each method has its limitations. Experiments, tests, and survey interviews will produce highly controlled speech samples which are necessary for specific kinds of comparison. But even the most carefully contrived interview is still an interview and we cannot expect it to yield a reliable sample of spontaneous speech. Ethnographic fieldwork, and particularly participant observation, is very well suited to the study of everyday speech behavior. Its drawbacks are that some of the features we may wish to study occur less frequently than others. What this means is that fieldworkers who choose to use an observational approach have less control over the sociolinguistic factors which condition the speech they are studying. Conversely, this approach may yield insights less likely to be uncovered by elicitation. Real life is complicated and unpredictable; its study has the same shortcomings.

Thus, we see that although the study of social variation in speech made great strides in the 1960s, much more remained to be worked out. The idea of collecting samples of actual speech upon which to base analyses of variation, an idea carried over from the closely related field of dialectology, had a profound and extremely salutory effect on the study of speech differences among various social groups. Careful use of sampling techniques, adapted from the field of sociology, was an extremely important step. Much remained to be learned about the study of language as it is actually used in social contexts as opposed to the test situation of the interview. It is not surprising that insights drawn from anthropology and, more specifically, from the ethnography of speaking should have thrown new light upon this difficult problem. The kinds of questions raised by an approach that takes cultural as well as specifically interactive factors into account need to be answered before we can claim to understand the true meaning of variation in speech.

CHAPTER

10

Dialects and Standards

INTRODUCTION

The longer an area is inhabited by a population speaking the same language(s), the more dialect diversity we can expect to find. Thus, the differences among the various regional dialects in Great Britain are more extreme, as a rule, than those found in such countries as the United States, Canada, Australia, New Zealand, and South Africa, where English has been spoken by the dominant group for only a few centuries. Similarly, if we look at the regional differences within the United States, we see that the greatest distinctions are to be found along the eastern seaboard, the area which has been inhabited by English speakers for the longest period of time. Indeed, most dialect geographers would distinguish three broad dialect areas in the United States: the New England dialect, the Southern dialect, and the General American. Obviously, much finer distinctions are possible and those who have worked to describe dialect divisions have provided a great number of detailed studies of regional pronunciation and other features which are too numerous to be gone into here. Although regional differences in pronunciation, lexicon, and even syntax may be quite pronounced, these distinctions between the English of one area and that of another are not usually great enough to prevent mutual intelligibility. It is true that an English speaker from the Highlands of Scotland would have considerable difficulty understanding an English speaker from Appalachia, but even such extreme regional dialect differences as these can be overcome with effort. Enough linguistic structure and basic vocabulary are shared for mutual comprehension to take place. In a less industrialized era, perhaps, such divergent dialects would long since have become separate languages. In the twentieth century, however, public education, geographic mobility, and, above all, the distribution of radio, television, and cinema productions around the English-speaking world have worked against the development of regional dialects into separate, mutually unintelligible languages.

One of the more difficult problems to be faced in teaching English as a second or foreign language has to do with the variety of English to be taught, a policy issue which is of considerable interest for nations everywhere in the world. Since the variety of English taught will depend heavily on who is doing the teaching, the choice is to a large degree inseparable from decisions about the origin, education, and general background of the teachers who will be employed, and this, of course, is of extreme concern to the TESOL profession in general. Obviously, teachers have social and regional identities and, whether or not they are native speakers of En-

211

glish, they come from a great variety of national and geographic origins. As we have seen, languages vary greatly from region to region and, within regions, from social group to social group. Since these differences involve pronunciation, vocabulary, and, to some degree, syntax, it is clear that not all English teachers can be expected to present all students of English with the same linguistic model on which to pattern their speech.

STANDARD ENGLISH

Wherever English is spoken as a native language, dialect differences emerge as they do in any other language spoken over a wide area. For this reason it is difficult to justify a claim that such an entity as a spoken standard exists for the English language as a whole. Indeed, the very idea of a standard is, in many respects, an abstraction rather than a concrete reality. If we accept the idea that standard speech is equivalent to the speech of the educated or the prestige group, we are left with the fact that educated people come from virtually everywhere in the English-speaking world and that therefore educated speakers speak in many different regional dialects. Thus, we must recognize that if we apply the notion of a standard to spoken English, we are dealing with an ideal in terms of syntax rather than with any specific model of pronunciation. In the United Kingdom, Canada, and the United States, in Australia and New Zealand and South Africa, and in dozens of areas within these grander subdivisions of the English-speaking world, there are people who grow up acquiring the best usage of the best representatives of local cultural traditions. Taking the United States as our example, the cultural facts are that there is inherently nothing to place the prestige usage of Massachusetts above that of Minnesota, that of Texas above that of Tennessee, that of Virginia above that of California. American presidents have represented our country's highest office in the accents of the Piedmont area of Virginia, of central Ohio, of Vermont, of Iowa transplanted to the San Francisco Bay area, of the Hudson Valley, of Western Missouri, of Boston, of Southeast Texas, and of Southern California—all within the last half century, when broadcasting has made a candidate's accent instantly accessible to a national audience. This is not to suggest that subjective reactions on the part of the general population do not exist or that presidents and other public figures have not been ridiculed for their speech patterns. Indeed, it is almost axiomatic that one regional dialect will constitute an object of amusement or scorn for speakers of the others. Thus, it is difficult for us to accept the idea of nonnative speakers being taught to speak with an accent and a vocabulary very different from our own conception of what standard English should be like. Purists are often outraged at the notion that one dialect is as good as another, and most people, if asked, would deny that they speak a dialect at all. This is because, in most language communities where a more or less rigid standard speech is assumed to exist, the very word *dialect* is derogatory since it refers to an uneducated or quaint way of speaking. To linguists, the term *dialect* has no such pejorative meaning since it is understood that each regional and social group has its own set of features of pronunciation, vocabulary, and syntax.

However, because the everyday meaning of the word *dialect* continues to carry negative meaning, most linguists prefer to use the term *variety* to refer to the differences which set one group's speech habits off from those of another.

Regional varieties, however unusual they may sound to someone coming from a different area, are not corruptions of standard forms. Rather, as McDavid says:

> . . . each regional and local variety, on whatever level, has its own history, and is the result of a complex of forces such as (a) settlement history, (b) routes of migration and communication, (c) prestige or isolation of the community, and (d) its social structure and educational system. In the United States, every local variety of English—to say nothing of the more important regional ones—has developed from a mixture of various British dialects, plus foreign-language settlements, plus varying degrees of contact with the Standard English of the British Isles and with other varieties of American English. In each area, thanks to the tradition of cultural and political autonomy of the various colonies and states, a prestige group developed. And one might say that in each community the standard variety of speech is essentially a modification of the basic local type of speech by the tradition of Standard English. (McDavid 1980:192)

Regional speech patterns, then, do not represent degenerations or corruptions from some perfect standard form of speech that exists or used to exist somewhere. Rather, they are the result of normal linguistic divergence. And, just as this is true of regional varieties of Standard English, so is it true for social differences in language use within a region. Because such social differences are markers of an individual's position in his or her social world, and because they tend to reflect the speaker's cultural and educational background, they are generally regarded as even more important. Even within a specific region, social differences are very noticeable, especially with respect to syntax, and speakers tend to be much more self-conscious about the "correctness" of their grammar. As has been amply demonstrated (cf. Labov 1966), linguistic insecurity is most common among those who aspire to higher social status.

Insecurity of this type is, indeed, largely responsible for the great respect shown throughout the English-speaking world for dictionaries and grammar books and guides to "correct" pronunciation. In one respect, this is a healthy sign. If the social structure of our society were so rigid as to make movement into a higher class an impossibility, it is unlikely that people would pay much attention to attempting to "improve" their speech. Indeed, it was not until the middle of the fourteenth century in England that the social class system became fluid enough to permit upward mobility, and it is no accident that the following centuries saw increasing interest in the standardization of the language. Until that time, society had consisted of a small number of noble families who made up the upper class, controlling all political and economic power, and a great majority of lower-class people who were laborers and had no hope of moving into that upper class. It was only with the emergence of the middle class in the late fourteenth and early fifteenth centuries that social mobility became a possibility. Since speech then as now was an obvious clue to social background, those who aspired to move out of the social class of their birth needed to gain not only money and land but also the ability to speak like the upper classes. As time went on and social mobility became ever more possible, those who had social ambitions paid more and more attention to speech. Thus, although England never established an academy to rule on language as so many other countries did, dictionaries and grammars gained wide acceptance as the ultimate authorities on correct usage.

When we turn to the written language, we are on much firmer ground in speaking of a standard. Although a few small differences exist in the orthographies of England and the United States, for example, the rules for written Standard English are well established and vary little from region to region. And, as we have already pointed out, the written language is different enough from speech that all children must learn to express themselves through this medium as part of their schooling. That is, no matter how much the spoken dialect of a child may resemble that considered acceptable by the school, the child will still be ignorant of the conventions of the written language until he or she is taught them. Obviously, the closer the speech of the child to the speech of the school, the easier it will be for students and teachers to understand one another. This is not a trivial matter, since no matter how well-intentioned they may be, teachers often fail to distinguish errors in reading from differences in pronunciation or syntax. Further, many syntactic patterns of the speech of the educated are also acceptable in writing. Thus, the child from an upper-middle-class background whose native syntactic patterns are those of the prestige dialect accepted by the schools certainly has some advantage in learning to write Standard English. Nevertheless, as we all know, the ability to express oneself in an educated dialect of spoken English is no guarantee of an ability to write well.

With respect to the teaching of writing to nonnative speakers, there is much less divergence than one finds in dealing with the spoken language. Here, the difficulty lies more in recognizing that there are many types or genres of writing. The rules that govern the way descriptive narratives are written differ greatly from those used in business letters, and both differ enormously from academic discourse. Styles of argumentation or rhetoric are not the same across all forms of writing. The sociolinguistic and, indeed, the pedagogic implications of this fact are that nonnative speakers need to learn to express themselves according to rules of appropriateness for the particular task at hand. What this means is that we need materials which will help us teach students to master a variety of different genres and teachers well enough trained in the teaching of writing to be capable of training their students in the various kinds of writing they will be expected to do. Obviously, not all students have the same needs, and this fact should be taken into consideration when decisions are made concerning which types of writing are to be taught.

NONSTANDARD ENGLISH

A nonstandard dialect is, by definition, a language variety spoken by a group at the lower end of the social scale. This means that there is nothing intrinsic to the linguistic forms themselves which causes them to be stigmatized, but that the attitude toward the speech of certain groups is, in reality, a reflection of the way society regards the speakers. Those who do not have economic or political power lack the social prestige which would cause their way of speaking to be regarded as elegant. Put another way, language is heterogeneous and full of variability. One of the major factors influencing linguistic differences within a speech community is the socioeconomic background and educational level of the speakers. The variety of a language spoken by those who have wealth, power, and education—the language, that is, of the elite group—is generally regarded as the prestige variety by the entire speech community (cf. Labov 1966). When the prestige variety becomes codified in written form, with dictionaries and grammar books which prescribe "correct usage," and when it becomes the variety used by government, courts of law, the mass media, and the schools, it is referred to as the standard variety or the standard language. What this means, in effect, is that it is the institutionalized variety of the language and therefore the one which needs to be known by all who wish to participate fully in the political, social, and economic life of the English-speaking community. The fact that institutional English is referred to as Standard English carries the unfortunate implication that all other varieties of the language are non-standard, and therefore deviant insofar as they differ from the standard. This accounts, at least in part, for the popular conception of nonstandard dialects that has held them to be corruptions of the higher form, the standard language. The reasoning here is, like so much else which concerns classifications of human behavior, circular. That is, the prestige variety of language is defined as that variety spoken by the people in the society who have prestige—the elite group. Forms which are stigmatized are those which are used by people at the lower end of the social scale—those who are themselves stigmatized. Once the language of the prestige group becomes codified and given official recognition in textbooks, dictionaries, and grammar books, forms which differ from it are regarded as incorrect. Since the varieties of English which are called nonstandard are those spoken by people at the lower end of the social scale, it is clear that a social rather than a linguistic distinction is at the heart of the judgment. If what the lower classes speak is considered "bad English" because it is spoken by the lower classes, then there is really no way out of the trap except for the lower classes to learn to use the prestige or standard variety. This, of course, is the major reason it is considered important for children to be taught "good grammar" in school.

Unfortunately, the general public and even many teachers often regard the use of nonstandard varieties of English as a sign of stupidity or laziness on the part of speakers. The notion behind this attitude is that nonstandard speakers are attempting to speak English (the standard variety) but are too lazy and sloppy and ignorant to succeed.

This attitude toward nonstandard speech is hardly a new one. People have always recognized differences in dialects, both regional and social, and, depending on the prestige of the group that spoke a particular dialect, respected or ridiculed the manner in which they spoke. The speech patterns of the poor and powerless have never come in for much respect except in the rare cases in which they were believed to represent some older, purer form of a language. And, in holding their speech forms against them, more powerful groups were simply using this manifestation of social identity of groups lower in status than themselves as an example of why their low social status was justified. The fact that the reasoning here is utterly circular has never seemed to worry people much.

In the last two decades there has been considerable concern over the poor school achievement of children who came from lower socioeconomic backgrounds and who were, by and large, speakers of nonstandard English. Controversies over the reasons for school failure and possible solutions to it became extremely heated. As we will see below, rigorous linguistic investigations of nonstandard varieties of English have clearly demonstrated that there is nothing "sloppy" or "lazy" about these nonstandard varieties, and that they follow consistent patterns or rules of grammar and pronunciation which, while different from the standard, are just as clearly organized and just as capable of expressing the thoughts of speakers. Through these studies, it has been shown that nonstandard varieties of English have long histories, just as the standard does, and that the same kinds of historical forces have operated to change and form both standard and nonstandard varieties of the language. There is nothing intrinsic to the prestige varieties which has caused them to be held in esteem. Rather, it is a historical accident that certain forms of English have come to be codified and therefore to carry more prestige than others. There is nothing more or less pure about one variety of English over another. Nevertheless it must also be recognized that although the use of Standard English is not better in any objective sense than the use of any other variety, it occupies a privileged position because it is considered better by society.

From a linguistic point of view, then, any variety of English which is systematic or consistent in its grammar is good English. From the point of view of society, however, Standard English is the only good English. This means that children whose native dialect happens to be the standard will, through no effort of their own, know "good" grammar. Children whose native dialect is a nonstandard one will, through no fault of their own, not know "good English." That is, nonstandard-speaking children will be following sets of linguistic rules which are rather different from those considered acceptable by the school and by the wider society. From the point of view of school achievement, we are also faced with the undeniable fact that the tests given nationwide in the United States, such as the California Achievement Test, are heavily biased in favor of middle- and upper-class children who come to school speaking Standard English. Tests of this kind are intended to measure what children have learned in school. Since the correct answers to questions of grammatical usage are usually identical to the grammatical usage native to middle- and upper-class children, they need only consult their intuitions to find the right answers. Children whose native dialects make use of the very stigmatized forms considered to be wrong will, if they consult their intuitions, come up with exactly the opposite of what is wanted. For these children, the test does indeed provide a measure of the amount of standard dialect they have learned. Indeed, if they consistently marked wrong every item which they intuitively felt was correct, they would stand a rather good chance of being rated high achievers. Until quite recently, the middle-class bias built into the teaching and testing of English grammar in the United States was seldom questioned. It was assumed that there was only one correct way to speak and write and that all children would benefit equally by being drilled in the "logic" of Standard English grammatical rules.

THE DEFICIT/DIFFERENCE CONTROVERSY

Although the analysis of the speech behavior of specific ethnic groups in the United States is much less relevant for those concerned with TESOL than is the sort of social class dialectology just described, no textbook on sociolinguistics would be complete without some description of what came to be a major preoccupation of sociolinguistics in the late 1960s and early 1970s—that which was focused on the analysis of the speech of lower-working-class urban blacks in large northern and midwestern cities.

During the 1960s, a serious and important controversy arose over the increasing evidence that black children, particularly those who lived in northern urban ghettos, were showing heavy school failure and dropout rates. One of the most influential theories proposed as an explanation for this educational failure is the deficit or deprivation theory. Following this approach, educational psychologists theorized that the children were doing badly in school because they were linguistically and culturally deprived. In some cases, "deprivation" was understood to mean physical or material deprivation. The idea here was that children from families living in poverty were faced with a great many problems unknown to children from higher socioeconomic backgrounds. Living in overcrowded and insecure economic conditions, the child from the urban ghetto was likely to be too undernourished and tired to do much serious learning in school. More often, however, the term *deprivation* not only refers to material deprivation but is broadened in its meaning so that it includes cultural and/or linguistic deprivation. What this is understood to mean is that children from poor ghetto backgrounds are not only materially but culturally and linguistically deprived since their language and experience of the world is so lacking that they are unable to learn what the schools have to teach. The argument used to support this theory is that the child's early social and family environment is critical to successful performance in school. If children are brought up without the early childhood experiences which are considered to be necessary prerequisites to school success, they will lack the motivation to learn, be unfamiliar with the behavior and value system of the schools, have too little "language development" to be able to form concepts or express them, and similar deficits.

The theory of linguistic deprivation was given strong, if inadvertent, backing through the writing of the British sociologist Basil Bernstein. Since 1958 with the publication of his paper "Some sociological determinants of perception," the work of Basil Bernstein has become very important in the field of sociolinguistics and subsequently in education. His ideas are important for several reasons: (1) He has been concerned with explaining why working-class children (particularly in England) don't do well in school; (2) scholars in education, both in Britain and in the United States, have interpreted his ideas and used them to show why their own efforts have failed to raise the level of education for children from lower socioeconomic backgrounds in spite of huge expenditures for programs, consultants, and facilities; and (3) Bernstein has attempted to research and define the relationship of thought, language, and the class structure within society. From the first, Bernstein theorized that class membership had an important effect on the way children are socialized and, therefore, on the perceptual ability of children. According to Bernstein, the lower-class family is position-oriented, in the sense that family members are expected to behave in certain ways because of what, not who, they are. That is, boys are expected to behave like boys, not like specific individuals. Authority is arbitrary, and a very high value is placed on group conformity. In the middle-class family, the orientation is less toward roles and more toward persons. Authority is much less arbitrary, and children are taught to behave in certain ways not because of what they are, but because of how their actions will affect others. Bernstein labeled the different language forms used by the two classes as "restricted code," used by both lower and middle classes, and "elaborated code," used mainly by the middle class. He argued that the restricted code was concrete, visual, and full of short, simple statements, commands, and questions. Much of what is said in the restricted code is highly predictable. Middle-class children, while they too were sometimes exposed to the restricted code, and at the same time, access to the elaborated code, which was full of complex sentence structure, explicit explanations, individualized expressions, and a much higher level of logic. Thus, Bernstein argued, the socialization of the child and the code which he learns strongly affect his cognitive processes. The process of socialization of the child orients him toward speech codes which then control his ability to see meanings free of context. For this reason, lower-working-class children develop in a way which limits them educationally. They simply are not used to thinking and speaking in abstract terms. Although his work has been extremely influential, Bernstein has come under severe attack both in Britain and in the United States. Rosen (1972) criticizes Bernstein for leaving unexplained what he meant by the class system. According to Rosen, Bernstein has made no attempt to differentiate among the various subgroups which make up the working class and the middle class, in terms of their history, traditions, ethnicity, attitudes toward social class, and other factors. That is, Bernstein has a very stereotyped perception of working-class family life and language. As for Bernstein's claim that he is against compensatory education (1971) because this implies that there is something lacking in the children which needs to be compensated for by the schools, Rosen states that it is Bernstein's own theories which have given rise to notions of deprivation in the language of working-class children. Most critics agree that although Bernstein's theories are interesting and seem to contain some truth, he has very little evidence to support his suggestion that class differences in socialization and in use of language have a cognitive effect on children which causes them to be more or less educable. During the 1960s, however, many American educators and scholars interested in the educational problems of inner-city black children in the United States found a great deal in Bernstein's arguments which could be used to fuel their contention that these children did badly in school because they were culturally and linguistically deprived. That is, they spoke differently from middle-class children and came from a culturally different background. As we have seen, this extension of the deficit theory holds that poor inner-city children did poorly in school because they have been deprived in early childhood of the necessary linguistic and cultural experiences necessary to successful learning in school. The idea was put forth that black children could not learn well because they grew up speaking a nonstandard language which was itself cognitively deficient—primitive, unsystematic, and lacking in abstract vocabulary. For this reason, they argued, nonstandard speaking children were in a poor position to handle school tasks.

Linguists, well aware of the fact that all languages are systematic, were appalled at these arguments. A number of research projects were undertaken to study the dialect of inner-city black children and to try to analyze the reasons for the high rate of school failure. Thus, in 1968, Labov et al. carried out a study of Black English Vernacular (BEV) in Central Harlem with three main groups of speakers: (1) a random sample of 50 individual preadolescent speakers, (2) 6 preadolescent and adolescent peer group recording sessions, and (3) a random sample of 100 adults. The importance of this analysis was twofold; it gave concrete evidence that BEV is indeed a rule-governed linguistic system rather than the "sloppy English" it has so often been accused of being, and, in addition, it made use of more sophisticated fieldwork techniques than had previously been used in large-scale urban studies. Labov et al. analyzed a number of phonological variables (e.g., the -*ed* suffix) and found deletion rules to be quite systematic. In addition, they investigated the absence of the present copula and found it to be the result of regular phonological rules which operate to remove single consonants which remain after contraction. Their analysis of the invariant third singular -*s* is particularly interesting in view of the study of the same phenomenon carried out in Norwich, England, by Peter Trudgill (see below). Other studies of BEV by such scholars as Wolfram, Fasold, and Stewart, to name only a few, were responsible for gathering overwhelming evidence to show that BEV is indeed a separate linguistic system with its own set of rules.

On the basis of this study Labov wrote numerous articles, including a pamphlet for teachers entitled *The Structure of Nonstandard English* (1970a), published by the National Council of Teachers of English. Perhaps the most influential publication to come from these research findings is Labov's famous polemic, *The Logic of Nonstandard English* (1969), in which he argues that some educators have taken the old myths about nonstandard languages as their fundamental assumptions and have built programs based on them. Labov maintained that nonstandard speakers have the same basic vocabulary, possess the same capacity for conceptual learning, and use the same logic as anyone else who learns to speak and understand English. Using data from his 1968 study, he demonstrates how children in urban ghettos are "bathed in verbal stimulation," and he says that there is no connection between what children can do with language in their own neighborhoods and what they do in school. The problem, says Labov, is not that the children speak a cognitively deficient language but that the value system of their own peer groups is opposed to that of the schools. Labov's contention is that urban ghetto children are more influenced by their peer groups than they are by their families, and since peer pressures are particularly strong at the end of elementary school, the children are most likely to show a turn for the worse in school during fourth and fifth grades. From the point of view of education in the United States, such findings have been of tremendous importance. Controversies over the cause of the poor school performance of children from urban black ghettos have, as we have seen, centered around the issue of whether the children are or are not "verbally deficient." Studies such as the one described above and many others have made it plain that *verbal deficit* is an inappropriate term by which to describe a situation in which children coming into mainstream schools are nonnative speakers of the variety of English used by teachers, textbooks, and tests. The fact that linguists were able to present cogent evidence to show that speakers of BEV were not speaking ungrammatical English but were following grammatical rules of a different linguistic system has had a considerable impact on educators and on society generally. This does not, unfortunately, mean that the educational problems of black inner-city children have been solved, or even that the majority of educators have now adopted a more positive attitude toward children who are linguistically "different." What it does mean is that the evidence now exists to show that difference and not deficit is at issue and that attitudes and practices are gradually undergoing a change.

BLACK COMMUNITY ATTITUDES

Without wishing to go very deeply into a discussion of a particular ethnic variety of English spoken in the United States, it is important to mention that although the work of Labov et al. and that of such other researchers as Wolfram (1969b) and Fasold (1972) on the syntax of nonstandard Black English was an important contribution, it aroused serious controversy among both scholars and laymen. While the arguments for respecting the systematic nature of this dialect had a strong and positive impact on many educators, it is also true that a number of people have taken exception to this work. No one has suggested that the analysis done by these scholars on the grammar of vernacular Black English is faulty; rather, they have been offended because it leaves readers with the impression that inner-city black children speak only street language, and, indeed, that the street language reported in such work as Labov's is the common medium of interaction among blacks of all social classes in most situations. The fact is that speakers of Black English have a repertoire of varieties at their command, just as any speaker has. Linguists who had, themselves, grown up in black ghettos, were furious at the implication that black parents would permit their children to use street talk at home, and offended that Labov had not made it clear that all black children know the sociolinguistic rules which demand quite another variety in church than on the street. The point is that there are domains for different styles of speech, and native speakers know the rules. Simply because people speak a nonstandard variety is no reason to imagine that there are not subtle differences in vocabulary, grammar, and even phonology which vary depending on the situation. As Wright (1975), himself a black linguist, points out in his review of Labov's work:

> Linguists are quick to argue that there is nothing about any one dialect or language variety which makes it any more structured, logical, complex, superior, etc., to any other variety. If this is true, what accounts for the fascination of Labov and others with nonstandard data, especially nonstandard Black data. Is there no other variety of English spoken by Blacks of any interest to linguists than BEV. . . . The Black community, linguistically and sociologically, is a highly diverse and complex community, which among its varieties and language competencies include the nonstandard variety often quoted by linguists. The true challenge to the Black student in linguistics and/or communication is to extend research into areas of relevance which reflect the diversity and complexity of life and interpersonal interaction among Blacks. By focusing on the behaviors of the lower social segments, we project those very behaviors which carry the heaviest societal stigmatization, while, at the same time ignoring (by implication) other community behaviors which are highly valued and carry no such stigmatization.
>
> Labov's preference for the study of nonstandard language especially that of ghetto male adolescents has been a major factor in middle class Black rejection of the notion of an ethnically identifiable Black variety of American English. Such persons argue that they are Black, but deny that they use many of the characteristic features of "Black English." In such matters where linguistic research weighs heavily on social issues, some speakers prefer to be *un*represented rather than *mis*represented. (Wright 1975:192)

Thus, during the 1960s, there were those who said that the school problems of lower-class children could be explained by the fact that they had acquired less language than middle-class children, and there were others who maintained that these children had simply acquired a different language. Both theories assume that the child learns only one way to speak. Yet we know that even quite young children vary their speech to fit the situation—including the person they are speaking to.

The controversies over the reasons for the high rate of school failure among lower-income black children is far from settled. The upsurge of interest in research into the distinctive linguistic features of Black English Vernacular which was so prominent in the 1960s and 1970s has lost some of its impetus. Two major reasons seem to be responsible for this change in perspective.

On the one hand, as a number of language attitude studies have shown (see, for example, Hoover 1978), black parents and teachers are well aware that their children need to learn Standard English if they are to compete successfully for good jobs, and they rely heavily on schools to teach it. While the majority of black adults reject the approach of using BEV in the early grades as a stepping-stone toward teaching their children to read and write Standard English, there is, nevertheless considerable evidence that the black community believes it is important for teachers to be informed about Black English so that they will understand the children's speech and respect it as a separate linguistic system.

The second reason for the lessening emphasis on the study of Black English Vernacular has to do with the recognition that differences in language alone do not represent a sufficient explanation of the educational problems of poor black children. Recently, more and more attention has been paid to interactional styles within the home and the community, as well as to detailed observation of the way students interact with teachers and with one another. As the results of these studies become available, educators and researchers have come to recognize that sociocultural factors play at least as important a role in the school problems of black children as does their speech.

A recently published ethnographic study of children in two neighboring communities as they learn to speak and acquire the appropriate speech norms and behaviors (Heath 1983) points up the contrasts which eventually lead to different levels of school achievement. On the basis of her work in these two working-class communities, one black and one white, Heath argues that for the black children the style of school language conflicts with the style of language behavior children are socialized into at home. The result is that black students are at an immediate disadvantage when they enter school. As Heath puts it:

> No one lifts labels and features out of their contexts for explication; no one requests repetitions from Trackton children. Thus their entry into a classroom which depends on responses based on lifting items and events out of context is a shock. . . . Their abilities to contextualize, to remember what may seem to the teacher to be an unrelated event as similar to another, to link seemingly disparate factors in their explanations, and to create highly imaginative stories are suppressed in the classroom. The school's approach to reading and learning establishes decontextualized skills as foundational in the hierarchy of academic skills. . . . Thus the Trackton children receive little encouragement. . . . They fail in the initial sequences of the school-defined hierarchy of skills, and when they reach the upper grades, the social demands and habits of failing are too strong to allow them to renew for school use the habits they brought to their first-grade classroom. (Heath 1983:353-354)

Heath's study is a detailed exploration of the ways in which different communities socialize their children from the point of view of language. Her results clearly show that conflicts between the home language style of black children and the expectations they face in school result in their being evaluated as unable to use language effectively, and therefore destined to early failure. Far from supporting a deficit hypothesis, however, Heath has used an ethnographic approach to the study of ways of speaking in community and school which point up the differences that must be understood if teachers and administrators are to evaluate students' abilities and achievements in a way which will lead to real opportunities for school success. The ethnographic research that Heath and numerous other researchers (see, for example, Erickson and Shultz 1982, Cazden et al. 1980, Mehan 1979), have undertaken shows enormous promise in its ability to uncover and perhaps reverse the severe educational conflicts and problems that continue to face black children in our schools.

THE ANN ARBOR CASE

On July 28, 1977, a group of black parents from a low-income housing project in Ann Arbor, Michigan, brought suit in Federal Court against their children's school (The King School), the Ann Arbor School District, and the Michigan Board of Education. The grounds of this suit were that the authorities had failed to take into account the sociocultural and economic factors that would have prevented their children from failing in school. Judge Joiner dismissed these complaints on the basis that nothing in the Constitution gives the right to special educational services to overcome poor academic performance based on social, cultural, or economic background. However, the judge did retain one complaint—that the defendants had not taken appropriate action to overcome linguistic barriers that impede students from participating in instructional programs. He agreed with the plaintiffs that the dialect differences between the lower-income black children and the other children as well as the teachers might be a cause for action. Thus, the language problem came to be the central focus of the "King School case," or, as it is now commonly known, the Ann Arbor Case. Large numbers of linguists were called upon to testify to the differences between Black English and the mainstream standard with respect both to its present-day form and to its origins and history. The outcome of this famous case is now history. As Labov has described it: "Judge Joiner delivered his opinion on July 12, 1979. He found for the plaintiffs, and directed the Ann Arbor School Board to submit to him within thirty days a plan defining the exact steps to be taken to help the teachers (1) to identify children speaking Black English, and (2) to use that knowledge in teaching students how to read standard English" (Labov 1982:193).

Although this was a landmark case in the history of the struggle over educational opportunities for children who are native speakers of Black English, the final upshot left many problems still unresolved. Most important of these is the question of how best to provide the help so badly needed if these children are to succeed in school. Many controversies still revolve around the problem of what constitutes the best instructional approach. One important and very healthy outcome was the recognition that teachers themselves must be given adequate background knowledge about how and in what ways Black English differs from the standard, and an adequate understanding of the origins and history of this distinctive variety of American English. If there is to be any serious improvement in the instructional opportunities of inner-city black children, this must begin with a change in the attitude of teachers and other school authorities responsible for their education, an attitude that can change only for the better with the respect that comes from knowledge about it.

BIDIALECTALISM

We have gone into the issues surrounding the educational problems of inner-city black children at some length, primarily because BEV represents the most extreme case of dialect diversity in the United States. For this reason, and because of the political and social issues concerning civil rights, more attention has been paid and therefore more is known about this variety of English than about the many other nonstandard varieties of English. This does not mean that other varieties have been ignored. Indeed, nonstandard varieties of English around the world have been and are continuing to be studied. The dialects about which least is known are, unfortunately, those nonstandard regional varieties of White English spoken by lower-socioeconomic groups everywhere. Much more linguistic and sociolinguistic description must be undertaken before we have a true picture of the language diversity which exists everywhere English is spoken.

However much or little is known in a systematic way about the many dialects that constitute what may be thought of as the linguistic tradition known as the English language, there is no doubt that speakers of these nonstandard dialects are at a serious disadvantage in terms of socioeconomic mobility and their ability to participate fully in the mainstream society. As we have described in some detail in the case of BEV, it is the general assumption of the public, and, indeed, of the government, that the major responsibility for providing equal socioeconomic opportunities for children who are speakers of nonstandard dialects rests with the educational system.

As we have indicated, a great deal of disagreement has been attached to the question of how the schools should deal with children who speak nonstandard dialects of English. The schools are, in the eyes of the community, responsible for teaching all children the standard language so that they will be able to go out into the world and get good jobs or go on to higher education. Very few people seriously question the need for young people to have command of standard or institutional English. As Shopin and Williams (1980:xiii) point out: "It is true that every society with a rich written tradition eventually develops something it calls a 'standard written dialect,' which in fact can influence speech as well as writing. We have such a standard—it is our 'institutional English' "—and we cannot responsibly ignore it when we teach young people to read and write. We should give everyone who wants it the linguistic means to move up the economic and social ladder, and for that one must learn "institutional English." Clearly, the work of teaching Standard English to all children in the society is a worthwhile endeavor. On the other hand, a very normative approach which seeks to change completely the way a child speaks is not only unwise but probably doomed to failure. What needs to be understood by educators and by the community at large is that the dialects spoken by nonstandard speakers are not in themselves "bad" English and that no attempt should be made to eradicate them. If children stopped speaking the way their families and friends do, they would be ostracized. We have no right to expect children to reject the ways of speaking of their homes and communities. Rather, what is needed is the addition of another dialect, the standard dialect, to the children's repertoires. Children already have several speech styles available to them, and they know the appropriate use for these. What is needed is to teach them the style which is appropriate for use in the school. It is necessary to make it clear to schoolchildren that they are not expected to stop speaking their own native dialects in all appropriate varieties and that they are not looked down on for doing so. It should be understood that children need to speak the way their friends and families do when they are with them and that educators know that school language is inappropriate in such contexts. On the other hand, children need to learn school language, not only because that is the variety used in school but because control of what we refer to as Standard English has come to be one of the most obvious marks of an educated person—and teachers and schools have long been seen as the most important and influential agencies in transmitting that mastery to the next generation. What was once the dialect of the social elite, and thus dominantly exclusive in its social functioning, is seen in today's democratic societies as an essential passport to the "good" life—to wider society. Thus, it becomes something that everyone has the right to acquire. And it becomes the duty of teachers, particularly the English and language arts teachers, to facilitate this process as much as possible.

ETHNIC IDENTITY AND DIALECT DIVERSITY

The issue of how Standard English should be taught in the schools is one which has been fraught with controversy. To begin with, not all educators and community members agree that nonstandard dialects should be permitted to exist. Many people believe that nonstandard dialects are in some way sinful or evil and, as we have seen, are convinced that speaking them leads to serious cognitive disabilities. For this reason, it is argued, nonstandard English dialects should be completely eradicated if at all possible. The eradicationists want the schools to use their influence to convince children that they must forget their home dialect and speak "correct" English at all times. They believe that teachers should spend a great deal of time correcting children's spoken language. Children should be cautioned constantly to use only "correct" English both in school and outside it. Indeed, it is not unusual for teachers to try to persuade children to go home and correct their parents!

Leaving aside moral issues, it seems clear that those who believe it is feasible to carry out a policy of eradicating all dialects but the standard have a very limited understanding of the social factors which condition language use. Speech is, after all, a very important factor in group identity. For members of nonstandard-speaking groups, this does not necessarily lead to a greater attempt to speak according to the rules of Standard English but rather may lead to an attempt to emulate the speech style of those with whom they wish to be accepted and identified. There are numerous examples in the sociolinguistic literature which show the effects of speaker attitude on pronunciation and other linguistic features. In a now-famous study of the linguistic consequences of social change on the island of Martha's Vineyard, Labov (1963) demonstrated precisely this phenomenon. In his analysis of local pronunciation, Labov found that the younger men, especially those who had worked for a time on the mainland and then returned to make their homes on their native island, not only use the rather low-prestige pronunciation of the island but exaggerate it so that their speech is even more divergent from that of the mainland. Resentful of the increasing numbers of vacationers who come to Martha's Vineyard, these young islanders have chosen to use an extreme form of the island's dialect to signal their separate identity. This study points up the fact that linguistic change does not always move in the direction of the prestige variety. Language is a very important manifestation of group identity and solidarity. When a group believes itself to be discriminated against or otherwise vulnerable to pressures from outside, it may unconsciously or consciously choose to exaggerate the use of speech features which signal group identity. That is, the speech of the group in question will diverge from, rather than converge with, the more prestigious mainstream speech.

A study which is even more pertinent to the present discussion is that by Edwards (1985), in which she describes the situation of West Indian migrants in Britain and the linguistic reaction to it on the part of their school-age children. After nearly 30 years of living in Britain, people who came from the Caribbean with the hope that they would find better educational and occupational opportunities for their children have been frustrated in these expectations. By and large, West Indians still occupy positions with little status and relatively poor earnings. Further, West Indian children, of all immigrant groups in Britain, are generally performing least well in school. The fact that the newly arrived migrants from the Caribbean are speakers of West Indian Creole, a nonstandard variety of English which has, within itself, many regional dialects, has worked very much to the disadvantage of this group, serving as a symbol of their difference from other members of the population. Language attitude studies have revealed that Creole carries extremely low status among other English speakers and among West Indians themselves, a clear reflection of the low status of this group in society. For West Indian schoolchildren, the situation is particularly difficult. As Edwards says: "The insistence of British schools on standard English has done nothing to help the West Indian child. In addition to the linguistic insecurity and confusion to which it has sometimes given rise, it has conveyed very clearly the message that his own language, which, after all, is the most valuable resource which he brings to school, is inacceptable" (Edwards 1985:329).

As a result of discrimination, frustrated expectations, and their generally unfavorable position in society, West Indian children have shown an increasing tendency to "talk Black," exaggerating the Creole features of their speech as they become adolescents. The most likely explanation for this phenomenon is that, as

Edwards says, "children, consciously or unconsciously, are martialing this Creole speech as a defense mechanism, a symbol of defiance of and alienation from mainstream society" (Edwards 1985:331).

Thus we see that pressures to conform to mainstream speech and other forms of social behavior may work along with other forms of discrimination to cause speakers to use an even more extreme form of the low-status variety in question. An increase in divergence from the standard is often a signal that a nonstandard-speaking minority group feels itself to be under attack. Any attempt to denigrate, much less to eradicate, the nonstandard speech patterns of children in schools is an invitation to widen the social and cultural gulf that already separates these children from their standard-speaking peers. Not only is it unrealistic to expect children to react favorably to such treatment, it may also be dangerous and even immoral. To suggest that children give up their home dialects for the sake of social and economic advancement is tantamount to suggesting that they reject their families and communities for the same reason.

A second way of approaching the educational problems raised by dialect diversity is to accept the fact that nonstandard dialects have always existed and are unlikely to disappear, and to work at teaching children Standard English as a second dialect. This approach has come to be known as bidialectalism, and it has much to recommend it. On the one hand, those who believe that children should be taught English as a second dialect are clearly ready to accept and respect the fact that nonstandard dialects have a right to exist. What they advocate is to teach the standard for school and institutional use generally, recognizing that there will always be situations in which a variety of the nonstandard home dialect is the only appropriate one to use. Given our present knowledge about code switching and about the ways in which countries such as Norway and Switzerland have managed to retain their nonstandard regional dialects while at the same time ensuring that everyone is capable of using the standard where appropriate, this approach seems to be the most promising. A more practical problem arises when we consider how best to accomplish the goal of bidialectalism. Here we are in rather murky waters, for not enough is known. Attempts have been made to use ESL teaching methods such as grammar drills, but these have not proven successful. The teaching of a second dialect is not really comparable to the teaching of a second language. Nonstandard-speaking children already know how to speak English quite as fluently as any standard-speaking child. Further, they are quite capable of comprehending spoken Standard English. Even if they have had little exposure to standard speakers, non-standard-speaking children have, almost without exception, been watching television nearly all their lives. Their passive competence is very high. What these children do not have is the ability to consistently produce standard grammatical forms. The differences between standard and nonstandard speech are not nearly so great as we have come to believe. They are different systems, true, but the structural differences between them can be described and taught, not as though they were foreign to one another but as two very similar systems. One of the most difficult aspects of making such comparisons, however, is that we have very little in the way of descriptive analyses of spoken Standard English. We know from existing studies that the patterns used in the speech of even the most prestigious groups in a given society differ sharply from those used in most written discourse. Lacking anything approaching full analyses of any variety of standard spoken English, we have no choice but to rely on our native speaker intuitions. However faulty these may turn out to be, intuitions do help in these situations, however, and efforts at contrastive analyses have been made. It is now necessary for educators themselves to be trained to understand the structural differences among the various dialects they are likely to encounter so that they can teach in the most effective way possible. We are a very long way from solving the problem of dialect diversity in the classroom. Much of what is needed lies in the realm of teacher education and materials development. The educational system cannot erase social prejudice against minority ethnic groups, but it can give children the educational background they need to make use of their talents.

NONNATIVE ENGLISH SPEAKER ATTITUDES TOWARD DIALECTS AND STANDARDS

Although most investigation into the proficiency of nonnative speakers in comprehending spoken English focuses on some variety of standard English, the likelihood is that most, if not all, learners of English will often have occasion to interact with nonstandard speakers. Taking this fact into careful account, Eisenstein (1982, 1986) and Eisenstein and Verdi (1985) have investigated the intelligibility of three dialects for adult learners of English. Studying groups of learners who came both from working-class backgrounds and from a range of other socioeconomic levels, Eisenstein tested learners' abilities at different proficiency levels to discriminate among three dialects of English: the Standard, New Yorkese (New York nonstandard English), and Black English. It was found that learners are able to discriminate among the different dialects at a very early level, but that the attitudes and stereotypes toward these varieties which are common to native speakers are not acquired by learners until their proficiency in English increases. The most advanced learners in the study had acquired nativelike judgments of standard and nonstandard speech. With respect to intelligibility, Eisenstein and Verdi (1985) found that the listening comprehension of working-class learners of English at the intermediate level of proficiency was significantly affected by the dialect of the English speaker. Surprisingly enough, although the learners had had considerable contact with speakers of Black English, it was found that this dialect was the least intelligible to them of the three. Even more striking was the finding that the attitudes of English learners to speakers of the three dialects reflected their relative ability to comprehend. That is, when asked to make judgments regarding the friendliness, appearance, and job status of speakers of each of the three dialects, learners demonstrated attitudes which paralleled those of native speakers, rating the speakers of Standard English the highest, the New Yorkese speakers next, and the speakers of Black English lowest.

These results provide us with additional evidence regarding what we have learned about the effect of social attitudes on language performance. As we saw in the discussions of group identity and linguistic divergence, speakers are capable of making use of speech features which are more or less similar to those used by groups with whom they wish to identify. That intelligibility should also be affected by social factors is well documented in the anthropological literature, though not, until Eisenstein's investigations, in the literature on language acquisition. Wolff (1959) demonstrated that the objective linguistic similarity of a given dialect to another is not necessarily reflected by degree of mutual intelligibility. A dialect which, from the comparative linguistic point of view, is relatively different from another may, because of the social position of its speakers, prove to be more intelligible to the speakers of the first group. Conversely, dialects which appear, from the point of view of the linguist, to be very similar may be relatively unintelligible. In addition, closely related dialects are often nonreciprocally intelligible such that one group claims to be unable to understand the speech of the other but the reverse is not the case. In his study of the languages of Nigeria, Wolff found that intelligibility across dialects was deeply connected to social attitudes towards their speakers. The language or dialect of a high-status group was much more likely to be intelligible to other groups than was that of a low-status group.

It seems reasonable to assume that the findings reported by Eisenstein concerning intelligibility of nonstandard dialects among language learners is closely related to the findings described by Wolff. Language learners are clearly affected by social factors, and their relative ability to comprehend the speech of different groups reflects their motivation to identify with the group in question. Since learners' attitudes towards different social groups parallels those of native speakers, it is not surprising that these attitudes rather than the actual amount of contact with a specific group will determine the degree to which the speech of the group is intelligible.

It should be noted that Eisenstein's work points up an extremely important issue for TESOL. While it is clear that learners prefer to identify with speakers of the target language whom they perceive to have the highest status, it is nevertheless true that a large number of learners of English, particularly newly arrived immigrants, will themselves become members of the working class. For this reason, they will need to interact extensively with other members of this class, both black and white. However much they may choose to identify with nonstandard white speakers, they will be working side by side with speakers of Black English as well. Given the sociolinguistic evidence, it is not clear that classroom instruction will help to solve the intelligibility problem learners have regarding Black English. It is, nevertheless, clear that learners should be given as much background information and help with comprehension as possible so that both their language attitudes and their ability to comprehend nonstandard English may be improved.

CONCLUSION

From the preceding discussion, it seems clear that the TESOL profession has a responsibility to be sure that teachers and administrators are well informed about the enormous dialect diversity within the English-speaking world. As we have seen, linguistic diversity is a manifestation of social and ethnic differences as well as regional ones. Learners of English need to know as much as possible about the distinctions which exist within the language they are learning. Information about language diversity is not only of intrinsic importance to second language learners, it is also an excellent introduction to social and political facts about the society whose language they are learning.

CHAPTER 11

Bilingual Education

INTRODUCTION

One of the most heated debates going on at this time in the United States is one which specifically concerns language policy as it relates to the education of children whose native language is not English. Since this issue is of direct concern to the TESOL profession, we will examine it in some detail. This matter is of intrinsic relevance to TESOL since it affects the composition of the school population we will be called upon to teach and the question of whether English is to be the medium as well as the goal of instruction. In addition, the debate over bilingual education is almost equally important as an exemplar of the ways in which politics and education are inextricably interwoven with language.

Although we do not frequently think of it in these terms, the United States is an immigrant country. With the exception of the American Indians and their descendants, we are all immigrants and children of immigrants. Thus, by the very nature of things, the United States is and always has been a multilingual and multicultural country. In spite of this well-known historical fact, there persists an illusion that the United States is a monolingual English-speaking country. Although every school-child learns that the United States was colonized not only by the English but by Spanish, French, German, and Dutch settlers as well, it is often forgotten that English was far from being the only colonial language spoken by Europeans who came to live in this part of the "new world." The fact that there were hundreds of American Indian languages spoken here before the Europeans came to these shores is recognized at one level but rarely taken into consideration in the context of the multilingual/multicultural composition of the population. In addition, as we all know, millions of immigrants speaking literally hundreds of different languages have been coming to settle here ever since. So far from monolingual are we that by the late seventeenth century, approximately 20 different languages were spoken here apart from the many Native American languages already mentioned. Two centuries later, at the height of the great wave of immigration which took place during the end of the nineteenth and the beginning of the twentieth century, the United States Immigration Commission reported that almost 50 percent of all students in secondary schools were of foreign-born parentage. Indeed, "a July 1975 survey by the National Center for Educational Statistics found that thirteen percent of the U.S. population lives in households in which languages other than English are spoken" (Glazer 1978:32). In fact, census reports from 1970 showed that well over 16 percent of the United States population claimed a language other than English as their mother tongue. Given the negative attitude toward many of our minority languages, it is impossible to know how many of those people asked chose not to admit to their "foreign" background. What this means is that in spite of great efforts made to Americanize and de-ethnicize both Native Americans and immigrant groups in this country, large numbers of people in the United States have continued to speak a great variety of languages other than English.

At the present time, for example, there are approximately 150 American Indian languages still being spoken in this country, and this after more than a century of the most stringent efforts to eradicate them. Even today, many Indian adults can remember being taken to off-reservation boarding schools run by the Bureau of Indian Affairs. These schools were run entirely in English, and Indian children were punished and even beaten if they were heard speaking their own languages. In spite of these and other pressures, both social and economic, many Native American and immigrant groups have made strong and often successful attempts to maintain their ancestral languages.

A striking example of a successful attempt of one Indian nation to maintain its own tongue, an attempt that was eventually suppressed by the United States government, is the educational program developed by the Cherokee Indians in the early nineteenth century. Having devised their own alphabet (or, more accurately, syllabary) to write their language, the Cherokee established a system of education which resulted in almost total literacy of the population in the Cherokee language. English literacy was taught as part of the program, and so effective was it that the Cherokee had a higher literacy rate in English than did the English-speaking populations of neighboring states. By the latter part of the century, however, the policy of taking children away to boarding schools where they were not permitted to use any language but English had effectively put an end to the educational achievements of the Cherokee Indians, with the result that their present literacy rate is among the lowest of all Indian groups.

Although the policy of requiring that only English be spoken by the Cherokee and by all other Native American groups was, as we have seen, extremely damaging, the intention was to protect the Indians, not to harm them. The prevailing view of bilingualism was that it led to cognitive deficiency. The Indian languages themselves were generally regarded as crude and illogical, and it was argued that speaking these languages resulted in an inability to think clearly. Apart from these "intellectual" reasons, the language policy adopted toward Native Americans clearly had a strong political motivation. In suppressing Indian languages, the government was attempting to integrate the Indians into the mainstream English-speaking society.

Although English-only boarding schools were not set up in the Southwest, Mexican-American school children were forced to experience many of the same techniques of language suppression. In schools where virtually all of the children were Spanish speakers, students were discouraged in every way possible from using their home language, even on the playgrounds during recess. Again, the intentions were laudable, even though the policies were not. It was the sincere belief of school officials that if they could only force children to speak English, their improved fluency would have a strong positive effect on generally low reading levels and, by causing them to perform school tasks more successfully, would put a halt to the extremely high school dropout rate for Hispanic children. The possibility that the childrens' reading scores might have improved dramatically had they been permitted to learn this skill in their own language was apparently not considered. Children, no matter what their first language, were evaluated according to their ability to read in English, and their literacy scores were compared with those of other children in public schools, regardless of language background. If children fell behind in school subjects because their English proficiency was too low for them to follow the instruction offered in that language, it was widely held that the only answer was to insist that the children have more and more exposure to English.

The recent upsurge of immigration into this country of non-English-speaking people from Asia, Africa, and Latin America as well as from Europe has greatly added to and strengthened the multilingual/multicultural composition of our society. In many of our more densely populated states it is not unusual to find that 50 or 60 separate languages other than English are spoken. Many of these groups have made a concerted effort to maintain their ancestral languages, some through supplemental schools (often sponsored by churches or other cultural organizations) and some through privately supported day schools which offer instruction both in the ethnic language and in English. The fact that children attending such ethnic day schools have recently been found to achieve as high or higher reading scores in English, in spite of (or perhaps because of) being biliterate presents an interesting challenge to public schooling, and one which we will discuss later in this chapter.

The important point to be made here is that the United States has been, since long before it became an independent nation, both multilingual and multicultural. From the time of earliest colonization until this moment, there has been a continuous flow of immigration and a continuing effort on the part of the indigenous population and of many of those who have migrated here to maintain some aspects of their heritage. Often, this effort has manifested itself in language maintenance efforts. According to Joshua Fishman (1980), the foremost authority on language loyalty among immigrant groups in the United States, there are approximately 6000 ethnic community-sponsored mother tongue schools currently operating in all areas of the country and in every state of the union. It is Fishman's thesis that the ethnic community mother tongue schools "represent an American way of being ethnic and an ethnic way of being American. . . . Rather than being reflections of foreignness, these schools now represent the indigenization of ethnicity as an American way of life" (Fishman 1980:10). As Fishman also points out, it is not so much the newly arrived immigrant groups which tend to operate and support such schools. Rather, they are most commonly supported by groups which have lived in this country for several generations and by parents and teachers who are themselves dominant in English. According to Fishman, ethnic community mother tongue schools usually teach children who are second-, third-, and even fourth-generation Americans. What this means is that the image of the melting pot, comforting as it has been to those who believe in assimilation to a single dominant English-speaking society and regard multilingualism as a threat to national unity, is a false one which needs to be replaced in the public mind with a true picture of the pluralism which we see all around us. As Glazer and Moynihan have said, "the point about the melting pot is that it did not happen" (1970:xcvii). Hundreds of separate ethnic groups continue to exist and to maintain their mother tongues even though they may be more fluent and frequent speakers of English. On the other hand, many, especially among the more recent arrivals, have little or no command of English, the dominant language of our society.

The question of how best to provide publicly sponsored education to children whose English language proficiency is limited has led to a group of instructional approaches which, taken together, have come to be called bilingual education. By and large, bilingual public schooling in the United States today is viewed as a means to remedy the very serious inequality of educational opportunity for children who have little or no English language proficiency. That is, bilingual education as it is currently known came into being and continues to be viewed largely as a means of compensatory education for children who are regarded as "handicapped" by their lack of fluency in English. As will be described in the following pages, there has been and continues to be considerable controversy over the best means to accomplish this goal.

The fact that much recent research has shown that for many children there are distinct cognitive advantages to be gained from bilingualism has important implications for bilingual education and for the general belief that bilingualism is a handicap to children from minority language backgrounds. Considerable research has been carried out in order to ascertain the effects of bilingualism on children's cognitive abilities. In 1962, Peal and Lambert found that bilingual children did significantly better on both verbal and nonverbal intelligence tests than did monolingual children. They explain this superior performance by suggesting that the ability to formulate thoughts in more than one language improves children's ability to be flexible in their thinking. Still another positive consequence of bilingualism in childhood is that it has a positive influence on the foreign language learning ability of these same people when they become adults. Reporting on the results of a rigorously controlled study which she had carried out, Eisenstein states:

> All significant findings point towards the conclusion that bilingualism in childhood is indeed a positive factor in adult second language learning aptitude. Formal education may be a positive factor for formal learning situations although it may have a negative effect on the self confidence of the learner. Learning several different languages in childhood appears to have a cumulative positive effect. Also, bilingualism and language learning aptitude seem to correlate with the view of the individual that speaking a foreign language is an asset. (Eisenstein 1980:169)

In spite of such encouraging research findings, it is nevertheless the case that bilingual education has had a stormy history in this country over the last 15 years. Perhaps the most important point to recognize before we enter into a discussion of the history, the instructional problems and approaches, and the debates surrounding this issue is that there is, among scholars and laymen alike, no consensus as to what bilingual education is, or what should be achieved through it.

EARLY APPROACHES TO THE EDUCATION OF LANGUAGE–MINORITY CHILDREN

Before World War I, bilingual education existed in various parts of the United States, much of it publically supported. German-English bilingual schools were common (Kloss 1966) in the Middle West; Spanish in New Mexico and French in New England and in Louisiana were used as languages of instruction in public schools. As immigration increased, negative reactions toward linguistic and cultural pluralism increased. Efforts at the "Americanization" of new immigrants emphasized the use of the English language as a major means toward the accomplishment of this goal. A prime example of this attitude is embodied in a statement made by President Theodore Roosevelt in which he said: "There is no room in this country for hyphenated Americanism . . . Any man who comes here . . . must adopt the institutions of the United States, and therefore he must adopt the language which is now the native tongue of our people, no matter what the several strains in our blood may be. It would not be merely a misfortune, but a crime to perpetuate differences of language in this country" (*Education Week,* April 1, 1987:22).

It was not until World War I, however, that the practice of permitting bilingual programs, both public and private, began to be questioned by state legislatures in any serious way. Because the United States was at war with Germany, ethnic Germans in this country were seen as a potential fifth column, and it became unsafe, and in some places criminal, to use the German language in public. It was during this period of xenophobia that the use of English as a language of instruction in public schools was enforced by law. It was not until the early 1960s, when another political event, the Cuban Revolution, brought in its wake a sudden influx of Spanish-speaking refugees, that publicly funded bilingual education again became legal in the United States. Thus, between 1917 and 1963 there was no government support for education in any language but English. Foreign languages continued to be taught, of course, but school subjects were not taught in other languages. Rather, it was the clearly stated aim of our educational system to cause all children to speak English in school. An example of this policy is that until 1973 it was a crime in the state of Texas to use any language but English as the medium of instruction in public schools.

In its efforts to assimilate them, the American school system very often destroyed the cultural identity of the children they sought to educate, thereby causing untold personal damage and wasting a rich and important national resource. The irony of it is that at the same time as the schools were doing everything in their power to discourage use of the various ethnic languages, they were making sincere efforts to teach foreign languages in secondary schools. This situation is an example of what appears to be an inverse prestige ratio for languages in this country such that the ability to speak a foreign language is admired if that language is not one spoken by a local ethnic group. As Rolf Kjolseth (1975) put it: "This might be formulated as the Law of Anglo love of ethnic irrelevance . . . the more locally irrelevant an ethnic language and culture is, the higher its social status, and the more viable it is locally, the lower its social status." As noted in Fishman (1966), this attitude is typical in the United States with respect to the most diverse ethnic languages and concluded that "as long as these languages and cultures are truly foreign our schools are comfortable with them. But as soon as they are found in our own back yards, the schools deny them . . . this amounts to honoring the dead while burying the living." As we have seen, for a large number of Americans, the efforts made to assimilate them into the mainstream language and culture simply did not work. At the present time, there are at least 5 million school-age children who have limited English proficiency. The great majority of these children come from low-income homes. In order for them to have a chance for socioeconomic advancement in today's increasingly industrialized labor market, these children must be given the opportunity for a meaningful education. Insofar as language presents a barrier to educational opportunity for language minority children, this barrier must somehow be overcome. In the next section of this chapter, we will survey recent attempts to solve this problem.

HISTORY OF BILINGUAL EDUCATION IN THE TWENTIETH CENTURY

It was not until 1963 that the massive immigration of largely middle-class Cubans into Dade County, Florida, touched off an effort which resulted in a wave of new interest in bilingual education. Cuban refugees were arriving in Florida by the thousands, and among them came children whose only language was Spanish and well-trained teachers who were perfectly capable of instructing them in their own language. Special schools were set up in response to the needs of the children of these political refugees from Cuba, and these schools were bilingual. The first and most famous of the new bilingual programs was begun at the Coral Way School in the Miami area. Here, half the instruction in all elementary grades was given in Spanish by Cuban teachers; the other half of the instruction was given in English by American teachers. The student body in 1963 was representative of the neighborhood of which it was a part; approximately 50 percent of the children were Cubans and 50 percent were Anglos. At the end of the first three years of elementary school, both groups of children were bilingual. The success of this early enterprise was extremely influential. A year after the Coral Way School was begun in Florida, two bilingual programs began in Texas, one in Laredo and one in San Antonio. Bilingual programs began in New Mexico in 1965 and in California and Arizona in 1966. In 1967, New Jersey was added to the growing list. All the above programs were at the public elementary school level, and, with the exception of Navajo, which is taught at the Rock Point School in Arizona, all have Spanish as their language of instruction along with English. Although the immediate impetus was provided by the success of programs begun for the Cuban refugees, the upsurge of interest in bilingual education which led to the passing in 1968 of the Bilingual Education Act had its roots in the sociopolitical changes which were taking place throughout American society. A complex web of factors was involved. To begin with, the civil rights movement, long in the making, brought with it an awakening pride in ethnicity. Traditional mainstream values and assumptions were being called into question. The constitutional right to equality of opportunity for all citizens was tested and affirmed by the courts. Growing demands on the part of minority groups everywhere in the United States led to legislation aimed at removing barriers to full participation in the social, political, and economic life of the nation. For minority groups striving toward greater prosperity, public education has always held both hope and frustration. Language is a focal issue. Education provides the means for occupational and social advancement, but if the only institutionalized medium of instruction in public school is Standard English, children who are "linguistically different" are automatically blocked from taking full advantage of the educational opportunity which is their constitutional right.

The deeply rooted tradition of monolingual English schooling would have been impervious to change without strong political pressure. Numbers count in politics, and it is therefore not surprising that Hispanic Americans, the largest of the non-English-speaking language groups in the United States, should have led in the struggle for a more advantageous language policy in the nation's schools. Of all Hispanic Americans, the two largest ethnic groups are the Mexican Americans of the Southwest and the Puerto Ricans in the Northeast. Both groups experienced heavy additions to their numbers through large-scale immigration during the 1950s and 1960s. Although differing in a number of important ways, both groups shared certain problems. They were (and continue to be) concentrated at the lower end of the socioeconomic scale. They are subject to severe discrimination. Their children experience a heavy failure and dropout rate at school. And, within both groups there are large percentages of people who have a strong desire to preserve their linguistic and cultural heritage. Given these problems and aims, bilingual education appeared to be the best possible solution. Taking advantage of the educational efforts made by the U.S. government to aid the Cuban political refugee population in their struggle to adapt to life in this country, efforts which included the encouragement of bilingual education, the other Hispanic groups pressed hard for similar benefits. Unlike the Cubans, who were a largely middle-class group among whom there were numerous trained teachers who could and did fill the needs of the educational system, the Puerto Ricans and Mexican Americans tended, as we have mentioned, to consist of a population that was from a largely lower socioeconomic and educational level. This meant that there were relatively few trained teachers qualified to teach in the bilingual programs being formed. A large-scale effort was necessary to recruit and train teachers who were members of the local population and could be expected to provide the most effective educational environments for the children from these groups.

The legislative basis for bilingual education was provided by the Bilingual Education Act of 1968, as amended by the Elementary and Secondary Education Amendments of 1974. With the enactment of the 1968 act, Congress declared it the policy of the United States to explore new educational approaches to meet the needs of children of limited English-speaking ability. The Office of Education established a Division of Bilingual Education to administer this act. The preliminary programs funded under the 1968 act revealed a greater need for bilingual education than anticipated, and it became clear that a stronger federal effort in assisting state and local agencies was needed.

Thus, the 1974 Bilingual Education Act, enacted as part of the Elementary and Secondary Education Amendments of 1974, announced a broader national policy on bilingual education. The act states that "special educational provision must be made for persons of limited English-speaking ability, because there are significant numbers of such children with unique educational needs which can best be met by bilingual/bicultural educational methods and techniques." The law declares it to be United States policy to (a) encourage bilingual educational methods and techniques and (b) fund state and local education agencies to develop and carry out such programs at the elementary and secondary level. The law directed the National Institute of Education and the Office of Education to jointly undertake a program of research directed toward developing methods of measuring the success of individual projects, approaches, and the program as a whole.

Litigation arising under Title VI of the 1964 Civil Rights Act, which bans discrimination in the operation of any federally assisted program, has stimulated the growth of bilingual education. Title VI of the Civil Rights Act states that participation in, or receipt of the benefits of, federally sponsored programs may not be restricted upon the basis of race, color, or national origin. In *Lau* v. *Nichols,* in 1974, the Supreme Court held that the failure of the San Francisco Unified School District to provide English language or other adequate instruction to 1800 Chinese American students who did not speak English denied them meaningful participation in the school program and thus violated Title VI. *Lau* v. *Nichols* was a class action suit which claimed that the constitutional rights of the Chinese students of San Francisco had been violated, rights guaranteed under the fourteenth amendment of the United States Constitution. The Supreme Court, in relying on Title VI of the Civil Rights Act, said:

> There is no equality of treatment merely by providing students with the same
> facilities, textbooks, teachers, and curriculum; for students who do not under-
> stand English are effectively foreclosed from any meaningful education. Basic
> English skills are at the very core of what these public schools teach. Imposition
> of a requirement that, before a child can effectively participate in the education-

al program, he must already have acquired these basic skills is to make a mockery of public education. We know that those who do not understand English are certain to find their classroom experiences wholly incomprehensible and in no way meaningful. (U.S. Supreme Court, 414 U.S. 563)

This landmark decision for bilingual education directed the district to remedy the situation, although no specific remedy was mandated. In *Serna* v. *Portales Municipal Schools* in 1974, under similar circumstances to those in Lau, but with Spanish-speaking plaintiffs, the circuit court affirmed a district court ruling requiring the establishment of a bilingual/bicultural education program to remedy the consequences of past discrimination. The school system was ordered to offer courses in English as a second language and to teach other courses in Spanish.

Unfortunately, these judicial and legislative initiatives were often vague and even ambiguous with respect to educational policy. Thus, although the courts and the legislature made clear their concern for the rights of children who spoke little or no English, they remained silent on the issue of how these children's rights were to be protected. More questions arose than could be answered and no one solution seemed appropriate for all groups. Unclear laws, insufficient preparation and research, internal political conflict, and most of all an unhealthy national economy have combined to threaten the future of bilingual education in the United States. Congress's initial enthusiasm for bilingual/bicultural instruction became severely decreased by the late 1970s partly because the government had become increasingly conservative with respect to fiscal matters and partly because research evaluations had found serious shortcomings in bilingual programs. By the early 1980s, in reponse to dissatisfaction with federal guidelines voiced by local school district, the administration began to back down on earlier threats of enforcement. In 1981 Secretary of Education Bell announced that he planned to rewrite federal regulations in order to give local school districts the option of using methods they considered most appropriate. Enforcement of the Lau remedies was sharply reduced. The Reagan administration was, according to information gathered by the civil rights office in 1986, nine times less likely to monitor school districts for Lau violations than either the Ford or the Carter administrations. At the same time, an organization called U.S. English led by a former senator from California, S. I. Hayakawa, gained increasing public support in its efforts to make English the official language of the United States. Hayakawa's group is strongly opposed to bilingual education, believing that it impedes immigrants from assimilating to American society. The English-only movement currently represents the most well organized opposition to bilingual education.

In addition to the federally mandated and publicly funded bilingual education programs in this country, a wide variety of ethnic groups have, as we have seen, maintained private schools in which their ethnic languages have been taught and used for teaching along with English. In a recent study, Fishman (1980), one of the foremost advocates and scholars of bilingual education, has investigated five ethnic day schools in the New York area. Interested in the successful acquisition of literacy in both English and the ethnic language, Fishman found that the major features leading to the success of these schools are community support and involvement in schools, commitment on the part of teachers, and strong administrative and community support of teachers. A major point is that the children do not necessarily come from middle-class backgrounds. The schools are not very well equipped, the tuition is generally low, the communities are often lower middle class. One interesting finding from the ethnographic studies done by Fishman and his team is that the children actually do more reading in school than the adults in the home community and that the children are not motivated by the need to do very much reading in their adult lives. Still the community and the schools are very supportive of their becoming biliterate as well as bilingual. The fact that the children in these schools do as well or better in standardized tests of reading than children in monolingual public schools presents an important challenge to public education.

PHILOSOPHICAL DIFFERENCES

One of the most serious problems facing bilingual education in the United States is the lack of agreement as to the purpose, aims, and even the validity of the enterprise. Viewpoints on these issues are linked to general political philosophy and to ideals of what it means to be an American. Language is an important symbol of group identity and the decisions we make concerning the teaching of our young people represent our hopes and goals for the future.

Broadly speaking, there are two major philosophical orientations toward the education of children from non-English-speaking homes. On the one hand, we have the viewpoint which holds that the United States is an English-speaking country and that federally funded schools should be responsible for assimilating diverse linguistic groups into the mainstream language and culture. On the other hand, we have the viewpoint that the United States is and always has been a pluralistic nation and that it is the obligation of the government to protect the rights of minority groups to maintain their ethnic heritage, including language. Given the difference between these opposing views, it is not suprising that opinions should vary greatly concerning the approach to be taken in the education of minority-group children. Several alternatives are possible, and we will examine each in turn.

THE SUBMERSION APPROACH

Not all who espouse the philosophy of assimilation agree that public funds should be spent on bilingual education of any kind. Indeed, many feel strongly that we should continue to follow the precedent of earlier generations and insist that all children, regardless of language proficiency or background, be placed in mainstream classrooms together and taught only in English. No special provisions to give additional English-language help to children coming from non-English-language backgrounds were considered necessary. From the point of view of educational opportunity, the argument is made that millions of poor immigrant children managed to become educated under the system of all English instruction and that there is no good reason why non-English-speaking children today should not do the same. There are few facts and figures either to support or to refute this line of reasoning. It is known that in the early years of the twentieth century, children of foreign-born parentage accounted for a large percentage of the school population. In some large cities, indeed, the figure was as high as 50 percent. Every effort was made to assimilate these children into the mainstream English-speaking culture, and one of the major vehicles of assimilation was instruction in English. It is difficult to calculate how successful this policy was. School dropout rates were extremely high, but it is not known how much this was due to economic necessity and how much to difficulties and frustrations caused by the language barrier. A powerful argument against submersion today is that in our increasingly industrialized society, education is more and more a necessary prerequisite to employment. Given that the school failure and dropout rate is much higher for non-English-speaking minority-group children, particularly Hispanics, and that unemployment rates for these groups is also disproportionately high, it is clearly incumbent upon the society to attempt to find a solution.

ENGLISH AS A SECOND LANGUAGE

Since bilingual education is exactly that—instruction in two languages—and since English is the dominant or mainstream language of U.S. society, it stands to reason that English as a second language (ESL, or, as it is sometimes called, English to speakers of other languages—ESOL) is always part of a bilingual program. To what extent it should be used is one of the major questions that must be dealt with in developing a bilingual program. That is, children may receive special instruction in ESL as a part of monolingual schooling, or ESL may be one component in a system in which most of the early instruction is given in the children's mother tongue. After the Bilingual Education Act of 1968 was passed, many school districts sought to conform to the new legislation by insituting ESL classes within the framework of regular mainstream schooling. This policy, however, soon came under attack by proponents of bilingual education. Following the *Lau* v. *Nichols* decision in 1974, the office of Health, Education and Welfare (HEW) laid down guidelines (the so-called Lau Remedies) which explicitly stated that instruction in ESL alone could not be considered a substitute for bilingual education.

There were several arguments against using ESL as the sole means of improving education for children from non-English-speaking backgrounds. To begin with, very few states had certification requirements for ESL teachers, and not many public school teachers were professionally trained in the pedagogical approaches and methods of teaching English to children from different language backgrounds. Thus, even if special instruction in English as a second language had been pedagogically and politically acceptable as a means to equalize educational opportunities for children from language-minority backgrounds, the dearth of trained ESL teachers would have precluded this as a viable alternative. A further objection was that all content instruction would have continued to be given in English, and those children who were unable to understand their teachers and their textbooks would inevitably fall behind in their work in spite of additional English-language instruction. Further, many ESL programs operated in such a way that children designated as having limited English proficiency were taken out of their regular classes in order to be given instruction in English-language skills. Since this ESL instruction was often not relevant to the children's regular classwork, it was argued that such "pull-out" classes caused children to miss important instruction in regular content areas and therefore had the effect of putting the children even further behind their English-speaking classmates. Further, it has been effectively argued that the children who were being "pulled out" of their classes in order to be given special instruction in English as a second language were not only speakers of minority languages but members of ethnic groups against whom there was often considerable prejudice. To call attention to their special language needs could only exacerbate the stigma attached to their minority-group membership. Added to these objections is the strong, though controversial, argument that reading and language arts are best taught first in the native language of the child, who will then easily transfer these skills to reading in English. Supporters of bilingual education, then, were strongly opposed to the substitution of ESL for programs which involved the use of the mother tongue in conjunction with English. That some type of instruction in English (or ESL) must be intrinsic to all models of bilingual education has, however, not come into question.

THE IMMERSION MODEL

A rather different model for teaching non-English-speaking children is that known as immersion. In an immersion program, all instruction in the early grades is given in the target language, while reading and content classes in the native language are gradually introduced in the later grades of elementary school. Although the teacher is bilingual, children are urged to speak only the target language during class hours. The difference between this model and the earlier practice of putting non-English-speaking children directly into mainstream schools (submersion) is that immersion programs are carefully designed as bilingual programs. The fact that the children are being taught in a language which is not their mother tongue is not ignored, and instruction is carefully planned to encourage the learning of the target language through the teaching of content courses. Furthermore, as soon as the children are competent in the target language, instruction in the mother tongue is introduced. The aim of the immersion model is to educate children to be biliterate as well as bilingual. The first and most famous bilingual immersion program was the

St. Lambert experiment headed by Wallace Lambert in Canada (Lambert and Tucker 1972). There, middle-class English-speaking children were, at the request of their parents, given all instruction in French. The children's progress was carefully monitored and compared with that of control groups who were receiving traditional mother tongue instruction. The upshot of the St. Lambert experiment was that important empirical evidence was found to show that children taught under this system achieve the same level of ability in content areas as do those taught in their native language. Immersion bilingual education has been clearly demonstrated to have no disadvantages with respect to the development of cognition. In terms of language skills, the immersion model proved to be vastly superior to more traditional models of second language teaching. Following the original St. Lambert experiment, other communities in Canada have asked for and received immersion bilingual education programs in their own communities. Because the results of these immersion bilingual education programs in Canada have been excellent with middle-class speakers of English, an important debate has arisen among educators and researchers as to the appropriateness of making use of this model of bilingual education for children of minority-language backgrounds in the United States. The controversy over transferring the Canadian immersion model of bilingual education to educational settings in the United States turns primarily on the very different socioeconomic backgrounds of the pupils and on the attitudes and motivations of the communities from which they come. The Canadian immersion programs were specifically designed at the request of middle-class parents who wanted their English-speaking children to become bilingual in French. The goal of these programs was clearly and explicitly that of providing the children with what is known as "additive bilingual education." That is, it was never the intention or the expectation that pupils in the immersion programs would lose proficiency in their mother tongue. Reading and language arts in English were introduced in the early grades and given serious attention thereafter. Students were regularly tested to compare their English language arts abilities with those of students receiving instruction in schools where English was the sole medium of instruction. The children who took part in the Canadian immersion bilingual education programs came from backgrounds where educational and economic levels were relatively high. The programs were entirely voluntary, and, as a result, there was strong support on the part of the parents, who saw this form of bilingual instruction as a means of enriching the educational backgrounds of their children. Few of these criteria hold for the populations in the United States for whom such programs were being attempted. In general, the children came from lower-socioeconomic backgrounds and from families and communities where educational levels were relatively low. Their native language, usually a variety of Spanish, was the nondominant language, and there was a long history of discrimination toward them in social, political, and economic terms.

The question of whether the immersion model of bilingual education so successful in Canada could be appropriately and effectively transferred to the United States has, therefore, raised some interesting and important questions.

TRANSITIONAL BILINGUAL EDUCATION

The legislation of the 1960s and 1970s which demanded that school systems develop programs to ensure equal education to students of non-English-speaking backgrounds was clearly both assimilationist and compensatory in its aims. Although the laws did not explicitly restrict such educational programs to children from lower-socioeconomic minority groups, the guidelines laid down by the United States Office of Education made it clear that this was exactly the population they were intended to serve. Federally mandated bilingual education programs were seen by legislators and by a large majority of the public as a means by which poor, non-English-speaking children could be given the help they needed to "overcome the language barrier" and to become fully fluent and literate in English. This approach is widely referred to as transitional bilingual education (TBE). Proponents of this approach see instruction in the children's native language as a necessary first step, not as an end in itself. Programs which fall into the category of transitional bilingual education are normally designed so that the children's native language is used for instruction in the early grades only, with content area instruction in English gradually increasing as the children become proficient enough to learn in it and teaching through the medium of the children's mother tongue being decreased accordingly. Reading is taught both in the child's first language and in English. Except where newly arrived immigrant children are concerned, it is expected that elementary school children in transitional bilingual programs will be completely "mainstreamed" by the time they reach high school. Transitional bilingual education often has an ESL component to facilitate the children's learning of English. It is, however, different from ESL-only programs in that the children's first language is used as a medium of instruction during the early grades and they are taught to read and write in both their first and second languages.

Although transitional bilingual education has received considerable support from the courts, from the legislature, and from government agencies, there are a number of structural problems which, combined with recent cutbacks in education generally, raise serious questions regarding its future. Some of these questions have to do with specific problems in implementing TBE, while others have to do with whether or not this form of instruction has been effective at all. With regard to the implementation of TBE, two of the most critical specific problems have to do with ethnic diversity and equality of opportunity—the two issues most central to the development of bilingual education. Put simply, the difficulty is that unlike some so-called bilingual countries in the world, the United States does not have only one major ethnolinguistic minority group but rather embraces several different language groups, both large and small. What this means in concrete terms is that while the majority of children come from backgrounds where a variety of Spanish is the home language, there are scores of other ethnic, often recently arrived minority groups, each with its own language or dialect. With the great increase in immigration from Asia and Africa as well as from Latin America, the larger cities in the United States are becoming ever more heterogeneous with respect to the ethnolinguistic composition of their populations. In some areas such as Southern California and Southern Florida, 50 or more languages may be represented within the student body of a single school district. A frequently cited example of the impracticality of bilingual education is Fairfax County, Virginia, a suburb of Washington, D.C., in which there are 50 different languages spoken by children enrolled in public schools. In 1980, Fairfax County won a four-year dispute with the Office of Civil Rights in which it was agreed that English as a second language could be substituted for bilingual education in this school district.

A further complication with regard to the implementation of bilingual education programs is that some of the most recent immigrant groups come from backgrounds where little or no tradition of formal schooling was in existence. This is true for a number of groups which come from rural communities in developing nations where literacy rates are extremely low. At least one group, the Hmong, an agricultural people from the highlands of Southeast Asia, speak a language which has only recently been put into written form. Although a small percentage of Hmong had received schooling through the medium of one of the neighboring languages in the area from which they came, most adults as well as children had no familiarity with any sort of formal schooling. Admittedly, this is an extreme case, but it remains true that both the number of different language groups and their levels of education are enormously diverse. For this reason, even if the funds were made available to develop bilingual education programs for each of these groups, it is almost impossible to imagine finding enough qualified teachers with the necessary linguistic backgrounds to meet the needs of such a diverse population. Even if community members are employed as aides in linguistically heterogeneous classrooms, it is difficult to see how instruction could take place in such a wide variety of languages at the same time.

It seems clear that in cases of extreme linguistic diversity, transitional bilingual education is not possible. Although such cases are relatively rare, they do present a strong argument against a government policy which would mandate transitional bilingual education as the only acceptable model. Where we have classrooms composed of children from a variety of ethnolinguistic backgrounds, a combination of native language support from bilingual teaching aides along with some form of ESL seems to be the only realistic alternative.

Another thorny problem has to do with the choice of linguistic variety to be used in instruction. Even when there is a large homogeneous minority language community, the linguistic variety spoken by the children may be very different from the standard or prestige variety used in school. Dialect diversity within languages is so great that it is perfectly possible for a Spanish-speaking teacher from one region of the Spanish-speaking world, for example, to be nearly unintelligible to children whose native speech represents a different regional and/or social dialect. It is possible, of course, to insist that teachers have the same linguistic background as the children they teach, but this is not always feasible in terms of available personnel, and, even if it were, it could easily lead to charges of discriminatory hiring practices.

Still another difficulty revolves around the issue of language proficiency. Even in areas which are heavily populated by members of the same ethnic groups (e.g.,the Southwest), it is still the case that the dominant language of the wider society will be English. Depending on their own life histories and even on the amount of television they have watched, children will have varying levels of proficiency in English and in their mother tongue. In addition to this, immigration is a continuing process which brings newly arrived children into all levels of the public schools. These facts make it difficult to determine the amount of mother tongue instruction appropriate to any one grade level. None of these problems is entirely insoluble, but together they require an expenditure in time, effort, and money that may be greater than the public is willing to invest. Transitional bilingual education has lost a good deal of its earlier popularity, but it nevertheless remains an important educational movement, particularly in areas where there are large numbers of school-age children who share a common ethnic background and language.

MAINTENANCE BILINGUAL EDUCATION

While no one seriously questions the need of minority-group children to learn English, many proponents of bilingual education do not see this as the major aim of such schooling. For this group, the true purpose behind bilingual education is the maintenance of the minority language and culture. Unlike transitional programs, what have come to be called maintenance programs aim at teaching children to be both bilingual and biliterate so that they are able to fully appreciate their own ethnic heritage while at the same time participating in the life of the wider society to the extent that they wish to do so. Those who argue for this view point to the fact that economically advantaged groups have always regarded bilingualism as a means of cultural enrichment. As Joshua Fishman (1976) has pointed out:

> Those who are relatively secure in their social, economic and political power can afford and, indeed, often seek an additional educational and cultural exposure to that afforded by their own mother tongue and immediate milieu. Thus, rather than merely being a palliative for the poor, bilingual education has been long and widely viewed by advantaged groups as "an elitist thing." Whether we are interested in the classical world or the modern, in the West or in the East, bilingual education has been savoured by the fortunate few and, apparently, found to be very good indeed.

In spite of the prestige attached to the ability to speak, read, and write in more than one language, the purpose behind the bilingual education legislation of the past 15 years has been to help children speaking minority languages to enter the mainstream English-speaking society, not to develop their native language abilities. Although it has often been argued that by supporting and maintaining our minority languages, the United States would be making use of and developing a resource which could be of enormous value in terms of international relations, this argument has not overcome the public's fears of sociopolitical fragmentation. With respect to general public support, it must be said that maintenance bilingual education has never done very well. Ideologically committed to the maintenance of ethnic identity through education of children in the language and culture of their own groups, this model of bilingual education requires that the children's mother tongue be used as a medium of instruction and as a subject of study from kindergarten through high school. Strong emphasis is placed on teaching students to read and write in their mother tongue as well as in English, and the ethnic heritage is an important area of study. Of all the models so far discussed, maintenance bilingual education is the one that arouses the most public controversy. Supporters see it as the logical outcome of true democracy, protecting the right of minority communities to self-determination with respect to language use and ethnic identity. Opponents see the maintenance model of bilingual education as culturally and politically divisive. The specter of political instability and even warfare along linguistic lines is raised again and again by the popular press. The deep conviction that being American means assimilation into the mainstream language and culture leads critics to strident demands that ethnic minority groups accept federally funded schooling in English or "go back where they came from." The fact that at least some groups, like the American Indians and the Mexican Americans, *are* where they came from is rarely recognized. To those who believe that maintenance bilingual education is harmful to national unity, it seems ironic and even absurd that federal money should be spent on programs that will encourage cultural separatism and perhaps lead to secessionist movements. The fears that are most often expressed in this context are that the present cultural goals of linguistic minority groups to maintain their own identities will be translated into a desire for political separatism. Despite historical evidence showing that unless minority language groups are severely repressed, cultural and linguistic differences tend to remain stable rather than lead to political separatism, maintenance bilingual education is seen by many as an invitation to disaster.

CONTROVERSIES OVER BILINGUAL EDUCATION

Given the many differences of opinion both among educators and among the general public, it is to be expected that controversies over the goals, models, methods, and evaluation of bilingual education programs would be many and heated. In this section, we will review some of the major debates concerning bilingual education which are at present unresolved.

As we have already pointed out, the legal and legislative decisions which have led to the present programs in public bilingual education were largely based on the civil rights issue of equality of educational opportunity. Underlying court decisions and governmental policy decisions at various levels was the strong belief that providing special programs for children from minority language backgrounds was the best way to compensate for their lack of proficiency. Since most of the children who fell into this category were not only from minority ethnic groups but from lower socioeconomic backgrounds, it was believed that such programs would help them to move into the mainstream English-dominant world and, not incidentally, give them the means to find good jobs and to move from poverty into the middle class. In fact, one of the main concerns that led to bilingual education legislation was the extremely high school dropout rate of children with minority-group backgrounds. From the political point of view, the idea that these children would be encouraged to assimilate and helped to leave the more obvious aspects of their ethnicity behind them was regarded as a healthy move toward a more cohesive society.

If we were to base our evaluation of public opinion toward bilingual education on the many negative newspaper articles, letters to the editor, and political statements to be read and heard, we would be forced to conclude that there is virtually no public support for bilingual education. However, as Hakuta (1986) has pointed out, "letters to the editor are not random samplings of public opinion." In an effort to discover the true state of public opinion, Hakuta and his students at Yale University did a telephone survey of local attitudes toward bilingual education. The subjects of the telephone interviews were selected randomly from the telephone directory in New Haven, Connecticut (Hakuta 1984). Somewhat to his surprise, Hakuta found that the great majority (70%) of those sampled said they believed that bilingual education was the best way for a Spanish-speaking child to learn English, and, as Hakuta says, "there was even considerable support for the notion that bilingual programs should maintain the Spanish language and culture of the children (58%)." What Hakuta found most interesting about the results was the effect of the background attributes of the respondents who expressed negative views toward bilingual education. What he found was that three characteristics seemed to be the most important determining factors. To begin with, sex had an important part to play in people's opinions. Men, he found, were much more likely to oppose bilingual education than were women. After sex, age was an important conditioning variable. Both men and women over the age of 50 were more opposed to bilingual education than were younger people. The third and perhaps most interesting factor was that both men and women who themselves came from homes where foreign languages had been spoken were more opposed than those respondents who had grown up in English-speaking households. Hakuta concluded that "although the majority supported bilingual education, the most strongly held sentiments were the negative ones" (Hakuta 1986:213).

A nationwide survey conducted by Cole (1982) at Columbia University also found that there was widespread support for bilingual education in some form. As in the Hakuta study, the age of the respondents was an important factor, with younger people much more supportive of bilingual education than the older members of the group studied. In addition, Cole found that attitudes toward bilingual education were, not surprisingly, linked to the general political ideology of the respondents, since those respondents who supported bilingual education were also those who held more politically liberal attitudes in general. The most significant result of the study, however, was that two-thirds of the people surveyed said that they supported some form of bilingual education.

The high convergence between these two surveys of public attitudes toward bilingual education is striking. Both report on findings of studies scientifically designed to sample of the views of the general public. On the surface, it is difficult to reconcile the positive attitudes reflected by these reports with the opinions written so forcefully against bilingual education which appear in newspaper columns and letters to the editor. However, letters to newspapers are not written by a balanced sample of the population, and, as is so often the case, it is apparent that the people who go to the trouble to write do so because they are outraged and are seeking a forum for their protests. The much greater percentage of the population that appears to support bilingual education has no need to express its views. The only exception to this general state of affairs is that people who are deeply committed to supporting bilingual education do frequently respond to some of the more violent attacks on it. In light of the studies by Hakuta and Cole, it would appear that additional empirical studies of public opinion regarding bilingual education are badly needed. If the findings regarding public support for this form of instruction revealed in the two studies mentioned are replicated in other studies, such findings would provide valuable information to the government agencies and local school authorities responsible for making critical policy decisions regarding the future of bilingual education.

However, it must be recognized that even if public willingness to support bilingual education can be documented, it is still the case that a great many questions, controversies, and challenges must continue to be addressed. The most serious of these is the question of whether bilingual education is actually effective in improving the educational opportunities for language-minority children. Embedded in this question is the critical issue of how such programs have been and ought to be evaluated.

Beginning in the early part of the 1970s, there was a growing demand for concrete evaluation of bilingual education programs in attaining the goals of improving the educational achievement of language-minority children. A study (Danoff et al. 1977/1978) was commissioned by the Office of Planning, Budgeting and Evaluation of the Office of Education, to be conducted by the American Institutes for Research. This study, usually referred to as the AIR Report, compares the scores in math and English of two groups of elementary school students, one which came from a number of different bilingual programs and one which had received no bilingual education at all. The major conclusion of the AIR Report was that although there were some cases of positive results, the overall analysis of student performance showed no consistent results in favor of bilingual education.

There were numerous criticisms of the AIR Report, many having to do with the validity of the measures used, the selection of the sample students, and other methodological issues (see, for example, Cardenas 1977, Swain 1979). Further, and perhaps deeper, criticisms were expressed by Hakuta in which he pointed out that the programs studied by the AIR Report were heterogeneous in type, such that "Whatever was funded by Title VII was considered bilingual education, but depending on the school district, there were different manifestations of the program" (Hakuta 1986:220). The issue of the type of evaluation used was also called into question. Paulston (1980:41) pointed out that although English and math are important, the overall aim of bilingual education is not to improve scores in these school subjects but rather to improve the effects of this education on the lives of the children who had received it. Such figures as employment rates after leaving school, dropout rates, drug and alcoholism figures, and other economic and social measures are, she stressed, much more important and meaningful indications for the evaluation of a program's success than are psychometric tests of children's school performance. In spite of the fact that these larger and clearly more critical issues were not addressed by the AIR Report, it was nevertheless regarded as having presented extremely damaging evidence against bilingual education. In the June 1982 issue of the *TESOL Newsletter,* Ramon Santiago, president of the National Association for Bilingual Education, made a statement which only five years before would have been unimaginable:

> . . . we must not allow ourselves to say that we oppose English-only options under Title VII because bilingual programs constitute the ONLY way to serve LEP (limited English proficiency) or NEP (non-English proficient) children. The evidence simply is not on our side. . . . We believe that bilingual education has numerous advantages beyond contributing to the acquisition of English by LEP children, but if we are to be professionally honest, we cannot claim that it is the ONLY method or the BEST method in ALL circumstances. We have to admit (and we do admit) that under certain circumstances non-bilingual approaches may be more feasible and cost-effective than bilingual programs.

Further support for the conclusions of the AIR Report came in 1983 with the publication of an internal Office of Education Report, authored by Keith Baker and Adriana deKanter, which showed that when math and English scores are used to evaluate bilingual education programs, the results are not encouraging.

As Baker and deKanter (1983) argued, research evidence to support the effectiveness of transitional bilingual education programs has been very weak. In reviewing the literature on transitional bilingual education (TBE), the authors focused on two major questions: whether TBE leads to better performance in English and whether TBE leads to better performance in educational content areas not connected directly to language abilities. The issue underlying the study undertaken by Baker and deKanter had to do directly with United States government policy, and the question they sought to answer was whether there was a strong enough case, given research conducted over the past 15 years, to justify the government's requiring TBE through a legal mandate. The other side of this question was to discover whether alternatives to TBE have been found to be effective and, if so, whether it made sense for the government to require TBE to be used as the exclusive approach to improving educational opportunities for children whose proficiency in English was limited. In addition to the submersion approach, Baker and DeKanter identified three other approaches to the education of language minority children: English as a second language (ESL), immersion, and transitional bilingual education (TBE). As we have seen, the submersion approach is one in which all instruction is given in English, with no special help offered the language-minority child, an approach that was found by the Supreme Court to violate these children's civil rights in *Lau* v. *Nichols*. The ESL approach differs from submersion, as we have seen, only in that children are given special instruction in English during part of the school day. The immersion approach differs from submersion in that the teacher is expected to be bilingual in the children's home language, which is used for clarification when necessary, and that the instruction is planned to provide for the fact that the students are not well acquainted with the language in which their subjects are being taught. Thus, the students learn both the second language and the content of the subject matter at the same time. In contrast, TBE, or transitional bilingual education, is organized in such a way that reading is taught in both the children's first language and in English, and subject matter is taught in the native language until the children's English is proficient enough for them to go into mainstream classrooms.

In their study of the effectiveness of TBE, Baker and deKanter reviewed several hundred studies and evaluation reports and, of these, found only 39 which they considered sound enough methodologically to use in their own assessment. The large majority of the reports examined found no difference in second language performance between groups that had received bilingual education and those which had not. A few studies reported positive results and a few also reported negative effects. Given the mixed results and the overall lack of positive impact found in studies reporting on transitional bilingual programs, Baker and deKanter conclude that there is no justification for mandating TBE as the sole approach to bilingual education. They further conclude that only additional experimenting with various approaches at the local level will make it possible to determine which type of bilingual education works best in which situation. Given the very strongly positive reports (mainly from Canada and a few from the United States) on the results of the immersion approach, Baker and deKanter advocate a widespread "structured immersion" demonstration program to test empirically whether this approach can be successfully transferred from the Canadian to the U.S. situation. The idea here is that there is no support for the claim that children need to be taught in their first language while they are learning their second. If, they argue, the curriculum is properly structured, "carefully conducted" English-language instruction in all subjects may be preferable to bilingual methods. They cite Tikunoff (1983), who studied the characteristics of outstanding bilingual programs and found that two common features of successful programs were that they used the children's first language to help them understand what was being taught and that they integrated language and content area instruction. From this, Baker and deKanter conclude that teaching English through immersion is a key component of the successful programs investigated by Tikunoff. As a final point, Baker and deKanter reiterate their own findings that the general quality of bilingual education research and evaluation is extremely poor. They make a strong argument to the effect that more and better research and improved program evaluations in bilingual education are essential if the needs of language-minority children are to be adequately met.

A strong proponent of the immersion model, Cummins (1979, 1980, 1982) has sought to provide a theory of language proficiency and academic development which will explain the underlying causes for the success or failure of different approaches to bilingual education. Cummins's argument revolves around the fact that bilingualism has been shown to have distinct cognitive advantages for some children but not for others. To explain this, Cummins has developed the "threshold hypothesis," which holds that in order for their bilingualism to be advantageous rather than harmful to their cognitive development, children need to have attained a "threshold level" of linguistic competence. To add to this, Cummins also puts forth the "developmental interdependence hypothesis," which says that the level of second language competence gained by a bilingual child is directly related to the type of competence the child has developed in his or her first language. In order to clarify what he means by level or type of language competence, Cummins posits two kinds of language abilities: CALP (cognitive/academic language proficiency) and BICS (basic interpersonal communicative skills). CALP includes such aspects of language proficiency as are related to the development of literacy, such as the ability to process decontextualized language, and of vocabulary concepts, while BICS includes sociolinguistic competence and oral language fluency. All normal speakers acquire BICS, but it is CALP which must be developed if children are to do well in school-related tasks. As Cummins explains his theory:

> In summary, there exists a reliable dimension of language proficiency which is strongly related to literacy and to other decontextualized verbal-academic tasks. This dimension of cognitive/academic language proficiency appears to be largely independent of these language proficiencies which manifest themselves in everyday interpersonal communicative contexts. These latter forms of language proficiency are either near universal across native speakers or unrelated to cognitive/academic skills. (Cummins 1980:86)

Since his "developmental interdependence hypothesis" states that CALP transfers from one language to another and that the amount of competence in the second language will be directly related to the level achieved in the first language at the point when the second is introduced, immersion bilingual programs which are aimed at developing this sort of proficiency have been highly successful. Cummins then goes on to argue that the educational assumptions upon which transitional bilingual programs are based are contradicted by a large number of research evidence involving immersion programs in both majority and minority languages groups from a great many areas around the world. The idea that children should be switched to a majority language program so that they will develop literacy skills in that language has, according to Cummins, been proven to be inaccurate and often detrimental to the very aims it professes to serve. The solution to the problem of improving the educational opportunities of language-minority children is to work toward developing their bilingual cognitive/academic proficiency.

A major criticism of the AIR Report, the Baker and deKanter report, and the evaluation of successful bilingual programs by Tikunoff—which seem to work best and why—is that in all these studies, programs are evaluated on the basis of children's grades in standardized tests. The theory to account for inconsistencies in children's school achievement which has been proposed by Cummins (1979) and argued for by Swain (1981) is also based on data from tests. Perhaps the most serious critique of this means of evaluating children's proficiency in school-learned skills is that put forth by Edelsky et al. (1983), in which they examine the premises underlying the theory proposed by Cummins.

While agreeing that some minority-language children who attend bilingual programs become very skillful in using academic language while others do not, and that a basic aim of education for all children should be to acquire the ability to write and to engage in formal speech events, Edelsky et al. disagree with the basic premise, the data, and the constructs underlying the recommendations put forth by both Cummins and Swain:

> Underlying both Cummins' and Swain's attempts to account for differential school success among second language learners is the premise that the predominant current definition of success in school and particularly success in literacy is right, acceptable, reasonable, etc.; that what is, should be. They do not question the usual definition of reading as the ability to perform well on a reading achievement test, the definition of writing as the ability to do work-sheet type exercises on mechanics, vocabulary, synonyms, analogies, etc.; definitions that equate literacy with performance in discrete, otherwise purposeless tasks intended as practice for some other time when the "real event" occurs. This unquestioning acceptance of current school definitions and current school curricula is the flaw that we believe leads to all the rest of the errors. It accounts for Cummins' . . . choice of data and for his need to blame the learner for failure by establishing a spurious language proficiency dichotomy. Of course, once one accepts the equivalences *reading test = reading* and *exercises-with-artificial-texts = proper literacy instruction,* then it becomes necessary to explain failure on the tests and exercises by blaming the learner, the teacher, the language of instruction, the materials, etc.—*anything* but examining the validity of how literacy (or language proficiency or learning) was conceptualized in the first place. (Edelsky et al. 1983:4)

Given this very deep criticism, it follows that Edelsky et al. do not accept what Cummins refers to as CALP as anything substantive. Their position is that the very construct is a tautology since the definition of CALP is the willingness and ability to do what schools define as achievement in the first place. As they point out, "The definition of school achievement is cognitive academic language proficiency, which often amounts to scores on standardized reading tests. What explains scores on reading tests is cognitive academic language proficiency. This circularity is hardly illuminating" (Edelsky et al. 1983:8). In other words, they hold that cognitive academic language proficiency is actually the ability to perform well on tests. And, since Cummins implies that cognitive academic language proficiency is at the top level of cognitive ability, they point out that Cummins is indirectly saying that since children from low-socioeconomic minority groups regularly get lower scores on tests which display cognitive academic language proficiency, children from these backgrounds have generally lower intellectual ability than children from higher economic, language majority backgrounds. What Edelsky et al. are saying, then, is that Cummins's construct of CALP and BICS as an explanation of why some children do well in bilingual programs and others do not is, in reality, a new version of the deficit theory. The danger they see is that these notions give substance to existing prejudices and create classroom environments for poor language-minority children which discourage them from attaining true literacy.

What Edelsky et al. advocate is that research into bilingual schooling be based not on data from tests, which they consider meaningless, but rather on new ways of assessing school-related skills. They cite a body of naturalistic research already in existence and argue strongly for greater attention to be paid to the results of this work and for more research in this tradition of naturalistic observation.

A major aspect of the controversy over how bilingual education programs should be evaluated turns on the question of the validity of the various research paradigms used. In arguing for more research in the ethnographic or naturalistic tradition, Edelsky et al. are referring to a body of work which has made deep and important contributions to our understanding of the school problems of language-minority children. For this reason, the ethnographic approach to the study of schooling has gained more and more of a following over the past decade.

One of the first, and still most widely known, ethnographic studies of classroom interaction and the problems faced by children from minority-group backgrounds is that carried out by Susan Philips in 1970 at the Warm Springs Indian reservation in Oregon. By a rigorous investigation of the way Indian children interacted in classrooms and comparison of behavioral patterns in the Indian community, Philips was able to demonstrate why Anglo teachers perceived their Indian students as silent and uninterested in classroom participation. Using her observations of interaction among community members on the reservation, Philips showed that the children's school behavior was based on cultural differences in patterns of learning and in interactions with adults. The children were silent and reluctant to participate in one-to-one interactions with the teachers because Indian children are expected to learn by observing their elders and then practicing what they have learned alone until they have mastered the skill in question. They are more comfortable working in groups because that is the culturally appropriate way to work in their communities. Insights such as these have gone a long way toward dispelling the notion that Indian children are indifferent or unintelligent.

Since Philips's study, there have been numerous others which have investigated classroom dynamics through direct observation and comparison with the cultural norms of the communities from which children come. Increasingly, the focus has turned to cultural factors other than language to explain the school problems of minority-language children (see, for example, Trueba et al. 1981, Trueba 1987, Hornberger 1987a,b). The studies reported on in these books all follow the ethnographic tradition in their investigations into the classroom behavior and community cultures of children from a great variety of backgrounds both in the United States and in other countries where there are bilingual education programs. The result of these studies has been the increasing recognition of Trueba's opinion: "We can no longer assume that the knowledge and skills that mainstream children bring to our schools are readily transferable to language minority children by means of regular schooling. The language, culture, and values acquired in the home environment have a direct impact on children's school learning activities and successful adaptation" (Trueba 1987:v).

If bilingual education is to succeed in its aim of providing equal educational opportunities for language-minority children, it now seems very clear that we will need to depend heavily on the kind of information to be gained by ethnographic methods of study.

CONCLUSION

We have seen that the motivation for bilingual education comes from several sources. Compensation for educational and economic disadvantage is a major theme. Minority group maintenance, though less well accepted by the general public, has nevertheless played an important role in the new educational movement. Cultural enrichment bilingual education, much prized by the well-to-do, is supported by intellectuals. The fact that the languages of poor ethnic minority groups cannot, by definition, be regarded as prestigious enough to enrich the education of majority-group children is an unfortunate reality. Bilingual education of all types is currently suffering from lack of funding, insufficient research, a lack of trained teachers, administrators, and materials developers, and most of all from a lack of public agreement as to the acceptability of its goals. If this important new educational movement is to be successful in the long run, a careful evaluation of policy is essential. School situations differ greatly from one another, and it is of critical importance to recognize that no one model of bilingual education is appropriate to all. Whatever the merits and the disadvantages of bilingual programs as they are now constituted, it is clear that the controversy has at least as much to do with political ideology as with education.

In spite of the difficulties currently facing bilingual education in the United States, it is clear that the larger aims of providing good educational opportunities for language-minority children and breaking down ethnic barriers are worth the struggle. It is to be hoped that the public will, increasingly, see the advantages of encouraging the development of multilingualism in the United States as an important resource in such areas as international trade and diplomacy.

From the point of view of TESOL, the English language movement and the public and educational controversy over the efficacy of bilingual education has important implications. Bilingual education is, by definition, education in two languages. In the United States, the dominant language, and that which is always coupled with a minority language in bilingual education programs, is, unarguably, English. And, since one of the major aims of all bilingual programs is to enhance the fluency in English of children from minority-group backgrounds, it seems clear that TESOL will always play an important role in this area. For this reason, it is critical for professionals in the field of TESOL to be well informed concerning the issues and outcomes of the debate over how and whether bilingual education programs are to be implemented.

CHAPTER

12

Multilingualism

INTRODUCTION

One of the most persistent misunderstandings about language has to do with the notion that there is, or should be, a one-to-one correspondence between language and nation. That this myth exists in spite of all evidence to the contrary is very revealing in itself, for the fact is that we would be hard pressed to find a single example of a completely monolingual nation. There are majority languages and minority languages, dominant languages and oppressed languages, but there is hardly a country in the world in which only one language is spoken. Far from being a deviant phenomenon, multilingualism is, in actuality, the norm. How does it happen that English speakers, often of recent immigrant background themselves, should find it difficult to accept the fact that linguistic diversity is a fact of life? Probably this is due, at least in part, to the historical accident which has made their language the most important in today's world for the purposes of commerce, technology, education, and even diplomacy. The fact that English is, in our lifetime, the dominant world language, puts native speakers of English into an unusually fortunate position. And this seems so normal to native speakers of English, so much the way things are and should be, that we seldom stop to consider that this situation is only a recent development and that it is anyone's guess how long it will continue. Although there are countless cases in which a single language has been accepted by diverse populations within widespread areas, this does not alter the fact that multilingualism has been part of the fabric of human society throughout recorded history.

No one knows at precisely which point humans began to communicate by means of spoken language, and the origins of language are impossible to trace. In comparison with the spoken language, writing is a relatively recent innovation, going back no more than eight thousand years. Although our knowledge of how it all began is extremely scanty, we do know from very early records that ancient peoples lived in multilingual societies. Ancient cuneiform writings have been found in which the same message is written in three different languages, for example, demonstrating clearly that at least this many were of importance to the rulers of whom they spoke. The story of the Tower of Babel has many counterparts in other cultures as well, making it clear that our ancestors were quite cognizant of multilingualism but had, as do many people today and throughout history, the belief that the world would be a better place if everyone spoke the same tongue.

THE ORIGINS OF LINGUISTIC DIVERSITY

How, then, does multilingualism arise in the first place? We have spoken about dialect differentiation within a single language, and discussed the fact that people speak what is thought of as the same language very differently from region to region. We know that until quite recently travel was difficult, expensive, and often dangerous. Except for traders, and a very small number of the most privileged members of society, people tended to live out their lives in the same neighborhood where they were born. There were, of course, nomadic peoples whose way of life involved moving from one location to another within a resticted area, and there were wars which often ended in the conquest of a foreign territory, with armies of occupation moving in and residents taken as slaves to faraway places. In addition, we know that as a result of wars and famines or other natural disasters, there have been, throughout history, movements of peoples from one area to another, just as there are today. These factors all enter into the picture of how linguistically different populations come into contact with one another.

If, within a specific geographic area, there are communities of people who speak different varieties of the same language, and if these smaller speech communities are separated from one another by great distance or by geographical impediments such as mountains or large bodies of water, it usually happens that their dialects become more and more different from one another as time goes on. Language is always in the process of change, and when speakers of what was once the same language are separated by time and space, their pronunciation, vocabulary, and syntax are likely to change in different ways, so that eventually the dialects are no longer mutually intelligible to one another and come to be regarded as separate languages. We have already mentioned the differences among the speech patterns of English speakers of different countries (and within these, of different regions) today. And, because we have written records, we know that the first English settlers in what was to become the United States spoke a number of different regional dialects of British English when they arrived as colonists. The same is, of course, true for the English-speaking colonists of such recently settled countries as Australia, New Zealand, South Africa, and Canada. A few hundred years of separation, however, has been sufficient to cause changes in the speech patterns used in all these countries. Thus, because language is always in the process of change, it is clear that if speakers do not have the opportunity to interact with one another because of differences in location, their dialects will slowly diverge. If there were no air travel, no telephones, radios, television sets, or films, it is very likely that the dialects of the English-speaking nations of the world would have diverged much more sharply than they have. A few centuries of isolation from one another would have been sufficient to make them into mutually unintelligible languages.

These are rather extreme examples, of course, and it is not necessary to imagine such great distances in order to see how dialects of the same language may diverge into separate languages. All that is necessary is a lack of communication between two or more dialects over a considerable amount of time. As we know, rural people who seldom travel have the most extreme dialect differences from one another. The Latin spoken in Europe during and after the Roman Empire, for example, must have shown some regional dialect differences almost from the beginning. When the empire fell, however, and the steady flow of soldiers and administrators who spoke the Latin of Rome was halted, each region gradually developed its own divergent dialect. Conquests by non-Latin-speaking groups aided the change. Great care was taken in the attempt to preserve Latin as the classical language, but since only a tiny elite could write, this had little effect on the spoken vernaculars. Since few but the wealthy had the means or the motivation to travel, the poor—illiterate, tied as they were to their villages and farms—began to speak more and more differently from one another. Thus, the Romance languages, all modern forms of Latin, came to be separate, mutually unintelligible languages. A form of Latin continued to be spoken by the wealthy and the educated, but it was no longer anyone's mother tongue. Kept artificially alive, it served as a means of communication, a lingua franca for the Catholic Church, for scholarship, administration, diplomacy, and commerce.

When the speakers of one language migrate or conquer the territory of speakers of another, the two groups are forced into contact with one another. If the area is small and there are only two major languages in question, they may continue to coexist for centuries, as Norman-French and English did in England during the Middle Ages. In such a situation, it is clear that those in power have the ability to impose their language to the extent that a considerable number of the conquered group must become bilingual. In cases of conquest of speakers of one language by those of another, however, there is no way to predict which of the languages will survive. In some cases both do, and in other cases it is the dominant or the subordinate language which has the staying power. What we do know is that if the dominant language survives, it will show very few traces of the contact. Speakers of the dominant language rarely have the need to learn the language of those whom they rule. There will be some historical evidence of the contact in that words for unfamiliar items and concepts will be borrowed into the vocabulary of the dominant language, and there are nearly always traces of the earlier language left in the form of place names, such as those for towns and rivers. Otherwise, the dominant language, if it survives, does so with very little linguistic influence from what is called the lower or subordinate language. If, on the other hand, it is the lower language which survives, it will, like English after the Norman Conquest, show the scars of the contact in the form of huge numbers of borrowings, which will have far-reaching effects not only on the lexicon but also on the phonology and even the syntax of the surviving language.

As another example of what can happen in a situation of conquest and colonization, let us consider the fate of the Native American Indian languages in the United States. In this case, we are speaking not of a single language but of a great number of unrelated languages. Many did not survive at all. Those which did (approximately 150) have been heavily influenced by English. As we have seen, it is almost impossible for Native Americans not to become bilingual in English, the language of the dominant society. One result of this bilingualism and close contact with the language spoken by the mainstream population is that innumerable vocabulary borrowings from English have entered all of the Native American languages still spoken in the United States. To complicate the picture, many of the Native American groups in the Southwest, for example, who had occupied territories first conquered and colonized by Spain, came into contact with Spanish before these lands were won by English speakers. The effect of this contact with one European language after another was that the Indian languages now spoken in these areas have been influenced by both Spanish and English and are likely to contain vocabulary items and other linguistic material from both. In contrast, the English language as spoken in the United States has been almost untouched by contact with Native American languages. The only two areas in which traces of the contact can be found today are in the vocabulary borrowing that has occurred both in place names and in words for which English had no equivalents, such as *moccasin* and *tepee*. This kind of cultural borrowing is common in situations where the conquering group meets with items of material culture or with concepts which are either altogether unfamiliar or different enough to seem quaint. Rarely do such borrowings have more than a superficial effect on the language.

Multilingualism, then, arises through the separation and gradual divergence of regional dialects of the same language, and through language contact. These phenomena are not mutually exclusive, and, indeed, they usually act together. When, for example, speakers of Polish migrated to the United States, they came from many different areas of Poland and spoke a number of nonstandard regional dialects. As they came together in the United States, the dialect differences among them tended to level out so that the resulting variety was different from any in existence in their original homeland. In addition, as immigrants to an English dominant society, they needed to learn to communicate in English. Since English was the language of the government, the media, the schools, and, above all, the workplace, words and phrases were quickly learned and often found their way into the Polish of these new Americans. The next generation, bilingual and schooled in the United States, was even more likely to borrow words from English into Polish. In the end, the combination of being separated from Poles living in Poland and the heavy influence of borrowing from English made the dialect spoken by Polish Americans considerably different from any form of the language spoken in Poland. We will discuss the issue of immigrant languages in some detail below, but for now, suffice it to say that language contact which comes about through migration is one of the major means by which linguistic diversity arises.

BILINGUALISM

As we have seen, conquest by speakers of a different language will also result in multilingualism in that at least some speakers of the dominated language(s) will become bilinguals. If, as is often the case, the conquerors insist on making theirs the language of administration and commerce, the incentive to learn the new language will be great. When there is considerable linguistic diversity in the area at the time of the conquest, with numerous different ethnic groups all speaking their own languages, it may well happen that the language of the conquering group becomes accepted as the major medium of communication throughout the region, taking on the role of lingua franca or second language for the diverse dominated groups. In cases such as this, there is great political and economic pressure to become bilingual in the language of conquest. For some members of conquered population, economic survival may be at stake, and certainly the potential for achieving a foothold within the new sociopolitical power structure will depend heavily on the ability to communicate effectively in the language of the conquerers. This does not necessarily mean that each and every member of the conquered groups will have the motivation, or, indeed, the opportunity, to learn the new language. What it does mean is that a significant proportion of that population, especially those whose occupations bring them into contact with the new group, will become more or less proficient in the new language. Although, as we have pointed out, the conquered area may be populated by speakers of a single language or by a number of different language groups, the phenomenon of language contact resulting in members of each of the groups becoming bilingual in the dominant language is usually viewed from the point of view of each of the individual groups interacting with the dominant one.

As we have seen, populations speaking different languages come into contact with one another not only through conquest but also through the effects of large-scale migration. Such resettlements frequently result in situations in which different ethnolinguistic groups live side by side in the same geographic area, each maintaining its own language and culture, sometimes for centuries. Interactions occur, and, depending on a variety of factors, one or more of the populations in question may become bilingual in the language(s) of the other. In some such situations, the languages are roughly equal in status. More often, however, it happens that at least one of the groups has greater prestige than the other(s). In cases where groups from many different language backgrounds migrate to an area where there is already a population firmly in place which has a strong language tradition of its own, it is usually expected that the immigrant groups will learn the dominant language, that of the host community.

The term used to refer to bilingualism among populations (as opposed to situations where individuals become bilingual for one reason or another) is *societal bilingualism*, and it takes many forms. In describing the various types of bilingualism which may result from language contact, it is usual to refer to the languages in question according to their status. Thus, Bloomfield (1933) distinguished between a high or prestige language, which he called the *upper language*, and the language(s) of the dominated group, which he termed *lower languages*. It is important to recognize that the use of these terms implies nothing whatever about the intrinsic value of the languages in question. In this context, "upper" and "lower" refer to the status of the speakers and not to such linguistic attributes as relative size of vocabulary, for example.

In order to describe the complexity of the situation, however, we need to go much further. Indeed, as Fought (1985) has pointed out, "what is still lacking is a single system of classification integrating the dimensions of social stratification, situation, and code diversity." As Fought suggests, a truly satisfactory classification of types of bilingual situations would take into account not only that two or more languages are in use in the same speech community, but that their use varies according to the social position and ethnic group of the speaker on the one hand, and to the social situation on the other.

One of the most widely known types of bilingual situation is that which Ferguson (1959) has classified as *diglossia*. In his description of this phenomenon, Ferguson defines it as a stable sociolinguistic situation in which two languages are used in mutually exclusive domains by the same speech community. One of the two, the high language (H), has a standardized writing system, possesses a well-developed literature, and is used in government and in education. The low language (L), characterized by Ferguson as a nonstandard variety of H, is the everyday spoken language of the community and rarely appears in written form at all. In a diglossic situation it is usually the case that the lower language is the mother tongue of the entire speech community while H is learned through formal schooling, often by only a privileged few, but in some cases by the entire population. The low language is usually regarded with a combination of affection and scorn, both prized and despised for symbolizing the mass culture. With respect to functional distribution, the low language is used at home and among family and friends, as well as in other speech situations which are private and informal. The high language, on the other hand, is culturally accepted as the only appropriate medium of communication in public or formal settings, such as church, government, or school. Since formal instruction is nearly always the means by which H is attained, and since full participation in a diglossic society requires competence in both languages, education is of critical importance. The examples chosen by Ferguson (1959) to illustrate the way in which diglossia has been found to operate are Swiss German, Arabic, Modern Greek, and Haitian Creole. In each of these cases, there is a standard written variety, often with strong religious and/or classical roots, while the vernacular or lower language has no such traditions. As Ferguson puts it:

> In all the defining languages there is a strong tradition of grammatical study of the H form of the language. There are grammars, dictionaries, treatises on pronunciation, style, and so on. There is an established norm for pronunciation, grammar, and vocabulary which allows variation only within certain limits. The orthography is well established and has little variation. By contrast, descriptive and normative studies of the L form are either non-existent or relatively recent and slight in quantity. Often they have been carried out first or chiefly by scholars OUTSIDE the speech community and are written in other languages. There is no settled orthography and there is wide variation in pronunciation, grammar, and vocabulary. (Ferguson 1959:329)

Although Ferguson's original definition of diglossia holds that the languages which bear such a relationship to one another are varieties of the same language, more recent scholarship into pidgin and creole languages (see below) have demonstrated that at least one of the language situations he gives to illustrate his point does not fit this criterion. In giving Haitian Creole as an example of a lower language (L) in diglossia with standard French, Ferguson is making the assumption that the Creole is a variety or a dialect of French, an assumption which rigorous analyses have shown to be unfounded. Rather, Haitian Creole, although much of its vocabulary derives from the French spoken by plantation owners in Haiti, owes much of its structure and phonology to a combination of languages of African origin and is so different in these respects from French that it cannot be considered anything but a separate language.

Related to the issue of whether or not languages which exist in a diglossic relationship are necessarily varieties of the same language is the fact that many stable bilingual situations have been noted in which unrelated languages bear very much the same relationship to one another as that originally described by Ferguson. The characterization of diglossia, encompassing the functional distribution of two languages within a single speech community, is an important one. The term and the concept underlying it is such a useful one, however, that it has been extended in recent years so that it is now used to refer to a variety of very different bilingual situations.

In order to clarify some of the resulting ambiguity and to give descriptive clarity to a complex picture, Fought (1985) has provided a preliminary classification of nine distinctly different types of bilingual situation: (1) a postconquest situation in which the upper group uses one language and the lower group another (the community is bilingual but individuals are monolingual); (2) a situation in which all individuals in the community are bilingual and all use both languages in a variety of speech situations; (3) diglossia, a situation in which everyone in the society knows two languages but one is used in formal and the other in informal domains; (4) a situation similar to (1) above except that only a portion of the population among the dominated or lower group are bilingual in the upper language; (5) a situation similar to (1) and (4) except that, in this case, it is members of the upper group who have become bilingual while the lower group remains monolingual; (6) similar to the diglossic situation described in (3) except that the higher social groups use H more often and in more situations or domains, while the lower social groups use more L; (7) split diglossia of what Fought calls the "superstrate" type (in this case, the lower-status group(s) use H very little or not at all, while the upper-status group follows the behavior typical of the classical definition of diglossia originally described by Ferguson, such that they use both H and L, but in different domains); (8) split diglossia of the type called "substrate" by Fought (this situation is the opposite of "superstrate diglossia" in that only the lower social group is diglossic while the upper group uses H in all situations); (9) "mixed diglossia," a situation in which the upper group is diglossic with members using H in formal situations, but different from the classic model in that they code-switch or alternate languages in informal domains. At the same time, the lower group(s) is diglossic in formal situations using a mixture of both languages, and in informal situations using L alone. The complexity of the various types of diglossia classified by Fought reveals the need for a sophisticated approach toward any discussion of problems related to bilingualism.

ETHNIC DIVERSITY AND LINGUISTIC IMPOSITION

To add to the complex picture presented above, it must be recognized that many societies in the world are made up of a great variety of ethnic groups, each with its own language, all sharing the same political boundaries. A concrete example of an extreme case of multilingualism is described by Spencer (1985):

> Africa, particularly sub-Saharan Africa, is probably the most linguistically complex area of the world, if population is measured against languages. It is possible that Africa contains well over a thousand languages. They cannot yet be counted with any certainty or precision, for about many of them too little is known. . . . Indeed, Africa's linguistic condition is a monument to innumerable conquests, incursions, peaceful interaction, hegemonies, vassaldoms, cultural or religious movements, migrations, from time immemorial. And European colonial rule in Africa, much of it during only a century or so—or less in certain areas—planted a bold and arbitrary superstructure of European languages, as well as arbitrary political boundaries, on top of an already stratified or layered multilingualism; and in some areas, where settlement of Europeans and other non-Africans was encouraged, also planting powerful minorities speaking non-African languages as mother tongues. (Spencer 1985:387)

Conquest, migration, reconquest repeated again and again, cultural contacts bringing new religions, new trading patterns, and with them new languages—these are the forces which produce the extreme multilingualism so often found in third world countries. The resulting mix of large numbers of ethnic minorities is compounded by the development of trade languages necessary to interethnic communication. These wider languages, often called lingua francas, usually begin as the mother tongue of one ethnic group and are then learned, in somewhat simplified form, by an ever-widening circle of other ethnic groups. The adoption of a lingua franca does not mean that the ethnic mother tongue is lost but rather that a new language is added to serve a specific function. In recent centuries, colonization and the resulting imposition of languages not native to the area have added yet another linguistic layer to the already complicated sociolinguistic picture.

Colonization and language imposition are not, of course, European inventions. Long before Europeans arrived in East Africa, Arabic traders had already established settlements throughout the area (Wald 1985), and the Berber-speaking populations of North Africa had been conquered and colonized by Arabic speakers long before the French arrived. In Central and South America, one great civilization followed upon another, each with its own imperialistic ambitions. An excellent example of non-European imperialism is that of the Inca conquest in Peru. Hardman (1985) describes the linguistic history of Peru in this way:

> The Inca expansion wiped out many local languages, but not as an absolute policy. If there was resistance, then the residents were scattered and others brought in which resulted in loss of one language and the introduction of some variety of the general language (Quechua). . . . Another policy of the Incas was to send the children of community leaders to Cuzco for a four-year higher education program, of which one year was devoted to language learning. This is high incentive . . . for speaking Quechua when they returned as leaders themselves. . . . Not all takeovers were so peaceful. The flourishing Chimu on the North Coast were bloodily subdued, leaving only remnants of the language to disappear when the Spanish arrived not too many years later. Thus we see that patterns of multilingualism are complex and everchanging, as one group after another gains and then loses the political, military and economic power necessary to impose its language on the group it dominates. (Hardman 1985:190)

Thus we see that policies of linguistic imposition have roots which go further back than recorded history. Linguistic minorities have probably always existed. Those nations that have had the power to extend their borders have done so without regard for the rights or desires of the ethnolinguistic groups whose territories they took. Conquest was nearly always followed by some form of linguistic imperialism, and the result has always been to add to already existing linguistic diversity. As Haugen (1985) has so clearly stated:

> The policy of ethnic incorporation is of course not limited to modern Europe. It appears to be immemorial: China, Mongolia, Japan followed it in the Far East, India in South Asia, the Egyptians, the Chaldeans, the Assyrians, anyone you can mention in the Middle and Near East, the Incas and the Aztecs in the Americas and in some far-distant time, our most remote linguistic ancestors, the Indo-Europeans. Within historical time the Greeks, Romans, French, Germans, Russians, Spaniards, Portuguese, and English have carried on the grand tradition of encircling and suppressing racial and linguistic minorities wherever they had the power to do so. Even the small and now pacific nations of the Scandinavian North, cradle of my ancestors, have a history that does not in the least free them from an accusation of linguistic and cultural suppression. (Haugen 1985:6)

PROBLEMS OF LINGUISTIC INEQUALITY

As we have seen, not all languages are equal with respect to power and the prestige it brings. Further, some languages are spoken by small political minorities, others by large and thriving populations. Some languages represent ancient cultures with long literary traditions; others have never been written at all. Some languages are used as vehicles for administration, commerce, and education, while others are spoken only as home languages by humble minority groups. What this means is that within a multilingual society one or more groups will be more powerful and therefore more prestigious than others, and will thus be in a position to impose their language(s) on other, smaller groups. Even when a nation is politically independent, it is difficult, if not impossible, for all language groups to receive equal treatment in such a situation.

To give a concrete example, let us take India, a country seriously beset by problems of linguistic inequality. As in the case of the African continent, no one is able to give an accurate count of the number of languages spoken in India. Census reports are more confusing than helpful. The census of 1951, for example, reported some eight hundred languages in existence, but in 1961 the census report listed more than twice that number. Clearly, the number of languages spoken in India did not double within 10 years. Rather, the discrepancy between the two reports reflects considerable confusion and uncertainty as to which linguistic varieties "deserve" to be labeled languages. In addition, uneducated respondents to the census questions frequently gave the names of their castes, localities, and even occupations when asked what language they spoke. For these reasons, it is still not possible to give a complete account of the number of languages currently in use in India.

The languages spoken in India belong to four families: Indo-European, Dravidian, Austroasiatic, and Tibeto-Burman. The Indo-European family (to which the Romance and Germanic languages of Europe, including English also belong) contains the major literary languages of North India and Pakistan. The Indo-European or, as they are sometimes called, the Indo-Aryan languages, are spoken by approximately 75 percent of the population. The second major language group is the Dravidian, which is comprised of the four most important literary languages of South India as well as approximately 20 others. Dravidian languages are spoken by about 140 million people (approximately 23 percent of the population). They are not genetically related to the languages of the Indo-Aryan group or, for that matter, to any other known language group in the world. The third linguistic group in India consists of the Munda languages, spoken by some 8 million people in tribal areas. These are related to the Austroasiatic family of languages. There are also languages belonging to the Tibeto-Burman family.

Among the languages of India, 33 have over 1 million speakers each. Out of these, 14, which account for more than 90 percent of the population, are listed as official state languages by the constitution. Another 49 languages have over one hundred thousand speakers each, and many within this group have considerably more. Within each of the major languages of India there are speech variations based on geographical location, age, sex, education, caste, religion, and occupation. Nevertheless, for each of the official state languages there is a recognized standard variety used for literature and journalism, for administration and for education. English, the language of colonialism, continues to be recognized as one of the most important languages used in India, and it coexists, along with Hindi, as the official language of the federal government. Approximately 25 million Indian people have at least some working knowledge of English. Since independence from colonial rule, the states of India have been redrawn, largely on linguistic considerations. Of the present 21 states, 6 are Hindi-speaking. Although divided by several dialects, Hindi is spoken by over 40 percent of the population of India. Next in order within India are Bengali, Telegu, Marathi, and Tamil, each with over 40 million speakers. Since independence, arguments have raged over whether and to what extent English should be maintained in India. At the heart of the controversy lies the unarguable fact that whichever local language is chosen as the official language of the federal administration, its speakers would have clear economic and political advantage over speakers of the other languages of India. For this reason, although Hindi has by far the largest population base, speakers of the other languages have been extremely reluctant to see Hindi become the only official language of the government. In order to avoid discrimination along regional and linguistic lines, a compromise has been reached in which English, widely known among educated speakers from all regions, continues to be used for official purposes.

Because English was the prestigious language of the colonial empire, access to the expense of English schooling has long been a privilege of the wealthy and powerful, irrespective of regional background. For this reason, the compromise solution to retain English as an official language of the government has the virtue of avoiding discrimination along regional and linguistic lines by giving members of the various language groups of India an equal opportunity to participate in national affairs. Although no one ethnolinguistic group is favored by the choice of English, its continued use operates to keep political power in the hands of the elite, excluding those from lower-socioeconomic backgrounds who have had relatively little opportunity to attain mastery of the language. Thus, although it is true that the retention of English is an excellent means of avoiding regional discrimination, it is also the case that discrimination along socioeconomic lines is unavoidably maintained by such a choice.

Linguistic inequality along socioeconomic lines is a worldwide phenomenon. We have only to look at our own society to see the difficulties faced by speakers of nonstandard dialects. The extreme linguistic diversity which exists in India greatly compounds this ever-present form of linguistic discrimination. Thus, although the major regional languages serve as the vehicles of administration and education at the state level in India, the varieties in use are always those native to the regional elite. These elite varieties are often so different from the languages of the lower strata as to be unintelligible to them. As Southworth (1985) points out:

> . . . it is clear that traditional attitudes have triumphed over egalitarian ideology, with the result that language education continues to function as an exclusive mechanism. This effect has been achieved by defining much of normal spoken language as "nonstandard," legitimizing this claim by various intellectual and pseudo-nationalistic arguments, and then refusing to look at the results. Thus the ruling groups in each region, however much they may appear to support the principle of equality, have in fact given higher priorities to social status, economic self-interest, and political expediency. (Southworth 1985:235)

The pattern of linguistic inequality discussed above is not an uncommon one. Although the multilingual nations of the world, most of them newly independent, are striving to overcome the obstacles to national unity and to equality for all groups, the route to personal advancement and to power continues to be an education which leads to mastery of the prestige language.

PIDGINS AND CREOLES

Perhaps the most dramatic example of the way social forces shape language use is the phenomenon known as pidginization. More than any other category of languages, pidgins and creoles owe their existence to exploration and conquest, trade and slavery, colonialism and nationalism. As Hymes (1971a) has said: "And while these languages have come into being and existed largely at the margins of historical consciousness on trading ships, on plantations, in mines and colonial armies, often under the most limiting or harshest of conditions—their very origin and development under such conditions attests to fundamental characteristics of language and human nature" (Hymes 1971a:5).

What, then, are the languages which are classified as pidgins and creoles? How can they be defined and described? To begin with, it must be admitted that there is no general agreement on this issue. Indeed, with the best will in the world, scholars have not been able to arrive at a satisfactory linguistic definition of pidgin and creole languages in the sense that it truly serves to distinguish them from other languages. Thus, although pidgins and creoles share certain linguistic features which make them typologically different from most other languages, these same features are found to exist in languages which do not have the linguistic or historical background common to pidgin and creole languages.

While it is not possible to give a satisfactory linguistic definition of pidgin and creole languages, there is considerable agreement concerning the social definition of these languages. Because creoles are, by definition, derived from pidgins, it would be well to begin our discussion with a description of the characteristics of pidgin languages and of the theories which have been advanced to explain their origins and development.

To begin with, pidgins are no one's native language. They arise in situations of contact between speakers of mutually unintelligible languages and develop into relatively stable linguistic systems with their own syntax, lexicon, and phonology. The fact that a pidgin has, by definition, no native speakers has two important implications. On the one hand, it follows that in order for a language to qualify as a pidgin it must be sufficiently different from the native languages of its speakers to be mutually unintelligible with them. This is an important point since, despite widespread popular wisdom on the subject, pidgins cannot be counted as dialects, or as "deviant" or "broken" forms of the source languages from which much of their vocabularies derive. On the other hand, there is the equally important corollary to this fact. That is, because pidgin languages are native to no one, it follows that all of their speakers are bilinguals.

Pidgins, then, are contact languages which develop as vehicles of communication between people who have need to interact and who have no common language. As long as the need for communication across groups speaking different first languages continues, the pidgin language may continue to exist. If, however, pidgin speakers intermarry and form a community where the pidgin becomes the common language, the children of these speakers acquire the language in the way all children acquire first languages, and, because the language must now function as the main or only means of communication, it develops a much more extensive vocabulary and syntactic system. Once a pidgin gains native speakers, it becomes classified as a creole language. As DeCamp (1971) puts it:

> If the interlingual contact is prolonged and institutionalized, however, as in the case of slavery, the presence of foreign military troops, or the marriage of Tarzan and Jane, then the pidgin becomes fixed, and newcomers to that interlingual scene must learn it as they would learn Esperanto. The pidgin may then be expanded to make it suitable for a greater variety of speech situations, either externally by borrowing additional features from the standard language or internally by analogical improvizations on the resources of the original pidgin—and so begins the process of evolution which may someday result in a creole if speakers begin using it as a native language. (DeCamp1971:21)

The historical situation in which pidgin and creole languages came into being was the European colonialism of the eighteenth and nineteenth centuries. Under this system, dominated peoples were frequently transported as cheap or free labor to distant places. In the Americas, where slavery was practiced, these displaced populations were unlikely ever to return to their original homes. In the Pacific, under the indentured labor system, the work force was almost exclusively male and the term of labor was a fixed number of years rather than a lifetime. What slavery and the indentured labor system had in common was that people from a great many different (though often neighboring) ethnolinguistic groups were transplanted from their homes and forced to work together in distant lands. A common means of communication between fellow workers and between workers and masters was clearly a necessity. As the dominated groups, the workers were expected to bear the burden of learning to understand and, when necessary, to respond to their European masters. Had all the dominated peoples thus thrown together been speakers of a single language, the outcome would very likely have been bilingualism, however imperfect, in the language of the ruling class. In these cases, however, the workers themselves were usually from many different language backgrounds, and the languages which developed were not simply varieties of the prestige languages but new linguistic systems altogether. Indeed, it has been postulated (cf. Whinnom (1971) that: "since it would appear to be true that no pidgin has ever consolidated itself in other than a multilingual situation (New Guinea Pidgin, Hawaiian Pidgin, the Caribbean Creoles, Sango, Chinook, etc., etc.) it may well be that no simple bilingual situation ever gives rise to a pidgin" (Whinnom 1971:104).

Given their historical background, there are a number of theories as to how pidgin languages originated. Todd (1974) gives a clear description of these different theories, which we summarize here.

1. The baby-talk or foreigner-talk theory holds that the masters, in accommodating their speech to make it intelligible to their workers, used a much reduced morphological and syntactic system which then served as the model for these language learners. Although this process may well have had some part in the creation of the new languages, there is evidence to suggest that this process could only have been one ingredient in their development. As scholars specializing in pidgin and creole languages have pointed out, one important piece of counterevidence is the fact that although pidgin languages are characterized by morphological reduction, they are also frequently found to contain some features which are morphologically more complicated than the European language which serves as their source. Here we must remember that although the workers spoke many different languages, they often came from the same geographical areas, and their native languages therefore would have shared certain morphological and semantic distinctions which carried over into the developing new language.

2. The independent Parallel Development Theory or the theory of polygenesis (Hall 1962) holds that since pidgins arose in separate situations, each must be considered to have developed independently. Thus, according to this viewpoint, the pidgin languages "come from" French or English or whatever European language served as the source for the lexicon, and they should be considered varieties of these languages. The difficulty with this theory is that it cannot account for the well-known fact that European-based pidgin languages are very similar to one another in spite of the fact that some are spoken along the shores and islands of the Atlantic Ocean and others in the Pacific Ocean area, with little likelihood of contact between speakers in the two far-distant regions. In the case of French-based creoles, for example, there is a considerable degree of mutual intelligibility among languages which could not possibly have come into contact. Clearly, the polygenetic theory is a difficult one to defend.

3. Pidgin languages arose from the nautical jargon used by sailors during the period of extensive exploration which began in the fifteenth century. Because the men who made up the crews of these ships came from a great variety of language backgrounds and nationalities, a common language developed among them. This was then passed on to the many different populations with whom these sailors came into contact during their travels, creating a common core upon which speakers of a host of different languages could expand through combining it with elements from their native tongues.

The evidence for this theory is the existence of nautical items in pidgins and creoles which derive their lexicons principally from European languages, but since only a few such elements exist, the theory cannot be considered adequate to explain the many structural similarities among European-based creole and pidgin languages.

4. In the case of the theory of monogenesis, the above-mentioned similarity among the pidgin and creole languages of both the Atlantic and the Pacific has given rise to a related, but far more comprehensive, theory concerning the origin of this category of languages. The most extreme or strong version of this theory holds that all pidgins had a single common origin in Sabir, a Mediterranean trade language which flourished during the fourteenth and fifteenth centuries and which appears to have had a comparatively stable linguistic structure, resembling those of present-day pidgins and creoles and, like them, differing in vocabulary from one area to another. Thus, according to the monogenetic or relexification theory, the various colonial languages supplied their own vocabularies to this one basic trade language, serving as a basis for the development of a large number of pidgin languages with essentially the same linguistic structure but with quite different lexicons. That is, Sabir was relexified to accommodate to contact situations involving different European language groups, and the resulting versions of the same essential language are known as French or Dutch or English pidgins according to the language from which their vocabulary was borrowed. The strong version of the monogenetic theory is quite controversial, and most scholars are unready to accept it. What many do accept, however, is the idea that relexification of a widely known trade language probably had its part in the development of present-day pidgins and creoles.

As Todd (1974) points out, another explanation of the origin of pidgin and creole languages would look toward a synthesis of the theories so far discussed and add to them the fact that languages and language learning in contact situations have in common much that is universal. As she puts it:

> The similarities revealed by all pidgins and creoles so far studied and the difficulties encountered in trying to locate their historical origins, suggest that it is, perhaps, shortsighted to look to the past, to look for a "common" origin in the sense of their being descended from one parent language. Perhaps it would be more profitable to look for a "common" origin in another sense; that is by examining the possibility that there are universal patterns of behavior appropriate to contact situations. One could express this view more positively by suggesting that pidgins and creoles are alike because, fundamentally, languages are alike and simplification processes are alike. Seeing in the structural simplicity of pidgins and creoles a similarity due to inherent universal linguistic constraints precludes the necessity of postulating a proto-pidgin, whether of African, European or any other origin. The similarities in all pidgins from the past as well as the present, and from all continents, may well be accounted for if one can show that human beings are biologically programmed to acquire *Language* rather than any particular language, and that the programming includes an innate ability to dredge one's linguistic behavior of superficial redundancies where there is a premium on transmitting facts, on communicating, as it were, without frills. It is not being suggested that one is consciously aware of how one adjusts one's language behavior. But the fact that one does adjust and the fact that people of different linguistic backgrounds adjust their language behavior in similar ways, suggests that the behavior is rule-governed and may be the result of linguistic universals. (Todd 1974:42)

The theory put forth by Todd is closely related to the argument proposed by Bickerton (1981) in his famous book, *Roots of Language*. Here Bickerton argues that the origin of creoles and the way children acquire their first language are basically similar and that both are similar to the origin of language itself. Thus, the origin of creole languages and their striking similarities to one another are explained by postulating a universal cognitive map, much like that proposed by Chomsky (1968). Bickerton's theory, generally known as the bioprogram hypothesis, makes use of an analysis of second language acquisition studies, data from a number of creole languages with an emphasis on that of Hawaii, and a discussion of what is known about the origin of language itself. In his argument that Hawaiian Creole English (HCE) is syntactically different from Hawaiian Pidgin English (HPE) from which it derives, he points out that the syntactic differences between HCE and HPE cannot be explained with reference to the dominant language, English, or the less prestigious languages, mainly those of the Philippines and of Japan, which have contributed to the development of HCE. These syntactic differences can be explained, Bickerton claims, only by recognizing that there are universal cognitive strategies at work in the development of creole languages. As Bickerton explains, the bioprogram at the heart of his theory of language development that accounts for the origin of language, the way children acquire it, and the way in which creole languages develop works in the following way:

> The child does not, initially, "learn language." As he develops, the genetic program for language which is his hominid inheritance unrolls exactly as does the genetic program that determines his increase in size, muscular control, etc. "Learning" consists of adapting this program, revising it, adjusting it to fit the realities of the cultural language he happens to encounter. Without such a program, the simplest of cultural languages would presumably be quite unlearnable. But the learning process is not without its tensions—the child tends to hang on to his innate grammar for as long as possible—so that the "learning trajectory" of any human child will show traces of the bioprogram, and bioprogram rules and structures may make their way into adult speech whenever the model of the cultural language is weakened.
>
> This, then, in outline is the unified theory of language acquisition, creole language origins, and general language origins for which the present volume has amassed numerous and diverse types of evidence. (Bickerton 1981:297)

Bickerton's theory is both interesting and clearly described, albeit impossible to prove. It has attracted widespread interest and deserves to be mentioned in a book of this sort since it touches on so many issues of concern to scholars interested in language acquisition. However, this, no more than any other theory described, can be accepted as fact since the very nature of the question of pidgin/creole origins (let alone the issue of the origin of language itself) preclude the possibility of providing data adequate to prove their validity. From my own point of view as a linguist (though certainly not a creole specialist), the most appealing theory, given the evidence that can be brought to bear on the question, is a weak version of the monogenetic/relexification hypothesis. However, since the historical information needed to support any theory of pidgin/creole origin is far from complete, we can only hope that future studies will reveal more convincing evidence.

Although we may never know if all European-based pidgin and creole languages have a common linguistic origin, there is no doubt that they have much in common from the social point of view. With few exceptions, these languages are spoken by people at the very bottom of the socioeconomic structure. Many pidgin and creole speakers lack formal education. Where one of these languages exists side by side with the standard language from which its vocabulary is derived, it will nearly always occupy the position of the subordinate language. In general, pidgin and creole languages are seen, by their own speakers as well as by others, as corruptions of the infinitely more prestigious standard languages. Thus, a Jamaican Creole speaker, who calls his language a *patois,* will be quick to describe it as "broken English." Often ridiculed by standard speakers, pidgin and creole languages are rarely recognized as being separate, highly regular languages. The fact that they are spoken by poor and powerless people is thus reflected and perpetuated by negative attitudes expressed about the languages themselves. In this respect, the scornful viewpoints manifested toward pidgin and creole languages are similar to those held about most languages and dialects spoken by groups at the bottom of the social scale in a given society. Painful as it may be, we must always recognize that the low esteem accorded these languages is symbolic of sociocultural attitudes toward their speakers.

THE POST-CREOLE CONTINUUM

In some areas, creole languages are beginning to merge with their corresponding standard languages in such a way that depending on their education and the amount of exposure to the standard, people will control a range of varieties of a creole language. People with the least education and exposure to the standard, usually those from rural areas, will speak the variety furthest from standard, known to creolists as the *basilect*, while those in the opposite position will speak a form of creole which is very close indeed to the standard—that known as the *acrolect*. Each individual along this continuum will control a range of varieties, from most to least similar to standard, and acrolect speakers will often control a variety of the standard as well.

Not all creole languages develop such a continuum. DeCamp (1971) suggests that in order for a postcreole continuum to develop, two conditions are necessary. First, the official language of the community must be the standard language which has served as the source for the creole so that speakers have continuing exposure to the prestige variety as their model. Second, and most important, the rigid social differentiation which separated creole from standard speakers must have loosened considerably. The point here is that in order for people to want to attempt to change their speech patterns in the direction of the prestige variety, there must be sufficient social mobility to motivate them. Thus, the fact that a postcreole continuum exists reflects the desire of the creole-speaking population to model their speech on that of the prestige group, a desire fueled by the expectation that standard speech will lead to upward mobility.

As Craig (1985) describes it, this striving for increased social status through the acquisition of the standard language has created severe educational problems. Convinced that the creole is corrupt and that its use reflects the laziness and stupidity of its speakers, teachers and educational administrators enforce rigid examination standards for "proper English" in Jamaica. Those children who are not successful, the great majority from rural areas, especially, are automatically blocked from further education. Since education is the route to socioeconomic advancement, and since expectations of what schooling can accomplish are very high among the population at large, disappointment is extreme. Children from urban areas and from higher socioeconomic backgrounds have a clear advantage over those from rural areas. As long as the educational system continues to stress command of Standard English while refusing to recognize the creole as a separate linguistic system, social mobility will be restricted, talent will be wasted and political discontent will grow.

Closely related to the ongoing investigation of postcreole continua is the increasingly widespread agreement among scholars that the variety of English spoken by inner-city blacks in the United States is itself an example of just this phenomenon. Indeed, one of the strongest arguments made by linguists testifying in the Ann Arbor Case (see Chapter 9) was that Black Vernacular English, the variety used by the children of the defendants and classified as deviant by the school system, was in reality derived from a linguistic system separate from that of Standard English, and therefore needed to be understood on its own terms. If this is indeed the case, and if Black Vernacular English is in a relationship of what Fought (1985) has called "split diglossia" with Standard English, then it is clear that educators need to take a much closer look at the current linguistic situation in our schools.

CONCLUSION

For teachers of English as a second or foreign language, a firm grasp of the origins and implications of linguistic diversity is essential to an understanding of the world language situation and the place of their students within it. Insight into the history of language contact, and especially into the age-old struggle between dominant and dominated, provides a perspective on the ways in which language can serve as both an instrument of control and a symbol of social inequality. When we see how and why it happens that certain languages have or lack social prestige, we gain a deeper understanding of the importance to language learners of prescriptive grammars, dictionaries, and manuals on "proper" pronunciation. We all have our own views about the beauty or value of different languages, but it is important to recognize that these are largely based upon the status of the speakers. Respect for other languages and cultures is a necessity for all teachers in our pluralistic society. For teachers of English in the present world situation, it is especially critical.

CHAPTER
13

English as a World Language

WHY ENGLISH?

Given the difficulties which arise from situations of extreme multilingualism and the fact that modern technology has made geographical distance almost irrelevant to ease of communication, it is not surprising that a single language should have emerged as a worldwide medium in our day. The fact that it is English which has become *the* international language should not be seen as a reflection of intrinsic merit in the linguistic system but rather as a historical accident. Other languages have been imposed or spread through the military, cultural, and economic supremacy of their speakers but never before has the spread of a single language been so wide or so deep. The success of the British colonial empire and the subsequent rise of American industrial and technological power have combined and interacted to create a situation in which English, alone of all the world languages, has come to be accepted as the tool and the symbol of modern technologically advanced society. Not only does English have some 300 million native speakers, it is now regularly used as an additional language by at least as many nonnative speakers throughout the world. Nearly 40 nations use English in an official capacity within their own borders, and an untold number of others require that it be learned as a second or foreign language by schoolchildren. As Conrad and Fishman (1977) point out: "Growing school age populations coupled with a growing percentage of that population in fact enrolled in secondary school amounts to a demand for English instruction which is growing at a substantially greater rate than the population itself . . . in Asia . . . the percentage of age-appropriate population in secondary schools doubled in the decade 1960–1970, a fact doubly significant for these purposes since overall 97% of that secondary school enrollment is in English classes" (Conrad and Fishman 1977:14).

With respect to international interaction, it is fair to say that a working knowledge of English is imperative. Whether the matter at hand is diplomacy, commerce, or science, it is now usually taken for granted that meetings at the international level will be held in English. The fact that English has been accepted so widely and by such vast numbers does not, of course, imply that it serves the same functions for all groups. Thus, although the net effect is that a single language has gained worldwide provenience, it is certainly not the case that it is used in the same way everywhere.

In order to see how use of English varies, it will be helpful to consider the three main groups of nonnative English speakers: immigrants to English-speaking countries, newly independent multilingual nations where English serves as the link language, and nations where English is learned and used as a foreign language.

IMMIGRANT GROUPS

Immigrants who take up residence in countries where English is the language of the dominant majority must, if they are to participate fully in their new homes, learn to speak the language. As we have seen, many immigrant groups make great efforts to maintain their ethnic languages along with English and to educate their children in schools where they will learn to read and write both English and the ethnic language. Other groups tend to shift languages much more quickly, and some make little or no effort to maintain the original language. In examining the factors which influence language shift, Clyne (1985) has found that in Australia: "of the factors discussed, those most influential in determining the rates of language maintenance and shift appear to be: cultural core values, degree of cultural similarity to the dominant group (including common rules of communication), and extent of intermarriage" (Clyne 1985:201).

The maintenance of ethnic languages in an English-dominant society has been investigated by examining public manifestations of its use as well as by questioning native speakers. Thus, Fishman (1966) in his volume entitled *Language Loyalty in the United States*, included reports on ethnic radio programs, theater, newspapers and other periodicals printed in ethnic languages, and on enrollments in ethnic language schools. This and other more recent studies have shown a strong tendency for immigrant groups to shift languages over time so that as new generations are born in an English-speaking country, use of the ethnic languages decreases steadily. As Weinreich (1953:35) points out, however, vestiges of the immigrant group's linguistic heritage remain in the maintenance of fossilized phrases and interjections which serve as markers of in-group membership, as well as in terms which are borrowed into English and become part of the general vocabulary of the dominant group.

Although they were accepted and often welcomed into this country as a source of much-needed labor, immigrant groups from southern and eastern Europe, from Latin America, and later from Asia were generally despised for their old-country ways and for their ignorance of English. Indeed, it was taken as a matter of general agreement that immigrants would adapt themselves to the language and culture of the host country as quickly as possible and that until they did so they could not be considered fully "American." Not all immigrant groups were willing to accommodate themselves in this way. For many, the threat to their mother tongues gave rise to what Weinreich (1953) has termed language loyalty: "It might be said accordingly that if a group considers itself superior but in practice has to yield to the other group in some of the functions of its language, a resentful feeling of loyalty may be fostered" (Weinreich 1953:99).

Weinreich further suggests that, like nativism, language loyalty will be strongest among those groups which occupied the highest social positions before immigration. Certainly it is true that the immigrant groups which have abandoned their mother tongues most quickly have come from the lower classes in their countries of national origin. In order to see how the status of a language variety spoken by an immigrant group interacts with language maintenance and shift, it will be useful to look more closely at more recent immigrant groups and to trace the history of one of them.

By the 1880s, vast numbers of poor immigrants from southern and eastern Europe were arriving in the United States. Of the millions who came between 1880 and 1920, the great majority came from the lower strata of old world society. Thus, although the languages they spoke often had highly respected standard forms and well-known literary traditions, the immigrants themselves often spoke regional and social varieties which had been regarded as nonstandard in their home countries. Knowing themselves to speak stigmatized varieties, and aware that upward mobility in the new country depended to a great extent upon their learning to function in English, they attached great prestige to the education of their children. The example of Yiddish as an American immigrant language is a case in point.

YIDDISH: CASE HISTORY OF AN IMMIGRANT LANGUAGE

Yiddish, a language which has a history of almost a thousand years and was once spoken by more than 11 million people over a wide geographical area, a language with an impressive literature which has continued to be produced up to the present moment, is now considered by many to be in a state of imminent demise. Although there have been numerous efforts at language maintenance, the attitude of erstwhile speakers and their descendants has largely been one of indifference to its disappearance.

That an immigrant group in the United States should have given up its language in favor of the English spoken by the dominant majority is not surprising but is, in fact, a feature common to the acculturation of almost every immigrant group to reach these shores. Like other immigrant languages, Yiddish was treasured for its ability to express intimacy, humor, and old-country values, while at the same time it was scorned as a symbol of poverty and powerlessness. Generations of speakers who knew almost nothing of its history have felt quite justified in ridiculing this rich and ancient tongue for being "nothing but a corrupt jargon." What is the history of this much maligned language and what are the reasons for the negative attitude of so many of its speakers?

The Yiddish language began in the eleventh century as the speech of Jews who had come from the Romance-speaking areas of France and Italy and settled in the regions of the middle and upper Rhine. There they acquired the language of their Germanic-speaking neighbors, a dialect of middle High German. Other components of this new language were items from the Romance dialects they had spoken earlier and terms borrowed from Hebrew, the language of their sacred texts and prayers. Later, as persecution drove them eastward, Slavic components were also borrowed into the language.

The Jews who came to settle in communities along the Rhine River were carriers of an ancient tradition, and they brought with them certain religious and cultural habits which set them apart from their non-Jewish neighbors. Literacy, for example, was a rare accomplishment among Christians in this era. For Jews, religious observance necessitated the ability to read Hebrew, and for this reason literacy was nearly universal among male Jews, a fact which had several important consequences for Yiddish. On the one hand, Yiddish became a written language very early, and the alphabet in which it was written was adapted from the Hebrew one with which Yiddish speakers were already familiar. It follows from this that Yiddish speakers were to a great extent bilingual and biliterate. It also follows that although Yiddish eventually attained a large population of speakers and extended over a wide geographical area, it did not and could not replace Hebrew in the minds of its speakers, and therefore its functions were restricted from the beginning. It was, throughout most of its history, the daily or "lower" language of a people who reserved their "higher" language for prayers and for scholarly work. It functioned as the vehicle of entertainment literature since Hebrew was considered too sacred to be used for any but the most serious writings, and it served as the language of instruction. More important, it came to embody and symbolize an entire cultural tradition.

Toward the end of the nineteenth century, increasing numbers of East European Jews were brought into contact with the more general European cultural developments. Prime among these was the great nationalist movement of the age. Many Jews came to see themselves in terms of other national-ethnic groupings, and since this often meant a rejection of religion, a cleavage was created between traditional religious Jews and those who identified the new secular Jewish peoplehood as a completely ethnic entity with the Yiddish language as the central, unifying element of the entire culture. However, the high value placed on the Yiddish language by these secular Jews never became the attitude of the masses of Yiddish speakers. Although the intellectual philosophy of Jewish ethnicity caused an increased awareness of language and group identity in those who came into contact with it, it did not basically alter the traditional view of Yiddish as a daily language of no particular value or importance. Thus, although it was in the name of the Yiddish-speaking masses that the intellectuals worked to create an exalted position for the language, the masses continued to regard it as an inferior vernacular.

This persistence of the general population in considering Yiddish an inferior vernacular was rooted in two important factors. On the one hand, we have the

previously mentioned fact that Yiddish had, throughout its history, competed un-
favorably with Hebrew, which continued to be valued as both the sacred and the
ancestral language. On the other hand, it is important to recognize that no matter
how wide a geographical area Yiddish covered, and no matter how many speakers it
had, it was never the dominant language of any political territory. The millions for
whom Yiddish was a native language were never in control of the lands in which
they lived. Throughout its long history, the Yiddish language was spoken by people
who were subject to speakers of other languages and were constantly exposed to
every sort of pressure against them and the culture which their language
represented.

Thus, not only did the Yiddish secular nationalist not have the status or political power gained by other nationalist groups, not only were they the intellectual
elite of a poor and powerless people, but the very population whose cultural and
linguistic identity they were seeking to protect were being increasingly oppressed.
The hapless victims of every sort of political and economic persecution, the object
of ever more bloody pogroms, dislocated both physically and culturally from the
towns and villages which had been their world for centuries, the Jews began, in ever
greater numbers to seek safety and a new life overseas.

For most of the Jews who migrated to America between the years 1881 and
1924, Yiddish was a daily language which was widely used but of no particular
value in itself. As the language of destitute and insecure immigrants, Yiddish
provided a link with the life in the old country and with countrymen here. Jewish
fraternal and mutual aid societies grew up with Yiddish as their language, a large
Yiddish press was established with 11 daily newspapers in the 1930s, the Yiddish
theater developed with Second Avenue in New York as the Yiddish Broadway,
Yiddish radio programs became popular, and Yiddish cultural organizations were
transplanted to New York.

In all of these developments, Yiddish was seen, by the majority of its speakers
here, as a comfortable and familiar vehicle which provided a temporary route to
Americanization, adjustment to American life, and the learning of English. Thus,
although Yiddish served the cultural, intellectual, social, and material needs of the
new immigrants, very little of the activity in this language was directed toward
establishing and maintaining it as the expression of a separate Jewish culture. On
the contrary, the vast majority of Jewish immigrants, religious in orientation if not
always in practice, continued to honor Hebrew as their sacred language and to
assign an increasingly negative role to Yiddish.

Because it was the language of their daily lives, most Yiddish speakers came to
regard it as the symbol of their low immigrant status. Far from wishing to make
efforts on behalf of retaining Yiddish, most speakers were only too eager to give it
up as quickly as possible. In this desire, they were aided and encouraged by the
prevailing American point of view.

Thus, to most Jewish immigrants, for whom Americanization held the promise
of a better life, Yiddish was, far from being a treasure, an impediment which stood
in the way of economic and social advancement. To the children of these immi-

grants, Yiddish became a source of shame, a mark of immigrant parentage. For this first American-born generation, Yiddish was a language spoken with family and immigrant neighbors, but English was the language of school and the work world, and the preferred language of social interaction. All this is not to say that this first American-born generation had no positive attitudes toward the language of their parents; indeed it is this generation which shows the greatest ambivalence. Yiddish was seen as both foreign and intimate. It was the spoiler of American accents and the source of colorful idioms which expressed one's deepest feelings. An intense linguistic self-hatred warred with the powerful feeling of comfort and group identity which Yiddish provided.

The following generation, much more secure in their status as Americans, looked on the immigrant past as only a dim memory of stories told by old grand-parents with funny accents. For this generation, Yiddish stood for the customs and language of the old people, and as such it could be regarded more as a source of amusement than as a badge of shame. Although the number of second-generation American Jews who retain fluency in Yiddish is comparatively small, isolated words and phrases continue to be used for the sense of identity and the affective function they serve.

By the third generation, Yiddish, like other immigrant languages, is usually regarded with very great detachment indeed. Hebrew, the ancient language of prayer, has emerged as the official language of the State of Israel and therefore has received ever-increasing interest and respect. Nevertheless, efforts at maintaining Yiddish continue, and its emotional connotations continue to be treasured.

Since the Jewish migration from eastern Europe to the United States was in every sense a mass movement, many intellectuals who had been members of the secular-nationalist Yiddishist movement were among those who came here, and with them was transplanted the idea of Yiddish as an ethnic treasure. Although they constituted only a small percentage of the total number of Jewish immigrants, their devotion to the retention of the Yiddish language as the symbol of a separate Jewish culture caused them to make great efforts in this direction. It was this secular ideology which caused groups of intellectuals, writers, and journalists to create and support a sophisticated Yiddish literature and press, scientific institutions and jour-nals, cultural organizations of every sort, as well as a network of Yiddish schools, summer camps, and adult education classes.

Although these efforts achieved moderate success as long as new waves of Yiddish-speaking immigrants were arriving to read the newspapers, join the organizations, attend the classes, and fill the lecture halls and theaters, subscriptions and membership rates have fallen off very considerably in more recent decades. The Yiddish press has been reduced, attendance in Yiddish schools has decreased, and the professional Yiddish theater has virtually ceased to exist. For the children and grandchildren of Yiddish-speaking immigrants, the language has, in effect, ceased to function except as the idiom of reminiscences, humor, endearments, and certain signaling devices of in-group ethnic identity.

Thus, the secular intellectuals were unable to win a following among American Jews, for whom religion rather than ethnicity was the preferred element of self-identification and for whom participation in American life precluded a desire for linguistic separation. At the same time that the efforts of the secular Yiddishists to maintain the language have met with disappointments, their work has borne fruit in the respect that a number of universities, colleges, and high schools have, in the last two decades, introduced academic courses in Yiddish language, literature, and folklore.

Once the mother tongue of immigrant masses in the United States, Yiddish was despised and rejected by most of their children, who, at the same time, felt a deep nostalgia and emotional attachment to it. The grandchildren and great-grandchildren of these immigrant Jews have, with the exception of a few fringe groups, all but forgotten the language, but they now view it with greater respect and welcome its recent introduction into colleges and universities as a language of study. Although secular Yiddishists have worked devotedly in behalf of its retention, efforts to keep it in use have met with limited success at best. No longer associated with the negative status of the immigrant or with true cultural identity for the majority of American Jews, it has become for many the reminder of a disappearing culture.

No two immigrant languages have exactly the same history. Nevertheless, the story of Yiddish is an example, resembling in many aspects the fate of the languages spoken by the millions of immigrants of different backgrounds who have chosen to give up the languages of their ethnic heritage in the process of becoming Americans.

POSTCOLONIAL SOCIETIES

As we have seen, the importance of English as a major world language does not rest with native speakers, whatever their linguistic heritage. Indeed, a very large proportion of English users have it as an additional language while maintaining their mother tongues in functionally different roles. The fact that English is widely used as a lingua franca in third world nations is due to the interaction of a number of factors. We have seen that most of the lands of Asia and Africa which fell under British colonial rule were ethnically and linguistically complex long before the arrival of the Europeans. As these areas were carved into colonies, the already diverse language situation was further complicated by the fact that ethnic and tribal boundaries were largely ignored by the new rulers. Thus, when colonies at last began to achieve independence, linguistic diversity was one of the major factors to be reckoned with. Under colonial rule, the imposition of English worked to keep internal language rivalries latent. With political independence, however, came the necessity of choosing languages to replace it in the governing of the new countries. As a result, open language conflict soon became acute in many postcolonial nations. At the same time, the colonial period had left behind political, economic, and legal institutions which it was convenient for the new states to make use of. Clearly, a common language was necessary to the functioning of a national government, and, for reasons which we will discuss, it was often the erstwhile colonial language which was chosen to serve this function. In order to gain perspective on the use of English as a second language in so many of the previously Anglophone colonies, and to understand its maintenance as an important factor of postcolonial life, it would be well to turn our attention back to India as an example.

ENGLISH IN INDIA

Since 1947, when India attained independence from British colonial rule, arguments have raged over whether English should be maintained in India and, if so, to what extent and for what functions. Although there are a number of different positions on this subject, their supporters can be roughly divided into two categories: those who hold that English must and should be maintained as an official language, and those who believe that it is only through the development of one or more indigenous languages that India can realize her full potential. Because the controversy has engaged the attention of so many of India's intellectual leaders, a large literature exists in which arguments for both sides are put forth. A representative example of the argument for the maintenance of English appears in *India Without English*, by T. K. Dutt (1967) of the Nehru Foundation.

Beginning his discussion with the political implications of language diversity, Dutt raises the point that if the regional languages of India are made the media of instruction in the various states, ethnic and linguistic loyalties will be emphasized. Further, members of different language groups will be left without a common language in which to communicate, and political fragmentation or Balkanization will be the ultimate result. As we have seen, this fear of linguistic pluralism leading to political divisiveness is a constant theme in debates concerning language policies in multilingual nations. Some, like Indonesia or Tanzania, have chosen to develop an indigenous language to fulfill the role of linking diverse ethnic populations. Dutt, however, considers this solution inadequate. To begin with, he points out that the use of Indian languages in the areas of technology, commerce, industry, and so on, would require the constant translation of the literature in these fields into languages which have no scientific tradition and which are not developed for these purposes. Further, he points out that even if the necessary vocabulary were to be developed in each area, there would be no possibility of keeping up with translation of the constant flow of high-level literature in all the sciences. A particularly strong argument is that only individuals who are themselves well trained in the various disciplines are capable of translating technical material. As Dutt reminds us, there are far too few trained scientists in India as it is, and these people are desperately needed to develop India's technology. Clearly, it would be a serious misuse of their time and energy for them to be made responsible for translating the constant flow of scholarly literature in their disciplines.

Moving on to a discussion of the value of education in the regional languages, Dutt points out that since very little is translated into these languages, students who elect to take their studies and examinations in the regional languages have not gained the habit of reading and are therefore deficient in general knowledge about the world. Further, he says, the irony of the present system is that although they are allowed to have their education in their regional languages, graduating students are unqualified for higher-level jobs if they do not have a good command of English.

A proponent of using English as a medium of instruction in secondary schools, Dutt does not hesitate to say that the standard of education in India has fallen very low since independence. This he claims is at least partly because English is no longer used as it was in high schools and universities. Worse, if English is not well known to students, he warns, the exchange of scientists and technologists would be impossible between the states of India or between India and other countries. India is a developing country and needs to send students to study abroad; obviously they must be proficient at English in order to do so.

It is undeniable that English is the vehicle of progress in areas of science and technology and that knowledge of English is associated with power and prestige. It is Dutt's view that for this very reason the privileged class who do have English education themselves and who can afford to send their children to English schools are unwilling to make English available to the masses through education. If the rest of India is educated only in Indian languages, the number of people at the top in government and industry will be limited to the elite group, who already have access to it. Thus, he sees the motive for advocating education in the state languages as less than honorable; English speakers want to keep the language of power for themselves.

Many of these arguments seem very convincing, but to understand the intricacy of the language problem in India, it is necessary to look now at the arguments advanced by proponents of the national languages. In a book called *The Language Revolution*, Vaasamoorti (1974) claims that the future of India is tied up with its own languages, which are the symbols of its freedom and honor as a nation. He explains that he and other members of the National Language Movement have no hatred for English or, for that matter, for Hindi, but that they naturally love their own languages much more. That is, there is no wish to abolish English from India, but rather to see it take its place as a foreign language instead of as a medium of instruction in the schools of the nation. Taking up the issue of the need for mastery of English on the part of young scientists and scholars, Vaasamoorti denies the validity of the argument which holds that the attainment of mastery in the language requires that students have their education through it. He points out that Japan, a most successful example of an industrialized non-Western nation, offers instruction at all levels of education only in and through Japanese. Foreign students, he points out, commonly learn new languages in order to study abroad without having had their schooling in the language before.

With respect to terminology and its development for modern use, Vaasamoorti points out that all the regional languages have, at one time or another, served as languages of administration, and although this vocabulary has fallen into disuse, it can be brought back. The important point here is that a government must be carried on in the language of the people. English might be a useful link language among the educated, but rather than promote unity, its use in government can only create a barrier between the administration and the people.

The core of the language controversy here is the question of which language should serve as the medium of higher education. All admit that there has been a steep fall in educational standards since independence, but the reason for this situation is explained differently by the two sides. The advocates of English blame the replacement of English with the national languages, but the National Language Movement disagrees. Standards, they say, have fallen because there has been a huge growth in student population which it has not been possible to match with a growth in teacher education and in facilities. This has nothing to do with knowledge or use of English. Indeed, there is no possibility for the great majority of Indians to learn English well enough to make it a viable medium of instruction or even of communication. If education is to reach the masses of India, the regional languages must be used.

Vaasamoorti's major argument then is that the regional languages can bridge the gulf between the intelligentsia and the masses. If a foreign language continues to be used in government and education, the gulf will grow ever greater, and the elite will do all in its power to keep the masses under control. The people of India, however, have become awakened to their political rights, and only conflict can result from attempting to deny them the opportunities they demand. Further, there is considerable talent among the people which has so far not been exploited. If this is encouraged and developed through education, the whole country will progress. Thus, although vested interests will always oppose change, Vaasamoorti insists that it would be to the benefit of all to make education available in the national languages rather than in English alone.

These arguments are deeply emotional and go to the heart of national aims and philosophy. The fact that each side accuses the elite of wanting to keep power out of the hands of the people is very striking. There seems no easy solution to this problem in a country where well over a thousand languages are spoken. Obviously, the ideal would be to give each child an equal opportunity to learn through his or her native tongue. Not even proponents of the National Language Movement would consider this realistic, however. In spite of their arguments concerning the dangers of using an alien language for government and education, there is no attempt to deal with the fact that the national or state languages are, in fact, the mother tongues of the regional elites and are, as Southworth (1985) has pointed out, largely unintelligible to all but the most well educated. For most others, the varieties used by schools and government offices are, to all intents and purposes, foreign languages. To be sure, English is much more foreign to the majority of people, but it is not clear that it is any less accessible than the educated varieties to those at the lower end of the socioeconomic structure. Clearly, a great deal of effort will continue to be needed before a viable solution can be found to India's language problems. That English will go on playing a major role in Indian life is unarguable.

It is important to recognize that the spread and use of English in India has not been due entirely to linguistic imperialism. Certainly English gained the strong foothold it has because it was the language of the colonial administration, and therefore of all political power. However, this situation in itself would not have sufficed to maintain its importance once independence had been achieved. It is because of the extreme linguistic pluralism and the intense interethnic rivalries which exist that English has been of such great value. As a non-Indian, or extra-ethnic language, native to only a tiny fraction of the population, English has served as a link language, a neutral means of communication across ethnic groups. In this capacity it was English, the erstwhile language of oppression, which became the means of political unification, of wider communication with the rest of the world, and, more recently, of science and technological development. In this sense, even those who are least in favor of having it used for official purposes readily acknowledge its usefulness. In India, English has come to be accepted from within rather than imposed from without.

This development has not been without linguistic consequences. During British rule, the standard for pronunciation, structure, and lexicon was external, and although such values die hard, Indian English has, in recent years, come to be recognized as a variety in its own right. Spoken by millions of people using many regionally and socially differentiated forms, Indian English has developed in its own way. As Mehrotra (1982) puts it:

> IE (Indian English) often poses a problem of intercomprehensibility. It is generally believed that dialects are mutually intelligible and hence IE should be intelligible to the speakers of all other varieties of English. This is not always the case. There is a great deal in IE, particularly at the phonological and lexical levels, that is incomprehensible in varying degrees to the speakers of English outside the Indian subcontinent. At times, English spoken in one part of the Indian territory is not correctly understood in another part. The presence of mutual intelligibility therefore is not an absolute fact and should admit a range of wide variations. . . . it may be asserted that only a small fraction of the Indian population, consisting mostly of academicians, scientists, diplomats, top industrialists, and business executives, is bothered about intelligibility at the international level. What primarily concerns the majority of speakers of English in India is the comprehensibility of their speech and writing on a pan-India basis . . . there is no denying the fact that it is much more important to understand one's own countrymen than to understand outsiders. (Mehrotra 1982:167)

Although the use of English in India has many unique characteristics, several general problems parallel those in other multilingual postcolonial countries. The conscious decision to continue using English is due in large part to the fear that choice of a single majority indigenous language would be divisive; in either case, English is seen as emotionally neutral and therefore useful to the promotion of national unity. A further problem, much discussed, has to do with the fact that none of the indigenous languages are regarded as being sufficiently well developed or modernized and that the difficulty of producing the necessary teaching materials would require too great an investment. The problems of using English, however, appear to be almost equally heavy. Few teachers are well enough trained to help students toward mastery of the language, and there is little or no opportunity for reinforcement outside of school. This means that most students are unable to understand the language of instruction if it is English which serves this function. Dropout rates and failure rates are high, and much time and talent is wasted. Thus, although knowledge of English is undeniably important at higher educational levels, most developing countries are now becoming convinced that indigenous languages should be used in public schools.

ENGLISH AS A FOREIGN LANGUAGE

Because English has become the most important language of wider communication (LWC) in the world, and because so much of the world's work is done and published in it, there has been a tremendous increase in the teaching of English as a foreign language (Fishman et al. 1977). The teaching of English as a subject of study in countries where its function is limited but where it is nevertheless regarded as an important and prestigious medium of communication carries implications which have rarely been investigated. Perhaps more important is the lack of knowledge concerning the needs of those to whom English is taught as a foreign language. One excellent example of the kind of study which is so desperately needed is that reported in Harrison et al. (1975).

What is particularly useful and important about this study is that Jordan represents a language situation which is almost the mirror image of that which exists in the multilingual nations and which we have exemplified through a description of the language problems of India. That is, nearly everyone in Jordan shares the same mother tongue, Arabic, which not only is the major medium of communication within the country but also is widely spoken by Arabs in neighboring countries. In Jordan, then, linguistic diversity is not an issue. Furthermore, Arabic is the only medium of instruction in government schools and English is the only foreign language taught widely. Because the school-going population is so homogeneous in this regard, the Ministry of Education was in a position to ask for a survey which would enable them to gear their language teaching curriculum to the needs of the population. In describing the rationale for the study, the authors say:

> The Field Study [was] conducted to collect information for a large group of Jordanians about their patterns of language use. Specifically, we wanted to obtain a detailed description of the extent to which they use English in a wide variety of situations, for both business and non-business matters; and then to assess the relationship between their actual use of English and factors such as educational attainment, occupation, location of business, age, sex and salary. Furthermore, we wanted to collect reasonably complete information about their educational history, their language training, and their reported English proficiency.

Basing their analysis on a questionnaire given to a large random sample of public and private sector employees, stratified by level of educational attainment, Harrison et al. (1975:81) found that 57 percent of the total use of English was reported to occur at work while 43 percent was not work-related. Nearly 40 percent of the population reported using English every day for listening to radio, television, and movies, while over 20 percent claimed to use English daily for professional advancement. Since English use is associated with prestige, it is impossible to know how the responses of subjects correspond to their actual use. Indeed, the reliance on self-report is the most serious flaw in the study. Ethnographic observation of at least some segment of the population surveyed would have provided an important dimension to the study and might well have revealed that perceptions of use differ in certain ways from the reality. What does seem to be quite clear from the results of the study is that mastery of English is associated with occupational mobility. That is, the greater the mastery of English, the more likely that the individual will be employed at a high level, and the higher the level of employment, the greater the use of English at work. "Overall the respondents who report using English most are administrative or managerial personnel with university degrees (87%), while those who report using English least are production or related employees with less than preparatory completion (14%)."

Another important finding of this study is that people at all educational levels regarded knowledge of English as extremely useful to occupational advancement. Further, the fact that people at all levels reported using English for entertainment purposes makes it clear that knowledge of the language is valued not only as a means of upward mobility but also for the access it gives to English-speaking culture.

From this report and from our knowledge of the ways in which English is used in other countries where it is a foreign language, we see that it has attained a position of extreme importance in the lives of those who use it. Ease of communication and modern electronic media have had a deep and important effect on linguistic habits and attitudes. Further, ease of travel makes it ever more likely that people who learn English as a foreign language in classrooms rather than in naturalistic situations which occur spontaneously will nevertheless be in a position to use the language for purposes of interaction.

ENGLISH AS A SHARED RESOURCE

We have seen that English has come to serve a great variety of functions in today's world and that it is currently being learned and spoken by large numbers of people for whom it is not and never will be a primary means of communication. Those of us who are native speakers are fortunate in being spared the time and trouble of learning English as a second language, but we must also recognize that our native use of the language gives us no superior rights over it. Because English has gained worldwide use, it can no longer be regarded as the exclusive property of a few nations for which it happens to serve as the dominant native language. New nonnative varieties of English have become stabilized and institutionalized in many different areas of the world. These nonnative institutionalized varieties of English (NIVES, as Williams 1987 has termed them) are now recognized as having their own integrity as linguistic systems and most linguists and language teaching specialists agree that they should not be criticized for being different from native speaker models (Kachru 1982a).

That there is a tension here is apparent, and many would consider it a contradiction. The very value of English as a world language rests on a certain amount of unity and standardization, for clearly if English is to continue to serve as an international medium of communication, mutual intelligibility must be maintained. Yet the fact that English now belongs to the world and that nonnative varieties, often quite different linguistically from any native variety or standard, have become institutionalized in schools, government, and the media means a lessening of the unity which has been so highly valued. That this variation has always existed is seldom mentioned in discussions of this troublesome subject. What is new is not the fact that Indian or Nigerian English differ from British or American but that they are no longer held in contempt for being unlike native varieties. Before we become too pessimistic over the threat of a decrease in ease of communication across varieties of English, it would be well to remember that regional and social dialects have always existed in native as well as nonnative varieties and that the speaker of Scots' English is probably less intelligible to the native of Appalachia than either would be to an educated speaker from Nigeria or India.

Sociolinguistic studies have made it clear that intelligibility is heavily dependent upon extralinguistic factors such as attitudes and motivation. As we saw earlier, Wolff (1959), in reporting on work done in Nigeria, made the important point that linguistic similarity in terms of lexicon and structure may have less effect upon intelligibility than does the relative prestige of the speakers.

Thus, people have been shown to be capable of understanding those with whom they are most willing to identify and not to understand those they prefer not to interact with. What this means is that adherence to an ideal linguistic model is probably less effective in promoting intelligibility than is the prestige which comes from successful national development.

Given our shared writing system and the ever improving technology which allows us to communicate with one another across enormous distances, it is not likely that the many varieties of English will diverge to the point where the language will lose its usefulness as a means of wider communication. We know enough about dialect differences to know that it is not necessary for nonnative speakers to follow native models in order to be understood. Rather, different groups of English users, native speakers or not, must recognize that variation in language, like blood pressure in a human body, is a vital sign of life.

Bibliography

Akere, F. 1982. Sociocultural constraints and the emergence of a standard Nigerian English. In *New Englishes,* ed. J. B. Pride, pp. 85–99. Rowley, MA: Newbury House.

Alatis, J. E. (ed.). 1978. *International Dimensions of Bilingual Education, GURT.* Washington, DC: Georgetown University Press.

Alatis, J. E., and K. Twaddell (eds.). 1976. *English as a Second Language in Bilingual Education.* Washington, DC: TESOL.

Albert, E. M. 1972. Culture patterning of speech behavior in Burundi. In *Directions in Sociolinguistics: The Ethnography of Communication,* eds. J. J. Gumperz and D. Hymes. New York: Holt, Rinehart & Winston.

Alt, R. R., and M. L. Kirkland. 1973. *Steps to Composition.* Washington, DC: Georgetown University Press.

Apte, M. L. 1974. "Thank you" and South Asian languages: A comparative sociolinguistic study. *International Journal of the Sociology of Language* 3:67–89.

Apte, M. L. 1976. Multilingualism in India and its sociopolitical implications: An overview. In *Language and Politics,* eds. W. M. O'Barr and J. F. O'Barr, pp. 141–164. The Hague: Mouton.

Aratake, Y., Y. Okushi, and N. Susuki. 1987. *Analysis of Observational Data on Compliment Responses.* Paper presented in course on Cross-Cultural Variation in Speech Behavior, University of Pennsylvania.

Austin, J. L. 1962. *How to Do Things with Words.* Oxford: Clarendon Press.

Bailey, R. W., and M. Gorlach. 1982. *English as a World Language.* Cambridge: Cambridge University Press.

Bailey, R. W., and J. L. Robinson (eds.). 1973. *Varieties of Present-Day English.* New York: Macmillan.

Baker, K. A., and A. A. deKanter. 1983. An answer from research on bilingual education. *American Education* July:40–48.

Baroni, M., and V. D'Urso. 1984. Some experimental findings about the question of politeness and women's speech. *Language in Society* 13:1.

Bauman, R., and J. Sherzer (eds.). 1974. *Explorations in the Ethnography of Speaking.* Cambridge: Cambridge University Press.

Beebe, L. M. 1977. The influence of the listener on code-switching. *Language Learning* 27(2):331–339.

Beebe, L. M. 1980. Sociolinguistic variation and style shifting in second language acquisition. *Language Learning* 30(2):433–447.

Beebe, L. M. 1981. Social and situational factors affecting communicative strategy of dialect code-switching. *International Journal of the Sociology of Language* 32:139–149.

Beebe, L. M. 1985. *Speech act performance: A function of the data collection procedure?* Paper presented at the 18th Annual TESOL Convention, New York, April.

Beebe, L. M., and H. Giles. 1984. Speech-accommodation theories: A discussion in terms of second language acquisition. *International Journal of the Sociology of Language* 46:5–32.

Beebe, L. M., and T. Takahashi. 1987. *Do you have a bag?: Status and patterned variation in second language acquisition.* Paper presented at the XIth University of Michigan Conference on Applied Linguistics: Variation in Second Language Acquisition. Ann Arbor, Michigan.

Beebe, L. M., and J. Zuengler. 1983. Accommodation theory: An explanation for style shifting in second language dialects. In *Sociolinguistics and Language Acquisition,* eds. N. Wolfson and E. Judd, pp. 195–213. Rowley, MA: Newbury House.

Beebe, L. M., T. Takahashi, and R. Uliss-Weltz. 1985. *Pragmatic transfer in ESL refusals.* Paper presented at the Second Research Forum, UCLA. To appear in *On the Development of Communicative Competence in a Second Language,* eds. R. C. Scarcella, E. Andersen, and S. C. Krashen. Rowley, MA: Newbury House.

Beeman, W. 19 6. Status, style, and strategy in Iranian interaction. *Anthropological Linguistics* 18:305–322.

Bell, A. 1984. Language style as audience design. *Language in Society* 13(2):145–204.

Berko-Gleason, J. 1987. Sex differences in parent–child interaction. In *Language, Gender and Sex in Comparative Perspective,* eds. S. Philips, S. Steele, and C. Tanz, pp. 189–199. Cambridge: Cambridge University Press.

Berko-Gleason, J., and E. Grief. 1983. Men's speech to young children. In *Language, Gender, and Society,* eds. B. Thorne, C. Kramerae, and N. Henley. Rowley, MA: Newbury House.

Bernstein, B. 1958. Some sociological determinants of perception. *British Journal of Sociology* 9:159–174. Reprinted in *Class, Codes, and Control,* 1971. London: Routledge & Kegan Paul.

Bernstein, B. 1970. A sociolinguistic approach to socialization: With some reference to educability. In *Language and Poverty: Perspectives on a Theme,* ed. F. Williams, pp. 25–61. Chicago: Markham. Reprinted in *Directions in Sociolinguistics,* eds. J. J. Gumperz and D. Hymes, 1972. New York: Holt, Rinehart & Winston.

Bernstein, B. 1971. A critique of the concept of compensatory education. In *Class, Codes and Control,* vol. 1, 1971. London: Paladin.

Bickerton, D. 1981. *Roots of Language.* Ann Arbor, MI: Karoma.

Blom, J. P., and J. J. Gumperz. 1972. Social meaning in linguistic structures: Code-switching in Norway. In *Directions in Sociolinguistics,* eds. J. J. Gumperz and D. Hymes, pp. 404–434. New York: Holt, Rinehart & Winston.

Bloomfield, L. 1933. *Language.* New York: Holt, Rinehart & Winston.

Blum-Kulka, S. 1982. Learning to say what you mean in a second language: A study of the speech act performance of learners of Hebrew as a second language. *Applied Linguistics* 3(1).

Blum-Kulka, S. 1983a. Interpreting and preforming speech acts in a second language—A cross-cultural study of Hebrew and English. In *Sociolinguistics and Language Acquisition,* eds. N. Wolfson and E. Judd, pp. 36–55. Rowley, MA: Newbury House.

Blum-Kulka, S. 1983b. The dynamics of political interviews. *Text* 3(2):131–153.

Blum-Kulka, S., and E. Olshtain. 1984a. Pragmatics and second language learning: Preface. *Applied Linguistics* 5(3).

Blum-Kulka, S., and E. Olshtain. 1984b. Requests and apologies: A cross cultural study of speech act realization patterns. *Applied Linguistics* 5(3):196–213.

Blum-Kulka, S., and E. Olshtain. 1985. *On utterance length of learners.*

Blum-Kulka, S., and E. Olshtain. 1986. Too many words: Length of utterance and pragmatic failure. *Studies in Second Language Acquisition* 8:47–61.

Blum-Kulka, S., B. Danet, and R. Gherson. 1985. The language of requesting in Israeli society. In *Language and Social Situation,* ed. F. Forgas. New York: Springer-Verlag.

Blum-Kulka, S., J. House-Edmondson, and G. Kasper (eds.). In press. *Cross-Cultural Pragmatics: Requests and Apologies.* Norwood, NJ: Ablex.

Bodine, A. 1975a. Androcentrism in prescriptive grammar: Singular 'they," sex indefinite "he," and "he or she." *Language in Society* 4(2):129–146.

Bodine, A. 1975b. Sex differentiation in language. In *Language and Sex: Difference and Dominance,* eds. B. Thorne and N. Henley, pp. 130–151. Rowley, MA: Newbury House.

Borker, R. 1980. Anthropology: Social and cultural perspectives. In *Women and Language in Literature and Society,* eds. S. McConnell-Ginet, R. Borker, and N. Furman. New York: Praeger.

Borkin, A., and S. Reinhart. 1978. Excuse me and I'm sorry. *TESOL Quarterly* 12(1):57–76.

Borstein, D. 1978. As meek as a maid: An historical perspective on language for women. In *Women's Language and Style,* eds. D. Butturff and E. L. Epstein. Akron, OH: L & S Books.

Bosmajian, H. L. 1974. *The Language of Oppression.* Washington, DC: Public Affairs Press.

Bough, A. C., and T. Cable. 1963. *A History of the English Language,* 3rd ed. Englewood Cliffs, NJ: Prentice-Hall.

Breen, M., and C. N. Candlin. 1980. The essentials of a communicative curriculum in language teaching. *Applied Linguistics* 1(2):89–112.

Briggs, C. L. 1986. *Learning How to Ask: A Sociolinguistic Appraisal of the Role of the Interview in Social Science Research.* Cambridge: Cambridge University Press.

Brosnahan, L. F. 1973. Some historical cases of language imposition. In *Varieties of Present-Day English,* eds. R. W. Bailey and J. L. Robinson, pp. 40–55. New York: Macmillan.

Brouwer, D., M. Gerritsen, and D. DeHaan. 1979. Speech differences between men and women: On the wrong track? *Language in Society* 8(1):33–50.

Brown, G., and G. Yule. 1983. *Discourse Analysis.* Cambridge: Cambridge University Press.

Brown, P. 1980. How and why women are more polite: Some evidence from a Mayan community. In *Women and Language in Literature and Society,* eds. S. McConnell-Ginet, R. Borker, and N. Furman. New York: Praeger.

Brown, P., and S. Levinson. 1978. Universals in language usage: Politeness phenomena. In *Questions and Politeness: Strategies in Social Interaction,* ed. E. N. Goody, pp. 56–289. Cambridge: Cambridge University Press.

Brown, R. 1965. *Social Psychology.* New York: Free Press.

Brown, R. W., and M. Ford. 1961. Address in American English. *Journal of Abnormal and Social Psychology* 62:375–385.

Brown, R. W., and A. Gilman. 1960. The pronouns of power and solidarity. In *Style in*

Language, ed. T. Sebeok, pp. 253–276. Cambridge, MA: M.I.T. Press. Reprinted in *Readings in the Sociology of Language*, ed. J. A. Fishman. The Hague: Mouton, 1968. Also reprinted in *Language and Social Context*, ed. P. Giglioli. New York: Penguin Press, 1972.

Brumfit, C. J. 1980a. Being interdisciplinary—Some problems facing applied linguistics. *Applied Linguistics* 1(2):158–164.

Brumfit, C. J. 1980b. From defining to designing: Communicative specifications versus communicative methodology in foreign language teaching. In *The Foreign Language Syllabus and Communicative Approaches to Teaching: Proceedings of a European-American Seminar*, ed. K. Muller. Special issue of *Studies in Second Language Acquisition* 3(1):1–9.

Brumfit, C. J., and K. Johnson (eds.). 1979. *The Communicative Approach to Language Teaching*. Oxford: Oxford University Press.

Burling, R. 1973. *English in Black and White*. New York: Holt, Rinehart & Winston.

Canale, M. 1983. From communicative competence to communicative language pedagogy. In *Language and Communication*, eds. J. Richards and R. Schmidt, pp. 2–27. London: Longman.

Canale, M., and M. Swain. 1980. Theoretical bases of communicative approaches to second language teaching and testing. *Applied Linguistics* 1(1):1–47.

Candlin, C. N. 1976. Communicative language teaching and the debt to pragmatics. In *Georgetown University Roundtable 1976*, ed. C. Rameh. Washington, DC: Georgetown University Press.

Candlin, C. N., H. Coleman, and J. Burton. 1983. Dentist–patient communication: Communicating complaint. In *Sociolinguistics and Language Acquisition*, eds. N. Wolfson and E. Judd. Rowley, MA: Newbury House.

Cardenas, J. A. 1977. *An IDRA Response with Summary: The AIR Evaluation of the Impact of ESEA Title VII Spanish/English Bilingual Education Program*. San Antonio, TX: Intercultural Development Research Associates.

Cazden, C. B., R. Carrasco, A. A. Maldonado-Guzman, and F. Erickson. 1980. The contribution of ethnographic research to bicultural bilingual education. In *Current Issues in Bilingual Education*, ed. J. E. Alatis, pp. 64–80 (Georgetown University Roundtable of Languages and Linguistics). Washington, DC: Georgetown University Press.

Cazden, C., V. John, and D. Hymes (eds.). 1972. *Functions of Language in the Classroom*. New York: Teachers College Press.

Cherry, L. 1975. Teacher–child verbal interaction. An approach to the study of sex differences. In *Language and Sex: Difference and Dominance*, eds. B. Thorne and N. Henley. Rowley, MA: Newbury House.

Chick, K. 1984. *Interactional sociolinguistics: Insights and applications*. Paper presented at the Annual Conference of the Linguistic Society of South Africa.

Chick, K. 1985. The interactional accomplishment of discrimination in South Africa. *Language in Society* 14(3):299–326.

Chomsky, N. 1968. *Language and Mind*. New York: Harcourt, Brace and World.

Christopher, R. C. 1982. *The Japanese Mind: The Goliath Explained*. New York: Simon & Schuster. Reprinted in 1984 by Fawcett and by Ballantine.

Cicourel, A. 1980. Language and social interaction: Philosophical and empirical issues. *Sociological Inquiry* 59(3–4):1–30.

Cicourel, A., K. Jennings, A. Jennings, S. Leiter, R. MacKay, H. Mehan, and D. Roth (eds.). 1974. *Language Use and School Performance*. New York: Academic Press.

Clark, H., and J. W. French. 1981. Telephone goodbyes. *Language in Society* 10(1):1–19.

Clyne, M. G. 1977. Intercultural communication breakdown and communication conflict: Towards a linguistic model and its exemplification. In *Deutsch im Kontact mit anderen Sprachen,* eds. C. Molony, H. Zobl, and W. Stolting. Kronberg: Scriptor Verlag.

Clyne, M. G. 1979. Communicative competences in contact. *ITL* 43:17–37.

Clyne, M. G. 1982. *Multilingual Australia: Resources, Needs, Policies.* Melbourne: River Seine Publications.

Clyne, M. G. 1985. Language maintenance and language shift: Some data from Australia. In *Language of Inequality,* eds. N. Wolfson J. Manes, pp. 195–206. Berlin: Mouton.

Cohen, A. 1975. *A Sociolinguistic Approach to Bilingual Education.* Rowley, MA: Newbury House.

Cohen, A. D., and L. M. Laosa. 1977. Second-language instruction: Some research considerations. In *Bilingual Multicultural Education and the Professional: From Theory to Practice,* eds. H. T. Trueba and C. Barnett-Mizrahi, pp. 75–88. Rowley, MA: Newbury House.

Cohen, A. D., and E. Olshtain. 1981. Developing a measure of sociolinguistic competence: The case of apology. *Language Learning* 31(1):113–134.

Cole, P., and J. Morgan (eds.). 1975. *Syntax and Semantics.* New York: Academic Press.

Cole, S. 1982. *Attitudes Toward Bilingual Education Among Hispanics and a Nationwide Sample.* Final Report, Center for the Social Sciences, Columbia University.

Conklin, H. 1964. Hanunoo color categories. In *Language in Culture and Society,* ed. D. Hymes. New York: Harper & Row.

Conklin, N. F. 1973. *Perspectives on the dialects of women.* Paper presented at the American Dialect Society.

Conrad, A. W., and J. A. Fishman. 1977. English as a world language: The evidence. In *The Spread of English: The Sociology of English as an Additional Language,* eds. J. A. Fishman, R. L. Cooper, and A. W. Conrad, pp. 3–76. Rowley, MA: Newbury House.

Cooper, R. L. (ed.). 1982. *Language Spread: Studies in Diffusion and Social Change.* Bloomington, IN: Indiana University Press in cooperation with the Center for Applied Linguistics, Washington, DC.

Coulmas, F. (ed.). 1981a. *Conversational Routine.* The Hague: Mouton.

Coulmas, F. 1981b. Poison to your soul: Thanks and apologies contrastively viewed. In *Conversational Routine,* ed. F. Coulmas, pp. 69–93. The Hague: Mouton.

Coulthard, M. 1977. *An Introduction to Discourse Analysis.* London: Longman.

Craig, D. R. 1971. Education and Creole English in the West Indies: Some sociolinguistic factors. In *Pidginization and Creolization of Languages,* ed. D. Hymes, pp. 371–391. Cambridge: Cambridge University Press.

Craig, D. R. 1985. The sociology of language learning and teaching in a creole situation. In *Language of Inequality,* eds. Wolfson, N., and J. Manes. Berlin: Mouton.

Craig, J. 1979. *Culture Shock.* Singapore: Times Books International.

Crosby, F., and L. Nyquist. 1977. The female register: An empirical study of Lakoff's hypotheses. *Language in Society* 6(3):313–322.

Cummins, J. 1979. Linguistic interdependence and the educational development of bilingual children. *Review of Educational Research* 49:222–251.

Cummins, J. 1980. The construct of language proficiency in bilingual education. In *Current Issues in Bilingual Education,* ed. J. E. Alatis, pp. 81–103 (Georgetown University Roundtable on Language and Linguistics). Washington, DC: Georgetown University Press.

Cummins, J. 1982. Tests, achievement, and bilingual students. *FOCUS* 9:2–7.

Cummins, J., and M. Swain. 1983. Analysis-by-rhetoric: Reading the text or the reader's own prejudices? A reply to Edelsky et al. *Applied Linguistics* 4(1):23–41.

Daikuhara, M. 1986. A study of compliments from a cross-cultural perspective: Japanese vs. American English. *Penn Working Papers in Educational Linguistics* 2(2):103–134.

Dalsheim, J., V. Ephraimson-Abt, Z. Provenzano, and J. Spiegel. 1986. *Investigation of inappropriate questions*. Paper presented at a seminar in sociolinguistics, University of Pennsylvania.

D'Amico-Reisner, L. 1983. An analysis of the surface structure of disapproval exchanges. In *Sociolinguistics and Language Acquisition*, eds. N. Wolfson and E. Judd, pp. 103–115. Rowley. MA: Newbury House.

D'Amico-Reisner, L. 1985. *An Ethnolinguistic Study of Disapproval Exchanges*. Ph.D. dissertation, University of Pennsylvania. To appear in the series Topics in Sociolinguistics, eds. M. Gerritsen and N. Wolfson. Dordrecht, The Netherlands: FORIS Publications.

Danoff, M. N., G. J. Coles, D. H. McLaughlin, and D. J. Reynolds. 1977/1978. *Evaluation of the Impact of ESEA Title VII Spanish/English Bilingual Education Program*, 3 vols. Palo Alto, CA: American Institutes for Research.

DeCamp, D. 1971. The study of pidgin and creole languages. In *Pidginization and Creolization of Languages*, ed. D. Hymes, pp. 13–39. Cambridge: Cambridge University Press.

Dillard, J. L. 1972. *Black English: Its History and Usage in the United States*. New York: Random House.

Donovan, J. 1980. The silence is broken. In *Women and Language in Literature and Society*, eds. S. McConnell-Ginet, R. Borker, and N. Furman. New York: Praeger.

Doroshkin, M. 1969. *Yiddish in America*. New Jersey: Associated Press.

Doughty, C., and T. Pica. 1986. Information-gap tasks: Do they facilitate second language acquisition? *TESOL Quarterly* 20(2):305–325.

DuBois, B. L., and I. Crouch. 1975. The question of tag questions in women's speech: They don't really use more of them, do they? *Language in Society* 4:289–294.

Dutcher, N. 1982. The use of first and second language in primary education: Selected case studies (World Bank Staff Working Paper No. 504). Washington, DC: World Bank.

Dutt, T. K. 1967. *India Without English*. Ambala City, India: Nehru Foundation.

Eakins, B., and G. Eakins. 1976. Verbal turn-taking and exchanges in faculty dialogue. In *The Sociology of the Languages of American Women*, eds. B. L. Dubois and I. Crouch. San Antonio, TX: Trinity University.

Eakins, B., and G. Eakins. 1978. *Sex Differences in Human Communication*. Boston: Houghton Mifflin.

Eble, C. 1975. Etiquette books as linguistic authority. *The Second LACUS Forum*, pp. 468–475. Columbia, South Carolina: Hornbeam Press.

Edelsky, C. 1978. Question intonation and sex roles. *Language in Society* 8(1):15–32.

Edelsky, C. 1981. Who's got the floor? *Language in Society* 10(3):383–421.

Edelsky, C. 1982a. *Genderlects: Beliefs, behavior, and a few research and application issues*. Paper presented at VTEP, Colloquium Series on Women and Languages.

Edelsky, C. 1982b. Writing in a bilingual program: The relation of L1 and L2 texts. *TESOL Quarterly* 16(2):211–228.

Edelsky, C., S. Hudelson, B. Flores, F. Barkin, B. Altwerger, and K. Jilbert. 1983. Semi-lingualism and language deficit. *Applied Linguistics* 4(1):1–22.

Education Week. 1987. Special Report on Bilingual Education. April 1.

Edwards, A. D. 1976. *Language in Culture and Class: The Sociology of Language and Education*. London: Heinemann.

Edwards, V. K. 1979. *The West Indian Language Issue in British Schools: Challenges and Responses*. London: Routledge & Kegan Paul.

Edwards, V. K. 1985. Expressing alienation. Creole in the classroom. In *Language of Inequality*, eds. N. Wolfson and J. Manes, pp. 325–334. Berlin: Mouton.

Eisenstein, M. 1980. Childhood bilingualism and adult language learning aptitude. *International Review of Applied Psychology* 29:159–174.

Eisenstein, M. 1982. A study of social variation in adult second language acquisition. *Language Learning* 32(2):367–391.

Eisenstein, M. 1983a. *Language Variation and the ESL Curriculum*. Washington, DC: Center for Applied Linguistics.

Eisenstein, M. 1983b. Native reactions to nonnative speech: A review of empirical research. *Studies in Second Language Acquisition* 3(2):160–249.

Eisenstein, M. 1986. Target language variation and second-language acquisition: Learning English in New York City. *World Englishes* 5(1):31–46.

Eisenstein, M., and J. W. Bodman. 1985/in press. May God increase your bounty. To appear in *Cross Currents*.

Eisenstein, M., and J. W. Bodman. 1986. "I very appreciate": Expressions of gratitude by native and nonnative speakers of American English. *Applied Linguistics* 7(2):167–185.

Eisenstein, M., and G. Verdi. 1985. The intelligibility of social dialects for working-class adult learners of English. *Language Learning* 35(2):287–298.

Ekka, F. 1984. Status of minority languages in the schools of India. *International Education Journal* 1(1):1–19.

Erickson, F. 1977. Some approaches to inquiry in school-community ethnography. *Anthropology and Education Quarterly* 8:58–69.

Erickson, F. 1981. School-community ethnography. In *Culture and the Bilingual Classroom*, eds. H. T. Trueba, G. P. Guthrie, and K. H-P. Au, p. 29. Rowley, MA: Newbury House.

Erickson, F. 1982. The cultural organization of participation structures in two classrooms of Indian students. In *Doing the Ethnography of Schooling*, ed. G. D. Spindler, pp. 132–174. New York: Holt, Rinehart & Winston.

Erickson, F., and J. Shultz. 1982. *The Counselor as Gatekeeper: Social Interaction in Interviews*. New York: Academic Press.

Ervin-Tripp, S. M. 1969. Sociolinguistics. In *Advances in Experimental Social Psychology*, ed. L. Berkowitz, vol. 4, pp. 93–107. Excerpt published in *Sociolinguistics*, eds. J. B. Pride and J. Holmes, 1972. Harmondsworth, England: Penguin.

Ervin-Tripp, S. 1972. On sociolinguistic rules: Alternation and co-occurrence. In *Directions in Sociolinguistics*, eds. J. Gumperz and D. Hymes, pp. 213–250. New York: Holt, Rinehart & Winston.

Ervin-Tripp, S. M. 1973. Children's sociolinguistic competence and dialect diversity. In *Language Acquisition and Communicative Choice: Essays by Susan Ervin-Tripp*, ed. A. Dil. Stanford, CA: Stanford University Press.

Ervin-Tripp, S. M. 1976. Is Sybil there? The structure of American English directives. *Language in Society* 5(1):25–66.

Farah, I., S.-C. Chen, G. Liao, W. Gallagher, and D. Boxer. 1987. *Ethnographic analysis of compliment data*. Paper presented in course on Cross-Cultural Variation in Speech Behavior, University of Pennsylvania.

Fasold, R. W. 1972. *Tense Marking in Black English: A Linguistic and Social Analysis.* Washington, DC: Center for Applied Linguistics.

Fasold, R. W., and R. Shuy (eds.). 1970. *Teaching Standard English in the Inner City.* Washington, DC: Center for Applied Linguistics.

Ferguson, C. A. 1959. Diglossia. *Word* 15:325–340. Reprinted in *Language Structure and Use,* 1971, pp. 1–26. Stanford: Stanford University Press. Also reprinted in *Language and Social Context,* ed. P. P. Giglioli, 1972. Harmondsworth, England: Penguin.

Ferguson, C. A. 1971. Absence of copula and the notion of simplicity: A study of normal speech, baby talk, foreigner talk, and pidgins. In *Pidginization and Creolization of Languages,* ed. D. Hymes, pp. 141–150. Cambridge: Cambridge University Press.

Ferguson, C. A. 1976. The structure and use of politeness formulas. *Language in Society* 5(2):137–151.

Fisher, E. 1974. Children's books: The second sex, junior division. In *And Jill Came Tumbling After: Sexism in American Education,* eds. J. Stacy, S. Bereaud, and J. Daniels. New York: Dell.

Fishman, J. A. 1965a. *Yiddish in America.* Bloomington, IN: Indiana University Press.

Fishman, J. A. 1965b. Yiddish in America. *International Journal of American Linguistics* 31(2).

Fishman, J. A. (ed.). 1966. *Language Loyalty in the United States: The Maintenance and Perpetuation of Non-English Mother Tongues by American Ethnic Religious Groups.* The Hague: Mouton.

Fishman, J. A. (ed.). 1968. *Readings in the Sociology of Language.* The Hague: Mouton.

Fishman, J. A. 1972. *The Sociology of Language.* Rowley, MA: Newbury House.

Fishman, J. A. (ed.). 1976. *Bilingual Education: An International Sociological Perspective.* Rowley, MA: Newbury House.

Fishman, J. A. 1979. Bilingual education: What and why? In *Bilingual Multicultural Education and the Professional: From Theory to Practice,* eds. H. T. Trueba and C. Barnett-Mizrahi, pp. 11–19. Rowley, MA: Newbury House.

Fishman, J. A. 1980. Bilingual education in the United States under ethnic community auspices. In *Current Issues in Bilingual Education,* ed. J. E. Alatis, pp. 8–13 (Georgetown University Roundtable on Language and Linguistics). Washington, DC: Georgetown University Press.

Fishman, J. A. 1985. The lively life of a "dead" language (or "Everyone knows that Yiddish died long ago"). In *Language of Inequality,* eds. N. Wolfson and J. Manes, pp. 207–220. Berlin: Mouton.

Fishman, J. A., R. L. Cooper, and A. W. Conrad. 1977. *The Spread of English: The Sociology of English as an Additional Language.* Rowley, MA: Newbury House.

Fishman, J. A., C. A. Ferguson, and J. Das Gupta. 1968. *Language Problems of Developing Nations.* New York: Wiley.

Fishman, P. 1978a. What do couples talk about when they're alone? In *Women's Language and Style,* eds. D. Butturff and E. L. Epstein, pp. 11–22. Akron, OH: L & S Books.

Fishman, P. 1978b. Interaction: The work women do. *Social Problems* 24:397–406. Reprinted in *Language, Gender and Society,* ed. B. Thorne, C. Kramarae, and N. Henley, 1983, pp. 89–110. Rowley, MA: Newbury House.

Fought, J. 1985. Patterns of sociolinguistic inequality in Mesoamerica. In *Language of Inequality,* eds. N. Wolfson and J. Manes, pp. 21–39. Berlin: Mouton.

Frank, F., and F. Anshen. 1983. *Language and the Sexes.* Albany, NY: SUNY Press.

Fraser, B. 1978. Acquiring social competence in a second language. *RELC Journal* 9(2):1–26.

Fraser, B. 1981. On apologizing. In *Conversational Routine*, ed. F. Coulmas, The Hague: Mouton.

Fraser, B., E. Rintell, and J. Walters. 1980. An approach to conducting research on the acquisition of pragmatic competence in a second language. In *Discourse Analysis in Second Language Acquisition*, ed. D. Larsen-Freeman. Rowley, MA: Newbury House.

French, K. 1981. *The uses of first names or "Just ask for Janice."* Paper presented at the Annual Meeting of the American Anthropological Association, Los Angeles, December.

Gal, S. 1978. Peasant men can't get wives. *Language in Society* 7:1–16.

Garfinkel, H. 1964. Studies of the routine grounds of everyday activities. *Social Problems* 11(3).

Garfinkel, H. 1967. *Studies in Ethnomethodology*. Englewood Cliffs, NJ: Prentice-Hall.

Garfinkel, H. 1972. Remarks on ethnomethodology. In *Directions in Sociolinguistics: The Ethnography of Communication*, eds. J. J. Gumperz and D. Hymes. New York: Holt, Rinehart and Winston.

Gass, S., and L. Selinker. 1983. *Language Transfer in Language Learning*. Rowley, MA: Newbury House.

Geertz, C. 1972. Linguistic etiquette. In *Sociolinguistics*, eds. J. B. Pride and J. Holmes, pp. 167–179. Harmondsworth, England: Penguin.

Geertz, C. 1973. *The Interpretation of Cultures*. New York: Basic Books.

Giglioli, P. P. (ed.). 1972. *Language and Social Context*. Harmondsworth, England: Penguin.

Giles, H., and P. F. Powesland. 1975. *Speech Style and Social Evaluation*. London: Academic Press.

Giles, H., and P. M. Smith. 1979. Accommodation theory: Optimal levels of convergence. In *Language and Social Psychology*, eds. H. Giles and R. N. St. Clair, pp. 45–65. Baltimore: University Park Press.

Giles, H., D. M. Taylor, and R. V. Bourhis. 1973. Towards a theory of interpersonal accommodation through speech: Some Canadian data. *Language in Society* 2(2):177–192.

Giles, H., P. Smith, C. Browne, S. Whiteman, and J. Williams. 1980. Women's speech: The voice of feminism. In *Women and Language in Literature and Society*, eds. S. McConnell-Ginet, R. Borker, and N. Furman. New York: Praeger.

Glazer, N. 1978. The proccess and problems of language maintenance: An integrative review. In *A Pluralistic Nation: The Language Issue in the United States*, eds. M. A. Lourie and N. F. Conklin, pp. 32–43. Rowley, MA: Newbury House.

Glazer, N., and D. P. Moynihan. 1970. *Beyond the Melting Pot: The Negroes, Puerto Ricans, Jews, Italians, and Irish of New York City*. 2nd ed. Cambridge, MA: MIT Press.

Godard, D. 1977. Same settings, different norms: Phone call beginnings in France and the United States. *Language in Society* 6:209–219.

Godfrey, D. L. 1980. A discourse analysis of tense in adult ESL monologues. In *Discourse Analysis in Second Language Research*, ed. D. Larsen-Freeman. Rowley, MA: Newbury House.

Goffman, E. 1956. The nature of deference and demeanor. *American Anthropologist* 58(3):473–502.

Goffman, E. 1971. *Relations in Public*. New York: Harper Colophon Books.

Goffman, E. 1976. Replies and responses. *Language in Society* 5(3):257–313.

Goffman, E. 1981. *Forms of Talk*. Philadelphia: University of Pennsylvania Press.

Goldberg, P. 1974. Are women prejudiced against women? In *And Jill Came Tumbling After: Sexism in American Education*, eds. J. Stacy, S. Bereaud, and J. Daniels. New York: Dell.

Goodenough, W. H. 1964. Cultural anthropology and linguistics. In *Language in Culture and Society*, ed. D. Hymes, pp. 36–37. New York: Harper & Row.

Goodman, M. F. 1964. *A Comparative Study of Creole French Dialects*. The Hague: Mouton.

Goodwin, M. 1980. Directive-response speech sequences in girls' and boys' task activities. In *Women and Language in Literature and Society*, eds. S. McConnell-Ginet, R. Borker, and N. Furman. New York: Praeger.

Goody, E. 1978. *Questions and Politeness: Strategies in Social Interaction*. Cambridge: Cambridge University Press.

Gordon, D., and G. Lakoff. 1975. Conversational postulates. In *Speech Acts*, eds. P. Cole and J. Morgan, vol. 3 of *Syntax and Semantics*. New York: Academic Press.

Graham, A. 1973. The making of a nonsexist dictionary. *Ms* 2(Dec.):12–16. Reprinted in *Language and Sex: Difference and Dominance*, eds. B. Thorne and N. Henley, 1975, pp. 57–63. Rowley, MA: Newbury House.

Grice, H. P. 1975. Logic and conversation. In *Speech Acts*, eds. P. Cole and J. Morgan, vol. 3 of *Syntax and Semantics*. New York: Academic Press.

Grief, E. B., and J. B. Gleason. 1980. Hi, thanks and goodbye: More routine information. *Language in Society* 9(2):156–166.

Gumperz, J. J. 1968. The speech community. In *International Encyclopedia of the Social Sciences*, pp. 381–386. New York: Macmillan. Reprinted in *Language and Social Context*, ed. P. P. Giglioli, 1972. Harmondsworth, England: Penguin.

Gumperz, J. J. 1978. Dialect and conversational inference in urban communication. *Language in Society* 7(3):393–409.

Gumperz, J. J. 1982a. *Discourse Strategies* (Studies in Interactional Linguistics 1). Cambridge: Cambridge University Press.

Gumperz, J. J. 1982b. *Language and Social Identity* (Studies in Interactional Linguistics 2). Cambridge: Cambridge University Press.

Gumperz, J. J., and D. Hymes (eds.). 1964. The ethnography of communication. *American Anthropologist* 66(6), pt. II.

Gumperz, J. J., and D. Hymes (eds.). 1972. *Directions in Sociolinguistics: The Ethnography of Communication*. New York: Holt, Rinehart & Winston.

Hakuta, K. 1984. Bilingual education in the public eye: A case study of New Haven, Connecticut. *NABE Journal* 9:53–76.

Hakuta, K. 1986. *Mirror of Language: The Debate on Bilingualism*. New York: Basic Books.

Hall, R. S., Jr. 1962. The life-cycle of pidgin languages. *Lingua* 11:151–156.

Hall, R. A., Jr. 1964. *Introductory Linguistics*. Philadelphia: Chilton.

Hall, R. A., Jr. 1966. *Pidgin and Creole Languages*. Ithaca, NY: Cornell University Press.

Halliday, M. A. K. 1973. *Explorations in the Functions of Language*. London: Edward Arnold.

Halliday, M. A. K., A. McIntosh, and P. Strevens. 1964. *The Linguistic Sciences and Language Teaching*. London: Longmans.

Hardman de Bautista, M. 1985. The imperial languages of the Andes. In *Language of Inequality*, eds. N. Wolfson and J. Manes, pp. 182–193. Berlin: Mouton.

Harrison, W., C. Prator, and G. R. Tucker. 1975. *English-Language Policy Survey of Jordan: A Case Study in Language Planning*. Washington, DC: Center for Applied Linguistics.

Hartman, P. L., and E. L. Judd. 1978. Sexism and TESOL materials. *TESOL Quarterly* 12:383–393.

Hatch, E. M. 1978. Discourse analysis and second language acquisition. In *Second Language Acquisition*, ed. E. M. Hatch, pp. 401–435. Rowley, MA: Newbury House.

Haugen, E. 1972. *The Ecology of Language: Essays by Einar Haugen*, ed. A. S. Dil. Stanford, CA: Stanford University Press.

Haugen, E. 1973. The curse of Babel. In *Language as a Human Problem*, eds. E. Haugen and M. Bloomfield, pp. 33–43. New York: W. W. Norton.

Haugen, E. 1985. The language of imperialism: Unity or pluralism? In *Language of Inequality*, eds. N. Wolfson and J. Manes, pp. 3–17. Rowley, MA: Newbury House. Reprinted from *Language and Society* 1969, pp. 65–82, under the title *Linguistic Pluralism as a National Goal*.

Heath, S. B. 1983. *Ways with Words: Language, Life, and Work in Communities and Classrooms*. Cambridge: Cambridge University Press.

Henley, N. 1975. Power, sex, and nonverbal communication. In *Language and Sex*, eds. B. Thorne and N. Henley. Rowley, MA: Newbury House.

Henley, N. 1977. *Body Politics: Power, Sex and Nonverbal Communication*. Englewood Cliffs, NJ: Prentice-Hall.

Herbert, R. K. 1986a. Say "thank you"—or something. *American Speech* 61(1):76–88.

Herbert, R. K. 1986b. *Sex-based differences in compliment behavior*. Paper presented at the American Anthropological Association meeting, December 1986.

Herbert, R. K. 1987. *Form, frequency, and function in speech acts: Analyzing compliment structures*. 1987. Paper presented at Conference on New Ways of Analyzing Variation (NWAV—XVI), October, 1987.

Herbert, R. K., and A. Mickiewicz. In press. The ethnography of English compliment responses: A contrastive sketch. To appear in Oleksy, W. (ed.) *Contrastive Pragmatics*. Amsterdam: Benjamins.

Herbert, R. K., and H. S. Straight. In press. *Compliment-rejection versus compliment-avoidance: Listener-based versus speaker-based pragmatic strategies*. Paper presented at Sociolinguistics Symposium 6, April 1986, University of Newcastle Upon Tyne, England.

Hoenigswald, H. H. 1960. *Language Change and Linguistic Reconstructions*. Chicago: University of Chicago Press.

Holmes, J. In press. Compliments and compliment responses in New Zealand English. To appear in *Anthropological Linguistics*.

Holmes, J. Paying compliments: A sex-preferential positive politeness strategy. Submitted to the *Journal of Pragmatics*.

Holmes, J., and D. F. Brown. 1977. Sociolinguistic competence and second language learning. *Topics in Culture Learning* 5:72–82.

Holmes, J., and D. F. Brown. 1987. Teachers and students learning about compliments. *TESOL Quarterly* 21(3):523–546.

Hoover, M. 1978. Community attitudes toward black English. *Language in Society* 7(1):65–87.

Hornberger, N. 1985. *Bilingual Education and Quechua Language Maintenance in Highland Puno, Peru.* Ph.D. dissertation, University of Wisconsin-Madison. To appear in the series Topics in Sociolinguistics, eds. M. Gerritsen and N. Wolfson. Dordrecht, The Netherlands: FORIS Publications.

Hornberger, N. 1987a. Bilingual education success, but policy failure. *Language in Society* 16(2):205–226.

Hornberger, N. 1987b. Schooltime, classtime, and academic learning time in rural highland Peru. *Anthropology and Education Quarterly* 18(3):207–221.

Hymes, D. 1962. The ethnography of speaking. In *Anthropology and Human Behavior,* eds. T. Gladwin and W. C. Sturdevant, pp. 15–53. Washington, DC: Anthropological Society of Washington. Reprinted in *Readings in the Sociology of Language,* ed. J. A. Fishman, 1968, pp. 99–138. The Hague: Mouton.

Hymes, D. 1967. Models of the interaction of language and social setting. *Journal of Social Issues* 23(2):8–28.

Hymes, D. 1971a. Introduction. In *Pidginization and Creolization of Languages,* ed. D. Hymes, pp. 65–90. London: Cambridge University Press.

Hymes, D. 1971b. *On Communicative Competence.* Philadelphia: University of Pennsylvania Press. Appears in part in *Sociolinguistics,* eds. J. B. Pride and J. Holmes, 1972, pp. 269–293. Harmondsworth, England: Penguin. Also in *The Communicative Approach to Language Teaching,* eds. C. J. Brumfit and K. Johnson, 1979, pp. 5–26. Oxford: Oxford University Press.

Hymes, D. 1971c. *Pidginization and Creolization of Languages.* London: Cambridge University Press.

Hymes, D. 1972a. Editorial introduction to *Language in Society* 1(1).

Hymes, D. 1972b. Models of the interactions of language and social life. In *Directions in Sociolinguistics,* eds. J. J. Gumperz and D. Hymes, pp. 35–71. New York: Holt, Rinehart & Winston.

Hymes, D. 1973. Speech and language: On the origins and foundations of inequality among speakers. In *Language as a Human Problem,* eds. E. Haugen and M. Bloomfield, pp. 45–71. New York: W. W. Norton.

Hymes, D. 1974a. *Foundations in Sociolinguistics: An Ethnographic Approach.* Philadelphia: University of Pennsylvania Press.

Hymes, D. 1974b. Ways of speaking. In *Explorations in the Ethnography of Speaking,* eds. R. Bauman and J. Sherzer, pp. 433–451. Cambridge: Cambridge University Press.

Hymes, V. 1975. The ethnography of linguistic intuitions at Warm Springs. *Proceedings of the 1975 LACUS Forum.* Columbia, SC: Hornbeam Press.

Irvine, J. T. 1974. Strategies of status manipulation in the Wolof greeting. In *Explorations in the Ethnography of Speaking,* eds. R. Bauman and J. Sherzer, pp. 167–192. Cambridge: Cambridge University Press.

Irvine, J. T. 1986. *Domains of description in the ethnography of speaking: A retrospective on the "speech community."* Paper presented at the annual meeting of the American Anthropological Association, Philadelphia.

Jakar, V., P. Calzada, S.-L. Qiu, and K. Kim. 1987. *Summary of findings on compliment behavior.* Paper presented in course on Cross-Cultural Variation in Speech Behavior, University of Pennsylvania.

Jamaluddin, N., N. Nongshah, N. A. R. Taufek, and N. Zulkifli. 1986. *Inappropriate questions.* Paper presented at a seminar in sociolinguistics, University of Pennsylvania.

Jesperson, O. 1922. *Language: Its Nature, Development and Origin.* London: Allyn and Unwin.

Johnson, K. 1982. *Communicative Syllabus Design and Methodology*. Oxford: Pergamon.

Kachru, B. 1982a. Models for non-native Englishes. In *The Other Tongue: English Across Cultures*, ed. B. Kachru, pp. 31–58. Oxford: Pergamon Press.

Kachru, B. (ed.). 1982b. *The Other Tongue: English Across Cultures*. Oxford: Pergamon Press.

Kalcik, S. 1975. "Like Ann's gynecologist or the time I was almost raped": Personal narrative in women's rap groups. *Journal of American Folklore* January–March.

Kaplan, M. 1983. *The social implications of saying goodbye*. Paper presented at a seminar in sociolinguistics, University of Pennsylvania.

Katriel, T. 1986. *Talking Straight: Dugri Speech in Israeli Sabra Culture*. Cambridge: Cambridge University Press.

Katriel, T. 1987. *"Style gone wrong": Cultural barriers to communication between Israeli Jews and Arabs*. Paper presented at the Third Annual Conference of the Association of Israel Studies, Burlington, VT, June.

Katriel, T., and G. Philipsen. 1981. "What we need is communication": "Communication" as a cultural category in some American speech. *Communication Monographs* 48:302–317.

Keenan, E. O. 1974. Norm-makers, norm-breakers: Uses of speech by men and women in a Malagasy community. In *Explorations in the Ethnography of Speaking*, eds. R. Bauman and J. Sherzer, pp. 125–144. Cambridge: Cambridge University Press.

Keenan, E. O. 1976. The universality of conversational implicature. *Language in Society* 5:67–80.

Kipers, P. 1983. *Partings: A sociolinguistic perspective*. Paper presented at a seminar in sociolinguistics, University of Pennsylvania.

Kipers, P. 1986. Initiation and response in service encounter closings. *Penn Working Papers in Educational Linguistics* Fall:1–16.

Kjolseth, J. R. 1975. Bilingual education programs in the United States: For assimilation or pluralism? In *Bilingualism in the Southwest*, ed. P. R. Turner, pp. 3–27. Tucson: University of Arizona Press. Also appears in *The Language of Education of Minority Children*, ed. B. Spolsky, 1972, pp. 94–121. Rowley, MA: Newbury House.

Kloss, H. 1966. German-American language maintenance efforts. In *Language Loyalty in the United States*, ed. J. A. Fishman. The Hague: Mouton.

Knapp, M. L., R. P. Hart, G. W. Friedrich, and G. M. Shulman. 1973. The rhetoric of goodbye: Verbal and nonverbal correlates of human leave-taking. *Speech Monographs* 40:182–198.

Knapp, M. L., R. Hopper, and R. A. Bell. 1984. Compliments: A descriptive taxonomy. *Journal of Communication* 34(4):12–31.

Kolodny, A. 1980. Honing a habitual languagescape: Women's images for the new world frontiers. In *Women and Language in Literature and Society*, eds. S. McConnell-Ginet, R. Borker, and N. Furman. New York: Praeger.

Kramer, C. 1975. Sex-related differences in address systems. *Anthropological Linguistics* 17(5):198–210.

Kramerae, C. 1980. Proprietors of language. In *Women and Language in Literature and Society*, eds. S. McConnell-Ginet, R. Borker, and N. Furman. New York: Praeger.

Krivonos, P., and M. Knapp. 1975. Initiating communication: What do you say when you say hello? *Central States Speech Journal* 26:115–125.

Kurath, H., and R. McDavid. 1961. *The Pronunciation of English in the Atlantic States*. Ann Arbor: University of Michigan Press.

Labov, W. 1963. Social motivation of a sound change. *Word* 19:273–309.

Labov, W. 1966. *The Social Stratification of English in New York City*. Washington, DC: Center for Applied Linguistics.

Labov, W. 1969. *The Logic of Nonstandard English* (Georgetown Monographs on Language and Linguistics 22). Washington, DC: Georgetown University, Center for Applied Linguistics. Reprinted in *Language in the Inner City: STUDIES IN Black English Vernacular*, 1972, pp. 201–240. Philadelphia: University of Pennsylvania Press.

Labov, W. 1970a. *The Structure of Nonstandard English*. Washington, DC: National Council of Teachers of English and the Center for Applied Linguistics.

Labov, W. 1970b. The study of language in its social context. *Studium Generale* 20:30–87.

Labov, W. 1972. *Sociolinguistic Patterns*. Philadelphia: University of Pennsylvania Press.

Labov, W. 1981. Field methods of the project on linguistic change and variation. *Working Papers in Sociolinguistics* 81:1–41.

Labov, W. 1982. Objectivity and commitment in linguistic science: The case of the black English trial in Ann Arbor. *Language in Society* 11(2):165–201.

Labov, W., and J. Waletzky. 1967. Narrative analysis. In *Essays on the Verbal and Visual Arts*. Seattle: University of Washington Press.

Labov, W., P. Cohen, O. Robins, and J. Lewis. 1968. *A Study of the Non-Standard English of Negro and Puerto Rican Speakers in New York City*. Final Report, Cooperative Research Project 3288, vols. 1 and 2. Washington, DC: Office of Education.

Lakoff, R. 1973. Language and woman's place. *Language in Society* 2(1):45–80. Reprinted in *Language and Woman's Place*, 1975, pp. 3–50. New York: Harper Colophon Books.

Lambert, W. E., and G. R. Tucker. 1972. *The Bilingual Education of Children: The St. Lambert Experiment*. Rowley, MA: Newbury House.

Lambert, W. E., R. C. Hodgson, R. C. Gardner, and S. Fillenbaum. 1960, Evaluation reactions to spoken languages. *Journal of Abnormal and Social Psychology* 60:44–51.

Lau v. *Nichols*, 414 U.S. 563 (1974).

Leith, D. 1983. *A Social History of English*. London: Routledge & Kegan Paul.

Levinson, S. C. 1983. *Pragmatics*. Cambridge: Cambridge University Press.

Mackay, D. 1983. Prescriptive grammar and the pronoun problem. In *Language, Gender, and Society*, eds. B. Thorne, C. Kramerae, and N. Henley. Rowley, MA: Newbury House.

Mackay, D., and D. Fulkerson. 1979. On the comprehension and production of pronouns. *Journal of Verbal Learning and Verbal Behavior* 18:661–673.

Maltz, D., and R. Borker. 1983. A cultural approach to male–female miscommunication. In *Language and Social Identity*, ed. J. Gumperz. Cambridge: Cambridge University Press.

Manes, J. 1983. Compliments: A mirror of cultural values. In *Sociolinguistics and Language Acquisition*, eds. N. Wolfson and J. Manes, pp. 96–102. Rowley, MA: Newbury House.

Manes, J., and N. Wolfson. 1981. The compliment formula. In *Conversational Routine*, ed. F. Coulmas, pp. 115–132. The Hague: Mouton.

Martyna, W. 1978. *Using and understanding the generic masculine: A social psychological approach to language and the sexes*. Ph.D. dissertation, Stanford University.

Martyna, W. 1980. The psychology of the generic masculine. In *Women and Language in Literature and Society*, eds. S. McConnell-Ginet, R. Borker, and N. Furman, pp. 68–78. New York: Praeger.

Martyna, W. 1983. Beyond the he/man approach: The case for non-sexist language change. *Signs: Journal of Women in Culture and Society* 5:482–493. Also in *Language, Gender and Society,* ed. B. Thorne, C. Kramarae, and N. Henley, 1983, pp. 25–87. Rowley, MA: Newbury House.

Mazrui, A. A. 1973. The English language and the origins of African nationalism. In *Varieties of Present-Day English,* eds. R. W. Bailey and J. R. Robinson, pp. 56–76. New York: Macmillan.

McConnell-Ginet, S. 1978. Address forms in sexual politics. In *Women's Language and Style,* eds. D. Butturff and E. L. Epstein, pp. 23–36. Akron, OH: University of Akron Press.

McConnell-Ginet, S. 1980. Linguistics and the feminist challenge. In *Women and Language in Literature and Society,* eds. S. McConnell-Ginet, R. Borker, and N. Furman. New York: Praeger.

McConnell-Ginet, S. 1983. Intonation in a man's world. In *Language, Gender, and Society,* eds. B. Thorne, C. Kramerae and N. Henley. Rowley, MA: Newbury House.

McConnell-Ginet, S., R., Borker, and N. Furman (eds.). 1980. *Women and Language in Literature and Society.* New York: Praeger.

McDavid, R. I., Jr. 1980. *Varieties of American English,* selected and introduced by Answar S. Dil. Stanford, CA: Stanford University Press.

McDermott, R. 1977. Social relations as contexts for learning in school. *Harvard Educational Review* 47:198–213.

Mead, M. 1952. Preface. In *Life Is with People: The Culture of the Shtetl,* M. Zborowski and E. Herzog, pp. 22–28. New York: Schocken Books.

Mehan, H. 1972. Language using abilities. *Language Sciences* 22:1–10.

Mehan, H. 1979. *Learning Lessons: Social Organization in the Classroom.* Cambridge, MA: Harvard University Press.

Mehan, H., and H. Wood. 1975. *The Reality of Ethnomethodology.* New York: Wiley.

Mehrotra, R. R. 1982. Indian English: A sociolinguistic profile. In *New Englishes,* ed. J. B. Pride. Rowley, MA: Newbury House.

Mey, J. 1985. *Whose Language?: A Study in Linguistic Pragmatics.* Philadelphia: John Benjamins.

Miller, C., and K. Swift. 1976. *Words and Women.* Garden City, NY: Doubleday.

Milroy, L. 1980. *Language and Social Networks* (Language in Society 2). Oxford: Blackwell.

Milroy, L., and J. Milroy. 1977. Speech and context in an urban setting. *Belfast Working Papers in Language and Linguistics* 2(1).

Munby, J. 1978. *Communicative Syllabus Design.* Cambridge: Cambridge University Press.

Nader, L. 1968. A note on attitudes and the use of language. In *Readings in the Sociology of Language,* ed. J. Fishman. The Hague: Mouton. Also appeared in *Anthropological Linguistics* 4(6):25–29, 1962.

Nakane, C. 1972. *Japanese Society.* Berkeley: University of California Press.

Neustupny, J. V. 1971. A model of linguistic distance. *Linguistic Communication* 5:115–132.

Nichols, P. C. 1980. Women in their speech communities. In *Women and Language in Literature and Society,* eds. S. McConnell-Ginet, R. Borker, and N. Furman. New York: Praeger.

Nichols, P. C. 1983. Linguistic options and choices for black women in the rural South. In *Language, Gender, and Society,* eds. B. Thorne, C. Kramerae, and N. Henley. Rowley, MA: Newbury House.

Nilsen, A. P. 1977. Sexism in children's books and elementary teaching materials. In *Sexism and Language,* ed. A. P. Nilsen, H. Bosmajian, H. L. Gershuny, and J. P. Stanley, pp. 161–179. Urbana, IL: National Council of Teachers of English.

Nilsen, A. P., H. Bosmajian, H. L. Gershuny, and J. P. Stanley (eds.). 1977. *Sexism and Language.* Urbana, IL: National Council of Teachers of English.

O'Barr, W. M., and B. Atkins. 1980. "Women's language" or "powerless language"? In *Women and Language in Literature and Society,* eds. S. McConnell-Ginet, R. Borker, and N. Furman, pp. 93–110. New York: Praeger.

O'Barr, W. M., and J. F. O'Barr (eds.). 1976. *Language and Politics.* The Hague: Mouton.

Ochs Keenan, E. 1976. On the universality of conversational implicatures. *Language in Society* 5(1):67–80.

Olshtain, E. 1983. Sociocultural competence and language transfer: The case of apology. In *Language Transfer in Language Learning* (eds.) S. Gass and L. Selinker, pp. 232–249. Rowley, MA: Newbury House.

Olshtain, E., and S. Blum-Kulka. 1985. Degree of approximation: Nonnative reactions to native speech act behavior. In *Input in Second Language Acquisition,* eds. S. Gass and C. Madden, pp. 303–325. Rowley, MA: Newbury House.

Olshtain, E., and A. Cohen. 1983. Apology: A speech act set. In *Sociolinguistics and Language Acquisition,* eds. N. Wolfson and E. Judd. Rowley, MA: Newbury House.

Olshtain, E., and A. Cohen. 1987. *The learning of complex speech act behavior.* Paper presented at the Colloquium on TESOL and Sociolinguistics, Eighth Annual TESOL Convention, Miami, Florida.

Olshtain, E., and L. Weinbach. 1986. Complaints—A study of speech act behavior among native and nonnative speakers of Hebrew. In *The Pragmatic Perspective: Selected Papers* from the 1985 International Pragmatics Conference, eds. M. B. Papi and J. Verscheuren. Philadelphia: John Benjamins.

O'Neill, P. G. 1966. *A programmed guide to respect language in modern Japanese.* London: The English Universities Press Limited for the School of Oriental and African Studies, University of London.

Ovando, C. J. 1983. Bilingual/bicultural education: Its legacy and its future. *Phi Delta Kappan* 64:538, 564–566.

Owen, M. 1980. *Apologies and Remedial Interchanges.* The Hague: Mouton.

Paulston, C. B. 1974a. *Developing communicative competence: Goals, procedures and techniques.* Paper presented at the Lackland Air Force Base Defense Language Institute.

Paulston, C. B. 1974b. Linguistic and communicative competence. *TESOL Quarterly* 8(4):347–367.

Paulston, C. B. 1976. Pronouns of address in Swedish: Social class semantics and a changing system. *Language in Society* 5(3):359–386.

Paulston, C. B. 1980. *Bilingual Education: Theories and Issues.* Rowley, MA: Newbury House.

Paulston, C. B., and N. M. Bruder. 1976. *Teaching English as a Second Language: Techniques and Procedures.* Cambridge: Winthrop.

Peal, E., and W. Lambert. 1962. The relation of bilingualism to intelligence. *Psychological Monographs* 76:1–23.

Penelope, J., and S. Wolfe. 1983. Consciousness as style: Style as aesthetic. In *Language, Gender, and Society,* eds. B. Thorne, C. Kramarae, and N. Henley. Rowley, MA: Newbury House.

Philips, S. U. 1970. Acquisition of rules for appropriate speech usage. In *Report of the 21st Roundtable Meeting*, ed. J. Alatis, pp. 77–96 (Monograph Series in Languages and Linguistics, 23). Washington, DC: Georgetown University Press.

Philips, S. U. 1972. Participant structures and communicative competence: Warm Springs children in community and classroom: In *Functions of Language in the Classroom*, eds. C. Cazden, D. Hymes, and V. John. New York: Teachers College Press.

Philips, S. U. 1976. Some sources of cultural variability in the regulation of talk. *Language in Society* 5(1):81–85.

Philips, S. U. 1982. *The Invisible Culture: Communication in Classroom and Community in the Warm Springs Indian Reservation*. New York: Longman.

Philips, S. U., S. Steele, and C. Tanz. (eds.). 1987. *Language, Gender and Sex in Comparative Perspective*. Cambridge: Cambridge University Press.

Philipsen, G., and M. Huspek. 1985. A bibliography of sociolinguistic studies of personal address. *Anthropological Linguistics* 27(1):94–101.

Pica, T. 1983. The article in American English: What the textbooks don't tell us. In *Sociolinguistics and Language Acquisition*, eds. N. Wolfson and E. Judd, pp. 222–233. Rowley, MA: Newbury House.

Pica, T. 1985a. Communicative language teaching as an aid to classroom second language acquisition: Some insights from research. *Anglo-American Studies* 5:5–13.

Pica, T. 1985b. The selective impact of classroom instruction on second-language acquisition. *Applied Linguistics* 6(3):214–222.

Pica, T. 1987. Second language acquisition, social interaction, and the classroom. *Applied Linguistics* 8(1):3–21.

Pica, T., and C. Doughty. 1988. Effects of task and participation pattern on classroom interaction. In *Second Language Discourse: A Textbook of Current Research*, ed. J. Fine. Norwood, NJ: Ablex.

Pica, T., C. Doughty, and R. Young. 1986. Making input comprehensible: Do interactional modifications help? *I.T.L. Review of Applied Linguistics*. 72:1–25.

Pica, T., R. Young, and C. Doughty. 1987. The impact of interaction on comprehension. *TESOL Quarterly* 21(4):737–758.

Pomerantz, A. 1978. Compliment responses: Notes on the co-operation of multiple constraints. In *Studies in the Organization of Conversational Interaction*, ed. J. Schenkein. New York: Academic Press.

Prator, C. 1968. The British heresy in TESL. In *Language Problems of Developing Nations*, eds. J. Fishman, C. Ferguson, and J. Das Gupta, pp. 459–477. New York: Wiley.

Preston, D. 1986. Five visions of America. *Language in Society* 15:221–240.

Pride, J. B. 1979. *Sociolinguistic Aspects of Language Learning and Teaching*. Oxford: Oxford University Press.

Pride, J. B. (ed.). 1982. *New Englishes*. Rowley, MA: Newbury House.

Pride, J. B., and J. Holmes (eds.). 1972. *Sociolinguistics: Selected Readings*. Harmondsworth, England: Penguin.

Rabinowitz, J. 1983. *Parting talk in short face-to-face service encounters*. Paper for independent study in sociolinguistics, University of Pennsylvania.

Reich, A. 1974. Teaching is a good profession . . . for a woman. In *And Jill Came Tumbling After: Sexism in American Education*, eds. J. Stacy, S. Bereaud, and J. Daniels. New York: Dell.

Reisman, K. 1974. Contrapuntal conversation in an Antiguan Village. In *Explorations in the*

Ethnography of Speaking, eds. R. Bauman and J. Sherzer, pp. 110–124. Cambridge: Cambridge University Press.

Richards, J. C. 1980. Conversation. *TESOL Quarterly* 14(4):413–432.

Richards, J. C., and R. W. Schmidt (eds.). 1983. *Language and Communication* (Applied Linguistics and Language Study). London: Longman.

Rickford, J. R. 1979. *Variation in a Creole continuum: Quantitative and implicational approaches*. Ph.D dissertation, University of Pennsylvania.

Rickford, J. R. 1985. Standard and non-standard language attitudes in a Creole continuum. In *Sociolinguistics and Language Acquisition*, eds. N. Wolfson and E. Judd, pp. 145–160. Rowley, MA: Newbury House.

Rivers, W. 1973. From linguistic to communicative competence. *TESOL Quarterly* 7(1):25–34.

Romaine, S. 1980. A critical overview of the methodology of urban British sociolinguistics. *English World-Wide* 1(2):163–198.

Romaine, S. 1982. *Sociolinguistic Variation in Speech Communities*. London: Edward Arnold.

Rosaldo, M. Z. 1982. The things we do with words: Illongot speech acts and speech act theory in philosophy. *Language in Society* 11(2).

Rosen, H. 1972. *Language and Class: A Critical Look at the Theories of Basil Bernstein*. Bristol, England: Falling Wall Press.

Rubin, J. 1970. *National Bilingualism in Paraguay*. The Hague: Mouton.

Rubin, J. 1983. How to tell when someone is saying "no" revisited. In *Sociolinguistics and Language Acquisition*, eds. N. Wolfson and E. Judd, pp. 10–17. Rowley, MA: Newbury House.

Rubin, J. 1985. The special relation of Guarani and Spanish in Paraguay. In *Language of Inequality*, eds. N. Wolfson and J. Manes, pp. 111–120. Berlin: Mouton.

Rubin, R. B. 1981. Ideal traits and terms of address for male and female college professors. *Journal of Personality and Social Psychology* 41(5):966–974.

Sacks, H. 1972. An initial investigation of the usability of conversational data for doing sociology. In *Studies in Interaction*, ed. D. Sudnow. New York: The Free Press.

Sacks, H. 1974. An analysis of the course of a joke's telling in conversation. In *Explorations in the Ethnography of Speaking*, eds. R. Bauman and J. Sherzer. Cambridge: Cambridge University Press.

Sacks, H., E. Schegloff, and G. Jefferson. 1974. A simplest systematics for the analysis of turn-taking in conversation. *Language* 50:696–735.

Santiago, R. 1982. The future of ESL and Bilingual Education in the next decade. *TESOL Newsletter* 16(3).

Satell, J. W. 1983. Men, inexpressiveness, and power. In *Language, Gender and Society*, eds. B. Thorne, C. Kramerae, and N. Henley. Rowley, MA: Newbury House.

Savignon, S. 1972. Teaching for communicative competence: A research report. *Audiovisual Language Journal* 10(3):153–162.

Savignon, S. 1983. *Communicative Competence: Theory and Classroom Practice*. Reading, MA: Addison-Wesley.

Saville-Troike, M. (ed.). 1977. *Linguistics and Anthropology*. Washington, DC: Georgetown University Press.

Schegloff, E. 1968. Sequencing in conversational openings. *American Anthropologist* 70:1075–1095. Reprinted in *Directions in Sociolinguistics*, eds. J. J. Gumperz and D. Hymes, 1972, pp. 346–380. New York: Holt, Rinehart & Winston.

Schegloff, E., and H. Sacks. 1973. Opening up closings. *Semiotica* 8:289–327. Reprinted in *Ethnomethodology: Selected Readings,* ed. R. Turner. Baltimore: Penguin.

Scheman, N. 1980. Anger and the politics of naming. In *Women and Language in Literature and Society,* eds. S. McConnell-Ginet, R. Borker, and N. Furman. New York: Praeger.

Schmandt, L. 1983. *Leave taking in natural speech settings: A sociolinguistic study.* M. A. long paper, Department of General Linguistics, University of Pittsburgh.

Schmidt, R. W. 1975. *Sociolinguistic rules and foreign language teaching.* Paper presented at the Symposium on Sociolinguistics and Applied Anthropology, Annual Meeting of the Society for Applied Anthropology, Amsterdam.

Schmidt, R. W. 1983. Interaction, acculturation, and the acquisition of communicative competence: A case study of an adult. In *Sociolinguistics and Language Acquisition,* eds. N. Wolfson and E. Judd, pp. 137–174. Rowley, MA: Newbury House.

Schmidt, R. W., and J. C. Richards. 1980. Speech acts and second language learning. *Applied Linguistics* 1(2):129–157.

Schneider, D. M. 1968. *American Kinship: A Cultural Account.* Englewood Cliffs, NJ: Prentice-Hall.

Schulz, M. 1975. The semantic derogation of women. In *Language and Sex: Difference and Dominance,* eds. B. Thorne and N. Henley, pp. 64–73. Rowley, MA: Newbury House.

Schutz, A. 1967. *The Phenomenology of the Social World.* Evanston, IL: Northwest University Press.

Scollon, R., and S. B. K. Scollon. 1981. *Narrative, Literacy and Face in Interethnic Communication.* Norwood, IL: Ablex.

Scollon, R., and S. B. K. Scollon. 1983. Face in inter-ethnic communication. In *Language and Communication,* eds. J. Richards and R. Schmidt. London: Longman.

Searle, J. R. 1965. What is a speech act? In *Philosophy in America,* ed. M. Black. Ithaca, NY: Cornell University Press.

Searle, J. R. 1975. Indirect speech acts. In *Speech Acts,* eds. P. Cole and J. Morgan, vol. 3 of *Syntax and Semantics.* New York: Academic Press.

Searle, J. 1976. The classification of illocutionary acts. *Language in Society* 5(1):1–24.

Sears, P., and D. Feldman. 1974. Teacher interactions with boys and girls. In *And Jill Came Tumbling After: Sexism in American Education,* eds. J. Stacy, S. Bereaud, and J. Daniels. New York: Dell.

Serna v. *Portales Municipal Schools,* 351 F. Supp. 1279 (D.N.M. 1972), *aff'd,* 499 F.2d 1147 (10th Cir. 1974).

Shapiro, M. C., and H. F. Shiffman. 1981. *Language and Society in South Asia.* Delhi: Motilal Banarsidass.

Sherzer, J. 1977. The ethnography of speaking: A critical appraisal. In *Linguistics and Anthropology* (Georgetown University Roundtable on Languages and Linguistics), ed. M. Saville-Troike, pp. 43–57. Washington, DC: Georgetown University Press.

Shopin, T., and J. M. Williams (eds.). 1980. *Standards and Dialects in English.* Cambridge, MA: Winthrop.

Shuy, R. W. 1967. *Discovering American Dialects.* Urbana, IL: National Council of Teachers of English.

Shuy, R., W. Wolfram, and W. K. Riley. 1967. *A Study of Social Dialects in Detroit.* Final Report, Project 6-1347. Washington, DC: Office of Education.

Shuy, R., W. Wolfram, and W. K. Riley. 1968. *Field Techniques in an Urban Language Study.* Washington, DC: Center for Applied Linguistics.

Singer, M.R. 1987. *Intercultural Communication: A Perceptual Approach.* Englewood Cliffs, NJ: Prentice-Hall.

Smith, D. 1985. *A study of the distribution and acceptability of responses to thank you.* M.A. long paper, Department of General Linguistics, University of Pittsburgh.

Smith, P. M. 1985. Language and the representation of men and women. In *Language, the Sexes, and Society*, pp. 31–57. Oxford: Basil Blackwell.

Southworth, F. C. 1985. The social context of language standardization in India. In *Language of Inequality*, eds. N. Wolfson and J. Manes, pp. 225–239. Berlin: Mouton.

Spencer, J. 1985. Language and development in Africa: The unequal equation. In *Language of Inequality*, eds. N. Wolfson and J. Manes, pp. 387–397. Berlin: Mouton.

Spender, D. 1980. *Man-Made Language.* London: Routledge & Kegan Paul.

Spolsky, B. 1978. *Educational Linguistics.* Rowley, MA: Newbury House.

Spolsky, B., and R. Cooper. 1977. *Frontiers of Bilingual Education.* Rowley, MA: Newbury House.

Stanley, J. P. 1977a. Gender-marking in American English: Usage and reference. In *Sexism and Language*, eds. A. P. Nilsen, H. Bosmajian, H. L. Gershuny, and J. Stanley, pp. 43–74. Urbana, IL: National Council of Teachers of English.

Stanley, J. P. 1977b. Paradigmatic woman: The prostitute. In *Papers in Language Variation*, ed. D. L. Shores. Birmingham: University of Alabama Press.

Stewart, W. 1970. Toward a history of Negro dialect. In *Language and Poverty*, ed. F. Williams. Chicago: Markham.

Strodbeck, F. L., and R. D. Mann. 1956. Sex role differentiation in jury deliberations. *Sociometry* 19:3–11.

Stubbs, M. 1983. *Discourse Analysis: The Sociolinguistic Analysis of Natural Language.* Chicago: University of Chicago Press.

Sudnow, D. 1972. *Studies in Social Interaction.* New York: Free Press.

Swacker, M. 1975.The sex of the speaker as a sociolinguistic variable. In *Language and Sex: Difference and Dominance*, eds. B. Thorne and N. Henley, pp. 76–83. Rowley, MA: Newbury House.

Swacker, M. 1976. Women's verbal behavior at learned and professional conferences. In *The Sociology of the Languages of American Women*, eds. B. L. DuBois and I. Crouch. San Antonio, TX: Trinity University.

Swain, M. 1979. Bilingual education: Research and its implications. In *On TESOL '79: The Learner in Focus*, eds. C. Yorio, K. Perkins, and J. J. Schachter, pp. 23–33. Washington, DC: TESOL.

Swain, M. 1981. Time and timing in bilingual education. *Language Learning* 31:1–16. Also presented as a Forum Lecture, Linguistic Summer Institute, Albuquerque, New Mexico, July 1980.

Takahashi, T., and L. Beebe. 1987. Development of pragmatic competence by Japanese learners of English. *Journal of the Japan Association of Language Teachers* 8(2).

Tannen, D. 1981. New York Jewish conversational style. *International Journal of the Sociology of Language* 30:133–149.

Tannen, D. 1982. Ethnic style in male–female conversation. In *Language and Social Identity*, ed. J. Gumperz. Cambridge: Cambridge University Press.

Tannen, D. 1984. *Conversational Style: Analyzing Talk Among Friends.* Norwood, NJ: Ablex.

Tarone, E. 1979. Interlanguage as chameleon. *Language Learning* 29(1):181–192.

Taylor, B. P. 1974. Toward a theory of language acquisition. *Language Learning* 24:23–35.

Taylor, B. P., and N. Wolfson. 1978. Breaking down the free conversation myth. *TESOL Quarterly* 12(1):31–39.

Teitelbaum, H., and R. Hiller. 1977. Bilingual education: The legal mandate. In *Bilingual Multicultural Education and the Professional: From Theory to Practice,* eds. H. T. Trueba and C. Barnett-Mizrahi, pp. 20–53. Rowley, MA: Newbury House.

Thomas, J. 1983. Cross-cultural pragmatic failure. *Applied Linguistics* 4(2):91–109.

Thorne, B., and N. Henley (eds.). 1975. *Language and Sex: Difference and Dominance* Rowley, MA: Newbury House.

Thorne, B., C. Kramarae, and N. Henley (eds.). 1983. *Language, Gender and Society.* Rowley, MA: Newbury House.

Tikunoff, W. J. 1983. *An Emerging Description of Successful Bilingual Instruction: An Executive Summary of Part 1 of the SBIF Descriptive Study.* San Francisco: Far West Laboratory.

Todd, L. 1974. *Pidgins and Creoles.* London: Routledge & Kegan Paul.

Trudgill, P. 1971. *The social differentiation of English in Norwich.* Ph.D. dissertation, Edinburgh University. Published by Cambridge University Press, 1974.

Trudgill, P. 1972. Sex, covert prestige, and linguistic change in the urban British English of Norwich. *Language in Society* 1(2):179–195. Reprinted in *Language and Sex: Difference and Dominance,* eds. B. Thorne and N. Henley, pp. 88–104. Rowley, MA: Newbury House.

Trueba, H. T. 1977. Bilingual-education models: Types and designs. In *Bilingual Multicultural Education and the Professional: From Theory to Practice,* eds. H. T. Trueba and C. Barnett-Mizrahi, pp. 54–73. Rowley, MA: Newbury House.

Trueba, H. T. (ed.). 1987. *Success or Failure: Learning and the Language Minority Student.* Rowley, MA: Newbury House.

Trueba, H. T., G. P. Guthrie, and K. H-P. Au (eds.). 1981. *Culture and the Bilingual Classroom: Studies in Classroom Ethnography.* Rowley, MA: Newbury House.

Tuchman, G. 1979. Women's depiction by the mass media. *Signs* 4:528–542.

Turner, R. 1974. *Ethnomethodology.* Harmondsworth, England: Penguin.

Vaasamorti. 1974. *The Language Revolution: Let My Language Rule.* Madras, India: M. Seshachalam.

Wald, B. 1985. Vernacular and standard Swahili as seen by members of the Mombasa Swahili speech community. In *Language of Inequality,* eds. N. Wolfson and J. Manes, pp. 123–143. Berlin: Mouton.

Weinreich, U. 1953. *Languages in Contact; Findings and Problems.* New York: Linguistics Circle of New York. Reprinted by Mouton, The Hague, 1974.

Weinreich, M. 1968. Yidishkayt and Yiddish: On the impact of religion on language in Ashkenazic Jewry. In *Readings in the Sociology of Language,* ed. J. A. Fishman, pp. 382–413. The Hague: Mouton.

Weinreich, U., W. Labov, and M. Herzog. 1968. Empirical foundations for a theory of language change. In *Directions for Historical Linguistics: A Symposium,* eds. W. Lehman and Y. Malkiel, pp. 97–195. Austin: University of Texas Press.

Wesler, M. 1984. *Non-formulaic greetings among speakers of American English.* Paper presented at the Ethnography in Education Forum, University of Pennsylvania.

West, C. 1984. When the doctor is a "lady": Power, status and gender in physician patient encounters. *Symbolic Interaction* 7(1):87–106.

West, C., and D. Zimmerman. 1983. Small insults: A study of interruptions in cross sex conversation between unaquainted persons. In *Language, Gender and Society*, eds. B. Thorne, C. Kramerae, and N. Henley. Rowley, MA: Newbury House.

Wexler, P. 1981. Ashkenazic German (1760–1895). *International Journal of American Linguistics* 31(2).

Whinnom, K. 1971. Linguistic hybridization and the 'special case' of pidgins and creoles. In *Pidginization and Creolization of Languages*, ed. D. H. Hymes, pp. 91–115. Cambridge: Cambridge University Press.

Widdowson, H. G. 1972. The teaching of English as communication. *English Language Teaching* 27(1):15–18.

Widdowson, H. G. 1978. *Teaching Language as Communication*. London: Oxford University Press.

Wilkins, D. A. 1976. *Notional Syllabuses: A Contribution to Foreign Language Curriculum Development*. Oxford: Oxford University Press.

Wilkins, D. A. 1979. Notional syllabuses and the concept of a minimum adequate grammar. In *The Communicative Approach to Language Teaching*, eds. C. J. Brumfit and K. Johnson. Oxford: Oxford University Press.

Wilkinson, A. 1965. *Spoken English*. Birmingham: University of Birmingham Press.

Williams, F. (ed.). 1970. *Language and Poverty: Perspectives on a Theme*. Chicago: Markham.

Williams, F., N. Hewett, L. M. Miller, R. C. Naremore, and J. L. Whitehead, 1976. *Explorations of the Linguistic Attitudes of Teachers*. Rowley, MA: Newbury House.

Williams, J. 1983. *Partings: Elicited v. spontaneous*. Paper presented at a seminar in sociolinguistics, University of Pennsylvania.

Williams, J. 1987. *Production principles in non-native institutionalized varieties of English*. Ph.D. dissertation, University of Pennsylvania.

Wolf, M. 1973. Chinese women: Old skills and a new context. In *Women, Culture, and Society*, eds. M. Rosaldo and L. Lamphere. Stanford, CA: Stanford University Press.

Wolff, H. 1959. Intelligibility and inter-ethnic attitudes. *Anthropological Linguistics* 1(3):34–41.

Wolfram, W. A. 1969a. *Linguistic correlates of social stratification in the speech of Detroit Negroes*. Hartford Seminary Foundation thesis.

Wolfram, W. A. 1969b. *A Sociolinguistic Description of Detroit Negro Speech*. Washington, DC: Center for Applied Linguistics.

Wolfram, W. A., and N. H. Clarke. 1971. *Black-White Speech Relationships*. Washington, DC: Center for Applied Linguistics.

Wolfram, W. A., and R. W. Fasold. 1974. *The Study of Social Dialects in American English*. Englewood Cliffs, NJ: Prentice-Hall.

Wolfson, N. 1976. Speech events and natural speech: Some implications for sociolinguistic methodology. *Language in Society* 5(2):189–209.

Wolfson, N. 1978a. A feature of performed narrative: The conversational historical present. *Language in Society* 7(2):215–237.

Wolfson, N. 1978b. *Techniques for the analysis of sociolinguistic patterns: The study of compliments*. Paper presented at the 12th Annual TESOL Convention, Mexico City.

Wolfson, N. 1979a. The conversational historical present alternation. *Language* 55(1):168–182.

Wolfson, N. 1979b. *Let's have lunch together sometime: Perceptions of insecurity.* Paper presented at the 13th Annual TESOL Convention, Boston.

Wolfson, N. 1981a. Compliments in cross-cultural perspective. *TESOL Quarterly* 15(2):117–124.

Wolfson, N. 1981b. Invitations, compliments, and the competence of the native speaker. *International Journal of Psycholinguistics* 24(4):7–22.

Wolfson, N. 1982a. *CHP: The Conversational Historical Present in American English Narrative* (Topics in Sociolinguistics). Dordrecht: FORIS Publications.

Wolfson, N. 1982b. On tense alternation and the need for analysis of native speaker usage in second language acquisition. *Language Learning* 32(1):53–68.

Wolfson, N. 1983a. An empirically based analysis of complimenting in American English. In *Sociolinguistics and Language Acquisition*, eds. N. Wolfson and E. Judd. Rowley, MA: Newbury House.

Wolfson, N. 1983b. Rules of speaking. In *Language and Communication*, eds. J. C. Richards and R. W. Schmidt, pp. 61–87. London: Longman.

Wolfson, N. 1984. Pretty is as pretty does: A speech act view of sex roles. *Applied Linguistics* 5(3):236–244.

Wolfson, N. 1986. Research methodology and the question of validity. *TESOL Quarterly* 20(4):689–699.

Wolfson, N. 1988. The bulge: A theory of speech behavior and social distance. In *Second Language Discourse: A Textbook of Current Research*, ed. J. Fine. Norwood, NJ: Ablex.

Wolfson, N. In press. The social dynamics of native and non-native variation in complimenting behavior. To appear in *Variation in Second Language Acquisition: Empirical Views*, ed. Eisenstein, M. New York: Plenum Press.

Wolfson, N., and S. Jones. 1984. *Problems in the comparison of speech acts across cultures.* Paper presented at the AILA Convention, Brussels, Belgium.

Wolfson, N., and E. Judd (eds.). 1983. *Sociolinguistics and Language Acquisition.* Rowley, MA: Newbury House.

Wolfson, N., and J. Manes. 1978. "Don't 'Dear' me." *Working Papers in Sociolinguistics.* Austin, TX: SEDL. Reprinted in *Women and Language in Literature and Society*, eds. S. McConnell-Ginet, R. Borker, and N. Furman, 1980, pp. 79–92. New York: Praeger.

Wolfson, N., and J. Manes. 1980. The compliment as a social strategy. *Papers in Linguistics* 13(3):391–410.

Wolfson, N., and J. Manes (eds.). 1985. *Language of Inequality.* Berlin: Mouton.

Wolfson, N., L. D'Amico-Reisner, and L. Huber. 1983. How to arrange for social commitments in American English: The invitation. In *Sociolinguistics and Language Acquisition*, eds. N. Wolfson and E. Judd, pp. 116–128. Rowley, MA: Newbury House.

Wolfson, N., T. Marmor, and S. Jones. 1985. *Problems in the comparison of speech acts across cultures.* Paper presented at the 18th Annual TESOL Convention, New York. To appear in *Cross-Cultural Pragmatics: Requests and Apologies*, eds. S. Blum-Kulka, J. House-Edmondson, and G. Kasper.

Wong-Fillmore, L., and C. Valadez. 1986. Teaching bilingual learners. In *Handbook of Research on Teaching*, ed. M. C. Wittrock, pp. 648–685. New York: Macmillan.

Wright, R. 1975. Reviews of R. Burling, *English in Black and White*, and W. Labov, *Language in the Inner City: Studies in the Black English Vernacular. Language in Society* 4(2):185–198.

Yorio, C. A. 1980. Conventionalized language forms and the development of communication competence. *TESOL Quarterly* 14(4):433–442.

Zborowski, M., and E. Herzog. 1952. *Life Is with People: The Culture of the Shtetl.* New York: Schocken Books.

Zimmerman, D. H., and C. West. 1975. Sex roles, interruptions and silences in conversations. In *Language and Sex: Difference and Dominance,* eds. B. Thorne and N. Henley, pp. 105–129. Rowley, MA: Newbury House.

Author Index

Akere, F., 28
Alt, R. R., 184
Altwerger, B., 253–254
Anshen, F., 167
Apte, M. L., 21, 22, 103
Atkins, B., 178–179, 186
Au, K. H-P., 254
Austin, J. L., 56, 57

Bailey, R. W., 12
Baker, K. A., 250–252
Barkin, F., 253–254
Bauman, R., 14, 56
Beebe, L. M., 24, 71, 72, 100–101, 107, 133, 144, 146–149, 207–209
Bell, A., 207–208
Bell, R. A., 110
Berko-Gleason, J., 104
Bernstein, B., 217–219
Bickerton, D., 272
Blom, J. P., 38–40, 199
Bloomfield, L., 195, 261
Blum-Kulka, S., 69, 91, 93–94, 99, 150–154
Bodine, A., 183
Bodman, J. W., 69, 71–72, 102–103, 133, 152–154
Borkin, A., 73, 87–88
Bosmajian, H. L., 173–174
Bourhis, R. V., 207
Brouwer, D., 41, 179–180
Brown, D. F., 32
Brown, G., 62
Brown, P., 67–68, 85–86
Brown, R., 7, 81–84, 130, 170
Brumfit, C. J., 46

Canale, M., 47
Cardenas, J. A., 249
Carrasco, R., 223
Cazden, C., 223
Chick, K., 159–160
Chomsky, N., 272
Christopher, R. C., 19–20, 24

Cicourel, A., 58
Clark, H., 97
Clyne, M. G., 141–143, 276
Cohen, A. D., 69–70, 89–92, 143–144, 146
Cohen, P., 178, 219–220
Cole, G. J., 249
Cole, S., 248–249
Conrad, A. W., 12, 275, 286
Cooper, R. L., 12, 286
Coulmas, F., 22–23, 85–86
Coulthard, M., 63
Craig, J., 25, 274
Crosby, F., 178
Crouch, I., 180
Cummins, J., 252–254

Daikuhara, M., 110, 139
Dalsheim, J., 173
D'Amico-Reisner, L., 40, 71, 98–99, 118–123, 130–133
Danet, B., 91, 93–94, 153
Danoff, M. N., 249
DeCamp, D., 269, 273
DeHaan, D., 41, 179–180
deKanter, A. A., 250–252
Doughty, C., 160
DuBois, B. L., 181
Dutt, T. K., 282–283

Eakins, B., 180
Eakins, G., 180
Edelsky, C., 65–67, 180, 182, 253–254
Edwards, V. K., 226–227
Eisenstein, M., 69, 71–72, 102–103, 154–155, 228–229, 234
Ephraimson-Abt, V., 171
Erickson, F., 157–158, 223
Ervin-Tripp, S. M., 3, 7, 80, 83, 92–94

Fasold, R. W., 222
Ferguson, C. A., 85, 262–263
Fillenbaum, S., 194

Fishman, J. A., 12, 233, 236, 239, 246, 275–276, 286
Fishman, P., 181–182
Flores, B., 253–254
Ford, M., 7, 81–83, 170
Fought, J., 262–264, 274
Frank, F., 167
Fraser, B., 88, 94–95, 107, 150
French, J. W., 97
French, K., 83–84
Friedrich, G. W., 105–106
Fulkerson, D., 165

Gardner, R. C., 194
Garfinkel, H., 60–61
Geertz, C., 85
Gerritsen, M., 41, 181–182
Gherson, R., 91, 93–94, 153
Giles, H., 207–209
Gilman, A., 82, 84, 130, 170
Glazer, N., 232, 234
Gleason, J. B., 103–104, 133
Godard, D., 76, 95–97
Godfrey, D. L., 42
Goffman, E., 61, 65, 86, 127
Goodenough, W. H., 36–37
Gordon, D., 150
Gorlach, M., 12
Graham, A., 166–167, 183
Grice, H. P., 58–60
Grief, E. B., 103–104, 133
Gumperz, J. J., 14, 39–40, 56, 156–158, 199
Guthrie, G. P., 254

Hakuta, K., 248–249
Hall, R. A., Jr., 193
Halliday, M. A. K., 3, 28
Hardman de Bautista, M., 265
Harrison, W., 286–287
Hart, R. P., 105–106
Hartman, P. L., 184
Hatch, E., 118
Haugen, E., 265
Heath, S. B., 222
Henley, N., 169–170
Herbert, R. K., 134–137, 139
Herzog, E., 151
Herzog, M., 195
Hodgson, R. C., 194
Holmes, J., 32, 134, 136, 139
Hooper, R., 110
Hoover, M., 221

Hornberger, N., 254
Huber, L., 40, 71, 118–123, 130–131
Hudelson, S., 253–254
Huspek, M., 79–80
Hymes, D., 3, 5–9, 14, 44–51, 56, 59–60, 109, 126–128, 199, 268
Hymes, V., 59

Irvine, J. T., 20, 51–52

Jamaluddin, N., 18, 27
Jefferson, G., 61–66
Jesperson, O., 10, 163, 164
Jilbert, K., 253–254
Jones, S., 87, 137–138, 171
Judd, E. L., 184

Kachru, B., 12, 27, 288
Kaplan, M., 106, 131
Katriel, T., 152
Keenan, E. O., 21, 59, 99
Kipers, P., 106–107, 131–132
Kirkland, M. L., 184
Kjolseth, J. R., 236
Kloss, H., 237
Knapp, M. L., 104–106, 110
Kramer, C., 168
Krivonos, P., 104

Labov, W., 7, 11, 39–40, 177–179, 189–203, 205–208, 213, 215, 219–221, 223, 226
Lakoff, R., 150, 165, 173–174, 176–178, 180
Lambert, W. E., 194, 243
Levinson, S., 67–68, 85–86
Lewis, J., 178, 219–220

McConnell-Ginet, S., 168–169, 182
McDavid, R. I., Jr., 213
McDermott, R., 61
McIntosh, A., 28
Mackay, D., 165
McLaughlin, D. H., 249
Maldonado-Guzman, A. A., 225
Manes, J., 70, 74, 80–81, 110–117, 134, 171
Mann, R. D., 180
Marmor, T., 87, 137–138
Martyna, W., 165–166
Mead, M., 151
Mehan, H., 223
Mehrotra, R. R., 285
Miller, C., 167
Milroy, J., 199–202, 207

Milroy, L., 52, 127, 199–204, 207
Moynihan, D. P., 234

Nader, L., 177
Neustupny, J. P., 50–51, 96
Nilsen, A. P., 167
Nongshah, N., 18, 27
Nyquist, L., 179

O'Barr, W. M., 178–179, 186
O'Neill, P. G., 85
Olshtain, E., 69–70, 89–92, 99–100, 143–146, 153
Owen, M., 65, 86–89

Paulston, C. B., 45, 52–53, 80–81, 84
Peal, E., 234, 249–250
Philips, S. U., 59, 62–64, 67, 254
Philipsen, G., 79–80
Pica, T., 43, 160
Pomerantz, A., 110, 114–115
Powesland, P. F., 208–209
Prator, C., 28, 286–287
Pride, J. B., 12
Provenzano, Z., 171

Rabinowitz, J., 106, 131
Reisman, K., 63, 67
Reynolds, D. J., 249
Richards, J. C., 16–17, 19
Riley, W. K., 198
Rinehart, S., 73, 87–88
Rintell, E., 94–95, 107
Rivers, W., 46
Robins, O., 178, 219–220
Rosen, H., 218
Rubin, J., 18, 24, 108
Rubin, R. B., 168

Sacks, H., 7, 61–66, 97
Santiago, R., 250
Schegloff, E., 61–66, 95–97
Schmandt, L., 105–106
Schmidt, R. W., 77–78, 97
Schneider, D. M., 125
Searle, J. R., 56–57, 150
Sherzer, J., 14, 34–35, 56
Shopin, T., 224
Shulman, G. M., 105–106
Shultz, J., 157–158, 175, 223
Shuy, R. W., 198
Smith, D., 103

Smith, P., 208–209
Smith, P. M., 165
Southworth, F. C., 267, 284
Spencer, J., 264
Spender, D., 166, 174–175, 181
Spiegel, J., 173
Stanley, J. P., 174
Straight, H. S., 135–136, 139
Strevens, P., 28
Strodbeck, F. L., 180
Swacker, M., 180, 182
Swain, M., 47, 249, 253
Swift, K., 167

Takahashi, T., 24, 100–101, 107, 144, 146–149
Tannen, D., 64, 67, 91
Tarone, E., 4, 205
Taufek, N. A. R., 18, 27
Taylor, B. P., 149
Taylor, D. M., 207
Thomas, J., 15–20, 26, 31
Tikunoff, W. J., 251, 253
Todd, L., 270
Trudgill, P., 177–178, 198–199
Trueba, H. T., 254–255
Tucker, G. R., 243, 286–287

Uliss-Weltz, R., 100–101, 107, 146–149

Vaasamoorti, 283–284
Verdi, G., 228

Young, R., 160

Wald, B., 264
Waletzky, J., 7
Walters, J., 94–95, 107
Weinbach, L., 99–100
Weinreich, U., 141, 195–197, 276–277
Wesler, M., 105
West, C., 65, 78, 181
Whinnom, K., 269–270
Widdowson, H. G., 46
Williams, J., 28, 106, 131–132, 188
Williams, J. M., 224
Wolff, H., 229, 288
Wolfram, W., 198, 220
Wolfson, N., 7, 23, 40–41, 62–63, 70–71, 74–75, 78, 80–81, 87, 101, 103, 110–115, 116, 118–123, 129–131, 134, 137–138, 157–158, 169, 171, 178, 201, 206–208
Wright, R., 221

Yorio, C. A., 31–32
Yule, G., 62

Zborowski, M., 151
Zimmerman, D., 65, 78, 181

Zuengler, J., 211
Zulkifli, N., 18, 27

Subject Index

accommodation theory, 208–209
acculturation, 277
acrolect, 273
address/reference, forms of, 74, 79–86, 168–171
adjacency pair, 61–64
American Indian languages, 232
analytic frameworks, 55, 56
Ann Arbor case, 223–224
apologies, 22, 67, 69–70, 86, 128, 137–138, 143–146
approval, 23
articles, 43
assimilation, 234, 244
attention to speech, 191–192

basilect, 273
bidialectalism, 224–227
bilingual education, evaluation of, 249–255
bilingual education, public views of, 248–249
Bilingual Education Act(s), 237–238
bilingual public schooling, 234–235
bilingualism, cognitive consequences of, 234, 252–254
bilingualism, societal, 261
bioprogram hypothesis, 272
Bulge Theory, 129–139

CCSARP (Cross-Cultural Speech Act Realization Project), 87, 137–138, 153
channel, 8
Civil Rights Act, 238
code switching, 38, 227
cognitive deficiency, 232
communication breakdown (CB), 142, 156
communication conflict (CC), 142
communicative approach, 45–46
communicative competence, 3, 7, 36, 44–47, 51, 53, 56, 73, 118, 160, 188, 189
communicative language teaching, 46–47, 160
compensatory education, 218, 234, 244
complaints, 99–100, 109

compliment/response sequence, 62, 114–117, 133–137, 139
compliments, 22–23, 62, 67, 73, 75–77, 110–114, 128, 130, 171–173
contextualization cues, 157
conversational historical present, 41–42, 78
conversational implicatures, 59
conversational maxims, 58–59
cooperative simultaneous talk, 64
Coral Way School, 236
creole languages, theories of origin, 271–273

Department Store Study, 189–190
dialect(s), 3, 11, 212–213
dialectology, 188, 191
diglossia, 262–264
directives, 92
disapproval, 98–99, 132–133
discourse completion tests (DCT), 69, 72
domain, 262

elaborated code, 218
elicitation, 65, 69–70, 72, 201, 204
endearment, terms of, 169–171
English as an additional language, 281
English as an official language, 266–267, 273, 282
enrichment bilingual education, 255
equality of opportunity, 244
ESL in bilingual education, 241, 250
ethnic diversity, 244
ethnic language schools, 233, 276
ethnography of speaking, 5–9, 35, 51, 56
ethnomethodology, 60–61, 65–67

face, 67–68

gatekeeping encounters, 157
genres, 9
grammatical competence, 47
gratitude, expressions of, 21, 57, 69, 71, 102–104, 128, 133, 154–155
greetings, 57, 104–105, 128

he/man issue, 165–168
hypercorrection, 39, 177, 192–193

illocutionary act, 57
illocutionary force, 57, 150
immersion approach, 242–243, 250–251, 252
inappropriate questions, 26, 171
indirect speech act(s), 57
instruction, medium of, 278, 282–284, 286
interactional sociolinguistics (IS), 156–159
interference, 69, 141
interruptions, 65, 78, 181
interviews, 38–39, 206–209
intuition(s), 35, 38, 40–41, 43–44, 54, 68, 73, 164, 178
invitations, 17, 24, 40, 71, 75, 109, 118–124, 128, 130–131

keys, 8

language, dominant/upper/prestige/high, 261–262, 278–279
language, link, 284–285
language, lower/stigmatized, 261–262, 278
language, national, 283–284
language, official, 266–267, 273, 282
language, regional, 284
language attitudes, 220–222, 228–229
language change, 258
language contact, 258–261
language loyalty, 276–277
language maintenance, 233, 276–281
language policy, 231–232, 282
language shift, 276, 280
language of wider communication (LWC), 285–286
Lau v. Nichols, 238–239, 241
lingua franca, 281
linguistic diversity, 266–267, 281
linguistic imposition, 264–265
linguistic variety, choice of, 244

macrosociolinguistics, 2
maintenance bilingual education, 246–247
microanalysis, 160
microsociolinguistics, 2, 3
minority languages, 232
miscommunication, 3, 15–16, 22, 76, 140, 156–161
multilingualism, myth of, 257
mutual intelligibility, 229

negative politeness, 67–68
negotiation, 118, 120, 155
nonstandard English, 214–217, 219–220, 229
nonstandard variety, 215–216, 224–225
norms of interaction, 9

observation, ethnographic, 38, 40, 65, 201–205
observer's paradox, 202–203
overcorrection, 39. See also hypercorrection
overgeneralization, 149–150

participant observation, 75
participants, 8
partings, 105–107, 131–132
performatives, 56–57
philosophers of language, 56
pidgin languages, social characteristics, 268–269
pidgin languages, theories of origin, 269–273
pluralism, linguistic and cultural, 234–235, 282–285
positive politeness, 67–68
post-creole continuum, 373–374
powerless language, 179
pragmalinguistic failure, 16–17
pragmatic failure, 16–23
pragmatic transfer, 141–142, 154, 160
pragmatics, 15
prestige variety, 215–216

questionnaires, 69–70

refusals, 69, 71–72, 100–102, 133, 146–149
register, 3
requests, 67, 92–95, 150–154
restricted code, 218
ritualized expressions, 155–156
rules of speaking, 3, 6–9, 14, 17, 34, 37, 43–45, 49, 51, 53–56, 72, 74, 77, 91, 98, 109, 110, 126–128

St. Lambert experiment, 243
secessionist movements, fear of, 247
semantic derogation of women, 174–176
setting, 7
sex-related differences in speech, 163, 176
sexism in language, 160, 173–176
social-class variation, 39
sociolinguistic competence, 47
sociolinguistic diversity, 15, 17, 27
sociolinguistic/pragmatic transfer, 91, 140–156
sociolinguistic relativity, 2, 14, 26, 32

sociolinguistic rules, 14, 34–36, 40, 44, 48–49, 54, 69, 73
sociolinguistic variability, 140
sociopragmatic failure, 16–17
solidarity, 168–169
sound change, 195–197, 226
SPEAKING, 7–9
speech act(s), 6, 7, 58, 70–71, 77, 109, 110, 128–129
speech act set, 89
Speech Act Theory, 56–58
speech community, 40, 49–53, 59, 68, 76, 125–127, 128, 191
speech event(s), 6, 7, 43, 71, 189
speech situation(s), 6, 7, 76, 189
spontaneous interaction, 40, 70–71
spontaneous speech, 40, 70–71
sprachbund (language area), 50–51
spread of English, 285

sprechbund (speech area), 50–51
standard variety, 212
stigmatized varieties, 277
strategic competence, 47
style, 4, 189
style shifting, 39, 189, 207–209
stylistic variation, 189
submersion approach, 240–241, 250–251

telephone behavior, 76, 95–97
transfer, 141
transitional bilingual education (TBE), 242–244, 250–251
turn-taking, 61–63, 65–67

variety, 3, 211

women's speech, features of, 162, 176–182